Managing the Cultural Industries

An introduction to the business mechanics of the cultural and creative industries, this textbook provides a management-orientated, practice-based teaching and learning resource.

Aimed at students new to the study of the cultural industries and / or new to the study of business, the author introduces the reader to relevant academic insights and perspectives, without losing focus on the essentials of practical business and management. Designed for students who wish to develop a management and leadership career in the cultural and creative industries, the book incorporates coverage of key business ideas and disciplines, from strategy to accounting and finance, through management, human resources and innovation to marketing and consumer behaviour. Each chapter introduces a major new business topic. Key sectors covered included the music industry, television, video games and the performing arts. Relevant management tools and techniques are described and used.

Managing the Cultural Industries is a valuable resource for new students of the cultural industries, as well as providing insights for reflective practitioners in the industry.

Dr. **James Roberts** is currently a researcher and lecturer in strategy and leadership at the University of Leeds Business School, where he also led the Leeds MBA programme for eight years. Additionally, he developed and teaches a highly popular course on managing cultural industries. Prior to this, he completed his PhD and had a successful career as a strategy consultant. Throughout his consulting career, he worked with global clients in the entertainment and media sectors, advised leading law firms and provided guidance to regulators. He has also served as an expert witness for the European Commission.

Discovering the Creative Industries

Series Editor: Ruth Rentschler

The creative and cultural industries account for a significant share of the global economy. Gaining and maintaining employment and work in this sector is a challenge and chances of success are enhanced by ongoing professional development.

This series provides a range of relatively short, student-centred books which blend industry and educational expertise with cultural sector practice. Books in the series provide applied introductions to the core elements of the creative industries. In sum, the series provides essential reading for those studying to enter the creative industries as well as those seeking to enhance their career via executive education.

Human Resources in the Arts
Brea M. Heidelberg

Marketing Strategy for the Arts, 3e
Bonita M. Kolb

Doing (and Using) Research in Arts and Cultural Management
François Colbert, Jennifer Wiggins, Russell Belk, Ruth Rentschler, and Danilo C. Dantas

Arts Management
Managing a Culturepreneurial Organization
Carla Walter

Social Impact for Cultural Organizations
A Toolkit for Creating Change
Richard S. Andrews and Emilee Simmons

Race and Racism in the Cultural and Creative Industries
Nessa Keddo and Clive Chijioke Nwonka

Managing the Cultural Industries
An Introduction
James Roberts

For more information about this series, please visit: www.routledge.com/Discovering-the-Creative-Industries/book-series/DCI

Managing the Cultural Industries

An Introduction

James Roberts

Routledge
Taylor & Francis Group
LONDON AND NEW YORK

Designed cover image: Getty Images

First published 2026
by Routledge
4 Park Square, Milton Park, Abingdon, Oxon OX14 4RN

and by Routledge
605 Third Avenue, New York, NY 10158

Routledge is an imprint of the Taylor & Francis Group, an informa business

British Library Cataloguing-in-Publication Data
A catalogue record for this book is available from the British Library

ISBN: 978-1-032-81197-0 (hbk)
ISBN: 978-1-032-81196-3 (pbk)
ISBN: 978-1-003-49859-9 (ebk)

DOI: 10.4324/9781003498599

Typeset in Times New Roman
by Taylor & Francis Books

Dedicated to my mum, Yvonne Roberts, who believed above all in the value of lifelong learning.

Thank you to Adrienne, Jack, Rachel, Bazz, Annie and Bear for their constant support and patience.

Additional thanks to all the University of Leeds students on LUBS5249 who helped shape the contents of the book with their comments and insights.

Contents

Illustrations

Figures

1 Introduction

1.1 Introduction

In this introductory chapter we aim to do three things: describe the structure of the book and its general approach and aims; define what we mean by the cultural industries and associated sectors; and finally discuss why it might be important to study them from a business perspective, identifying potential gaps and biases in research conducted to date.

The cultural industries provide a fascinating setting for research and indeed a huge amount has been conducted on their operation and impact by academics. We will draw on this theory and, to the extent we can, critique it and indeed contribute to it in this book. The sector is also popular as a potential setting for career development, and the book aims to provide you with the type of insight into the operation of organisations in the sector that may help mark you out at interview, and hopefully help you secure that elusive first role.

We will cover a range of industry sectors, including electronic gaming, television and the performing arts. For those of you already active in a sector as a practitioner, there may be much to learn from how other sectors have dealt with the specific opportunities and threats you might currently be facing. Finally for those intent on mainly studying the sector, we hope to further explore an emerging but, at least until relatively recently, underrepresented voice in the canon of exciting research, the voice of the business community.

The book is designed to be read by those who have not studied business theory or the operation of the culture industries from an academic perspective before. You may have a background in performance. You may have graduated in a non-business subject and have decided to study for a higher degree in cultural industries and business. You may be moving into the cultural industries from another sector. As such it sets out to provide a basic grounding in key elements of business theory (e.g. how does business strategy work, what considerations are required when designing a new product?) and then apply them, where possible and helpful, to an analysis of the cultural industries.

1.2 Structure and approach

The overall structure of the book is based on the idea that it's important to understand the basic organisation of a business sector or industry, the types of company within it, how they operate and interact, its history and evolution, major business models and key processes, before we start to explore the broader themes and the issues that affect it and others. We need a basic level of knowledge before we can become more analytical.

DOI: 10.4324/9781003498599-1

Hence the book offers a series of 'deep delves' into specific cultural industry sectors (Chapters 3 to 6) including television, the popular music sector, electronic gaming and the performing arts. Clearly this is not a comprehensive review of cultural industry sectors, but the sectors we cover are useful in that they highlight major business models, organisational structures, challenges and changes that have been wrought across the industry in the last 20 years.

The book assumes that this is likely to be the first time you have studied business and potentially the first time you have explored the cultural industries from a business perspective. As such, Chapter 2 will be a brief overview of major business ideas and theories. We will describe some tools and techniques that can be used to analyse businesses and markets and utilise them in subsequent chapters to assess how they might be used in practice to enhance our understanding of the cultural industries. These tools and techniques apply to any business sector; they are relevant and potentially useful to you no matter how your career develops.

We also discuss further business ideas and themes that emerge as relevant as we work through the analysis of specific sectors—e.g. the management of stakeholders, business models, mergers and acquisitions etc. Thereafter, we explore some key areas of debate and enquiry at a more analytical level. Is the organisation of labour in the culture industries fundamentally different to that in other business sectors (Chapter 7)? How has the marketing function evolved and what is its future role likely to be (Chapter 8)? Throughout we will review large-scale changes in the industry as a whole, including the transition to digital and the move from distribution- to attention-based economies.

The general approach of the book is to look at the realities of day-to-day life in the cultural sectors from a business perspective. As we will see, many academics have explored the cultural industries from quite a theoretical perspective and relatively few have actually worked for companies in the sector for any length of time (if at all). They have, quite reasonably, sought access to and researched companies in the cultural industries for academic reasons, but this produces a very different perspective from working in them. Where possible we will draw on the lived experience of those working in the sector, which includes the author, who spent many years as a business consultant working in the performing arts, television, gaming and music industries. Equally, the research that has been conducted to date has typically been dominated by academics who have not studied business—they have tended to study sociology, anthropology, philosophy, culture, political economy, history and so on, using the cultural industries as a setting for their research efforts. Inevitably they bring their own discipline's focus (e.g. for a sociologist a focus on issues like gender, power, the operation of societal systems and structures, the role of institutions etc.), questions, theories and methods. Whilst these perspectives have hugely enhanced our understanding of the industry, and hence are vitally important to review, they don't tend to offer much detail about specific business processes or activities and are often produced without actually talking to those involved in them. Academics have been very interested in talking to creative constituencies in the sector, but apparently far less interested in seeking the views and opinions of business-related groups. For those of you intent on a business-related career in the industry, these latter perspectives are vital.

The book takes a very practice-based approach. We will of course draw on theory when necessary and useful, but we are focused more on understanding the practicalities of trying to make a profit as a video streaming company, the challenges of running a TV programme production company, understanding what are you likely to be doing if you work in the A&R (artists and repertoire) department of a record company, the challenges of running an opera company and the detail of how digital technologies have and might further transform these sectors. We draw on theory to the extent that it helps us understand these very practical issues. Academic articles are detailed in the references at the end of the chapter and, where possible, mention the original academic papers that first proposed a theory or idea, rather than the numerous articles that have typically followed, which comment on and critique elements of the theory. It is important that you understand the basic thinking behind each idea, theory or tool, before engaging with the inevitable academic commentary that subsequently emerges. References to more recent internet articles, commentaries and data sources are provided in the footnotes.

Ultimately, then, the book is designed for those who intend to one day to **work in these industries**, rather than those who are intent on studying them from a more academic and theoretical perspective. For those of you who wish to continue studying to a higher level, there are a multitude of books and research papers available, and we will mention some of them throughout the book. There are also sources if you want to work in a specific technical function, like video editing, sound engineering, stage management and so on. For those of you intent on an artistic career you can study dance, drama, film making, music, scriptwriting etc.

Unfortunately, those of you who want a business career in the industry are generally less well served. Getting a job in the sector can be extremely challenging—many people want to work in it and the routes into it are often convoluted and lengthy (see Chapter 10). By having a sense of the specific challenges faced by an organisation you might want to work for and the business ideas that might help address them, you will certainly stand out in an interview. Many of the ideas we discuss will then help you perform better and hopefully get promoted once you are in a job. In each chapter we will discuss a number of business theories and ideas that can help us understand the cultural industries. They are equally applicable to a vast range of other sectors and are designed to provide a broad overview and introduction to major business concepts. Whilst they cannot be comprehensive, it is hoped that they will broaden your perspective and perhaps even ignite your interest in a specific role or function, and where possible further references are supplied for you to continue your research.

Chapter	*Key business concepts*
Chapter 2: business 101	Profit and not for profit, customers and consumers, B2B and B2C markets, products and services, costs, revenues and profits, business organisation, hierarchies, roles and major functions, processes and systems
Chapter 3: the performing arts sector	Stakeholders, stakeholder management, value chain analysis, accounting, service-based businesses, business models
Chapter 4: television broadcasting and narrowcasting	New product development and innovation
Chapter 5: electronic gaming	Market attractiveness—Porter's five forces, mergers and acquisitions
Chapter 6: the popular music sector	Strategy, the resource-based view—assets and capabilities

Chapter	*Key business concepts*
Chapter 7: organisation and labour	Organisational behaviour and the role of the HR team
Chapter 8: marketing	The marketing mix (the four Ps), branding, market research techniques
Chapter 9: the future of digital media	Corporate foresight, annual budgeting, strategic planning systems, scenario planning, ScFi prototyping
Chapter 10: conclusions	Entrepreneurship

As we work through these chapters a number of significant questions emerge that are of direct relevance to those of you intent on a business career in the cultural industries. These might include:

- Are organisations in the cultural industries structured and operated in a similar or very different way to organisations in other business sectors (e.g. fast-moving consumer goods (FMCG), banking, consumer electronics etc.)? Do organisations have very different internal structures, processes and systems? This is significant, because if it is true (i.e. if they are really different) then perhaps many of the tools of business management that we find in business textbooks just won't work in the cultural industries—the subject organisations are just too different. Equally it may be that the sort of approaches to leadership and management taught in business schools won't work in cultural organisations because the nature of the organisations and the relationships between individuals at different levels are somehow unusual. The implication here is that the industry might have to develop its own approaches and tools and can't really borrow them from the body of business knowledge developed in other sectors, other than at a very superficial level.
- Are the products and services created in the cultural industries radically different to those created in other business sectors? Again, this has significant implications for those of you managing products and services in the sector. We might argue that the character of cultural products makes them very different (perhaps because of their cultural symbolism), that it's almost impossible to predict their success, or that they are created in such unusual ways that, again, traditional tools to help in new product / service development simply won't work in this context.
- Are the trends and developments currently evident in other business sectors equally applicable to the cultural industries? Whether this be the 'war for talent', globalisation, the radical implications of digital transformation or geopolitical developments, how is the industry likely to evolve over the short to medium term (5–10 years) and can we learn lessons from what's happening in other sectors and how other types of organisations are responding?
- Has the voice of the business community been sufficiently represented in the huge volume of academic work on the cultural industries that we find when we do our searches on Google Scholar or in our university library? Do we have a balanced, neutral and comprehensive understanding of how the industry functions, from a creative and a business perspective? Has the role of the business community been stereotyped as generally positive or negative? Has the academic community actually talked to people involved on the business side of the industry, or have they been content to get their perspectives on the influence of business from purely creative constituencies and other academics?

We will reflect on these questions throughout the book, and particularly in our conclusion (Chapter 10), and assess the implications of our findings for those of you with ambitions for a management or leadership role in the industry. But we can say that most academics like definitions—they are crucial for defining our scope of analysis, clarifying research questions and interpreting conclusions—so perhaps first we should start with how the cultural and creative industries have typically been defined.

1.3 Defining the industry

Definitions of the creative and cultural industries emerge from many sources. The two terms, cultural and creative, are often used interchangeably to describe the industry. Academics like to define things to improve the clarity of their thinking, delineate the scope of their enquiry and assess the implications of their findings. Trade organisations (UNESCO, WIPO) and government ministries are interested in the sector as a potential source of employment, as a tool to enrich (or perhaps monitor and control) the cultural lives of their populations, and as a key contributor to international trade. Defining sectors helps them to measure economic impact and focus their investment programmes and policy.

Article 4 (page 14) of the 2005 UNESCO (the United Nations Educational, Scientific and Cultural Organization) Convention[1], for example, defines cultural goods and services as those that 'embody or convey cultural expressions, irrespective of the commercial value they may have'. UNESCO's 2009 framework[2] for information collection suggests the industry covers cultural and natural heritage; performance and celebration; visual arts and crafts; books and press; audiovisual and interactive media; design and creative services; tourism (what they call a 'related domain'); and sports and recreation (another related domain). The WIPO's (World Intellectual Property Organization) definition includes organisations involved in the film industry, music sector, video games, publishing and advertising.

Each country's national ministry of culture (most have one), tends to define the cultural sector slightly differently. In the UK, this is typically the responsibility of the government's Department for Culture, Media and Sport (DCMS). Its 1998 definition[3] chooses to define 'creative industries' as those industries that have their origin in individual creativity, skill and talent, and that have a potential for wealth and job creation through the generation and exploitation of intellectual property. It's a very broad definition, including advertising, architecture, the art and antiques market, crafts, design, designer fashion, film and video, interactive leisure software, music, performing arts, publishing, software and computer services, television and radio.

China differentiates between 'cultural industries' and 'creative industries', though in many cases the terms appear to be used interchangeably. According to the National Ministry of Culture (which merged with China National Tourism Administration in 2018), cultural industries are those businesses that offer cultural productions and cultural services.[4] The National Bureau of Statistics of China collects data on two major categories of cultural organisations: **core companies** involved in news services, publishing and copyright, radio, TV and film, and those involved in the 'arts' (what we will subsequently call performing arts). **Related companies** include those involved in providing internet services, leisure and entertainment and cultural services, and those involved in the sales of related equipment.

India, following the definition provided by UNESCO, defines the cultural and creative industries as those 'sectors of organized activity that have as their main objective the production or reproduction, the promotion, distribution, or commercialization of goods, services and activities of content derived from cultural, artistic or heritage origins' (Dasgupta and Clini, 2023). The Economic Commission for Latin America and the Caribbean (ECLAC)[5] suggests the industry includes publishing, film, TV, radio, phonographics, mobile content, independent audiovisual production, web content, electronic games and content produced for digital convergence (cross-media).

These definitions seem determinedly broad and inclusive, though we end up with a relatively similar set of companies to study. Academics have tended to be more specific and focus particularly on the nature of these sectors, their products and services and their potential differences to other types of business in determining their definitions. This issue of definition is subject to significant academic debate and conflicting interpretations; entire research projects, academic papers, chapters and even books have been written on the subject. We can therefore only cover a small sample of them here.

Caves (2000), from an economics background, describes what he calls the 'creative industries' as a place where art and commerce meet. They produce products and services that are associated with cultural, artistic and entertainment value. He stresses two major processes: the creation of content and its distribution. Creation is very much the province of the artist, distribution that of the business organisation. They are brought together through contracts (something he focuses on) designed to align the interests of both parties. The industry includes organisations involved in book and magazine publishing, the visual arts, the performing arts, sound recordings, cinema and TV films, fashion, toys and games. Throsby (2008), describes an industry based on a core set of activities focused on the generation of creative ideas and activities—e.g. those focused on literature, music, performing arts, visual art or film, museums, galleries etc.—in addition to organisations with more commercial ends, including heritage services, publishing and printed media, sound recording, television and radio, video, computer games and those with a related interest in the sector, like advertising, architecture, design and fashion.

Garnham (1990) focuses more on the product / service characteristics of the industry and the way they are created, suggesting that such products are subject to unusual levels of risk, typically have high production costs but low reproduction costs and are often semi-public goods (that is, the use of a product by one person reduces its availability to another). Hence Garnham argues that cultural industries relate to institutions in society with characteristic modes of production and organisation, focused on the creation and dissemination of symbols in the form of cultural goods and services (Garnham, 1987).

Wackman and Lavine (1987) describe the often-perishable nature of the creative product, the presence of highly creative workers, unusual organisational structures and the unique societal role of the creative industries. O'Conner, in his 2000 paper, chooses to outline a definition partly in relation to government policy, and partly through the nature of the product itself, that is as a set of organisations whose activities 'deal primarily in symbolic goods – goods whose primary economic value is derived from their cultural value' (2000, p.20). He includes broadcasting, film, publishing, recorded music, design and architecture in his categorisation, along with visual arts, the theatre, concerts and performances, museums and galleries.

Hence definitions tend to vary depending on your starting point and aims for defining the sector. The interchangeable use of the terms 'cultural' and 'creative' to describe the industry seems very apparent. But as we can already see, no matter what academic, economic or policy lens we look through, we repeatedly end up with the same types of organisations as our unit of analysis. This then will be our starting point, so what companies will we focus on?

We choose to focus on those organisations involved in the **creation of cultural content** (in all its varied forms) rather than what are rather loosely described as the 'creative industries'. Every business, in every sector, requires creativity in some form, creative problem solving, creativity in product or service design, creative leadership and management, a creative approach to organisational design or business models etc., and so therefore every business might justifiably consider itself 'creative' and hence part of the creative industries. Apple sees itself as a creativity-driven organisation, as do fast-moving consumer goods companies, those involved in the energy sector dealing with the transition away from fossil fuels and so on. This does not help us focus our attention and research—it is too broad a unit of analysis to help us here. Our focus therefore will be on organisations involved in the creation of cultural content—that is, goods (products and services) that have symbolic meaning in some form, a significant artistic dimension and cultural significance, as well as the potential to generate economic returns.

We outline four potential sectors but focus on only two (see Figure 1.1). These are simplified categories and to a degree arbitrary, but they are a convenient way for us to divide up industry sectors and look at their dynamics. There is some blurring at the edge of each category; they are not necessarily mutually exclusive. Equally the size, scope and nature of each category is likely to vary in different regions.

1 **Core cultural organisations:** often traditionally 'not-for-profit' organisations (i.e. profit is not their sole or main goal; see Chapter 2), often in the past reliant on state or government support, often involved in the performing arts (e.g. theatre, opera, orchestras, dance companies), but also potentially organisations involved in cultural heritage (e.g. museums and galleries). They tend to be both **publicly** held, that is owned or significantly supported by governments and the state, and **privately** held, where the government has no ownership interest or involvement in

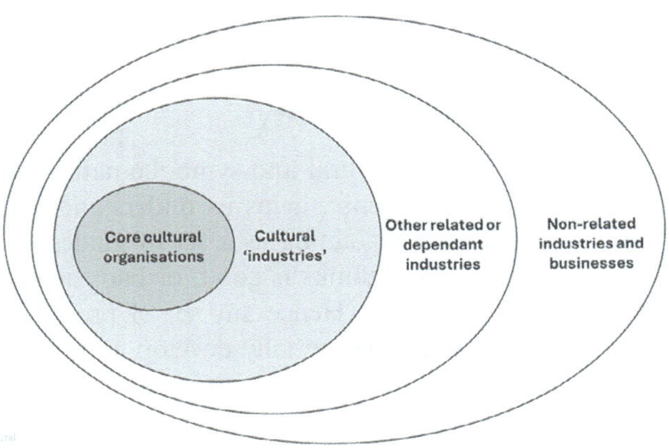

Figure 1.1 Scope of enquiry
Source: author.

their day-to-day operation. Museums in many European countries are typically reliant on state funding, for example, whereas museums in the USA all tend to be privately held. Hence, we will examine organisations involved in theatre, opera, dance, classical music and so on.

2 **Cultural industries:** those cultural sectors that have gone through a process, to some degree, of industrialisation, which might include film and television, popular music, electronic games etc. Typically, this means the increased involvement of companies with more of a focus on profit as a goal ('for-profit' companies), which are often large and multidivisional (e.g. Walt Disney Corp., Warner Bros.), major television companies like the BBC, games and technology companies like Tencent, record companies like Universal Music. They are often international in scope and typically are privately held (but, again, there are exceptions—e.g. public service broadcasters in Europe). Hence, we will look at television companies, record labels and games studios.

3 **Other dependent and related organisations** include companies that rely on cultural content to some degree to provide their services—e.g. telecoms companies, internet service companies or organisations supplying things like equipment and services to the cultural sector (accountancy firms, talent agencies, consulting companies, technology companies like IBM etc). This might also include related sectors such as advertising, architecture and the fashion industry. We will touch on these organisations when relevant.

4 Finally, those **companies least involved with the cultural sectors**, organisations involved in oil and gas, medical technology or retail banking, for example. We will not mention these very often, typically only if they help inform our understanding of more culturally orientated organisations and sectors.

We will focus our study particularly on categories one and two, though we will cover dependent and related organisations to some degree, particularly as many culture-creating companies end up being owned and controlled by related companies, such as those in the technology and telecoms sectors—e.g. Comcast, a global telecoms company based in the USA, owns companies such as NBC Universal (a TV, film and cable company), Amazon owns content studio MGM, or Tencent, which might have started out as an information technology company but is now one of the biggest video games publisher in the world.

1.4 Why it is important to study the industry?

In the previous section we noted the cultural and symbolic nature of cultural products and services. Culture, in its broadest sense, helps us understand the world around us and helps us function in our daily lives, acting as a set of guides to behaviour, norms and values. It tells us what our society thinks is good, or bad, how to interpret events, and how to behave in certain situations. Hence any set of products and services that significantly contribute to, express and potentially develop culture are likely to be significant in our understanding of the world around us and in our ability to navigate it successfully.

The cultural industries are key conveyors of understanding and meaning in society, they help us interpret the world around us. Further, they prompt key debates around things like power and politics, economics, gender and identity, crime and punishment or sexual mores. They force us to engage with issues around things like censorship—what are people allowed to see and consume, what they are denied and why? The media, typically defined as methods of mass communication including broadcasting, newspapers and the internet, tells us what is happening in our own and other countries, it helps us understand what is going on in the world and perhaps even how we should interpret events. Understanding how the media operates is therefore crucial to developing a sense of how it might be affecting our own personal views and behaviour.

In times of crisis, cultural products (e.g. music recordings, television programmes, books and films) can help us maintain our sanity and bring us moments of calm and happiness in an otherwise chaotic world. Such products can also enable us to further explore our inner worlds, helping us to examine our own emotions and personality, what 'makes us tick'. They can change our moods, making us feel ecstatic and happy, or gloomy and introspective, help us understand our own behaviour, and that of others, and even change it.

If nothing else, given this enormous significance, it is probably important to understand how such products and services are created, and the agendas of those individuals and organisations involved in producing and distributing them. Certainly, authors like Noam Chomsky (particularly in his book *Manufacturing Consent*, which is to be recommended to the reader) have suggested that we are in many ways controlled and dominated by mass media—it dictates, often in a negative way, how we see the world. Others suggest we have far more agency in our interactions with cultural content. But understanding how cultural content is affecting us, influencing us and perhaps even controlling us, seems a vital personal agenda for just about everyone living in the time of large profit-orientated culture-producing companies, and governments intent on fostering their own vision of a nation's culture. Beyond these quite personal reasons to examine the functioning of the cultural industries, there are other reasons we might wish to study the sector.

1.4.1 The economics

Cultural industries are hugely significant from an economic perspective. There are probably two issues that are most significant in this regard: their absolute size and contribution to the global economy and, perhaps even more significantly, their capacity for growth and change compared to other sectors.

Estimates vary hugely as to the size of the total global market for cultural content, with such estimates emerging from different governments, trade bodies, academics and statistics collection organisations. These variations occur partly because different data-collection organisations define the industry in different ways (see section 1.2), and hence they include different types of company. There are significant variations in what is measured and how it is measured, with further variations in the quality and consistency of that measurement. Some estimates focus on revenues to companies involved in the industry, others on measurements of economic benefit to the economy or consumer spending. As a general point it is important to note what is and is not included in any statistic you draw on in your analysis, so pay close attention to exactly what is being measured and how it is measured. The following then may be subject to debate and disagreement and may not even be precisely accurate in terms of what they describe (depending on your perspective), but they will provide a broad idea of the general size of the industry and its various sub-sectors compared to others.

Statista (a specialist statistics collection company) estimates that the total value of the media and entertainment market globally was $2.32 trillion in 2022[6], a growth of 5.4% compared to 2021, a figure broadly confirmed by consulting company PWC[7] drawing data from their own research and that of the IMF (International Monetary Fund). This compares to something like the global automotive industry at $4.7 trillion[8] or the global oil and gas market at $6.5 trillion.[9]

Within that huge figure of $2.3 trillion, there are some very large sub-sectors. Statista for example suggests that the global size of the television and video market was around $683bn[10] in 2023. This includes subscriptions, public sector funding, relevant packaged media (e.g. DVD, Blu-ray) sales and related advertising, but excludes cinema and consumer equipment (e.g. televisions). SkyQuest estimate the size of the global electronic gaming market to be approximately $230bn in 2023[11], with the mobile gaming sector making the biggest contribution to this total. The performing arts market, defined very broadly to include organisations involved in live popular music (so a company like Live Nation) as well as theatre, dance, orchestras, circuses and opera, covering productions in everything from tiny concert halls to large theatres and ultimately huge stadiums, was estimated to be worth approximately $193bn in 2024.[12]

Other sectors have had a more turbulent times in recent years. The popular music sector has gone through a relative period of stagnation and low growth for much of the last 20 years. We will discuss the reasons for this in Chapter 6, but current estimates suggest a global recorded music market value of around $28.6bn[13] in 2023, with streaming revenues contributing 67% of that total. The global cinema market, which went through a very difficult period during COVID, was generally estimated to be worth around $70bn in 2023.[14]

Expanding out from our core focus on organisations directly involved in cultural production and distribution, a significant number of related industries are driven by the cultural sector. Advertising, as well as arguably being a cultural sector in its own right, often relies on cultural content and its distribution to function. Advertisements need cinemas, television channels, internet services and newspapers in which to appear. The advertising market alone was estimated to be worth around $615bn in 2023.[15]

The cultural industries also drive sales of technology and equipment, from consumer electronics (televisions, DVD players, audio systems, games consoles and arguably even mobile phones), to sector-specific equipment like broadcast playout centres, specialist IT equipment, lighting and sound boards, audio equipment like PA systems and so on. The toys and games sector, estimated to be worth an enormous $37 trillion globally in 2022[16], has grown hugely in recent years partly due to its association with film and TV franchises. Even things like telecoms network traffic rely on the transmission of 'cultural' content (much of it user-generated) to help generate usage, retain customers and improve revenues. Hence the cultural industry helps drive value creation and growth in a wide variety of other large-scale industries.

So, some of these individual sectors are very large, and hence important to the economy. As well as their absolute size, the cultural industries are interesting from a growth perspective. Cultural industry sectors often grow faster (in size and value) than those in the rest of the economy, though it is worth remembering they can shrink equally quickly. Analysis from consulting firm Accenture[17], for example, noted that the media sector typically outperformed all other business sectors (including healthcare, retail, technology etc.) in the growth and value of returns to shareholders during the period 2010 to 2015. In relatively mature and stable economies, like the UK, overall growth in the total economy is typically very modest: PWC's 2022 forecast for its average growth rate to 2026 was less than 1% annually.[18] This compares with their estimate of growth in the entertainment and media sector at >4% growth annually. In the USA, Statista market insight data suggests that the average rate of growth of the entertainment and media sector in the USA (including all digital and non-digital content) was 17% annually during the period 2017–2023.[19]

The electronic gaming market in China grew at an annual rate of 7.3% annually during the period 2018–2023[20], with 66% of its value accounted for by mobile gaming (which has outpaced all other gaming sectors in terms of growth). Perhaps more significantly it is forecast to continue to grow from $66bn in 2024 to over $95.5 bn in 2029, an overall annual growth rate of over 7.5%. Annual growth rates for the entertainment and media industry in India are forecast at nearly 14% growth annually to 2027, to a market size of $644.9bn (PWC[21]). They forecast growth rates for the sector of >7% in countries such as Chile, Indonesia, Pakistan and Mexico, rising to >10% in countries such as Argentina and Turkey.

Whilst these figures may not necessarily seem significant in their own right, when compared to growth rates in economies more generally (typically 1–2% annually; even fast-growing economies tend not to consistently grow more than 4% each year), and those forecast for other business sectors—e.g. 3.6% annually to 2031 for fast-moving consumer goods[22], around 4% annually for global retail to 2026[23]—they become very significant and attract a lot of attention.

Strong growth prospects and potentially positive returns on investment usually attract investors and create business opportunities and deals. Investors like to invest in companies and markets that are growing, and the faster the better. Growing markets typically mean more consumers, more revenues and more companies in which to invest. This attracts the interest of investment banks, venture capitalists and private equity companies. It prompts deal making: there were 92 major deals (typically mergers and acquisitions; see Chapter 5) in the entertainment and media sector globally in 2020, growing to 158 in 2021 according to PWC.[24]

Indeed, some of the biggest global deals in business have been seen in the entertainment and media sector, from the merger of AOL and Time Warner in 2000, often seen as one of the worst deals of all time (see Chapter 5), to Microsoft's acquisition of Blizzard (a global games developer and publisher) for $68bn, the largest all-cash acquisition in business history at that time. China's Tencent has acquired stakes (ownership interests) in Universal Music Group, Warner Music, China Music Corp, Finnish games publisher Supercell, Spanish games company Tequila Works, Turtle Rock Studios and Ubisoft, and has significant plans for further expansion. The entertainment and media sector, then, is an attractive one to investors: growth rates are higher than other sectors, consumer spending is high and growing, it tends to be active and buoyant in terms of corporate activity and hence is also of significance to firms that service these companies and their deals, accountants, lawyers and business consultants.

Finally, and perhaps most significantly to you the reader, the cultural sector contributes to employment in an economy, as a provider of jobs, though the sheer number of jobs may be out of proportion with the overall economic impact of the industry. In the UK in 2021, for example, there were approximately 700,000 people employed by businesses in the arts, entertainment, and recreation sector[25], compared to approximately 3.5m in the retail sector or 2.5m in the manufacturing sector. The sector is relatively small, then, in terms of absolute number of jobs—about 2.1% of the total 33m workforce in the UK. Estimates in the USA suggest that there were around 3.5m people working in arts, entertainment and recreation in 2023[26], out of a total workforce of 158m[27], again around 2.2%. In India, estimates[28] suggest there are approximately 5 to 6 million people working in the industry, a tiny percentage of the total population of 1.4bn in 2022.

It's worth noting that many of those working in the industry are self-employed. They may work for large multinational companies but do so as external suppliers of skills and capabilities. DCMS figures on the UK suggest that just slightly less than half of the 700,000 people working in the sector are self-employed. They often work in very small companies they have set up themselves, perhaps with only two or three other employees (though more may be hired for specific projects). Statista suggests there were approximately 270,000 SMEs (small and medium-sized enterprises) in the arts and entertainment sector in the UK in 2023. This is a huge proportion of the estimate of the total number of business enterprises involved in the sector, around 280,000. Indeed, their analysis suggests that only 100 of the total number of enterprises in the cultural industry in the UK employ 500 people or more. This is characteristic of the industry globally; SMEs typically make up the vast majority of firms in the cultural industries.

This of course has been exacerbated hugely with the growth of user-created content on platforms like YouTube and TikTok. People who post their own content on these platforms, and internet influencers more generally, have found they can make a living by providing such content, securing revenue from advertising, product endorsement and sponsorship. They typically set up their own companies to manage their activities. Relatively little research has been done into the economic size of this sector or the number of people involved but it's clearly growing, and quickly. SkyQuest suggest a global value of $5.7bn in 2023 but growing rapidly to $35bn by 2030. We will come back to this issue as we describe market and industry structures in Chapters 3–6 and in the chapter dealing with labour and organisation in the sector, particularly in our discussion of the role of the 'independent' sector in cultural industries (Chapter 7).

Our conclusion at this point might be that despite its huge economic impact, there are relatively few jobs in the industry compared to other sectors. Yet given its appeal, dynamism and perhaps glamour, many people want to work in it. Competition for roles is therefore particularly intense, even at the lowest level, working in the post room of a record company, as a runner on a film set or as a junior researcher for a TV production company. Routes into the industry are many, varied and often convoluted. Volunteering is often a route in, doing a job for free to get experience and at least something on your CV. Some rely on knowing someone in the industry or having family connections, helping them find a job at the start of their career. Still others go through programmes of study, the type of programme that you may currently be enrolled on, at undergraduate, master's or doctoral level. Others work in quite different industries (e.g. fast-moving consumer goods, IT and technology) and then transfer into the sector later in life. Still others work in related sectors (consulting, accounting, legal) and transfer to work in their client's company full-time. Still others create their own businesses. Getting your first job or promotion is always a great challenge; doing so in the cultural industries seems even tougher. Hence it is our hope that in producing this book we will help you secure the role you hope for and speed your progression in your chosen industry once you have secured it. We will return to this issue in Chapter 10.

1.4.2 Previous research

As is the case with most books and research papers, we are already 'standing on the shoulders of giants'. A huge amount of research has already been carried out into the operation of the creative and cultural industries. So, who has been researching the sector to date? What is their specific discipline and perspective? What kinds of questions have they sought answers to? What are their key findings? Are there significant gaps in the current academic coverage of the industry? We won't try and include all of the major works of the authors we are about to discuss, which would take a whole chapter in itself and might well put you off reading the rest of the book; rather, the reference section offers direction to their most well-known and representative papers and books.

Some of the earliest 'modern' work on the role of business in the cultural industries in the West, particularly around the general effects of industrialisation on the sector, was probably that undertaken by Theodore Adorno and Max Horkheimer during the mid-1940s. Part of what would later be called The Frankfurt School, these Jewish refugees from the German occupation of Europe, and their analysis of the culture industries in the USA perhaps best described in their chapter 'The culture industry: Enlightenment as Mass Deception' (1944), were highly influential and remain discussed and debated to this day.

Their view of the effects of industrialisation (specifically the growth of business interests) on the culture industries was typically very negative. It was to 'dumb-down' cultural content, simplifying it to an easily produced and consumed commodity. They saw cultural content as subject to the negative effects of mass production, driven by a desire of business interests to produce profit, and nothing else. According to their analysis, the business community achieved this partly by forcing artists and other creatives to create content according to pre-existing formulas, blueprints for how a film, a theatre production or a piece of music should be structured, its content and how it should look or sound, based on previously successful commercial content. Business interests, in this sense, were seen very clearly as nothing more than a **constraint** on the creativity of artists and creators; they emerge from the literature as powerful bullies, exploiting the struggling artist, a theme which has been returned to again and again by academic commentors on the cultural industries. We will return to this issue, with a quite different perspective, in Chapter 7.

Adorno and Horkheimer were sociologists and philosophers, highly influenced by the previous works of writers like Karl Marx and Max Weber. Interestingly, in undertaking their research, they did not apparently venture out and actually talk to those involved on the business side of the culture industries, preferring to remain in various libraries in New York and California and make their observations, based on relatively little primary data, from a distance.

Sociologists, from various schools of study, have remained dominant in the academic study of the cultural industries ever since. From studying how content is produced thanks to researchers such as Peterson and Anand (2004), Paul DiMaggio (1977), Paul M Hirsch (1972) or Pierre Bourdieu (1993), to the cultural studies school populated by researchers like Stuart Hall (1980), to those studying the effects of culture on individuals including Denis McQuail (2010), if you are reading a chapter or paper on the culture industries, there is a good chance it was written by a sociologist or someone who has studied it extensively.

Inevitably they have their own areas of interest and critical questions they want to answer—e.g. the effects of media on individuals and society as a whole, how culture is linked to issues like social perceptions of power, race, gender, social class or if business interests do have such a negative effect on the production of cultural content. These are all very important questions, but in answering them such academics tend to focus minimally on generating a detailed understanding of relevant business processes.

Other disciplines have also contributed to our knowledge about the functioning of the culture industries, some a little more focused on business issues, like those working in the field of media and cultural economics (see work by Robert Picard (2002) or Gillian Doyle (2006) for example) or the study of political economy (see Deacon, Pickering, Golding and Murdock, 2007; or Nicolas Garnham, 1987). Their study tends again to be at a rather higher level than individual business processes or organisations. They are more concerned with the functioning of economies as a whole and the contribution of the cultural economy to them. They will often look at markets and market structures, concerned with issues around concentration, market dominance and market failure. If you like 'the big picture', papers and chapters written by economists can often give it to you. But you may still wish for more concrete detail about how companies are operating, as 'the literature of media economics is replete with studies at industry level and theoretical examinations of companies and their behaviour, but only a small portion explores media from the perspective of real firms and real choices' (Picard, 2002, p.1).

Another group of academics who often touch on, though don't necessarily focus on, business issues are those academics working in schools of music, theatre and the performing arts. Whilst many focus on performance issues, or the study of musicology, the historical evolution of the industry etc., some have focused more on how organisations in the sector are administered. Their interest has led to a particular focus on audiences, their composition, interaction with products and services, and particularly how to grow them. See for example work by Miranda Boorsma (2006), Ian Fillis (2011) or Mathew Reason (2010).

But only in relatively recent history have business academics begun to consistently look at the sector. This is partly due to the nature of career progression in academia, driven as it is by publishing in well-regarded and high-profile academic journals. Up until relatively recently these did not exist in the study of the entertainment and media sectors from a business perspective. Research had to be published in more general business journals, where competition was at its most intense, or in journals of sociology or cultural studies. Choosing to spend your career researching this sector was unlikely to offer as many publishing opportunities as studying other sectors, with a larger number of related journals and hence publishing opportunities, and as a result business academics typically chose to focus elsewhere. Equally business schools tend to be organised based around specific functions (management, marketing, finance, accounting etc.), so specialisation tends to be functional rather than sector-led. There were few dedicated research groups focused on the cultural industries when compared to other sectors (banking, fast-moving consumer goods, technology etc.). Finally, up until relatively recently there were few well-regarded degree programmes at undergraduate and master's level exploring business in the cultural industries—hence teaching opportunities were also limited. All in all, the cultural industries were not a sensible choice for any business academic in terms of finding a promising direction for their career.

Things have improved, however; good journals have appeared that do offer promising publishing opportunities (we will mention and draw from a number of them in this book), research groups are increasingly set up to focus specifically on the industry from a business perspective, the number of degree programmes concentrating on the cultural industries in universities has increased hugely, and its study has generally taken on a greater level of legitimacy in the academic community.

But still, those seeking an introductory and practical guide to the operation of businesses and their key processes in the sector may struggle. Much academic output is aimed at those intent on studying the industry, not necessarily those participating in it (other than as researchers). The arguments are academic, and at their most extreme resemble discussions of philosophy, rather than practical and usable advice for those working in the sector. Often the texts are designed almost exclusively to appeal to other academics and particularly journal and book editors, to support publication efforts and hence career development. Some excellent contributions are aimed at advanced-level readers and expect a reasonable level (and in some cases quite a sophisticated level) of business knowledge already; e.g. Aris & Bughin (2005) or Kung (2008). These are complemented by a range of very practical books focused on the detail of writing contracts, using social media for marketing or more technical activities like video editing or sound production. These latter texts tend to be less academic and often quite anecdotal—that is, based on the personal experiences of the author, rather than supported by rigorous academic research.

So, to answer the first question we posed in the chapter, it is important to study and contribute to business-orientated research in the industry because arguably this perspective is lacking when compared to views from other disciplines, so our understanding of the industry is still partial. Further it could be argued that business constituencies have generally not found a voice in the canon of existing research: they have often been ignored or consigned to the role of the 'bad guys', constraining the creativity of artists. To find out the degree to which this might be true, we at least need to give the business community a voice.

Our approach in this book will be to draw on all these sources. Where useful we will draw on more advanced and academic texts, if only to point you in the direction of the type of texts you might wish to review once you have finished this book. Fundamentally, however, our goal is to provide an introductory text to business management in the cultural industries, one that introduces major aspects of business theory as a first springboard to your further research, aimed at those of you hoping to work in the industry, not just study it.

1.5 Conclusions

So hopefully you now have a better idea of what you are getting into by reading this book. You may be reading it as part of a course of study; you may even be planning on having a career studying the industry as an academic. This book may provide some interesting insights into relevant academic theories and perspectives; it will certainly prompt some debate about the canon of existing research, and provide some different perspectives, but it's not primarily why it exists. There are already hundreds of other books that will help you build your academic skills.

Rather it primarily exists to help those who want to work in the sector, to get a job and build a career, particularly for those hoping to secure a role managing and leading in the cultural industries. The aim is to turn you from observer and bystander, to being an active participant in the cultural industries of tomorrow. It will introduce you to management thinking and innovation in a variety of different business sectors, as well as in the cultural industries. It will hopefully be the start of a lifelong engagement with management innovation, and prompt you to develop your own learning agenda and help identify your personal areas of interest. Equally, you may decide that you absolutely don't want a business career in the cultural industries—you may be put off business for life! It's useful to discover this sooner rather than later in your career, as whether you chose a more artistic and performative career, or one managing the business dimensions of a cultural organisation, it's going to take all of your energies and time to build it. Better not to waste time, then, and to start with a clear idea of what you hope to achieve and how you might achieve it. Hopefully this book will contribute to you achieving that clarity and focus.

1.6 Activities

- For the last TV programme you streamed, film you watched or song you played, identify the companies involved in its production and distribution.
- For the next academic paper you read, find out who wrote it, why they wrote it, what their discipline is and how the research was conducted. How did their background influence their research approach, research focus and findings?
- What contribution is the cultural industry making to the overall economy in your home country? Does it make a significant contribution in terms of things like revenue generated or employment? Is the government or state trying to encourage growth in the sector and, if so, how? How is it connected (if at all) to the tourism industry?
- Consider if constraint is always bad for creativity? How might it benefit creativity?

Notes

1 https://www.unesco.org/creativity/en/2005-convention.
2 UNESCO Framework for cultural statistics (FCS), 2009.
3 https://www.gov.uk/government/publications/creative-industries-mapping-documents-1998.
4 https://en.chinaculture.org/ministry.html.
5 https://www.cepal.org/en.
6 Statista Reports, 2023.
7 PWC Entertainment and Media Report 2022.
8 Precedence Research Report.
9 Kings Research Report.
10 Statista Reports, 2023.
11 SkyQuest Report, 2023.
12 Mordor Intelligence Report.
13 IFPI, 2023.
14 Global Market Insights, 2023.
15 Market Research Group, 2024.
16 RRW research group, 2023.
17 Accenture: The future of Broadcasting, 2016.
18 PWC UK Economic Outlook, 2022.
19 https://www.statista.com/outlook/amo/media/united-states.
20 Dezan Shira Associates: China Gaming Industry Report, 2024.
21 PWC global market forecasts, 2022.
22 SkyQuest Reports, 2024.
23 Statista Reports, 2024.
24 PWC Global M&A Industry trends analysis, 2021.

25 Statista Reports, 2022.
26 IBISWorld report.
27 Statista Reports, 2023.
28 See *The Emerging Media & Entertainment Industry*, Kailash B. Gupta, INOX Leisure, for example.

References

Adorno, T. and Horkheimer, M. 1977/1944. The culture industry: Enlightenments as mass deception, in Curren, J., Gurevitch M. and Wollacot J. (eds.). *Mass Communication and Society*. London: Edward Arnold.

Aris, A. and Bughin, J. 2005. *Managing Media Companies: Harnessing Creative Value*. London: Wiley & Sons.

Boorsma, M. 2006. A strategic logic for arts marketing: Integrating customer value and artistic objectives. *The International Journal of Cultural Policy*, 12 (1), pp. 73–92.

Bourdieu, P. 1993. *The Field of Cultural Production*. Cambridge: Polity Press.

Caves, R. E. 2000. *Creative Industries*. Cambridge, Massachusetts: Harvard University Press.

Dasgupta, R. K. and Clini, C. 2023. The cultural industries of India: An introduction. *Cultural Trends*, 32 (4), pp. 341–347.

Deacon, D. N., Pickering, M. J., Golding, P., Murdock, G. 2007. *Researching Communications: A Practical Guide to Media and Cultural Analysis*. Arnold, Second Edition.

DiMaggio, P. J. 1977. Market structure, the creative process and popular culture: Toward an organisational reinterpretation of mass culture theory. *Journal of Popular Culture*, 11, pp. 433–452.

Doyle G. (ed). 2006. *The Economics of the Mass Media*. Edward Elgar.

Fillis, I. 2011. The evolution and development of arts marketing research. *Arts Marketing: An International Journal*, 1 (1), pp. 11–25.

Garnham, N. 1987. Concepts of culture: Public policy and the cultural industries. *Cultural Studies*, (1) 1, pp. 23–37.

Garnham, N. 1990. *Capitalism and Communication: Global Culture and the Economics of Information*. Sage.

Hall, S. 1980. Cultural Studies: Two paradigms. *Media, Culture & Society*, 2 (1): pp. 57–72.

Hirsch, P. 1972. Processing fads and fashions: An organization-set analysis of cultural industry systems. *American Journal of Sociology*, 77 (4), pp. 639–659.

Kung, L. 2008. *Strategic Management in the Media: From Theory to Practice*. Sage Academic.

McQuail, D. 2010. *McQuail's Mass Communication Theory*. Sage.

O'Conner, J. 2000. The Definition of the Cultural Industries. *The European Journal of Arts Education*, 2 (3), pp. 15–27.

Peterson, R. A. and Anand, N. 2004. The production of culture perspective. *Annual Review of Sociology*, 30, pp. 311–334.

Picard, R. (ed.). 2002. *Media Firms, Structures, Operations and Performance*. Routledge.

Reason, M. 2010. Asking the audience: Audience research and the experience of theatre. *About Performance*, 10, pp. 15–34.

Throsby, D. 2008. The concentric circles model of the cultural industries. *Cultural Trends*, 17, pp. 147–164.

Wackman, D. B. and Lavine, J. 1987. *Managing Media Organizations: Effective Leadership of the Media*. New York: Longman Publishing, Inc.

2 Introduction to Business Theory and Practice

2.1 Introduction

For many of you, this will be the first time you have studied business and read a textbook on the subject. You may have learnt something about business by watching the news or reading newspapers, from your family, friends, even by starting your own business or participating in one as a part-time employee, but this may be the first time you have studied it in detail from a theoretical and practical point of view.

People go to university to study business as an undergraduate programme. This takes three or four years and some even spend their entire time studying just one element of business—e.g. a degree in marketing, or finance or human resources. Others go on to study it as an intensive master's degree—that's another one or two years. Some spend an additional three or four years studying it as part of a PhD! It's a long process. Equally, some of our most respected and successful businesspeople did not pursue this more academic route at all; they left school (often quite early in life) and learnt about the subject 'on the job', practising business from a relatively early age, perhaps augmenting their practice with a few professional training courses as they felt the need. There is no single 'best way' to learn how to be successful in a business career, but whatever your approach it is a lifelong learning process for all.

This is partly because it's a vastly complex discipline, drawing in ideas and theories from a wide range of different subjects, including economics, sociology, history, psychology, decision making, engineering, technology, information processing and management and so on. This diversity and scope are part of what makes the study of business so interesting, but also so challenging.

In this chapter we are going to outline some of the key fundamentals of business. It can't be as comprehensive as a three-year programme of study, or give you as detailed an understanding as actually working in a job for a few years, but it will start you on your learning journey and act as a solid basis for our more detailed analysis of business issues in the cultural industries in the rest of the book. Hence, we will define some critical terms, review some basic processes, highlight some relevant theories and start to develop your business vocabulary. Where useful, the chapter will provide further references for study if a particular idea or issue sparks your interest.

We will introduce some key tools and techniques that are likely to be useful in your business career. We'll then draw on those tools in subsequent chapters, to illustrate how you might use them, noting their strengths and weaknesses, and to enhance our understanding of specific cultural industry business sectors and issues. For those of you who have already studied business to some degree, you may wish to skip some sections

DOI: 10.4324/9781003498599-2

of this chapter but perhaps review the sections on tools and techniques to ensure you are familiar with them and to establish a common understanding as we apply them in the rest of the book.

There are a number of further issues we will discuss that are core elements of a basic business education (e.g. business models, stakeholder management, mergers and acquisitions) and we will address them as they become relevant in each subsequent chapter.

So, to business.

Almost all organisations can broadly be categorised as either '**for profit**', or '**not for profit**'. This describes their basic aims and ambitions, and why they exist. Typically, organisations in each category attempt to achieve their goals by providing **products and services** desired by **customers and consumers**.

2.2 'For profit' and 'not for profit'

The business world has for most of its history been associated with '**for profit**' organisations. These organisations exist primarily to make a profit, typically a financial reward, for their owners, employees and stakeholders (that is, individuals and groups with an interest in the activities of the organisation). Their aims are clear and unequivocal, and they are judged on their ability to produce increasing profits, consistently over time. Their founder wants to be rewarded for all their hard work and the risks they took (maybe by investing their life savings) to set up and run the business. Their employees expect to be rewarded for their efforts helping to produce profits and achieve organisational goals. Individuals and institutions may buy an organisation's shares (that is, a share in its ownership); they too want to be rewarded. These rewards typically grow as profits increase; hence, the search for profit defines these organisations' scope, activities, processes, organisational structure, values and goals.

There are also '**not for profit**' organisations, which don't have profit as their main or sole concern; they exist for other purposes. Such organisations may want to reduce world hunger, save a rare species of animal, provide services to the public like waste collection, education and health care, or enrich our cultural lives. Here then we are typically describing charities (sometimes called the third sector), government / state departments (often called '**public**' organisations, as opposed to **private** organisations in which the government typically has no ownership or involvement other than perhaps setting regulation and collecting taxes) or many cultural institutions like theatres, operas or ballet companies. Profit may feature in their objectives and will probably be considered in decisions about how the organisation operates, but it's typically not their primary goal. Whilst clearly an important part of the overall structure and economy of a country, you might ask: why even consider them in a discussion of business?

Well, partly because there has been a significant blurring of boundaries between the two categories which, as we will see, is particularly relevant to some of the sectors we will study in this book. For example, many performing arts organisations, theatres, dance companies and orchestras, often considered not-for-profit organisations, have only been able to focus on non-profit goals (creativity, audience engagement, developing artistic talent, maintaining our 'artistic culture') because they have been significantly supported by state funding. In the UK, for example, many such organisations rely on the Arts Council, a UK government-funded body, to support their activities with grants and other forms of financial support, along with support from local, geographically based councils that are involved in the civic management of cities and regions. In China artistic organisations might hope for support from the Ministry of Culture and the CNAF (China National Arts Foundation), in India via the Financial Assistance for the Promotion of Art and Culture programme, again run by their Ministry of Culture.

Ticket and merchandising sales alone did not typically allow these organisations to survive and grow. Believing such institutions had a significant role in maintaining and enriching the cultural life of the population, historically, governments intervened to support them. We will discuss the implications of this further in Chapter 3 but, suffice to say, such funding has typically been static or has declined significantly in the last 20 years in most territories, particularly during the COVID epidemic in 2020–2022 as government funds were diverted to health care. During the period 2010–2016, for example, some estimates suggest there was a 30% decline in Arts Council funding in the UK, and between 2007 and 2018 local council (part of the local government infrastructure) funding declined by 43%. Similar stories are heard in other regions of the world.

This has forced many traditionally not-for-profit organisations to become more business-like and profit-orientated, devising their own methods of revenue-generation to remain operational. The sector has sought ideas from more traditionally business-orientated sectors like those involved in producing fast-moving consumer goods (the FMCG sector). In both sectors (for-profit and not-for-profit) there are similar business-orientated processes, developing strategy, hiring and developing people, managing finances, serving customers etc. Not-for-profit businesses have increasingly sought ideas and guidance on how to operate these processes from more profit-orientated companies. This has been partially enabled by the movement of talent and skills from profit-orientated business sectors to non-profit ones, helping to blur the boundaries between the two.

Equally, profit-orientated companies have increasingly borrowed from the non-profit sector. They often now embrace a broader set of objects than just pure profit. An increasingly common term in the for-profit sector is the 'triple bottom line' approach to management, where companies have goals and missions in the development of society, the protection and enhancement of the environment, as well as making profits. They no longer assess their strategies and business plans purely on the basis of profit implications, but also their effects on society and the world around them. They are no longer purely for-profit companies. Equally, many such companies now face challenges in acquiring and managing creative talent; there is a much-discussed 'war for talent' in all business sectors. Many not-for-profit cultural organisations have been managing this delicate process (of working with creative talent) for hundreds if not thousands of years. Profit-orientated companies are looking to those involved in the cultural sector for answers to how to deal with the creative community, a group who often exist outside the boundaries of the traditional organisation in what is called, at least in the cultural industries, the 'independent sector' (see Chapter 7 for a further discussion of this).

Hence there has been increasing interaction between the two sectors in recent years, with ideas and people regularly moving between the two. It's getting harder and harder to draw up clearly defined boundaries between for-profit and not-for-profit organisations, but that may not be such a bad thing.

2.3 Customers and consumers

Businesses (for-profit and not-for-profit) typically achieve their goals by serving customers and consumers. It's worth mentioning this distinction and explaining it in a little more detail, as it brings us on to another issue, the differences between **business-to-consumer** and **business-to-business** organisations.

Consumers, as you might expect, are typically the end users of a product or service, the ones who consume it. You are the consumer of this book. But for the book to get to you, a chain (often called a **value chain**—see later in this chapter for a fuller explanation of the term) of organisations had to work together. The publisher had to commission the author, they might have used an external printing company to print the book (which in turn had to buy paper, printing ink and equipment from yet more companies); the publisher might have used another company to distribute the final book to retailers (those distributors had to buy lorries and vans, petrol from other companies etc.) and had to work with the retail organisation to market and finally distribute the book to you.

Whilst the retailer is ultimately the **business-to-consumer** (often call B2C) element of the chain, all of those other organisations are involved in the **business-to-business** (B2B) sector. They don't supply products and services to the ultimate consumer, but to other companies, their customers. Ultimately there are probably far more organisations in the B2B sector than the B2C sector.

For many of the core activities undertaken by organisations, there is not a lot of difference between B2B and B2C companies. Finance may run in broadly the same way, operations the same, human resource management etc. But big differences do emerge, particularly in things like marketing. The types of promotional activities, market research and product and service development activities undertaken are often quite different in B2B and B2C companies. We will come back to this issue in our discussion of marketing in Chapter 8.

2.4 Products and services

All organisations, whether B2B or B2C, serve consumers and customers by providing goods, things they need or want. We typically define goods as either products or services.

Products tend to be tangible and material; you can touch and hold them. You can choose if and when you want to use them. They can be stored by organisations for later sale or use (typically called inventory or stock). Their quality can generally be consistently maintained, even if thousands, tens of thousands or millions are made. Think of the tinned food you buy in the supermarket, stationery, cosmetics, your cell phone or computer, clothes, cars etc.

Services, on the other hand, tend to be intangible—you can't touch or hold them. Think about your last visit to a cinema, the maintenance service you received when your washing machine broke down or getting financial advice from your bank manager. There may be tangible elements in the delivery of the service (a cinema screen, a spare part to fix your computer) but the overall experience is ultimately intangible. Hence, they are often called 'experience goods'.

Typically, services have other characteristics that can complicate the process of producing and managing them. Generally, services cannot be stored, they are perishable—think of an airline seat on a specific flight from London to Paris: if it's not sold for that specific flight, it produces no value to the airline; you cannot 'store' the unoccupied seat. Equally a seat in a theatre for a specific evening's production can't be stored; if it's not sold before the performance, it is valueless for that night. Further, typically the delivery of the service requires the consumer to be in the presence of the provider—theatre productions need audiences, airline flights need passengers—they can't be separated, and delivery requires the cooperation and involvement of both parties. Finally, it can be difficult to consistently ensure the same level of quality for a service every time it's delivered. Often this is put down to the pivotal involvement of humans in the delivery of many services. Humans are variable and unpredictable: your hairdresser can have a bad day, the first violin in an orchestra can be feeling ill and may perform poorly, the bank manager may have just had an argument with their husband or wife. All of these can affect the quality of delivery of that specific service on that particular day.

This is partly why so many organisations are investing heavily in the search for technological solutions to the customer service challenge, with the increasing use of AI (artificial intelligence) to take on the customer interface, most evident in the service sector. You don't want your customer service associate to be grumpy, tired, frustrated, angry or sad when they interact with your customers. Hence the rise of automated systems, chatbots and a variety of other typically IT-based systems to take the unreliable human out of the provision of the service and (at least theoretically) improve the consistency of its quality.

In the past businesses were typically very clearly in one sector or the other, the supply of products or of services. Increasingly we are seeing a blurring of these traditionally clear boundaries. The last album you bought on Apple iTunes—is it a product (you own it, can use it whenever you like, it is consistent no matter how many copies of it are sold) or service (it is intangible, you can't touch it or hold it)? Arguably it's a hybrid good: it has qualities of both, the album might be considered the product (even more so when content tended to be sold in physical mediums, the CD, the DVD etc), enabled by the iTunes service.

Certainly, most business that traditionally only made products (let's say computer printers) are increasingly deliberately blurring these boundaries to add service elements to their offer (e.g. lifetime subscriptions for the provision of printer ink, enhanced maintenance contracts etc.). Basic products are always seen as vulnerable to lower-priced competitors, but adding service elements can add new revenue streams, make revenues consistent over time (the company receives a subscription fee every month from each subscriber), make the product more attractive to potential customers and help to maintain customer loyalty once it's sold.

2.5 Costs, revenues and profits

Whilst we will review the role of the finance function in a little more detail later in this chapter, we need a summary of some key financial terms and ideas before we proceed. **Revenue** is the money an organisation receives for selling its products and services. In providing them to customers and consumers **costs** are incurred: buying raw materials, employing staff, paying rent and utilities bills for the buildings they use, the costs of advertising their services etc. The difference between revenues and costs is the organisation's **profit** if revenues are higher than costs—or **loss** if costs are higher than revenues.

Such profits are used in a variety of ways. They can be invested back in the business (buying new equipment, hiring more people, developing new products and services, for example). They can be paid to shareholders in the form of dividends, handed out to employees in the form of bonuses or pay rises, or they can be saved up—that is, put into reserves. Such reserves might be subsequently used to help a company if it goes through a period of making losses, or to buy another company in the future.

Perhaps the most common challenge for most (certainly for-profit) businesses, and the thing that the leadership team focus on more than anything else, is how to increase revenues (by finding new customers, selling more to existing customers, increasing prices, expanding their geographical focus to new international markets etc.), decrease costs (through improvements in the efficiency and effectiveness of key processes, changing product / service design or making better deals with supplier organisations), and thus make bigger profits.

It sounds easy, but it's rather more challenging outside of a textbook, partly because there will typically be a range of competitive organisations trying to do exactly the same thing, trying to reach and secure the same customers, do deals with the same suppliers, utilise the same technologies etc. External events like economic downturns, major crises like COVID, wars and other geopolitical events can also make the search for consistent profits more challenging. It's even more difficult if you are a start-up company. They often don't make profits for years after their foundation as they incur costs to start the business but don't, at least immediately, generate sufficient revenues to cover them. Anecdotal evidence suggests that Amazon, now one of the largest and most successful companies in the world, did not make profits for the first 15 years of its operation. Music steaming site Spotify took nearly 10 years to make a profit. A lack of profitability (despite having great products and services, and even loyal customers) and poor financial management is the major reason why most start-ups fail. In larger organisations, most divisions will have profit targets that contribute to overall organisational profit aims. Specialist departments have emerged—typically the finance department—to carefully monitor and report on levels of revenue, costs and hence profits (we will come back to the finance team later in this chapter).

Not-for-profit companies are more concerned with **balancing costs and revenues**, and less on making high levels of profit. They don't want to consistently make losses (as eventually this would lead to bankruptcy), but equally they are not expected to make large profits. Those profits that are made are typically reinvested in the organisation, rather than being distributed to stakeholders. This is typically a requirement for many not-for-profit organisations that are classified as charities: they may have potentially significant benefits in terms of paying less taxation (corporation or capital gains), but any profit generated has to be reinvested in the organisation, rather than being paid as large salary increases or bonuses to staff, or dividends to investors.

2.6 Business structures: roles and functions

Now let's start looking at business organisations in a little more detail, and how they interact with their environment. We will start within organisations and work outwards. Most businesses have a fairly typical and predictable internal structure. These structures draw on ideas laid down during the earliest days of the emergence of organisation as a principle and particularly from the first major institutions that needed to evolve larger and hence more complex organisational forms: military, religious and civil bodies. Three ideas are critical: **specialised roles and responsibilities, hierarchies** and **working in teams**.

Within most organisations we find individuals with specific roles and responsibilities. In the earliest manifestations of this we lived in groups with other humans (tribes) where some individuals **specialised**, focusing on hunting or cooking, making tools, building shelters or dealing with and interpreting the actions of 'gods'. Tribes also had different **levels** of power and responsibility: a tribe had a leader, a chief who guided the behaviour and activities of the tribe as a whole, aided by some personal helpers who worked with the rest of the tribe to implement the leader's ideas and plans, attacking competing tribes, collecting the harvest or building new dwellings. Equally there would be someone in overall charge of building shelters or dealing with the gods (a chief priest), supported by a range of helpers and deputies. Hence at the top level of most organisations are its managers and leaders.

2.6.1 The management function

Definitions of what management actually is vary, but at its most basic level we can probably suggest that it is the organisation and coordination of the resources and activities of an organisation designed to achieve specific aims and objectives. It's typically associated with specific roles and a particular tier of employees in most organisations. Whilst the management function has always been of concern to those studying the administration of organisations, as a field of academic study in the West it became more significant as economies industrialised towards the end of the 19th century with the emergence of the factory system designed to support mass production of products. Early writers of the time like Frederick Taylor and Henri Fayol helped establish a field of study that continues to this day and their core view that the role of management is to forecast and plan, to organise, to coordinate and control has been endlessly debated and researched by academics and practitioners ever since. Let us examine some of these elements in more detail.

A key function of leadership and management is **planning**: identifying a clear set of goals or aims for the organisation and working out how it is going to achieve them. Typically, this involves forecasting (see Chapter 9 for more on corporate foresight) future developments in the market, the economy, potential new technologies, the behaviour of competitors and so on; hence, it is ultimately uncertain. In looking forward, the aim will be to identify opportunities and threats that may appear. Plans must then be set for how to deal with them, exploiting opportunities and neutralising threats. This in turn requires an assessment of the internal assets (what the company owns) and capabilities (what it's good at doing) of the organisation and whether they are sufficient to achieve its aims. Should they appear insufficient, plans will be set to develop the internal capabilities of the organisation, through recruitment, perhaps investing in the workforce's skill set or acquiring new equipment. New processes and systems may also be planned to improve performance in a specific area. Alternatively new skills and capabilities might be acquired through merging with or buying another company. The growth plans for an organisation often revolve around how more of an existing product might be sold, how prices might be raised or costs lowered, consideration of launching new products and services or trying to enter a new international market. Plans typically cover each major function, department, major territory and product or service group. These support an overall strategic plan for the organisation as a whole.

Once plans are in place, the attention of management turns to **organising**, ensuring that the right skills, internal structures and processes are in place to achieve the organisation's plan. From designing internal departmental structures, defining roles and responsibilities, to establishing the systems and processes that help coordinate activity across different individuals and groups, the aim will be to ensure the internal environment of the organisation is set up to best support employees as they work together to enact the plan. Once in place the planned structure will need support in the coordination of different activities and the allocation of resources, and the monitoring of performance over time (often called the **control** function) to ensure the plan is being implemented appropriately and results are as expected. Should this not be the case the management team are charged with finding solutions to emergent problems and getting the organisation back on track.

Finally, the management team are charged with **leading** the organisation. Here we encounter a major ongoing debate amongst academics and commentators on business: is management the same as leadership, or do they describe different roles and responsibilities? We will not delve into this major debate to any extent, but rather highlight that many academics claim they are different, with the management function more focused on the 'here and now', short-term coordination and implementation of plans, monitoring performance against them and correcting plans should it be deemed necessary. This is contrasted with leadership, which is more focused on creating a longer-term vision of the future for the organisation and securing the support of the workforce and other stakeholders in achieving it. Other commentators suggest that leadership is just one of the roles of management, that they cannot really be separated. Here leadership is seen as a set of behavioural characteristics, exhibited, to a greater or lesser degree by all managers and even those in the workforce without 'manager' in their job title, part of what is often called distributed leadership.

The roles of managers and leaders are multifaceted then. There is a strong focus on **interpersonal** aspects, communicating the organisation's goals, ambitions and plans to the rest of the workforce, motivating and inspiring people, solving problems and liaising with different departments and groups. There is a critical **informational** role, collecting information on the organisation and its environment, disseminating it and utilising it in planning. Managers and leaders are typically charged with significant **decision-making** responsibilities. Whilst everyone in the organisation will be making decisions daily, the management and leadership team are typically charged with making the most important and risky decisions, those involved in developing the company's strategic plan. The decisions often involve major organisational resources, affect everyone in the organisation and typically focus on the longer term. Hence they are the most important, uncertain and risky decisions. Getting the strategic plan wrong can spell disaster for an organisation.

It is worth noting here that we typically encounter different levels of management in an organisation, levels which multiply as the organisation gets larger and more complex. At the very top of the organisation are the most senior management, functional directors (the chief marketing officer, finance director, IT director etc.), and the person in overall charge of the organisation, the chief executive officer (CEO) or managing director. The group work together in what is typically called a board of directors, perhaps advised by non-executive directors (part-time experts whose role it is to represent major stakeholders and advise the board on strategy). This senior tier of management is typically charged with developing the organisation's long-term strategy.

Middle management act as intermediaries between the senior management and the rest of the organisation. They may be intimately involved in implementing strategic plans and organisational change, or overseeing the various control systems in place to monitor the organisation's performance against its plan. They will typically take on the more routine day-to-day running of specific functions like accounting or marketing (whilst senior management focus more on longer-term plans for how the function might evolve). In this regard they are sometimes called operational management, though other commentators see this as a further level of management, below middle managers, responsible exclusively for the operation of day-to-day activities within specific functions, with the middle manager more involved in the control function and implementing and overseeing major plans and change initiatives at the organisational level.

Management, then, requires a wide range of skills. From the ability to analyse and diagnose a situation, planning, to technical skills in particular functions (like finance or engineering), to skills around dealing with people (communication, persuasion, negotiation, motivation etc.). This partly reflects how research fashions have changed our focus on management, from an early focus on the role of managers as a technical function whose key role was maximising the efficiency and effectiveness of an organisation, what was often called scientific management, to a more recent focus on their role in maintaining and developing the human capital of the organisation (the human relations approach). These research foci change every few years, as new aspects of the managerial function are explored, and new issues and challenges take precedence, and it is partly the role of managers to track and exploit innovations in management knowledge when they emerge.

2.6.2 The evolution of organisational forms

The principles outlined over the past few pages were quick to emerge in civil society. Empires—large geographic territories run by a single dominant group, whether Mesopotamian, Egyptian, Roman, Mongolian, those emerging from the Indus Valley or the Xia, Shang or Zhou—needed to be organised. Taxes needed to be collected, food produced, cities built, laws implemented, armies raised and wars fought. Civil organisations emerged, typically based on **hierarchies**, to address these needs.

Hierarchies are an organisational form designed to divide up power and authority, find the right level and responsibility for an individual and help coordinate their actions with those of many others doing different things. Most military, religious and civil organisations are still based on hierarchies, as are most business organisations. Of course, in smaller organisations we may find individuals with multiple roles and responsibilities and a fairly 'flat' hierarchy (that is, not many levels). Often when business organisations are founded, the founder has to do everything—take care of marketing, developing the product or service, managing the finances, hiring people etc. They (see Chapter 10 for a fuller review of the entrepreneur) only have a few people working for them, so not many levels are evident in the organisation. As organisations get bigger and more mature, however (as the tribe or empire or business expands), these roles and responsibilities tend to be divided up amongst the growing workforce and new levels are added.

The detailed study of these hierarchies in a Western business setting was really begun by a French mining engineer, Henri Fayol (though some might argue his work was slightly predated by that of another writer and researcher, Max Weber). Fayol's seminal work, 'Administration industrielle et generale', was first published in 1916 (Fayol was 70 at the time) and is often seen as one of the founding works in the study of modern business organisations and how they should operate. He was an engineer at heart and, based on his engineering instincts and his experience running a large iron and steel company, he set out 14 principles for the efficient organisation and running of a 'modern' business. They included the division of work into distinct roles, responsibilities and specialisms, within an overall hierarchical structure (different levels), and clear leadership and direction from the top of the organisation. Weber coined a term to describe this, which has perhaps become more well known than Fayol's work, '**bureaucracy**'.

What does a typical hierarchy look like in a business organisation (see Figure 2.1)?

Firstly, we have distinct levels in a broadly pyramid shape. A smaller number of more senior, 'important' people at the top of the organisation, the leaders or 'bosses', and a larger number of workers at the bottom. Those people at the top are typically charged with running the organisation, developing its strategy, the overall direction it will follow, its goals, aims and ambitions. The rest of the workforce is there to implement these plans, to make them happen, and to run the business on a day-to-day basis (dealing with customers, suppliers and so on). In between we have a layer who connect these two up, middle managers, whose job it is to oversee the implementation of grand strategic plans, control the operations of the organisation and deal with day-to-day problems that those at the bottom of the organisation can't solve alone.

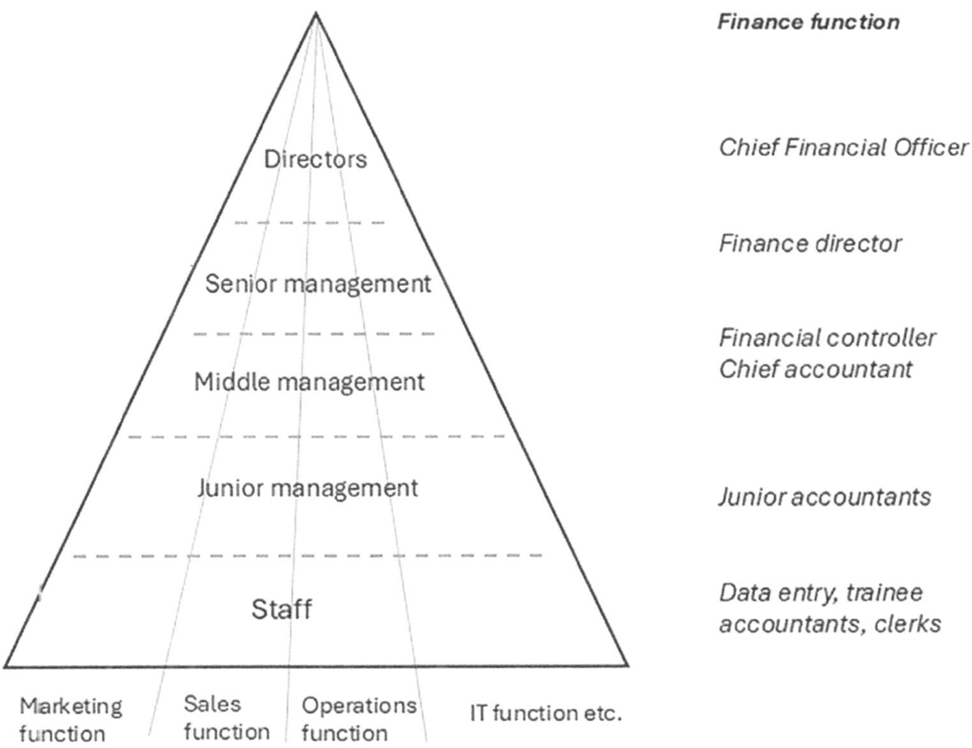

Figure 2.1 A typical organisational hierarchy in business
Source: author.

Overlaying these levels, we have specialisation based on function or activity (typically called a **functional structure**). Such functions are often called departments—e.g. the finance department, marketing department, IT department etc. Again, their presence is fairly standardised across most industry sectors, though what they do in different industries can vary significantly. Some industries have specialised functions you don't find in others; we will find a lot of these in the cultural industries—e.g. the A&R function in a record company, the commissioning function in a broadcaster, stage management in a theatre—and we will return to them in Chapter 7. Again, each function will have its own mini-hierarchy: in the finance function (or department) there will be chief financial officer (CFO), head of accounting, finance manager, all the way down to financial analysts, accounting clerks and finance assistants. Within the finance function there will often be further specialist teams focused on treasury, credit, mergers and acquisitions etc.

We will briefly describe some of the key functions that typically exist in most organisations and what they do.

Marketing: the marketing function is the voice of the consumer or customer in the organisation. It focuses on understanding them, through things like market and consumer research, and developing and promoting the company's proposition to customers. In marketing's earliest incarnation, often as an extension of pre-existing sales departments, those in the marketing department focused particularly on the promotion of the company and its products and services, through things such as advertising and brochures. Marketing's role has broadened dramatically, however. Marketing staff are now often deeply involved in analysing issues around pricing, distribution (particularly in FMCG companies like Coca-Cola), what products and services are developed and their features and characteristics. These are often called the marketing mix, or the four Ps of marketing: product, price, place (distribution) and promotion. Service businesses often add another P, for people, given their often-pivotal role in delivering services. Taken together, this is often described as the basis for the brand management approach, with each element supporting the others to create a brand—an overarching and unifying image and set of features for a product, service or company. Having historically often been the province of more visual and literary individuals, marketing has recently become much more quantitative in its approach, using data and analysis to help support decision making, partly as a response to the massive levels of consumer data generated by our interactions with digital systems. Indeed, as we will see, for some businesses, like Netflix, their business model and strategy are primarily based on their ability to collect and analyse consumer data—in this case, what we are viewing and what we think of it. We will come back to the four Ps, and marketing in general, specifically in the context of the cultural industries, in Chapter 8.

Finance: as has already been suggested, the finance function is traditionally responsible for monitoring and reporting on financial issues like revenues, costs and profits, though that role has expanded. Their vocabulary is numbers and the tools and techniques they use to investigate and assess them. They are typically involved at all levels of an organisation, from monitoring costs on the 'shop floor' where items are manufactured, to assisting in identifying and assessing strategic options at the very highest levels of the organisation. All business decisions typically have a financial dimension, and the finance team are involved. They might be assessing the relative cost implications of different suppliers of raw materials, how much it actually costs to produce a product or service, or the value of a company that might be a target for acquisition, analysing currency flows and valuations across international territories, working out how to optimise the level of taxes that an organisation pays or helping to decide what level salaries should be set at. Along with the CEO, the CFO is often the most powerful person in a company, and they often move on from being CFO to being CEO, given their involvement with and knowledge of all the functions of the organisation.

IT: the IT team are usually responsible for managing and developing the information technology infrastructure of the organisation. Since the first use of computers in business in the 1950s, through the evolution of desktop PCs and their widespread adoption, to the development of global information networks like the internet, the IT infrastructure has been a critical resource for most organisations. As a tool for storing or analysing data, managing workflow, enabling critical processes, communicating, or increasingly as the basis for automation, getting the IT system right is a minimum requirement for most organisations. It is typically a vital enabling resource for just about every other function. From deciding what IT systems and components should be used, to acquiring them, setting them up, training staff in their use and maintaining them, to planning the next evolution of the system, the IT team are usually busy in server rooms, working in incident management call centres (when things go wrong), interacting with technology suppliers, researching new technologies, training you or under your desk plugging everything back in. Again, their role has taken on a much more strategic perspective in recent times. Being innovative with IT and drawing on the latest technologies in new and creative ways can catapult an organisation ahead of its competitors, securing sustainable, at least in the short term, competitive advantage. IT has certainly taken on a hugely significant position in recent years as the infrastructure over which AI, in all its varied forms, will be deployed.

Human resources (HR): the HR function deals with the human capital in an organisation, the people. From designing specific roles and responsibilities, structuring the overall organisational form, to hiring the best talent, developing it and keeping it, to deciding what people are paid and what types of benefits they might have for working in a specific organisation, the HR department may well be the first function you encounter when you get a new job and the one department you interact most with beyond the one you work for. Emerging from the personnel function, which was typically involved in relatively mundane administrative issues around keeping data on employees and issuing employment contacts, HR is now a critical driver of competitive advantage in most organisations. It is generally agreed we are increasingly in a war for the best business talent. We want it and want to deny our competitors access to it. The HR team are charged with securing and keeping this talent. Often developing training programmes, devising incentive and reward schemes, solving contractual disputes, dealing with health and safety issues, and employee relations more generally, like the finance team, they tend to be deeply involved with all the other functions in an organisation.

Operations: the operations function covers a vast range of diverse activities. In a product manufacturing firm they may be responsible for the process of manufacturing or assembly. They are typically tasked with sourcing materials to make the product or run the business—that is, the purchasing function. They are often charged with ensuring the quality of the final product or service. They may be deeply involved in logistics and the distribution of products to customers and consumers. They are often responsible for developing and running global supply chains, drawing on supplier companies all over the world. They engage in planning, scheduling, inventory control and capacity planning. They maintain background systems and machinery. In service-based firms they are involved in planning, coordinating and controlling the resources necessary to deliver the service; hence, along with the HR department, they are often very involved in decisions around staffing and service process design. They may be involved in deciding how service staff should interact with consumers. They make decisions on issues like the level of standardisation or customisation of the service for different customers. Again, they may take a key role in managing service quality levels.

These are typically the core functions that just about all types of business share. But beyond this there are further departments and teams; some firms will have a legal function staffed by teams of lawyers, perhaps a lobbying function to deal with governments and public institutions, risk management teams, transformation teams, most will have some form of research and development (R&D) function (potentially huge in technology companies) and many are developing teams and functions around corporate social responsibility. We will deal with these as they appear to be relevant to our study of the cultural industries, in the rest of the book.

Again, in smaller and start-up companies, a single individual may need to cover a range of these divergent functions. As a founder, at least initially, you need to be a strategist, analyst, marketer, salesperson, accountant and head of HR. But as firms grow and diversify, they tend to form hierarchies to divide up this work and, as they expand, add new levels, specialist teams or even new hierarchies. If a new product or service is launched, for example, it will often need its own organisation (and hence hierarchy). If a product is launched in a fresh territory, it will evolve its own local hierarchy. Things can get extraordinarily complex, very quicky, so typically larger, more diverse organisations set up head offices, coordinating the activities of all of these different hierarchies across products, services and territories (see Figure 2.2).

In exploring how work gets done in these hierarchies, we typically think about teamwork, and often encounter the **matrix form** of organisational structure. Interest in this emerged as researchers looked at the reality of day-to-day life in these bureaucracies. They

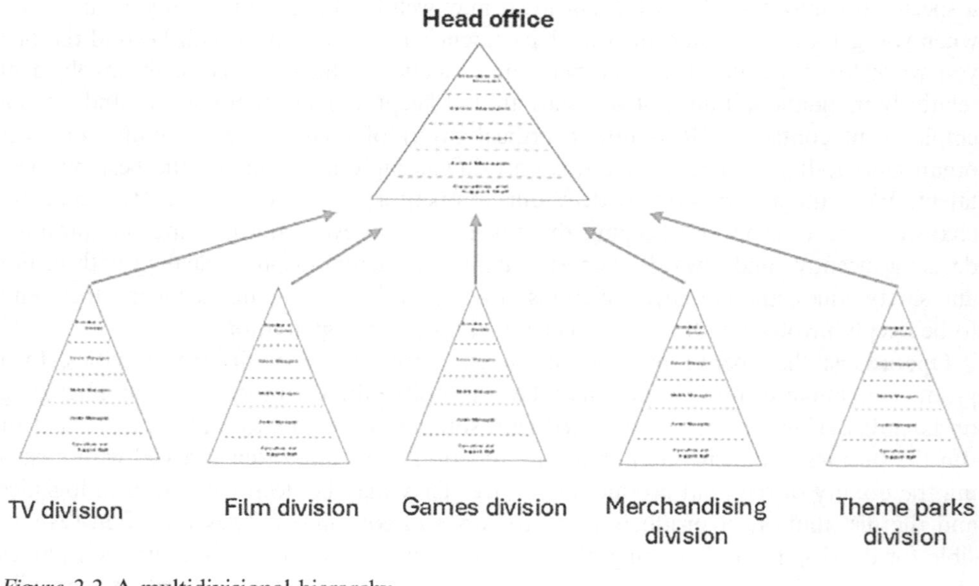

Figure 2.2 A multidivisional hierarchy
Source: author.

found that much work was organised in the form of team-based projects. These were specific initiatives, often with a limited timescale (they lasted a few weeks, months or years, but had a definite end point). The project might be to develop a new product or service idea, work out how to cut costs and improve profit, improve the efficiency of a particular function or how it interacts with other functions etc. Workers who were part of a particular function (marketing, operations, IT, for example) might also be working on a specific project. That project, often made up of staff from different functions, also had its team hierarchy: it had a project boss or team leader and specialist team members. Hence any individual within the organisation often had two bosses, their functional head and the leader of the project team they were temporarily working with (see Figure 2.3). This is the idea of a matrix.

Think of someone working in the property ('props') department of a theatre or opera company. They are part of a functional team (typically the stage management function: they normally report to the head of that department), but they may also be working on a specific production, let's say a production of Wagner's *Ring* cycle. The project (the production) will run for a set time. It will involve a team drawn from a variety of different functions (stage management, the orchestra, the chorus, the marketing team, finance team, programming team etc.). It will have its own leader, typically the director. Once the production is finished the team will be broken up.

Matrix structures appear to be the reality of how many functional hierarchies actually operate on a day-to-day basis. They operate through teams, working on projects in addition to the responsibilities of individuals based in specific functions. Matrix structures come with many challenges, including the potential for unclear roles and responsibilities (your functional head wants you to work on one thing, but your project leader wants you to work on something else!), conflict over resources (often people—each project wants access to the 'best' organisational talent), coordination of resources going to different projects and so on. A good place to start if you want to explore this in more detail would be the Davis and Lawrence (1978) paper available via *Harvard Business Review*. To finish this section it's worth mentioning a few key trends that currently occupy many senior staff responsible for designing and running these structures.

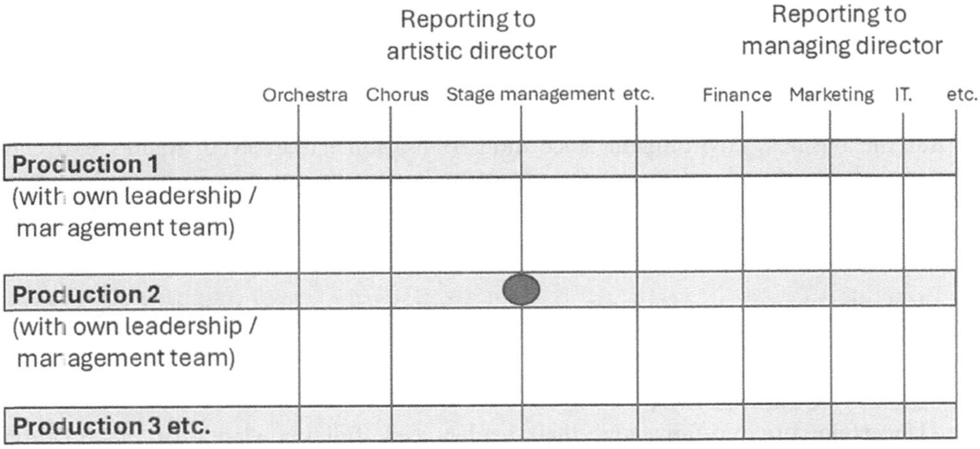

Figure 2.3 A matrix structure in a theatre
Source: author.

2.6.3 Trends in organisation

Firstly, are **hierarchies getting too big and complex**? The term bureaucracy is often used in quite a negative way, to describe an organisation that is too big, too complex, too difficult to deal with as a consumer or supplier. The term is often applied to government (public) institutions that are supposed to serve the public, but whom the public find exceedingly difficult to deal with. 'Bureaucrats' are rarely viewed positively. From a business perspective, having organisations with too many levels can add to difficulties of coordination, add significantly to costs and make it difficult for information to flow from the bottom to the top of organisation (and vice versa). A group who regularly come in for attention and often criticism in this regard are the middle managers. Research suggests that too many layers of middle management can add vast amounts of cost, slow down decision making and create too big a gap between the 'thinkers' at the top of the organisation and the 'doers' at the bottom for its efficient operation.

Since the days when author and businessperson Robert Townsend wrote his seminal text, *Up the Organisation* (first published in 1970), we have often viewed middle managers in quite a negative way. His suggestion was that huge hierarchies with multiple levels have an extremely negative effect on workers' motivation, energy and desire to innovate. Organisations, he suggested, needed to be 'flattened', reducing the number of levels, potentially by getting rid of as many middle managers as possible. How to flatten organisations, reducing cost and complexity, remains a big theme for senior executives and HR personnel.

A second major theme is adapting organisational structures and their operation to a changing business environment. An area of more academic research called 'organisational ecology', first posited by Hannan & Freeman (1984) and furthered by Hannan (2005), suggests that organisations built in the industrial era (typically the time when countries first industrialise and develop manufacturing on a mass scale) faced fewer external threats and disruptions than organisations today, and hence that their predominant aim (for someone writing at the time of Henri Fayol, for example) was to deliver stability, consistency and reliability—reflected in organisational forms (e.g. the fixed hierarchy) and the expected role of leaders. Organisational structures and routines were fixed and rigid, designed to perform in highly predicable and consistent ways, but potentially less adaptive to external pressures and changes (Hannan, 2005). Leadership was focused on hierarchical, 'command and control' models inherited from military and religious institutions: the leaders tell you what to do, and you do it, no debate or discussion.

But the business environment since industrialisation has evolved, thanks to trends like globalisation and advances in technology; hence, we are now in an environment characterised by the term VUCA. The new environmental context for business is described by four key themes. It is:

- **Volatile:** changes are frequent and cause instability—in the very first years of the 2020s we went through COVID, then the Russian / Ukraine war, conflict in Israel and Gaza, elections (and in some cases changes in the ruling powers) in Russia, India, UK and the USA.
- **Uncertain:** organisations and their leaders lack full knowledge of the potential impact of a development—e.g. AI.

- **Complex:** changes are difficult to understand and manage due to the interconnectedness of events, processes and information—e.g. the challenges of managing the supply of raw materials across the increasingly turbulent globe.
- **Ambiguous:** changes lack precedence or are novel or unusual.

As a response to this, organisations are, it is argued, changing their views of employee roles, responsibilities and how the organisation should operate. Organisations need to be more agile, (a quite common aim mentioned on many company websites); that is, quick to react, change and innovate. Huge, static and stable hierarchies are not necessarily suited to this. Hence, we are seeing a move from fixed, permanent hierarchy to temporary work teams in loosely formed, flexible organisational structures. From fixed, specialised roles and responsibilities to the dynamic division of labour. From fixed organisational boundaries to those that are more fuzzy, blurred and permeable (we will return to this issue when we explore 'open' innovation). From work processes that are routine and standardised to those that are improvised and flexible. From homogenous workforces (those that are essentially remarkably similar in composition), to those that are highly heterogenous (everyone is quite different). To this end, some organisations are exploring 'self-organisation' models to get things done, dividing up bigger organisational structures into small self-organising teams—for example, the 'holocracy' model utilised by Zappos, or the Rendanheyi (人单合) method being used by Chinese consumer electronics goods firm Haier Corporation.

From an ultimate focus on stability, predictability and inertia to one focused on speed, adaptability and change, many organisations are currently experimenting with these novel approaches to organisational design. It will be interesting to see how they play out, particularly during a period when the evolution of AI promises to further disrupt traditional roles, responsibilities and ways of working. Despite all of this, however, the hierarchical form remains remarkably resilient and evident.

Overlying these business structures are business systems and processes. If the structure is the skeleton of the organisation's anatomy, processes are the muscles and sinews. Each function will have its own set of processes and systems and, again, cultural industries often have their own unique ones, like commissioning (which we will explore in Chapter 4), but we will briefly mention a few critical ones here, particularly those that tend to happen throughout virtually all organisations.

2.7 Processes and systems

There are marketing processes, purchasing processes, finance and accounting processes etc. Every function will have its own set of core processes and systems, far too many to cover here. But we can briefly review some that all organisations share across functions.

Most organisations will go through some form of **planning process** each year, developing a set of goals—often for the next 12 months—and a plan to achieve them. Each function will do it: there will be a marketing plan, a finance plan, an operations plan etc., but there will also be a company-wide process of **strategic planning**. This is typically focused on working out the overall goals for the company, over a relatively longer time horizon, often three to five years, and for some companies like those involved in the oil and gas sector, or computer chip design and manufacturing firms, perhaps a 20–30-year plan in outline at least. For some companies in industries that develop and change more quickly, their strategic plan may not project forwards for more and one or two years.

These strategic plans are usually developed by the top management and leadership of the company, often aided by a specialist team of strategic planners and the senior people in each of the major functional areas. Individual functional plans (e.g. for accounting, for marketing, for HR) support these overall strategic goals: they are how these big aims and ambitions are to be enacted in each part of the organisation. Such strategic plans usually outline what the company wants to achieve over a relatively long timescale, and how they intend to reach these goals. They are usually focused on things like profit growth, launching new products and services, building new manufacturing plants, adding new parts to the business and expanding internationally. That is, big projects that are often quite risky, take a lot of time to implement, require a lot of resources, require significant coordination and will have a significant effect on the company as a whole (particularly if they fail). Such strategic planning processes are often supported by IT-based systems that collect and analyse data from multiple functions and assess the benefits of different strategic options (a key area where AI is expected to make an enormous impact over the next few years). Again, in small and start-up companies, the founder is likely to have to do all of this themselves, without much help. They will also need to take care of the next set of processes.

Organisations also typically go through a process of more routine **financial planning and budgeting** each year (see Chapter 3 for a detailed review of this in the context of the performing arts, and Chapter 9 for more detail on this in the context of strategic foresight). This often focuses on what costs are likely to be involved in running each department, function, product or service for the forthcoming 12 months. This might cover what raw materials will be needed and their price, the costs of the workforce (and if new people might be required or if people might be made redundant) or what new equipment might be needed. It will estimate costs for utilities (rent, rates, heating, cooling, electricity etc.). These costs are then reconciled with estimates (forecasts) of sales to work out how much profit the organisation expects to make next year. These budgets are then used as part of the organisation's control systems throughout the year, comparing actual ongoing (perhaps weekly, monthly or quarterly) results to forecast figures to make sure things are on track, and to prompt action if they are not.

Understanding how an organisation is structured, what the hierarchy looks like and its key functions and processes will provide you with a reasonable overview of how an organisation actually operates. But this misses quite a few things as well. To fully understand the internal workings of an organisation, we might use some further tools and techniques borrowed from academic and consulting commentators. We'll discuss two here that might be useful should you be asked to undertake a case study, research a company before a job interview or analyse a business for your boss.

2.8 The McKinsey 7S framework

McKinsey is a world-renowned consulting company that advises all types of organisations including businesses and governments on how to grow or operate more efficiently and effectively. In doing so they look at a variety of issues, best summarised in their 7S framework. It covers many of the issues we have already discussed: how the organisation is structured, what its strategy is, how its systems operate. But they also look at a few issues we have not covered, detailed here.

Staff: Unlike a lot of consulting companies, who focus almost exclusively on a very quantitative and data-driven analysis of financial and market data, McKinsey spend as much time looking at staff and skills when they analyse a company. When looking at staff they will identify key individuals and their contribution. They will look at how staff are trained and developed. They will look at issues like turnover (does the company regularly lose a lot of people who go to work for their competitors, and why might this be happening?), or if there are significant gaps in current staffing. Are there too many people working in the organisation, raising costs, and could the organisation operate more efficiently with fewer people? What's the organisation's reputation in the employment market? Do people want to go and work there, or avoid the company at all costs? Getting this right can have huge potential benefits for an organisation. For a lengthy period, Apple were seen as perhaps the most innovative and creative company in the world. Everyone wanted to work there. If you graduated in product design, marketing or electrical engineering and wanted to work in consumer electronics, the first place you sent your CV was Apple. They had the pick of the best graduate talent in the world and did not have to market themselves (a significant cost) to potential employees. This is a huge competitive advantage in the 'war for talent', though things may have changed at Apple in the last few years.[1]

Skills: what is the company best known for, what is it good or bad at? What is the company's skill set? Is the company able to acquire new skills where necessary (e.g. does it have a strong reputation in the market, does it pay competitive salaries and offer a good range of benefits)? How does the company develop and expand the skills of its workforce? Is it good at retraining staff with new skills? Are there significant skills gaps—e.g. lots of companies are hiring employees with expertise in AI at the moment; a few years ago it was in data analytics (using data analysis to improve decision making). Every few years organisations face the challenge of acquiring new skills and abilities to keep pace with and hopefully outdo their competitors. Are they doing this well? We will return to this issue when we discuss the idea of organisational capabilities later in the chapter.

Style: what is the organisation like to work for, what's its style? How do people dress—very formally or informally (e.g. for many years if you wanted to get on in IBM you wore a suit, a white shirt and a tie to work every day, and it had to be a white shirt—other colours were NOT acceptable). Is it ok (and even required) for you to turn up to work in torn jeans and a tee-shirt if you want to fit in? Is the organisation very bureaucratic with a multileveled hierarchy, or is it flatter, with fewer levels of management? Is the overall style of the organisation to encourage fierce competition between staff for things like promotions (a traditional feature often associated with investment banking) or is the style more cooperative? Are interactions between staff very formal or informal (with everyone using first names, including when you address the boss)? Is the boss just 'one of the guys / girls', or someone demanding respect and deference on all matters? What kind of language is used—does everyone use 'MBA speak' full of jargon and abbreviations, or is the language simpler and jargon-free?

These issues of style can vary hugely between different business sectors (e.g. working in an investment bank does not feel like working in an advertising agency), can vary hugely between different companies even in the same sector (Apple feels different to Samsung), can vary significantly depending on the nationality of the business (Scandinavian companies are different to Japanese companies), and perhaps most significantly they can vary significantly across different divisions, functions and teams **within the same company**—potentially leading to problems with communication and friction or bad feeling between departments. This was very apparent when retail and investment banks merged in the UK in the late 1980s. Whilst the strategic logic of the mergers was clear, retail and investment banks had very different styles of work, processes, systems, ways of rewarding staff, recruitment policies etc. and bringing them together often created discontent, bad feeling and unexpected leadership challenges. Style is important—don't ignore it when analysing companies, particularly when thinking about your next job.

Finally, **shared values:** what does the organisation think is important, what does it think is good or bad? This is often incorporated into the idea of an **organisational culture**. Culture in this sense is a set of values and norms of behaviour shared by a group, which evolves over time and is learnt by new employees. It's often extremely specific to an individual organisation because it evolved over time as a result of the organisation's very particular history—as such, it is unique. It links quite closely to issues around style. An organisation like Google has a strong set of values, expressed in its aim to do no evil, or that you can be successful as a business without doing bad things, or that you can be serious without a suit. Values can be subtle and powerful; Google, some would argue, also believes in maths, the importance of numbers (partly a reflection of the style of its founders, who were both doing doctoral studies in computer science when they met—indeed, Sergey Brin's father was a maths professor) and the value of generating data by measuring everything and using the data to run the company. More and more businesses see the benefit of having a set of shared values and principles around environmental, green and sustainability issues. Some organisations may have strong values around the benefits of meritocracy, in which the best and most able people are the only ones that are promoted. In other organisations tenure, age and family connections may take precedence.

Many of these values are often expressed in the form of organisational stories, descriptions of historical events, individuals and issues that are regularly discussed by staff and management, potentially around the watercooler or during after-work drinks. Stories proliferate, about a hugely successful employee who went from the bottom of the organisation to the top, or when the organisation tried something that turned out to be disastrous, or what the employees of a different department are like, or why that manager was sacked and should never be mentioned again. These stories help to guide our behaviour in different (particularly novel) situations. Key questions around shared values include what they are, why they exist (e.g. how did they evolve), the degree to which they help and support the other elements of the organisation, the degree to which they are genuinely shared by all employees (or if it's just the top management team telling everyone what their values should be), how values might vary across the organisation in different divisions or countries, and their ultimate strength: do they endure over time or change every year?

They key idea in this overall model is that all of the elements of the 7S framework—an organisation's systems, strategy, structure, style etc.—should be working together, each element supporting the others, pulling the organisation in the same direction, towards its strategic goals. It stresses the links between the elements and explores how they might vary across an organisation. A mismatch, perhaps where the systems don't support the strategy, or the style of the company may not suit the staff it has to recruit, can lead to inefficiency, ineffectiveness and ultimately failure.

It's an extremely useful little tool if you ever have to do a quick case study of a company, analyse a competitor or even look at your own organisation. It helps structure your thinking, providing a set of issues to consider, collect data on and analyse. Ensure you focus on the interconnectedness of the elements and if they work together to support overall strategic goals of the organisation.

2.9 Assets, capabilities and the resource-based view

The second perspective we will discuss in our review of how to analyse the internal functioning of an organisation is what has come to be known as the **resource-based view**. Developed partly by business academic Professor Jay Barney (see his 1991 paper for a good introduction), it suggests that to understand why companies succeed or fail in a particular market or industry, it is wise to look at their assets and how they use them, their capabilities.

Assets (sometimes called resources) are simple to understand: they are simply what an organisation has, what it owns. Assets are typically inputs into the organisation's production or operating processes.

Assets can be **tangible or intangible**. Tangible assets, as you might guess from our discussion of products and services, are things you can touch and feel: computers, offices, staff, raw materials, research equipment etc. They also include financial assets like cash reserves. Tangible assets are typically easy to trade: you can buy and sell them without too much trouble. If you want to copy Alibaba's IT infrastructure, you can, at least in theory, by buying the hardware and software from various suppliers. It's easy to identify who owns tangible assets and where they exist in the organisation: you can walk down to the relevant department and look at them. Finally, they typically need to be maintained, as without maintenance they often degrade over time.

Intangible assets are things that the company has, but that you can't really touch or feel: the organisation's reputation, its brand, its relationships with customers, suppliers and the government, for example. It may be the loyalty of its staff, or its energetic and innovative organisational culture. All of these are critical intangible assets. It also covers things like patents (which of course you can touch, in that they are written down, but for various accounting principles and rules they are generally considered intangible), copyrights, trademarks, knowledge assets, trade secrets and so on. This category of assets is not easily traded: you can't buy Alibaba's reputation, its relationship with its suppliers or how it actually uses its IT system. It's often difficult to identify where they exist in an organisation or who actually owns them: where, for example, does Walt Disney's formidable brand reside? It's been argued that because of these characteristics they are potentially more important to an organisation than tangible assets.

Why? Well partly because tangible assets can be easily identified and copied. It's easy for a competitor to copy us if they feel our success is based on our ownership of some tangible assets. If it's our culture that makes us successful, or our brand, or the knowledge in our organisation or our reputation (that is, intangible assets), it's much harder for a competitor to copy us as they are often a function of our very particular history, evolution and the way we use our assets, rather than the assets themselves.

If assets or resources are what we have, then **capabilities** are what we do with them, how we operate as an organisation, what we are good at doing. Like intangible assets (they share quite a few characteristics), capabilities are often difficult to acquire. They are learnt by an organisation, they evolve over time by combining resources or assets in different ways and trying things out. Authors Hill and Jones, who have contributed much to the analysis of organisational capabilities (see their useful 2012 book, *Strategic Management: An Integrated Approach*), suggest they reside in an organisation's rules, its routines, procedures and how it manages itself over time. Again, like intangible assets, they are difficult to trade and it's often difficult to identify precisely where they exist in an organisation. They tend to be organisationally specific and are often deeply embedded in it. That's why one of the most popular ways to acquire new capabilities is to just buy (or merge with) another company that has strong capabilities in a particular area, rather than trying to copy its various assets, systems and processes.

There are many distinct types of capabilities studied by academics. We will mention a few as they are terms you will see regularly in discussions of business, and we will use some of them subsequently in our analysis of the cultural industries. Hill and Jones (2012), for example, discuss **generic** capabilities that all organisations strive to develop around building superior efficiency, quality, innovation and customer responsiveness.

Other academics talk about **threshold** and **distinctive** capabilities. **Threshold capabilities** are the minimum an organisation needs to compete in a marketplace. To have a successful football team, for example, you need a minimum of 11 players and a plan for how they will work together. To provide a successful service you typically need a customer service function. But these capabilities don't necessarily make you a winner. Every football team has 11 players and a plan, but to win and be successful, particularly over a long period of time, you need **distinctive capabilities**, things other competitors don't have or find hard to copy. It might be a unique set of defenders in your football team, their formation and their experience of playing together that means your team never allows a goal in. It might be the way in which your customer service team works with the operations team, and the processes, routines and IT system you have built that support them, that make you better than anyone else at customer service. Hence threshold capabilities allow you to merely survive in a market; distinctive capabilities will help you flourish, grow and beat your competitors.

Interestingly there is some evidence that over time distinctive capabilities become threshold capabilities and don't secure you any competitive advantage. Over time all of the other football teams copy you and build a good defensive set of players, they build their experience in working together, work out the best formations etc. This no longer makes you a winner; it's just a necessary requirement to be competitive. Hence capabilities need constant attention, review and development to ensure they remain relevant and useful. In a similar vein, Gary Hamel and his associate C. K. Prahalad (1990) describe **core competencies**, the combination of **rare and distinctive resources and capabilities** that allow organisations to attain and maintain significant competitive advantage—arguably what the company is best at doing.

Finally, we might mention **dynamic capabilities**. This area of study partly emerged as the result of observations of the emerging VUCA-based business environment mentioned earlier. This work (review Teece's 2009 book *Dynamic Capabilities & Strategic Management* for a good overview) suggests that in order to cope with a rapidly changing business environment and high levels of uncertainty, companies need to develop capabilities focused on sensing changes in the environment, seizing opportunities and quickly reconfiguring their organisations. Taken together, they are called dynamic capabilities, the ability to rapidly identify, react to and capitalise on changes in your environment. We will return to this subject in Chapter 6.

As mentioned earlier, organisations can build capabilities by acquiring the right assets, building appropriate systems and structures, and finding and using distinctive resources in ways that competitors struggle to. This is typically called **internal capability development. External capability development** is typically about identifying another organisation with the capabilities you want and either entering into an agreement to work together (often called an alliance) or simply merging or acquiring them.

But not all capabilities are equally useful. We probably can't afford to invest in all of them, so we need to choose which to invest in and which to focus less on, as over time some become less valuable in a changing marketplace. Here we will introduce the **VRIO model** suggested by Jay Barney as a way to assess the relative value of different assets and capabilities.

2.9.1 The VRIO model

Barney (1991) suggests we need to assess our capabilities based on four key criteria: their value (V), rarity (R), inimitability (I) and level and type of organisational support (O) required.

Capabilities are **valuable** when they help us take advantage of opportunities (perhaps changes in the external environment) and minimise or remove threats. We want to build capabilities that customers value as well (there is not a lot of point in being good at something if no-one cares and it does not help you serve the customer or consumer), those that allow us to secure some advantage over our competitors in the minds of consumers. But the capabilities need to be developed and operated at a reasonable cost to us. If it's too expensive to maintain a valuable capability it will negatively affect our profitability as an organisation.

We want **rare** capabilities and assets, capabilities that are hard to find and develop. We might achieve this through having a patent on a process or product or a preferential relationship with suppliers that gives us access to raw materials and ways of processing them that our competitors don't have. We may have built the best research and development team over time, supported by unique processes and systems; we might have established the most trusted brand in an industry. These capabilities and assets are hard to find, often take significant financial resources to maintain and take time to establish. It's probably worth mentioning that we should not assume rarity will continue for ever: brands can suffer from bad publicity, people can leave our R&D team and go and work for a competitor, other companies may get access to your rare supply of raw materials or find a new material as a substitute. Hence the need to regularly review and refresh them.

Inimitable capabilities and assets are those that competitors find hard to copy or obtain. Whilst we've suggested it can be relatively easy for a competitor to copy an individual asset (e.g. a server in an IT system) it is much harder to copy how that IT system is used, how it interfaces with and supports the interaction of different functions, how it is used in things like budgeting and planning and how it is supported by the IT team. Sustainable advantage is typically found in capabilities built on specific ways of managing, developing, combining and improving assets, rather than the assets themselves. It can be hard for our competitors to identify just what makes us quite so good at marketing or customer service—the complex range of internal linkages and processes that enable it can be very hard for an external company to identify and copy. Sometimes it's even difficult for those in our own company to work out why something works quite so well.

Finally, we want to develop capabilities that our organisation can **support and develop**, at a cost that allows us to produce a profit. We can try and compete with Amazon by buying a huge IT infrastructure tomorrow, but are we able to support the functioning of that system in terms of people, skills and financial resources? If it is too expensive, like Amazon, we may not make profits for the next 15 years. Valuable capabilities and assets must help the organisation make a profit, not ensure that it doesn't, and capabilities and assets that are not actively supported by the organisation (financially, in terms of leadership attention or in terms of skilled workers) and used to further our strategic goals will eventually wither and die.

In all cases we want to have capabilities that allow us to develop sustainable competitive advantage over our competitor. Most of the time they are only likely to deliver temporary competitive advantage, or just competitive parity. Capabilities, then, need to be reviewed, assessed and invested in on an ongoing basis if they are to remain relevant and useful.

So, we have now taken a fairly lengthy view of the internal structure of business organisations. But businesses, whether for profit, not for profit, public institutions, or private ones, exist in a business environment, or a business ecosystem as it's sometimes called. Let's now start to work outwards from our individual institutions to explore the business environment in which they operate.

2.10 The business environment

Businesses typically operate in an environment that contains a range of different organisations, institutions, individuals and agencies. They are typically categorised into two groups—**the market environment** and the **non-market environment**.

The market environment includes the organisations and individuals that a business interacts with most regularly and which influence them daily, typically **customers and consumers, suppliers** and **competitors**. The non-market environment is composed of organisations that typically have less direct and regular interactions with our business, but that still may influence our operation, typically governments, legislators, the media, activists and consumer groups, and non-governmental organisations (NGOs). Taken together they are generally referred to as **external stakeholders** (entities that have an influence on or interest in our organisation), compared to our **internal stakeholders** like the labour force (see Chapter 3 for more about stakeholders in the performing arts sector).

In terms of the market environment, we'll discuss customers and consumers in much more detail as we work through each cultural industries sector and discuss marketing more generally in Chapter 8.**Suppliers** have a critical role to play in providing key inputs to a business's production and distribution activities. They may be supplying raw materials, equipment, software and systems, professional services and, in the case of the cultural industry, things like talent and ideas. Some authors have characterised these relationships as a 'supply chain', a chain of organisations (very similar to the value chain we described earlier) working together to supply a final product or service to the consumer. Sometime these chains extend across multiple regions and territories, often called global supply chains (GSCs). Apple, for example, source a great many of their materials and components from China, use other territories to assemble products, and all are linked to research, development and design activities in their California headquarters.

2.10.1 The value chain

One of the first academics to explore the workings of value chains in modern academic enquiry was Prof. Michael Porter in the mid-1980s. Porter is a hugely influential Western economist who has become one of the most widely read authors about business strategy. He characterised organisations as each having an **internal value chain** (see his 2008 book for fuller details) of primary activities to produce the product or service. The internal value chain of a computer manufacturer would be composed of several distinct stages, starting with design and engineering, securing raw materials and components, assembly, quality and testing, sales and marketing and so on. At each stage **value is added** to the final product or service (hence a value chain). The primary activities are supported by a series of secondary activities and functions: departments like human resource management, IT, finance and accounting etc. Figure 2.4 illustrates what this might look like for a theatre venue.

Markets and industries can be characterised as collections of these value chains, in different organisations, to create value networks. Our own organisation may be a supplier to another set of organisations (value chains) closer to the consumer (e.g. we may be supplying a retailer or distributor). This is illustrated in the context of a video game console manufacturer in Figure 2.5.

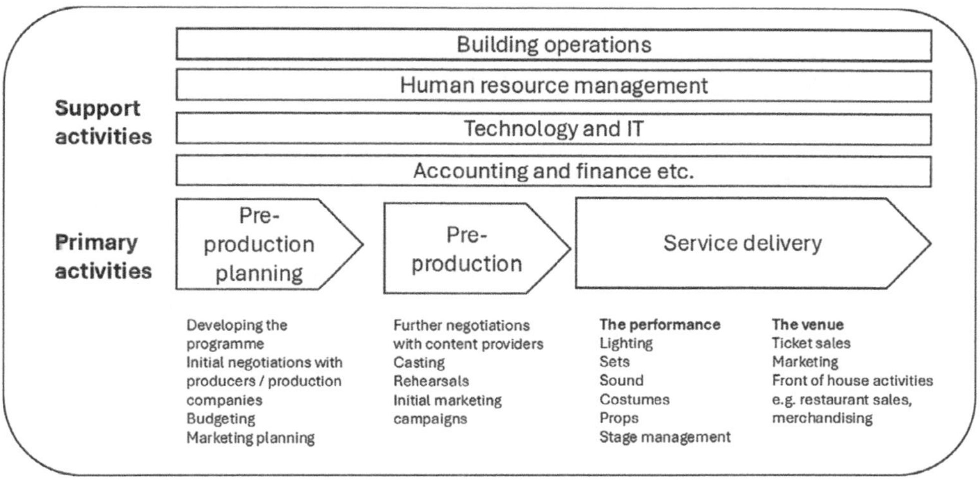

Figure 2.4 The internal value chain for a theatre venue
Source: author, adapted from Porter, 2008.

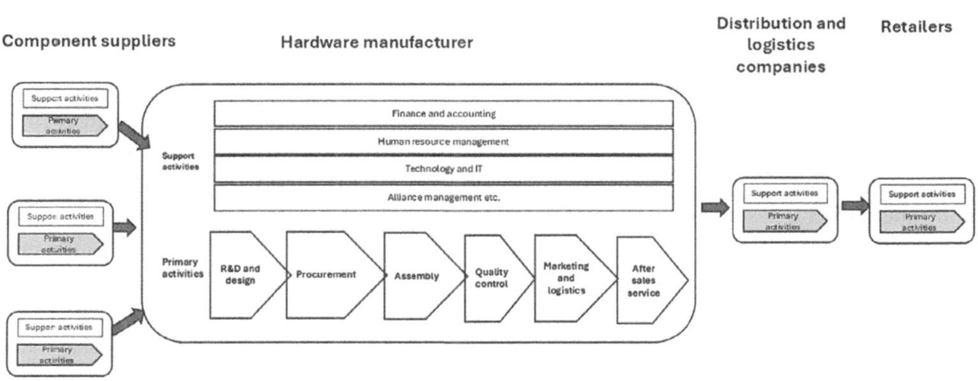

Figure 2.5 A value network in the gaming hardware sector
Source: author.

Analysing these value networks can help organisations understand the structure and dynamics of the market, work out how to manage things like their costs (e.g. you can explore the cost impact of different stages in product or service production in your own internal value chain), identify where other companies might be making large profits (perhaps retailers are generating the biggest profits in our value network) and hence look for ideas for expansion and diversification—perhaps we should buy that retailer in a process known as **vertical integration**. You will come across the term value chain in many business articles, papers and articles, but if you want to research it further it's probably best to go back to the source (Porter, 2008).

2.10.2 Positioning and alternative approaches to strategy

Porter also made huge contributions to answering the question of how organisations should fit into, or position themselves in, their environment, particularly in relation to **competitors and customers**—indeed, his theory of strategy is known as **the positioning model** (Porter, 1980). Porter suggested that in terms of business strategy, an organisation only has a small number of options to choose from in terms of positioning itself. Perhaps surprisingly, only four potential choices—generally referred to as Porter's **generic strategies**.

It could choose to be the **lowest-cost provider** (often called cost-leadership) in the marketplace, providing goods more cheaply and at a typically lower price than any of its competitors. It might achieve this through producing very simple products or services, sourcing raw materials at the cheapest price or having the most efficient manufacturing processes developed over time (benefitting from the 'experience curve' effect—the more of an item you manufacture, the better you get at manufacturing it, cutting down waste and improving efficiency). Whilst we might not make huge profits on each individual item, we have the lowest price in the market—after all, our company typically produces vast numbers of these individual products—and hence given the sheer volume we sell, despite the low margin (the difference between the cost of producing a product and its selling price), they produce significant overall profits.

Alternatively, organisations could **differentiate** their products and services, doing something that their competitors are not doing and that consumers are typically willing to pay a higher price for. Organisations can differentiate along things like product or service features (e.g. the latest Apple iPad in 2024 had a 'tandem OLED' screen which its competitors were yet to utilise and produced outstanding visuals), differentiate on things like customer service and relationships (e.g. a particularly beneficial loyalty programme) or differentiate based on how the product or service works with another one (e.g. the Apple iPhone and iTunes). Whatever way a product or service is differentiated, the critical thing is that the differentiation is valued by the customer. It's easy to come up with ideas to differentiate a product (we could build a rice cooker or toaster into our new range of audio equipment) but if it's not valued by the customer, it's not likely to lead to higher sales and profits. Equally, differentiation typically is a more expensive strategy than cost-leadership. New and unique features must be researched and developed, they often use new and expensive technologies or materials, new ideas go wrong, and resources and time are wasted, hence manufacturing the differentiated product or delivering the differentiated service may incur significant costs. This increased cost has to be reflected in the price that consumers are charged if the organisation is to secure reasonable levels of profit. Hence they typically cannot be the lowest-cost provider.

Finally, an organisation can choose to try and serve the biggest market it can (**a broad focus**) or a smaller part of the market, often called a market segment or niche (**a narrow focus**). We return to the idea of market segments and niches in Chapter 8.

Take a consumer goods company like Unilever, producing shampoo. Typically they are not the cheapest products on the market, they often have unique qualities (e.g. they are better than competitors in reducing dandruff, and they make your hair look glossy, or at least that's the claim) and they are typically aimed at as broad a market (often called the mass market) as possible. Hence Unilever are pursuing a broad, differentiated (rather than cost-leadership) market position. Another shampoo manufacturer might focus on a particular niche in the shampoo market, perhaps those dandruff-suffering consumers who put sustainability and green issues above all else (a differentiated, narrow focus). Still others will try and produce the cheapest shampoo possible for the mass market (a broad, cost-leadership strategy).

That's it—with all of the academic research done and books and papers written, Porter manages to reduce strategy to two choices, cost-leadership or differentiation, and broad or narrow focus. Of course, many authors and commentators have disagreed with this relatively simplistic analysis and produced their own interpretations of strategic options and explanations for why some companies are successful and some fail. The 'positioning' approach suggested by Porter is often contrasted with the 'resource-based view' and its focus on assets and capabilities mentioned earlier, for example. A lot of research has been conducted around how you might combine these different approaches in new and innovative ways, suggesting you don't have to choose one or another (cost-leadership OR differentiation) as Porter suggests, but can combine them in what are called hybrid strategies (see Bowman and Faulkner, 1997).

Others criticise Porter for his view of competition. Given that he is an economist, he is particularly focused on the rivalry amongst companies for scarce resources, including, of course, consumers and profit. Indeed, one of his other major contributions to a business leader's toolbox of techniques is his **5 forces** model (Porter, 1979), which is focused on assessing the attractiveness of a market or industry.

He argues that there are five forces we should consider in assessing the attractiveness of markets and industries: the threat of new entrants, threat of substitutes, bargaining power of suppliers and customers, and finally the degree of competitive rivalry in the market. This later point often refers to the number of competitors, how tough it is to find new customers, the level of price competition and hence the likelihood of being able to make a profit. Taken together they describe the attractiveness of a particular market. Low competitive rivalry, low buyer and supply power, the low threat of substitutes and high barriers to entry are all associated with attractive markets. High buyer power, low barriers to entry and intense rivalry are associated with less attractive markets. This can be a useful tool when first investigating opportunities in new markets and industries.

One of the major criticisms of this approach is suggested by authors Kim and Mauborgne (2005) with their 'blue ocean' strategy approach. Their argument is that Porter is too obsessed with working out how to secure competitive advantage in existing, what they term **red ocean**, markets. These are often highly established, relatively mature markets and industries in which many companies fight for advantage using tried and tested strategies that in many ways they all share. The 'ocean' of the market is red with the blood of their failed ideas and strategies, huge, potentially wasted investments in marketing and research and development, and ultimately their limited profits.

They in turn suggest a 'blue ocean' approach, searching for, and in some cases creating, new uncontested market spaces, creating and capturing new demand and making existing competition irrelevant. Only in these new markets, where competitive rivalry is (at least temporarily) at its lowest, is it likely that firms can consistently generate significant profits. This can partly be achieved by looking at existing products and services and working out which of their features might be improved, what new features might be created and what features might be reduced or eliminated. This latter point can seem somewhat illogical at first. Surely the aim is to constantly improve things, adding functionality, making things like computers or mobile phones ever more powerful, not to make them less powerful and feature-packed.

Perhaps the best example of the potential benefits of reducing functionality is the development and success of the Wii console by Nintendo. Rather than try to compete with the dominant existing companies Microsoft (Xbox) and Sony (PlayStation), companies who were fighting each other on the basis of who could spend the most on research and development to constantly increase the power and functionality of their consoles, and as a result losing money on each console they sold, Nintendo sought a new, uncontested **blue ocean**. This turned out to be one populated by families, who wanted to game together and who were happy to play games with relatively simple graphics (indeed, that was part of the appeal). Entering this market, Nintendo found they could produce consoles with relatively low specifications and functionality (compared to the Xbox and PlayStation) yet still fulfil the needs and wants of a significant market segment and make a profit on every console they sold. When other companies were obsessed with increasing the power and functionality of their products (a red ocean environment), by reducing its power and offering fewer functions Nintendo produced a console that ultimately created a new market segment (a blue ocean). We will discuss this example further in Chapter 5 (electronic gaming).

Perhaps the key message here is that the environment is a critical factor in considering our plan for how we will succeed as an organisation and that thinking about how we position ourselves in the environment, particularly with regard to customers and competitors, is key. This perspective suggests that our degree of **fit** with our environment will determine our progress and prospects. This chimes with theories from other disciplines; Darwin's theory of evolution suggests that the success of a species is largely determined by its fit with its environment and perhaps its ability to find a part of the ecosystem, a niche (a blue ocean), where competition for resources (e.g. food, shelter, a mate) is at its minimum.

Beyond the market environment, concerned with buyers, suppliers and direct competitors, we reach **the non-market**. This describes a range of institutions, individuals and agencies that might influence our organisation, directly or indirectly, and ultimately will play a role in determining our success or failure, but with which we don't necessarily deal every day. As already described it may include governments, regulators, the media and consumer interest groups and activists. Each will have their own way of influencing the environment. Regulators may introduce new safety rules for how products might be manufactured, ban the use of certain products or limit how products and services can be advertised; governments may want to introduce new taxes for businesses or introduce new economic policies (e.g. tariffs) that affect the overall state of the market. Consumer interest groups and activists may have particularly strong views on how our industry operates and its effects on society and the environment (e.g. the Just Stop Oil movement or groups opposing the use of high levels of sugar in fast foods etc.).

The key point is that we need to have a plan for how we will work with these organisations (typically known as external stakeholders). We must address issues raised by them, work out who the most powerful groups are and establish how best to influence and interact with them. Broadly, this is known as **stakeholder management** and several tools and techniques exist to assist in this process (see Johnson et al., 2023 for a fuller review). As we will see, in many parts of the creative industries external stakeholders like governments and regulators can have huge effects on the operation of the industry, so ignore them at your peril. We will discuss stakeholders and their management in more detail in Chapter 3, performing arts.

2.10.3 The PESTLE tool

All these stakeholders (including those in our own organisation, like the workforce) are affected by **major trends and developments** in a variety of areas at a regional and global level. All are typically affected by changes in technology or the global economic situation, social trends etc. At the time of writing, most organisations are trying to work out how to deal with and exploit technological developments in AI or to deal with the trade tariffs introduced by Donald Trump in the USA. These trends need to be examined and understood in a structured way. A variety of tools and techniques have evolved to help us with this; we'll discuss one here, the **PESTLE** model. There are a variety of different versions of the PESTLE model, e.g. PEST, but the PESTLE form tends to be most commonly used. The PESTLE model is used to identify and analyse important environmental trends and developments that might affect us and the markets we serve.

Typically these include:

Political issues: what is the role of the state and government in our industry? Do they own and control parts of our industry (e.g. the energy sector in Scandinavia, public broadcasters in many countries, the defence sector in some) and how do they want it to develop? Which political party is in power at a particular time? Might a new party take power? Might they impose significant and challenging new regulations? What's their view of things like taxation and economic policy? Is the political environment stable or is there a risk of political instability—e.g. in just three months during 2022, the UK, generally considered a very stable political environment, had three different prime ministers, each with their own policies and views on how to run the economy, compared with the previous record of three different prime ministers over the course of 28 years. How might such instability affect the economic climate? What is the state's view of international trade (and who are their key trading partners), are they intent on making huge investments in global economic programmes (e.g. China's Belt and Road initiative) that might benefit us? What's their view of the nature and benefits or drawbacks of competition in different markets etc.? How can we actually influence them as an organisation (e.g. on our own if we are big enough, or through a trade body)?

Economic: factors and trends to consider include things like economic cycles; global and local economies tend to go through cycles of expansion and contraction, so where are we now and what's going to happen in the next three years? What is happening to things like interest and inflation rates? Is consumer disposable income high or low currently? What are employment (and unemployment) rates like? How do all of these things vary in different territories (we may be seeing an economic recession in Europe, but Latin America may be buoyant)? This typically links quite closely to considerations of government involvement (one of those prime ministers in the UK during 2022 introduced new economic policies through a mini budget that had a hugely negative effect on the British economy for some years).

Social: how is society changing, in our specific territory and globally? Are there significant demographic shifts (more older people living longer, fewer young people in the population)? How is income distributed? How are lifestyles changing (e.g. the move in Japan away from the dominance of the salaryman career model to the existence and legitimacy of a more stable freelance culture)? What are the significant changes in culture and fashion? How are social values changing, what do we think is good or bad in terms of business behaviour (e.g. the emergence of the green and sustainability agenda for many consumers in the 2000s)? Are there major changes in critical social institutions and networks (families, religious groups, tribal or caste systems etc.)? The social effects of COVID, for example, including people staying at home, not visiting restaurants, pubs, cinemas or the theatre, often spending their time on self-development activities, not using public transport, turning to their phones and computers for much-needed personal interaction via social media, had a huge impact on the strategies and prospects of most businesses globally, some very positive (the gaming industry saw significant growth), some very negative (many bars and restaurants ceased trading).

Technology: developments in technology can rapidly reshape a market and industry. New discoveries, materials, methods and equipment can profoundly change what it takes to be successful in a market and suddenly make previously market-leading products, services and the companies that sell them irrelevant and in trouble. The emergence of a tiny piece of software that could be used to encode music in small digital files (mp3) radically changed the popular music market at the end of the 20th century, leading to huge consolidation in the market, many established and previously very successful companies being forced out of business, sector profits declining for almost 20 years and new organisations emerging as dominant players (e.g. the music streaming platforms). At the moment just about every company is exploring the potential of AI to reinvent their business. New materials in the field of nanotechnology offer to reshape a diverse range of industries, from medical technology to energy storage. Not identifying and making use of a new technology can quickly render your business a dinosaur, heading for extinction.

Legal: changes in regulation and legal requirements around things like labour, advertising, consumer protection and the environment can have significant effects on a business's prospects. At the moment, for example, the British government are considering introducing new laws to make it illegal for people born after 2012 to buy cigarettes (which is obviously of great concern to the tobacco companies). New, tougher rules are being introduced globally to prevent companies from damaging the global environment, particularly in the manufacturing, energy and farming sectors. Different countries have different laws around intellectual property, copyright and its infringement—particularly relevant to many cultural industries, as we will see. There may be tough laws around how companies are expected to manage themselves (corporate governance), rules around the ownership of companies and their potential to merge together (rules typically designed to stop companies becoming too dominant and powerful in any market—that is, 'market dominance'). Changes to these laws may open entirely new strategic opportunities for companies or shut down existing operations. At the very least legal systems establish some basic rules of operation (around governance, taxation, competition and ownership, intellectual property and copyright and workforce management) to which all companies must adhere, to operate in a specific market, industry or territory. Missing a major change in these can be catastrophic.

Environmental and ecological: green and sustainability issues have risen to achieve a significant level of importance in the functioning of most markets and industries. Issues around pollution, biodiversity, waste and climate change now occupy the minds of consumers, regulators and businesspeople as never before. From regulation around direct anti-pollution obligations and carbon emissions, through product stewardship issues (manufacturers are increasingly responsible for their products from creation to their final recycling or destruction) to sustainable development, business cannot afford to ignore these new trends and developments, particularly when they are enacted by governments through legislation and regulation. Seen perhaps originally as burdensome by businesses, a cost they just had to incur, changes in consumer attitudes to these issues are increasingly seen as a potentially huge opportunity for businesses to develop new products and services or change those they already supply. Equally, towards the middle of the 2020s we saw green initiatives and investments falling out of fashion to an extent, with support from governments (in the USA, for example) declining and investments from corporations being scaled back.

PESTLE is a simple model, but a useful one to start to undertake an environmental review. But a few points about its usage. Firstly, issues change in relevance and importance. Novel issues and themes emerge. Fifteen years ago, green and sustainability issues were hardly registering in reviews of external trends; now they are a critical issue for many. But enthusiasm for the green movement seems to be diminishing (at least as far as some governments and corporations are concerned) as we head towards the second half of the 2020s. Things change. Within each category, new events spur novel changes. So don't assume the range of PESTLE issues you covered and considered in your last planning cycle are the same ones you should be reviewing today.

Secondly, not all issues and trends have the same level of importance and relevance to an organisation. Part of the skill of conducting a good PESTLE analysis is prioritisation, identifying those issues with the most likelihood of having a significant impact on us; hence, issues are often categorised around level of impact and likelihood of happening. When doing a PESTLE analysis for your boss, volume of analysis (trying to cover all issues, whether relevant or not) is much less impactful than prioritising a few critical points and going into significant detail on them. This brings us to our last point, the use of data. PESTLE analysis is least effective when it looks like a collection of personal opinions, lacking any supporting evidence or data to establish their veracity. Issues need to be identified, prioritised AND supported by appropriate evidence if they are to have an impact.

Finally, the value of the work is less in the analysis of the themes and issues, and more in the assessment of their impact, the 'so what' part. The analysis itself is often the easy part; the assessment of priorities and conclusions tends to be much more challenging.

All of these external trends create the environment in which organisations operate and provide a context for their plans. Perhaps most significantly, their interaction often creates opportunities and threats for an organisation—a change in fashion, a new set of regulations or a change in economic policy. They must be addressed. We can combine this with our examination of our internal company structure and environment discussed earlier. Such an investigation will likely identify key strengths and weakness in our organisation. Taken together we have a list of strengths (S), weakness (W), opportunities (O) and threats (T). Add them all up and we have probably the most commonly and badly used business tool, which many of you will likely have come across already, the SWOT model.

2.11 Combining internal and external perspectives: the SWOT tool

The SWOT model is a simple tool to bring together our analysis of the internal and external environments of our organisation. It highlights opportunities and threats, typically though not exclusively drawn from an analysis of our external environment, and organisational strengths and weakness drawn from our internal analysis. It really is nothing more than an organisational tool to bring these ideas together, though there have been some attempts to turn this into a more useful tool to potentially develop strategies—e.g. the idea that strengths should be applied to opportunities, threats need to be neutralised, or versions like the TOWS matrix (see Johnson et al., 2023). It's very simple but perhaps that's why it appears at some point in just about every business report.

And again, like PESTLE, SWOT is often used quite badly. There is often a lack of data and evidence to support points: if something is a significant threat or opportunity, you need to show that it is through evidence and analysis. Further, it tends to be applied to everything—an analysis of a market, or a technology, or an opportunity etc.—but it's best used as a tool to compare our company to others (typically our direct and indirect competitors). What are our strengths and weakness **in relation to** our nearest competitor (often called benchmarking), are there opportunities that we are particularly well-placed to take advantage of given our strengths that they are not? Are there threats that we are particularly vulnerable to, but our competitors are not?

Hence SWOT is less of an analytical tool and more of a technique for organising our thoughts and presenting them as a summary. It's best used when we are comparing our prospects to those of our competition and should always be evidenced with appropriate data.

2.12 Conclusions

Over the course of this chapter, we've attempted to cover a lot of ground, cramming a mini business education into a few thousand words. As we proceed through the book, we'll introduce additional business concepts and theories (e.g. open and closed innovation, business models, mergers and acquisitions) and illustrate how issues around strategy, organisational structure and key processes and systems play out in the real world of the cultural industries. Hopefully this chapter is a useful start, though if you develop an interest in business you will quickly realise it is a lifelong learning journey, and this constitutes a very small first step. Hopefully, we've clarified a few key business terms, outlined some key business challenges and described a few tools, techniques and theories that you may find useful in your future business careers. We will attempt use some of these tools, such as PESTLE analysis, resource-based view (RBV) and value chains as we explore the structure and functioning of key sectors in the cultural industries in the next few chapters.

2.13 Activities

- Conduct a VRIO analysis of an organisation you work for or one you are familiar with. What are its key assets and capabilities? Which are most important?
- Review the key technological developments that are likely to impact a business sector you are interested in over the next five years.
- Apply the McKinsey 7S framework to your organisation, or one you might wish to work for. What is its structure, style and strategy etc.?

- Think of a product you use regularly; how might it be enhanced through the provision of service elements?
- What are the key social changes emerging in your country or region? How might they affect different businesses? Are they affecting the cultural industries?
- Look at the food retailing industry in your locality—identify companies pursuing each of Porter's different generic strategies.

Note

1 http://www.theguardian.com/technology/2016/jan/28/apple-quarterly-results-iphone-silicon-valley-developers.

References

Barney, J. 1991. Firm resources and competitive advantage. *Journal of Management*, 17 (1), pp. 99–120.

Bowman, C. and Faulkner, D. 1997. *Competitive and Corporate Strategy*. London: Irwin.

Davis, S. M. and Lawrence, P R. 1978. Problems of matrix organisations. *Harvard Business Review*, May.

Fayol, H. 1916. Administration industrielle et Générale. *Bulletin de la Societe de l'Industrie Minerale*.

Hamel, G. and Prahalad, C. K. 1990. The core competence of the corporation. *Harvard Business Review*, 68 (3), pp. 79–91.

Hannan, M. T. 2005. Ecologies of organizations: Diversity and identity. *Journal of Economic Perspectives*, 19 (1), pp. 51–70.

Hannan, M. T. and Freeman, J. 1984. Structural Inertia and Organizational Change. *American Sociological Review*, 49 (2), pp. 149–164.

Hill, C. W. L. and Jones, G. R. 2012. *Strategic Management: An Integrated Approach*. Cengage Publishers.

Johnson, G., Whittington, R., Regner, P., Angwin, D. and Scholes, K. 2023. *Exploring Strategy: Texts and Cases*, 13th edition. Pearson.

Kim, W. C. and Mauborgne, R. 2005. *Blue Ocean Strategy: How To Create Uncontested Market Space And Make The Competition Irrelevant*. Harvard Business Review Press.

Porter, M. 1979. How competitive forces shape strategy. *Harvard Business Review*, 57 (2).

Porter, M. 1980. *Competitive Strategy*. Free Press.

Porter, M. 2008. *Competitive Advantage: Creating and Sustaining Superior Performance*. Simon & Schuster.

Teece, D. 2009. *Dynamic Capabilities & Strategic Management*. Oxford University Press.

Townsend, R. 1970. *Up the Organisation*. Josssey-Bass.

3 The Performing Arts

3.1 Introduction

Core cultural organisations cover a wide variety of different entities that we might broadly categorise into two types: those institutions that are involved in curating existing, typically non-performance-based cultural content (art galleries, museums, libraries etc.) and those that are more performance-based (orchestras, opera, theatre and dance). For this chapter we will concentrate on those performance-based organisations, focused on presenting performance-based cultural content. For those interested in non-performance-based sectors we would recommend you review *Managing the Cultural Business*, a compilation of useful papers by Addis and Rurale (2021) or *Museums and Digital Culture* by Giannini and Bowen (2019).

In our review of the performance-related sector, we will consider both supply (organisations) and demand (audiences) sides. In terms of suppliers of performing arts goods, estimates of their number vary hugely across the world. This variation is compounded by differences in how each sector is defined, what organisations are included and how much and how regularly data is collected on them. Some data will only cover professional for-profit organisations, some only not-for-profit, and some includes both. Some countries have organisations dedicated to representing the industry sector that regularly research its size and activity; hence data is consistently produced and reasonably reliable. In others we rely almost exclusively on estimates and anecdotal evidence from individual researchers and commentators. Definitions vary—in some territories, for example, theatres are defined as those producing live plays, musicals etc., but in other territories figures can include the number of cinema screens (thus grossly inflating the size of the 'theatrical' sector).

Whatever our source, there do appear to be a significant number of organisations involved in the performing arts. In the USA, for example, estimates suggest there are 2,500 professional dance companies, though only 400 are relatively well established, with paid staff, salaried dancers and a track record of productions (Bathurst and Stein, 2008). The vast majority of dance companies are small, not for profit and have an annual budget of less than $500,000 (ibid). The same authors suggest 1,800 symphony, chamber, collegiate and youth orchestras, 114 professional opera companies and 1,893 professional theatre companies in the USA.

In the UK, the Theatres Trust estimate that in 2024 there were 1,100 active theatres in the UK, covering commercial (for-profit) and not-for-profit organisations. Open Concerts list 76 opera companies, with the vast majority small, regional organisations, and eight large-scale companies with international reputations (e.g. The Royal Opera

DOI: 10.4324/9781003498599-3

House or Opera North). The Association of British Orchestras list approximately 70 member organisations.

Data on the China Philharmonic website suggests that the number of professional Chinese orchestras has grown from less than 20 to over 100 in the last 20 years, though this seems to focus on orchestras presenting Western symphonic content rather than traditional Chinese music using indigenous instruments, for which there are few if any data sources. This compares to 38 orchestras in Japan (the Association of Japanese Symphony Orchestras) and 129 in Germany (unisono). Research on the Indian market appears to only provide data on the 'top performing' or most notable companies (e.g. in terms of theatre, companies like Kolkata, Asakta Kalamanch, Koothu-P-Pattarai etc.). rather than covering the entire sector. This is also the case for traditional classical music in India—e.g. Carnatic and Hindustani styles—where the focus is on researching the activities of specific artists and theatre companies, rather than data collection on the sector as a whole.

In many cases data appears to be most available and consistent on the major production companies and venues in the 'for-profit' sector who are legally required to publish data on their activities. Most traditional or indigenous forms of theatre and music are generally underreported in data sources. This may be because they don't have a body representing organisations in the sector whose job it is to collect and publish data, or performing arts organisations may be so small that they are difficult to identify and hence include in data collection, or their activities do not generate sufficient economic impact for their respective government to be interested in the often very expensive process of collecting data on them. Hence in general the for-profit performing arts sector tends to be reasonably well covered with reliable data sources, the not-for-profit sector far less so unless there is an active association representing organisations in the sector. Even cursory data does seem to suggest that in most performing arts sectors there is a clear distinction in terms of size and concentration of suppliers, with a few large well-established institutions vastly outnumbered by a huge number of smaller establishments, the latter often focused as much on participation in the arts (e.g. training and education) as performance.

The key lesson from a practical business perspective is that if you are researching the sector in your own territory, you will need to carefully review the data you uncover, be clear about what is or is not included, clearly identify definitions and assess who is producing the data along with the veracity of their data collection method. What is clear, even from this cursory analysis, is that there are a huge number and variety of organisations involved in the sector.

3.2 Organisational structures

There are a vast range of institutions involved in the performing arts. According to the structure we have laid out already, some might be classified as 'for-profit', others 'not-for-profit'. Many not-for-profit organisations in the performing arts are also classified as **charities** or '**third sector**' bodies—that is, their main mission is focused on generating social and particularly cultural rather than material wealth. As charities they may benefit from tax incentives (i.e. they may not have to pay corporation or capital gains tax) and other benefits (e.g. minimised financial reporting requirements, reduced rates on the use of buildings) supported by government initiatives and programmes. They do not focus on generating profits for their investors; rather their typical aim from a financial point of view is to 'break even' (that is, balance revenues and costs) or potentially deliver a modest 'surplus' (rather than 'profit', though it amounts to the same thing)—that is, a surplus of turnover compared to costs, typically reinvested in the organisation, rather than dispersed to its stakeholders.

But the sector does include large, international for-profit organisations like the Ambassador Theatre Group[1], which runs more than 58 venues in the UK, Germany and the USA, operating the venues and creating the productions hosted within them, with over 11,000 employees, generating £705m in turnover and £120m in profit for the year 2022–2023 according to its annual report. It would be considered a large company in just about any sector. Equally, the sector incorporates the Georgian Theatre Royal (in Richmond, North Yorkshire, UK[2]), operating with eight full-time staff, 100 volunteers and revenues of just £382,000, including donations of £88,000 and ticket sales of £232,000 (annual report, 2023), an organisation that would typically be classified as an SME (small or medium-sized organisation). It is worth noting here the often very significant role of volunteers in the operation of many performing arts organisations, particularly the smaller ones. They constitute a key group of **stakeholders**, and their good will and effort are typically vital to the ongoing operation of such organisations. We will return to this issue.

3.2.1 Stakeholders and their management

Stakeholders are any group, institution or individual with an interest in the performance of an organisation, or those who depend on an organisation to achieve their own ends. They are typically categorised as internal and external. **Internal stakeholders** include the workforce (which in our case may include a significant number of volunteers), management team and board of directors (or trustees). **External stakeholders** include those closely connected to the organisation, its customers and suppliers, and those typically more at arm's length (that is, those institutions and groups not typically involved in the day-to-day running of the organisation; earlier we described them as the non-market sector), potentially including local and national governments, shareholders, regulators, the media, civil and consumer groups.

In developing strategy and operating our organisation, it is important to keep our stakeholders happy. Typically, they need to be supportive of our business plan if it is to be successful. If key groups or individuals object, it can make it virtually impossible for a plan to be implemented efficiently and effectively. When organisational aims are clear and limited, this is relatively straightforward. If we are a for-profit company, then our aim is clear, to make profits, and our stakeholders normally align in support of this—e.g. our shareholders (those who have an ownership interest in the organisation), whether individuals or institutions, also want us to make profits and redistribute them, as do the leadership team, workforce etc. They may raise objections to a specific plan in terms of its profit potential, or how a particular function is operating and its contribution to profitability (e.g. pension funds, which are often major shareholders in for-profit organisations, may claim that the existing management team are not sufficiently profit-orientated and lobby for them to be replaced), but the overriding goal remains the generation of profit, and clear and logical plans to increase it are likely to be supported by all stakeholders.

Things become more complex when we are not a pure profit-orientated company, when we may have a diverse range of often less tangible goals, or when we are dealing with a diverse range of stakeholders. This is particularly so in the performing arts sector, given the high proportion of not-for-profit organisations. Take a theatre company, for example: our stakeholders are likely to include the management team, workforce, volunteers, suppliers, the government (at central and local levels), artistic talent who might want to work with us (writers, directors, actors, musicians and their management companies), touring companies, those individuals or institutions that have made donations or sponsorship deals, the audience, critics and the media, labour unions and even the local community in which our venue is based.

Each stakeholder group will have its own set of criteria by which to judge our activities. Central government may judge us on our contribution to increasing the appeal of the performing arts in the population as a whole and protecting key cultural activities. A local council may judge us on our ability to attract tourists to its area and our contribution to a city's or region's economic wellbeing. Artistic talent will often judge us on our capacity and willingness to innovate, to develop or promote new productions that push artistic boundaries. Donors want to ensure they are associating themselves with a well-regarded and progressive artistic establishment with a high and reliable public profile. The workforce wants to make sure it receives its pay every month. The audience is interested in things like value for money and the overall theatre experience.

Rarely can all of these demands be fully accommodated within the scope of a single business plan or initiative. Opinions and views will vary; what works for one group, may not work for another. We will probably have to compromise. Hence, we must navigate through this complex range of agendas, aims and ambitions. **Stakeholder management** begins this process by suggesting an approach which categorises stakeholders according to the issue being discussed. Stakeholders will vary according to two criteria: their level of interest in a particular plan or issue, and their power to influence decisions on it. For those stakeholders with a high level of interest and power, we need to prioritise their opinions and views. For those with low power and low levels of interest, we may be able to safely ignore them in terms of this particular issue. So, our first job is to categorise our stakeholders according to these criteria and prioritise the interests of those with high levels of interest and power.

It is worth noting that these categorisations should not be considered as static—they need to be monitored and adjusted over time. Stakeholders can change in their level of interest (from a complete lack of interest to an acute focus). They can change in their ability to influence the decision, perhaps by allying with a more powerful group. Local residents worried about the level of waste and rubbish produced by our audiences, immediately outside our theatre, may have relatively little power to influence our decision making around a plan to significantly increase those audiences—until, that is, they secure the interest and backing of the local council (who we may rely on for elements of funding) who typically have to deal with the waste, cleaning it up and incurring costs after each performance. Volunteers, engaged with a performing arts company for their love of a particular type of traditional theatre production, may object to new plans for our organisation to become much more commercial, presenting more popular but less traditional content, putting ticket sales before any other consideration. At the very least, if we do not take their views into consideration, we may lose the good will that their contribution rests upon.

So, when making a plan, or developing a new business idea for your organisation, think about the stakeholders. Think about how they might view your idea and how they are likely to react. Identify those voices you have to listen to and those that, at least for the moment, you can safely ignore. Try and secure the interest and support of powerful stakeholders who can sway opinions. Keep reviewing your analysis as things change. A fuller outline of approaches to stakeholder management can be found in Johnson et al., 2023.

3.2.2 Structure

Some organisations within the sector operate purely as a venue for performance, without the capability to produce productions themselves—e.g. the Leeds Grand Theatre. Hence they rely on external organisations to supply the content they host; such organisations may be touring companies who perform for a limited time at a venue and then move on, or others that may become 'resident', regularly producing performances in that specific venue (e.g. Opera North are consistent performers at Leeds Grand Theatre). Some companies will focus on productions only and often don't have a permanent venue (other than perhaps rehearsal rooms), others (like ATG mentioned earlier) combine both venue and production operations.

Most organisations of any size will typically have two broad parts in their overall structure: a team focused on productions and their execution led by an artistic director (who may hold the position for a limited and set time), and a team focused on more administrative and business elements led by a managing director or CEO. The production team will include those focused on planning productions and their execution (so often teams around stage management, orchestra management, sound and lighting design, costumes, props etc.). The administration business team will include those involved in activities like marketing, ticket and merchandising sales, fundraising and development, finance, human resources, and facilities and IT management.

Here we encounter the first function we have not already mentioned, **fundraising**. Fundraising is a vital activity for most charities. Given the charitable status of many performing arts organisations, it is perhaps inevitable that fundraising is a pivotal function for them. Ticket and merchandising sales are rarely enough for most organisations to survive in the not-for-profit sector, let alone provide the resources they need to grow. Hence historically, not-for-profit organisations have had to rely on other sources of revenue to maintain their operations. One such source is through donations from corporations, trusts, foundations or individuals. Securing these donations is generally in the hands of the fundraising function. In some organisations this function also includes fundraising from government sources. For some it also includes sponsorship, including everything from a local bar and restaurant to a major corporation.

The fundraising team will typically reach out to individuals (often high-net-worth individuals—though not exclusively) and organisations like the government, major corporations or charitable foundations, seeking donations (generally called 'contributed' income) to support the organisation's mission. The fundraising team focus on identifying potential donors, instigating a relationship with them and deepening it over time. Such relationships are often deepened by having a representative of the donor become part of the management team of the organisation, sitting on the management board and being allowed to influence strategic and operational decision making. Once the province of high-net-worth individuals, fundraising increasingly involves appeals to the general public too, particularly through platforms like crowdfunding apps Kickstarter or GoFundMe, with some smaller organisations raising funds for their entire schedule of productions through the platforms (e.g. HER Productions, a small theatre company based in Manchester that funded its entire production activity in 2022 through crowdfunding).

Organisations are typically structured according to the hierarchies we discussed in Chapter 2, based on different functions and levels—e.g. there will typically be a managing director at the top, focusing on business-related issues, combined with an artistic director (often for a set period), dealing with creative issues, both part of a board of directors. Below that will be the heads of each function (e.g. a chief financial officer, head of marketing), 'middle' management (more senior staff from each function) and below that more junior staff and workers. Within each function there will also be hierarchies: the fundraising function is likely to have a director of fundraising (who will sit on the board of directors) and a team below them of differing levels of seniority, focused on different specialist aspects of fundraising—some focused on working with institutions, some on high-net-worth individuals, some on events management etc. In smaller companies, this may all have to be covered by just one person, and that person may even be a volunteer, giving their time and efforts for free.

It is worth mentioning again that even at the highest levels of management in non-profit-orientated organisations, **volunteers are often critical** to their operation. Whilst we typically associate volunteers with those working at the bottom of such hierarchies, in the performing arts sector they often appear throughout organisational structures. As we have noted, most organisations (for- and not-for-profit) are ultimately run by a board of directors, a group sitting at the top of the hierarchy charged with running the organisation, achieving its mission and developing its plans. In the not-for-profit sector these directors (they may be called trustees) may be donors (or their representatives) to the organisation and often, though not always, may provide their time and effort as part of the board of directors for free as volunteers, receiving no monetary compensation. They may also raise further funds for the organisation by acting as ambassadors and its public face. One of their most significant roles may be in selecting other senior management—e.g. they may be involved in appointing a managing director or artistic director for the organisation. Bigger organisations typically have bigger boards, often with specialist sub-parts—there may be an audit part overseeing the organisation's finances, a group focused on external relations and fundraising or setting salaries etc. Such boards are typically present in most organisations in most business sectors, but relatively few are staffed by volunteers.

These boards are not typically involved in the day-to-day running of the organisation; they are more concerned with longer-term issues like developing strategies to achieve the organisation's mission and approving yearly plans and budgets. They may only meet as a board once or twice a year. Day-to-day management is usually devolved to a management team, made up of the heads of the major functions, all reporting into a managing and/or artistic director. We certainly see the prevalence of the matrix structures as an organising tool as discussed in Chapter 2, with employees part of an overall function (finance, marketing, fundraising, stage management etc.), but also working on a specific production or project for a period of time.

A very good overview of the various structures of specific organisations involved in the performing arts in the USA is included in Bathurst and Stein (2008, or the updated 2022 edition). Indeed, the book is a very useful resources for those interested in digging into any of the issues we deal with in this chapter in far more detail than we can afford here.

3.3 Value chain analysis

In our previous description of useful business tools and techniques we mentioned value chain analysis—looking at the primary stages and processes in the production of goods and services and how they are supported by other activities (secondary functions like human resources and finance) within an organisation. Let's explore some of the key primary activities for a venue in the performing arts sector. An outline of critical activities for a venue can be seen in Figure 2.4 (see Chapter 2).

3.3.1 The venue 'programme'

Venues need to plan their programme, their selection of events and productions, in advance, typically for the forthcoming year, or perhaps even longer for bigger organisations. This is usually the province of what is called the **programming function** or team. Influenced (as we will see) by issues around attracting audiences, managing costs and achieving the organisation's mission and goals, the process typically starts with incorporating the production plans of any resident companies who are permanently situated in the venue. Once that is done the programming team will reach out to other organisations (including touring companies and booking agents) to secure additional content for the rest of the year's schedule.

Generally programming teams try to achieve a balance of content that they know will secure good audiences—e.g. what might be called in the film sector 'blockbusters': well-known operas, plays or musical productions with recognised talent (actors, singers, conductors, directors etc.)—with innovative new, unproven content (e.g. premiers) that pushes artistic boundaries and raises the profile of the organisation in terms of the artistic community. Blockbusters guarantee, as much as is possible, ticket and merchandising sales and hence revenues, whereas new innovative content builds the organisation's artistic reputation. Getting the right balance is difficult to achieve. Too much innovative new content is a financially risky option, as it may attract small audiences, generating low revenues. Too many well-established and predicable productions risk accusations from the artistic community of a lack of artistic ambition. Equally, as in all things, venues need to take into account the wishes of a broad range of stakeholders; local councils may wish to see more of a focus on 'blockbusters'—those well-established pieces of content that are guaranteed to secure large audiences, hence attracting visitors to the local area or city and generating economic benefits (stays in hotels, visits to restaurants etc.). The venue's technical team may hope for productions that are relatively straightforward to stage. The marketing team will want productions to feature prominent talent as the basis for their marketing campaigns. The artistic director and their team will want to host innovative artistic creations that raise the profile of the venue and enhance their personal career prospects. Even for this limited range of stakeholders, it can be difficult to keep everyone happy all the time.

It is worth noting that in the past, thanks to higher levels of government support, venues could be less cautious in getting this balance right; they had been able to take quite significant risks in terms of programming new and innovative content. This was driven partly by their mission, to create such opportunities for new content to emerge, but just as significantly because they were often the beneficiaries of significant funding from state sources or donors. This funding meant that even if a new play or musical event failed to secure big audiences and generate significant revenue, the organisation could continue, buoyed up by these other sources of 'contributed' funds (e.g. grants from local councils). A not-for-profit organisation could afford to fail, far more so than a purely commercial for-profit company. As we have noted, however, such sources of funding appear to be declining across the globe, with resultant accusations that many venues and performance companies have become far less willing to take on the risk of funding and presenting innovative new content.

Things are perhaps simpler for for-profit companies, where programmes are typically designed to maximise audience numbers and hence ticket sales, maximising the chance of profit generation. There will be constraints imposed in terms of costs, however. Blockbuster content is often expensive to produce, it may require a major stage production, expensive rights acquisition, an extensive marketing campaign and often expensive talent. Having an entire year of such productions is typically beyond the resources of most venues. The programme team will therefore also include slots for content that is less expensive to produce in order to manage overall levels of organisational costs. They are further constrained if they wish to stage new and innovative content. If a new production fails to attract a significant audience, as many do, this can have a very significant effect on the organisation's overall financial health, and they do not have a buffer of funds from the government to rely on. It is a balancing act, then, between what the artistic team want to do, what the venue can afford to do, audience demand and the organisation's appetite for risk.

Of course it is possible for the two sectors to work together, with the non-profit sector acting in some cases as the R&D (research and development) department for larger commercial organisations. New content may be developed in the non-profit sector, given their relatively high-risk appetite and state support. Once proven as commercially viable, the content may then be picked up and supported in terms of perhaps a bigger venue, better staging, better talent and more marketing by a commercial company.

Programming may also be heavily influenced by cultural and market trends (e.g. the popularity of the Harry Potter franchise on film prompted the development of a stage play), what competitors are planning, the availability of talent (directors, writers, acting or musical talent) and the overall economic climate. If we are in an economic recession with limited consumer spending power, they may choose to spend their limited income on proven content that they know will deliver a predictable night's entertainment. Equally we may be in an economic boom wherein consumers have greater levels of disposable income and hence may be willing to experiment more, spending their hard-earned income on visits to innovative new content as well as the blockbusters.

Programming, then, is a multifaceted and complex task. We will also see a similar process when we review how television and games companies develop a 'slate' (or range) of planned products appealing to a variety of different market sectors, with different levels of associated risks and levels of innovation and costs, in subsequent chapters. Intimately linked to the programming process, will be the budgeting process.

3.3.2 Accounting and finance: the budgeting process

Developing a detailed plan of the potential costs and revenues for an organisation over the course of the next year, or budgeting, is a critical activity for all organisations. For performing arts companies these budgets typically track a 'season' of planned productions and activities and will cover aspects like the costs of overheads (these are costs that the venue may incur irrespective of the productions they support, also called fixed costs—e.g. the salaries of administrative staff, office supplies, utilities costs like heating or lighting); production-related costs associated with each individual production (typically pre-production and ongoing costs) and costs associated with marketing, fundraising and special projects (e.g. public outreach initiatives that might be designed to establish relationships with local educational establishments). These costs will be balanced by estimates of revenues from sources such as ticket, merchandising and food and drink sales, and what is called 'contributed income', which is donations and government aid. The overall aim is typically to at least balance the budget, matching costs to income. Not-for-profit organisations will often be happy just to secure this balance, but for-profit-orientated organisations aim to develop a budget where revenue outstrips costs, creating profit. A final 'budget' will be drawn up, reconciling the two, and will typically need board-level approval before it can be implemented.

Of course, as with most things, this seems easier to describe in a textbook than it is to achieve in the real world. A useful overview of the complexities of budgeting in the performing arts sector is provided by Amans et al. (2015) in their study of the activity in two French not-for-profit theatres, each with approximately 40 employees, each relying on the state for between 40% and 60% of their funding. They note the varying demands that need to be accommodated in such a budgeting process: artistic demands, business or management demands and demands from the public sector (as providers of funding) or other donors of funds (e.g. corporate sponsors). They note the use of artistic budgets (associated with repertoire planning, payments to artists etc.) and operational budgets, covering the costs of the theatre's operation. They note a variety of uses for these budgets, in some cases more as an information provision tool (e.g. this is what we intend to do), in others as a negotiating and monitoring tool. In some cases, the budget is partially developed and hotly debated by the board of directors; in others, the board are less involved in producing a budget, and more involved in simply approving it. In some the state funder may be involved in such negotiations, in others not at all (other than the requirement for them to receive a copy of the finalised budget). What emerges is that the budgeting process is one of the critical ways in which the demands of different stakeholders, each with potentially different desired outcomes and ways of measuring success, are brought together, negotiated over and ultimately reconciled.[3]

Drawing on our analysis from Chapter 2, what then are the key **capabilities** of these organisations? Certainly, such organisations will require threshold capabilities around the ability to produce and stage shows, market themselves to consumers, sell tickets and run the venue. For those in the not-for-profit sector, fundraising would also be a threshold capability. These are the types of capability that all organisations will display to some degree. More significant capabilities are likely to be those that are distinctive or rare. Often these appear to be intangible but based on tangible assets.

For example, a critical capability will be the organisation's ability to build a profile and identity for itself, a reputation amongst audiences, the artistic community and funders. This will partly be a function of its performance history and the relationships (e.g. with the artistic community or government) it has built over time. This in turn is partly built on key tangible assets, such as its artistic leadership, the marketing team, the activities of board members, the IT systems that allow data to be collected, stored and analysed on consumers, the nature and layout of its venue etc. Such capabilities are typically internally focused and built over time; external methods to acquire capabilities (e.g. mergers and acquisitions) appear to be relatively rare in the performing arts sector.

Many organisations are now turning their attention to developing dynamic capabilities—the ability to monitor their external environment, spot opportunities and threats, take advantage of them and reconfigure their organisations appropriately. This is particularly so in terms of monitoring changes in the consumer marketplace, through a greater interaction with audiences beyond the scope of an individual performance (see Chapter 8 on the role of marketing). Organisations, particularly those reliant to some degree on the tourism sector (often cultural organisations focused on traditional or regionally specific forms of content), need to be able to monitor and anticipate global trends to identify changes that may affect demand for tourism (these may be economic, political or social / cultural changes). Not-for-profit organisations need to be able to monitor and adjust to changes in the political environment and the dominant political party's attitude to support for the arts. Increasingly all organisations need to monitor technology trends as new ways of reaching and interacting with audiences develop.

Monitoring and analysing these changes is only the start, however (though that may be challenging enough); organisations may need to rapidly reconfigure their structures and processes to deal with these changes. As such, they increasingly need to be agile (something not necessarily associated with organisations in the performing arts sector), changing organisational structures, moving resources from one part of the organisation to another, developing new skills and acquiring new capabilities. This may need to be reflected in how roles and responsibilities are defined. It may require new capabilities at the board level and increasing levels of flexibility amongst the workforce. Having strong dynamic capabilities is likely to be a key requirement for all organisations in the performing arts sector (as it is in other business sectors) in the future.

3.4 The complex nature of the performing arts good

Organisations in the performing arts sell what we might describe as '**experience goods**' to consumers, composed of tangible and intangible elements—hence, they encapsulate elements that we have associated with both products and services. Some of the earliest work on the experiential aspects of consumption (and what is sometimes referred to by the term hedonistic consumption) was undertaken by Elizabeth Hirschman and Morris Holbrook, published in two papers (mentioned in the references section) in 1982, though working through their papers does require a good degree of knowledge around marketing and the analysis of consumer behaviour—it's a good place to turn if you want a slightly more advanced and academic perspective on the issue. Economics academic Prof. Philip Nelson (see for example his 1974 paper) was another commentator to note the differences between what he called search goods (where issues around the quality of the item can be easily ascertained before consumption—e.g. a new pair of shoes) and experience goods (wherein the quality of the good can only be ascertained in its consumption—e.g. a theatre production). The latter clearly applies to the performing arts sector.

A typical visit to a performance combines both tangible and intangible elements that all contribute to the overall quality of the experience. If we are visiting the theatre (to see an opera, play or musical performance, for instance), tangible elements include the venue itself, the quality and size of seats, legroom, if they provide good viewing angles of the stage, the temperature of the auditorium, the quality of the audio and lighting systems etc. We will be concerned about the availability of food and drink, toilets, easy parking—all very tangible issues to consider. In terms of service elements, we want it to be easy to buy tickets and find out about the performance, we want to be greeted and served by theatre staff who are knowledgeable and courteous, well dressed and presentable, and we don't want to wait too long in a queue for the bar or toilet.

The service aspects expand when we start considering the performance itself. Certainly, it is not a product that you will end up owning—once viewed you leave the venue with nothing other than a change in your mental state (hopefully for the better) and perhaps some merchandising and a programme. The performance cannot be stored, unless it is recorded and subsequently sold as an album of songs, or a video recording of a performance though, as we will see, consuming it in this way may not deliver the same experience as doing so in person, in the venue, surrounded by an audience. Given this inability to store the core service, the venue will certainly aim to sell every single seat it can before the performance to maximise revenue (hence the often-used technique of significantly discounting the price of seats immediately prior to a performance, a technique borrowed from the hotel industry and airlines).

Secondly, the presence of the consumer as part of the service delivery, in this case as a member of the audience, is critical. You have to be there but, typically, so do others. Watching a performance in the company of your peers is often vital to the full experience of a live performance. Jointly experiencing the thrill of a dramatic revelation in a play, a crescendo in a musical score or a particularly athletic jump in a ballet is very different to watching a recording or listening to music at home, alone. The social experience of being in a group, even in terms of watching a film at the cinema (think of the nervousness in the cinema during the last horror film you watched) contributes to the overall quality of the service experience. Hence there are three agents interacting in any performance: you, the performers and support staff, and the rest of the audience. Of course, sometimes having others that you share the experience with will negatively affect your overall experience. Sitting next to someone singing along to all of the songs in your favourite musical, out of key and out of time, is hardly likely to make you appreciate the performance more.

Finally, as we identified in Chapter 2 in our discussion of the general characteristics of services, it can be difficult, if not impossible, to guarantee the quality of the performance (the service). Actors can forget their lines, singers can have a throat infection, dancers may have pulled a muscle in rehearsals. Performers are generally human (though we will return to this issue in our analysis of the use of AI-based avatars in Chapter 9) and hence their performance is likely to vary from night to night. This can be compounded if such issues affect a number of those in the orchestra, dance company or ensemble of actors. They may simply not 'gel' (work together well) on a particular night, a certain vital spark may be missing, and the overall effect may be disappointing. This potential lack of consistency can also extend to those providing the service 'front of house', those involved in selling and collecting tickets, serving drinks and guiding visitors to their seats. If the team are having a busy night, perhaps are short-staffed, and have to deal with a problem with facilities (e.g. the toilets are blocked), their interactions with the audience may be brief and curt.

The challenge for organisations is that ultimately all of these elements need to work together to provide the consumer with the best experience, and whilst some may be in the control of the management team (e.g. hiring the best front-of-house staff, ensuring they are well trained, providing adequate facilities, securing the best artistic talent) many are not (e.g. the quality of the performance itself, and how the audience chooses to react to it). This presents a huge quality challenge for those running such venues.

Audiences themselves face a further challenge in that it can be difficult to assess the potential quality of a performance before it is enacted. How do you assess the quality of an intangible good and hence make the decision to purchase it in advance of its consumption, particularly when the price of a ticket for some performances can be very high? In many ways it's a very risky purchase decision. To a degree managing this issue is in the hands of the venue operator. By staging well-known productions and securing high-profile talent to direct or perform in them, consumers' concerns about quality can at least be partially ameliorated. The presence of 'star' performers can help to (at least in the minds of consumers) guarantee the quality of a performance in advance of ticket purchase. Of course, even these stars can have an off night, when they do not perform to the best of their ability, but the higher the profile and hence assumed quality of the star, the less likely this is to happen. We will see such practices used to reduce perceived risk in other sectors of the cultural industries, including the television sector, later in the book.

The nature of the good also has implications for potential competition. If we define performing arts goods as 'experience-based' then any potential experience might be considered an alternative. For the consumer the purchase decision may be less about comparing two opera companies when deciding which opera to visit, but comparing a visit to the opera to any other potential experience that would fill the time—a trip to the cinema, a sporting event, a restaurant, shopping or even spending time at home watching TV or listening to music. Hence undertaking a competitive review in which one theatre is compared to another, or orchestra, dance company etc. is likely to miss the vast amount of indirect competition potentially supplying the consumer.

Finally in this section, we raise a critical issue that we will return to repeatedly throughout the book, the issue of risk. Risk is a basic ingredient of all business. From the entrepreneur investing her life savings in setting up a new company, to a mature and established company investing its reserves in setting up a new manufacturing facility, risk is a key component of every decision and initiative an organisation undertakes. In each case, outcomes are essentially uncertain—we cannot be absolutely sure of the success or failure of a venture (this is particularly the case when launching new products or services, as we will see). Hence, it involves a degree of risk.

This is particularly relevant to our study as commentators often ascribe unusually high levels of risk to the operation of the cultural industries. Why might this be the case? We will look at two elements. The cost of developing cultural content (in this case in the performing arts, but we will look at other sectors subsequently) and the potentially high level of risk associated with its prospects with audiences.

It can be very expensive to develop a new piece of cultural content in the performing arts. Estimates suggest that it can cost at least £2–3m[4] to develop a new West End (referring to the West End of London, where there is a high concentration of theatres) musical. Broadway (referring to a part of New York where major theatres are clustered, typically with at least 500 seats) productions can cost even more; estimates[5] suggest $3–5m for plays and $10–20m for a musical. Some productions vastly increase this required initial investment; the *New York Post* suggested it cost $45m (though other estimates go as high as $70m) to stage the rock musical *Spider-Man: Turn Off the Dark*, with a score created by popular band U2, in 2011. *Shrek The Musical* cost $25m to stage. This is before the production even opens to the audience (typically called pre-production costs, or the cost to 'stage' a production). Ongoing costs when a production is running can also be very significant, amounting to $200,000–500,000 per week[6] made up of salaries, venue expenses, advertising costs and so on. The same source suggests that a major musical success like *Hamilton* had estimated weekly costs of $643,000. These costs are typically incurred irrespective of the size of the audience—they are incurred if 10 people attend a performance, or 1000.

Such significant investments in new products and services are common in all business sectors, however. Compared to some, those already mentioned might actually be considered quite low, as it will cost well over $1bn[7] to start to develop a new antibiotic in the pharmaceutical industry or $540m to develop a new computer chip, according to the Semiconductor Industry Association (2024). In all business sectors significant funds are regularly invested in new products and services.

What is potentially less common is the high level of uncertainty associated with how customers and consumers might react to the new product or service. In developing a new drug or computer chip, investors can be fairly certain of a reasonable level of subsequent demand for the new product; hence the risk of high investment is worth it. Particularly when only small changes are made in an existing product or service (what is typically called **'incremental' innovation**), the organisation can be fairly sure that historical levels of demand will continue even if the new enhancements do not radically increase overall levels of demand as intended.

Things seem much less predictable in terms of purely cultural content. New content is risky as audiences' responses are highly uncertain. New productions, even those created by well-established writers and directors, based on existing successful content (e.g. *Spider-Man* and *Shrek*) with high-profile artistic talent involved in its production and delivery (like U2), can fail. *Spider-Man: Turn off the Dark* ran for just over two years, closing in January 2014 due to falling ticket sales and ongoing costs of production (up to $1.3m per week). Estimates suggest investors lost up to $60m as a result.[8]

Highly successful industry figures can suddenly find themselves producing 'flops'. As we have already mentioned, Andrew Lloyd Webber made his reputation with a string of highly successful musicals during the 1990s. As the recipient of an Oscar, a Golden Globe, seven Tony awards, five Laurence Olivier awards, three Grammys and 14 Ivor Novellos for productions like *Jesus Christ Superstar, Evita, Cats* and *The Phantom of the Opera* during this period, he was as reliable (and hence low-risk) a source of new content as anyone in the industry. Investors were happy to pour their money into his new productions given their consistent success with audiences. But suddenly, almost overnight, it appeared he lost this ability to anticipate and deliver what audiences wanted. He had not changed, the type of content he developed had not changed, his ability to combine music and lyrics had not changed, but suddenly audiences were not responding positively to it. His production *Stephen Ward* cost £2.4m to stage and lasted less than four months.[9]

Given the very subjective nature of the audience's judgement of the quality and originality of a new piece of creative content, anticipating their response can be highly challenging. A fuller overview of why this might be the case can be found in a useful and accessible article by Chris Bilton (1999). Organisations respond in turn by drawing on pre-existing successful properties and franchises, investing in the best talent to develop the new content, producing a range of different types of content to reach as many different parts of the audience as possible and marketing their new content extensively. As we have seen, even this does not guarantee a 'hit'. We will go on to examine how the issue of risk emerges and is addressed in other sectors of the cultural economy in subsequent chapters.

3.5 Consumers: audiences

Attendance at performing arts events was radically affected by COVID, so drawing on data from the period 2020–2022 may provide an inaccurate picture of overall trends. We will therefore mostly use pre-and post-COVID data to try and build a more accurate picture of trends in attendance. Understanding the market as a whole is further complicated by the issue that (as with the supply side of the sector) different regions tend to collect different data about different parts of the performing arts market, reporting varying statistics that are not necessarily comparable. Equally the data that is collected tends to vary over time, with different data points and sources used to measure the audience. As such it's virtually impossible to produce an accurate global picture of attendance at performing arts events. Analysis is best done at a local or regional level where data is more likely to be consistent, particularly over time.

Here for example is some key data covering the UK, a developed and mature performing arts market, where data has been consistently collected by a variety of agencies (including governments and specialist data collection and analysis organisations like Mintel) over time. Prior to COVID, in 2019, it is estimated that approximately 56% of UK adults attended performance arts events at least once a year, with approximately 12% attending at least once per month or week.[10] This amounted to a total of 34m visits during 2019, generating a total of £1.3bn in revenue. It is worth noting that this attendance figure had remained at approximately the same level for the previous four years, with the only growth evident in overall revenue (largely because of increasing ticket prices).

Within that overall attendance figure, musical theatre was by far the most popular genre, with 37% of adults attending a musical during the year. Attendance at other types of performing arts event was far less common, with only 11% attending a dance event (including ballet) and only 8% attending an opera.[11] Much of this attendance is concentrated in cities, with London accounting for 40% of total theatre revenue in 2019.[12] This geographic concentration of performing arts activities in major cities is a common feature of the industry globally.

COVID inevitably hit the sector hard, with attendance declining to 7.5m in 2020, and box office revenues (ticket sales) falling nearly 80% to £274m.[13] Perhaps most significantly Mintel's forecast suggested that it would take the sector a significant time to return to pre-COVID attendance levels.

COVID was more positive in terms of the live streaming of performing arts events. To maintain a connection with their audiences whilst venues were closed, many performing arts organisations posted videos of performances or backstage activities. This was very much seen as a marketing cost that organisations were willing to absorb; the content was typically free to consumers. Mintel estimates that 30% of all adults in the UK (and 47% of regular theatre goers) watched a streamed performing arts event during COVID. The majority of this content was provided free by operators, though costs incurred were significant. Hence the next challenge will be for them to find ways in which such initiatives might be monetised to cover costs, a challenge when according to Mintel only 17% of adults suggested that they would be willing to pay to see a streamed event in the future. Further they were only willing to consider paying around £14 for a ticket according to the same study, significantly less than the typical price of a ticket to see a live event, implying an overall decline in ticket revenues unless a significantly greater audience can be attracted to such events.

The story is similar in other territories. In the Theatre Communications Group's (a group that represents the interests of 2,000 not-for-profit theatres employing over 82,000 artists, administrators and technical support staff in the USA) annual report[14] in 2023 they reported an 80% decline in audiences during COVID in the US. They also noted that whilst costs increased significantly once venues reopened, audience attendance has failed to return to pre-COVID levels. Total attendance in 2023 remained 5% below 2018 levels, and total ticket income 55% lower. This is particularly troubling as their estimates suggest that the costs of producing theatre rose significantly during the period (particularly in the areas of labour and equipment).

The annual report of the China Performing Arts Industry Association for 2021 appears to offer some more varied and in some cases encouraging results for the sector. The overall box office revenues of the performance market (though, significantly, this does include all live music, including live popular music events and festivals—which is typically measured separately in other territories) was estimated to be worth 14bn yuan (approximately £1.5bn) in 2021 (though they note this represents a decline of 30% compared to 2019). They also note a significant trend which we have already mentioned: a nearly 40% decline in government subsidy income compared to 2019.

Again, they note a concentration of revenues in key cities and urbanised regions, with 65% of all box office revenue accounted for by the top 10 regions (including Shanghai, Beijing, Jiangsu and Guangdong). One very interesting statistic suggests that young people aged 18 to 39 accounted for 76% of all ticket buyers. This would seem very unusual, given that similar statistics in other territories suggest a far higher proportion of older people responsible for purchasing performing arts tickets. It is probably explained by the fact that the Chinese data includes sales of tickets at 'pop' concerts and festivals, whilst this data is often excluded from measures of the sector in other territories.

In terms of genres, drama (though interestingly this category includes comedies) proves to be the most popular category of performing arts content in China, responsible for 30% of total box office revenues and 16,100 performances in 2021. This compares to 15,300 'musical' performances generating approximately 1bn yuan (approximately £107m). Even the dance market in China appeared relatively buoyant during COVID, with 4100 performances nationwide, generating 565m yuan.

Interestingly, one of the segments of the market that seemed to survive better than others in China was traditional opera, with the number of performances in 2021 exceeding pre-pandemic levels at 17,900, generating a box office revenue of 769m yuan (though this is still only 90% of 2019 figures). It is worth noting in this regard that according to the annual report, the average price for an opera ticket in China is 112 yuan, approximately £12 (around $16), far lower than the average price of an opera ticket in the UK or USA. In 2023, front row seats for Puccini's *Turandot* at the Royal Opera House, Covent Garden London, were £235 ($316)—over 2100 yuan. Metropolitan Opera (often performing at the Lincoln Centre in New York) seat prices start at $98 and could go as high as $1344 per performance in 2024.

We have noted that the high preponderance of younger audiences in China seems somewhat unusual given statistics from other markets. A review by the Arts Council in the UK, for example, suggested the 'core loyal audience' of performing arts in the UK, particularly for more traditional forms like opera, ballet, plays and classical music, are what they term 'culture vultures'. These individuals who are highly engaged with the arts and are more likely to attend an event each month, are typically in the age range of 45–74, highly affluent and educated, with two-thirds holding higher education qualifications.[15] They typically constitute 4% of all English adults. According to the same report, those least likely to be in the audience for an arts event are likely to be under 44 years old.

In the USA, research by The Broadway League examining attendance at Broadway shows in New York described in *The Demographics of the Broadway Audience 2022–2023 report* suggests that the average age of a Broadway theatregoer was 40.4 years (the youngest in the previous 20 seasons it had collected data on). Reviewing the rebound from COVID, several surveys have noted that younger people seemed more willing to return to live events in person than older audiences, perhaps leading to a skew towards younger audiences in immediate post-COVID research. Whether this trend will continue in the future is uncertain.

A word of warning here. When conducting this type of analysis of audiences in your own territory, be careful that you are not in fact analysing data on **participation** in the arts (e.g. getting singing lessons, attending a drawing or painting class, visiting a dance studio for a lesson on samba etc.). Such active participation (rather than viewing performances) leads to a much younger demographic profile for consumers (there are far more young people involved). This is troublesome as some studies of attendance at performances may be titled 'participation' in the arts, whereas others focus on those who actively engage in classes to learn about the arts. Ensure you are clear about exactly what a study is describing when using such data.

A final critical element to review in discussing performing arts audiences is the link to tourism—that is, travel for pleasure. The international tourism industry has grown hugely since the 1950s, when estimates suggested there were approximately 25m tourist visits globally. Its inexorable growth over the last 70 years meant that in 2019 there were approximately 1.5bn tourist visits globally.[16] Inevitably this figure was significantly affected by COVID, with visitors falling to less than 500m, but bounced back to just below COVID rates in 2023.

Tourism can provide a significant boost to local audiences for performing arts; indeed, it has its own moniker, TPA (tourism performing arts). The portrayal of local cultural elements through the performing arts, contributes, according to some commentators, to a sense of 'placeness', a specific local or regional identity that tourists seek when visiting a region (Hernández-Mogollón et. al., 2018), helping them develop a sense of affinity and connection with the region and its inhabitants (Chen and Dwyer, 2017). Hence a visit to London may not be complete without attending a West End play, or a visit to New York without attending a Broadway musical. A visit to China may not be complete without attendance at a live circus, or to Japan without attendance at a Noh or Kabuki performance. A useful paper to look at this in more detail is that by Luo et al. (2023). International performing arts festivals have also emerged, highlighting performing arts from different territories across the world (see Amorim et al., 2020 for a useful overview of consumer perspectives on this development).

Attention has also been particularly paid to the role of 'cultural tourism' in supporting local indigenous cultural activities (perhaps sundae masked plays and dances in Korea, classical dance in India, or a bambuco performance in Colombia), though concerns emerge around the degree to which such commercial tourism might distort more traditional forms of cultural expression, with changes to the content and presentation required by the demands of tourism. This is an area that requires further research by academics and governments, as does the rise of green and sustainable tourism and how this plays out in the performing arts sector.

We will return to the opportunities and challenges of tourism and particularly festivals when we explore 'music tourism' in our review of popular music in Chapter 6.

3.6 Trends, challenges and opportunities

Let us review some of the major trends impacting all sectors of the performing arts. These are issues that you may have to deal with directly in your career managing in the performing arts.

3.6.1 The fight for audiences

We have already noted that in selling 'experience goods', performing arts organisations open themselves up to a huge range of direct and indirect competition. They have to fight for consumers (audiences) not just with directly competing performing arts organisations, but with virtually any organisation or service that provides an experience. Such competition often emerges from different ways to spend an evening (so might include bars and restaurants or going to the cinema), or one's time more generally (like shopping or visits to a museum). We might include ways of watching or consuming any cultural content, including staying at home to watch TV with your family or even spending time on social media platforms. These latter categories have seen huge growth in the provision of services by new suppliers since the emergence of digital content in the late 1980s. As we will see in our chapter on broadcasting, the number of companies providing TV services, particularly streamed via broadband, has expanded hugely in the last 20 years. The sheer number of channels and hence content that audiences have access to has inevitably increased, and in some cases includes channels and content dedicated to the performing arts (e.g. Sky Arts channel in the UK, ARTE channel in France). Never before has there been so much competition for an audience's time, attention and spending.

This is particularly so when we consider younger audiences. As we have already seen, audiences for performing arts, at least in terms of the core audience that attend events regularly, tend to be older, typically over 40 and in some cases (like opera), much older than that. New younger audiences need to be secured if this element of older audiences that drive spending in the sector is to be continually replaced. Competition for these audiences, particularly those aged under 30, is severe given the emergence of new forms of digital platforms and content. The challenge is therefore how to make performing arts content relevant and interesting to these younger audiences. Many organisations turn to the issue of how we are educated about the performing arts as a key way to influence younger audiences, establishing initiatives with educational establishments in their local area to help raise awareness of the presence and importance of classical cultural content.

Further we have noted that much performing arts activity tends to be concentrated in major urban areas (cities and larger towns), forcing those in rural areas to travel significant distances to view performances. Accessing these large but distributed rural audiences (Statista suggest that up to one-third of the population of China, for example, still live in rural communities, a high proportion, but one that is dwarfed by India, in which estimates suggest 65% of the population still live in rural areas) also remains a challenge, particularly given that no matter how rural a community, they may have access to the type of streaming services and social media platforms mentioned earlier.

If the marketing function is typically charged with understanding consumers and securing their interest, then it will clearly have to play a significant part in addressing these challenges.

3.6.2 The growing importance of marketing

Organisations in the performing arts, particularly those in the not-for-profit sector, have in the past often been criticised for not paying enough attention to their audiences. As suggested by Addis and Rurale (2021, p.18) they 'rely [too much] on their unique cultural heritage, adopting the false belief that a unique cultural heritage means a unique value proposition. This is totally incorrect.' The accusation is that such organisations have been too inwardly focused on the cultural heritage they protect and represent, too obsessed with issues of creative and artistic endeavour, and too sure that the cultural content they create is relevant and meaningful to audiences, to the ultimate detriment of the consumer experience. To a degree this was enabled by the intervention of government and state authorities whose funding was reliant on this focus on the maintenance and development of a nation's cultural and creative wealth.

This funding allowed audiences to be ignored to some degree. No matter how innovative the content produced, how obscure or based on a society's deep cultural history, or how successful or unsuccessful such content was in terms of audiences, funding could still be provided. A string of highly innovative and culturally specific new performances, even if commercially unsuccessful, could be supported in the organisation thanks to funds secured from government, local councils and other sources. Hence understanding the audience and producing content that they might want to attend, took second place to staging performances that pushed creative boundaries and contributed to the maintenance of a country's cultural heritage, essentially keeping government agencies happy rather than the consumer.

Marketing, then, was focused largely on promotion of events. Marketing in the future will need to take on a bigger role, particularly in terms of understanding the consumer, their wants, desires and preferences, and the way in which they interact with content. This is certainly an area that in recent years cultural organisations have paid much more attention to, partly driven by increasing levels of indirect competition, but also due to declines in state funding for the arts. Even not-for-profit organisations increasingly need to produce content that is going to be reasonably successful with audiences, selling enough tickets to at least cover costs incurred. To do this they need to understand their consumers better but, arguably, there is a lack of marketing competence and expertise in the sector, particularly beyond issues like promotion and pricing, and particularly in the market research function—that is, around analysing consumers and competitors.

There is clearly a very tangible tension here for such organisations. If they become completely market-driven, only producing content that is assured of popularity with large audiences, they may end up ignoring cultural content that might be less successful with audiences, but which might help maintain a historically significant cultural movement. This is a tension that is played out every day in such organisations; we see it when developing the programme plan and when setting organisational budgets, as cultural, artistic, business and political issues and perspectives vie for prominence and a share of limited organisational resources. To help resolve these tensions, the marketing function may take on increasing significance, as will the development of new forms of business model.

3.6.3 New business models (and what exactly is a business model?)

We have already noted ongoing declines in the provision of state funding for the arts throughout the world. From the USA to China, governments increasingly struggle to maintain their support for the performing arts sector, given their vast range of other economic and social priorities. Whether it be the need to invest huge amounts of funds in the health care system (particularly during COVID), the transition from fossil fuels to greener energy sources, required investments in a country's infrastructure (a particular priority in India, for example), government funds are under pressure as never before. One of the areas that has typically been reduced in recent years is funding for performing arts. The funding that has been available has become more variable and unpredictable in terms of its allocation. Inevitably this has been particularly challenging for not-for-profit organisations, whose business model might have traditionally relied on such funding.

The term '**business model**' is one of the most-used terms when discussing businesses, but perhaps one of the least understood. The term is used regularly to describe just about every aspect of the operation of a business, so it is a blurry, ill-defined and often quite confusing term. In this brief section we will try and clarify it. Business models typically describe a **value proposition** for customers and consumers, typically in comparison to competing offerings, and the associated range of activities that produce that value, typically supported by an analysis of associated revenues and costs. Hence Johnson et al. (2023) describe three main components: the **value creation** element (what exactly is the proposition to the consumer?); **value configuration** (that is, the way in which resources and activities are organised to produce that value); and **value capture**—how that value is secured by the company (i.e. how is it turned into profits?).

But definitions vary hugely, with some commentators stressing the way in which business models link an organisation to its external environment (Zott and Amit, 2010) and others suggesting it should describe 'the logic' of a firm, the way it operates (Casadeus-Masanell and Ricart, 2010). A very good overview of all of these definitions is provided in a paper by Baden-Fuller and Morgan (2010) if you want a slightly more academic (but very comprehensive) analysis.

Barringer and Ireland (2016) stress four key components of a business model, including the core strategy of the company, its strategic resources, partnership network and customer interface. Gary Hamel (2000) points to the importance of focusing on the configuration (linkages) between these elements, with particular attention paid to how the organisation deploys the business model across its organisational boundaries to the ultimate benefit of the consumer. Osterwalder et al. (2005) see business models existing at the interface of an organisation's strategy, organisational structure and technology infrastructure and that devising a business model therefore involves consideration of the core product or service, the customer interface, the organisation of the company and financial aspects of its operation.

Teece (2010) stresses that business model development typically starts with consideration of the features and benefits (typically though not necessarily supported by an enabling technology) to be embedded in a product or service, identifying the range of potential consumer benefits, identifying relevant market segments, confirming the availability of revenue streams and identifying associated costs and finally designing mechanisms to capture value.

A useful tool to analyse the various dimensions of a business model is the Business Model Canvas (Osterwalder and Pigneur, 2010). This is a business tool developed by 470 practitioners from 45 countries led by Alexander Osterwalder. It is useful as it prompts good questions and integrated thinking. It can be used to establish where a company is at any point in time, and potential directions for future development. Rather than just downloading the template from the internet, we would recommend investing in the accompanying book, *Business Model Generation*, which offers are far more detailed and useful insight into the use of the Canvas and business models more generally. The Canvas model is particularly useful when combined with the Kim and Mauborgne (2005) 'blue ocean' perspective mentioned in Chapter 2, given its particular focus on value and its creation.

Business models often become standardised in an industry; they are adopted by many organisations and become a 'recipe' for how to do business. A good example might be the 'razor and blades' model adopted by Gillette, whereby shaving razors were sold relatively cheaply to encourage take-up, and the blades themselves are sold at a relatively high price point to secure profits. A similar model has helped pay-TV companies drive the penetration of their services, with the hardware (typically a set-top box) distributed for free or at a very low price point (driving take-up by consumers). Such a strategy incurs significant costs for the pay-TV operator. However, these costs are offset by subsequent sales of channel subscription services which generate relatively high levels of profit.

Another business model that has seen widespread adoption (it has become another recipe), and indeed has a very long history, is the freemium model, whereby basic services are offered by a company for free, attracting customers who are then encouraged to upgrade to more premium services, at a premium price. Such models have been adopted by the electronic games sector, particularly in the provision of games played on mobile devices like phones, with basic access to games being free, supported by significant opportunities for 'in-app' purchases of cosmetic upgrades, loot boxes and downloadable content. The 'platform' model has become another standardised business model, designed to bring together customers and suppliers of products and services, offering the service free to one group, and charging the other for access to them.

The importance of getting the right business model is regularly stressed by commentators. Teece (2010) argues that whilst entrepreneurs may be successful in developing an innovation or business idea, without a robust business model, they may fail to secure value from it. In turn, Chesbrough (2010) argues that a mediocre idea or technology with a great business model may be more valuable than an outstanding technology supported by a poor business model.

Business models, then, are defined in many ways. The core elements appear to focus on what value is delivered to customers / consumers, particularly in relation to competing offerings, and how the organisation is structured to deliver and capture value for itself. Perhaps the best advice whenever you read or hear the term is to try and establish what the author or speaker actually means by the term business model, what elements are they including and what are they not considering. Ensure the definition you use in any specific situation (e.g. business planning in your own company) is clear and shared with other participants.

Not-for-profit organisations are particularly concerned about their capacity to take risks and invest in new content and up-and-coming talent. Without the support of government funds, such investments arguably become too risky; the failure to attract significant audiences to a new production is likely to have too major an impact on the ongoing financial health of an organisation if it fails, particularly if they are not buffered by grants from state organisations. The tendency, perhaps inevitability, may be to turn to those proven performing arts properties and franchises that are likely to attract significant audience numbers, to the detriment of artistic creativity and innovation. This sounds very much like the situation forecast by Adorno and Horkheimer, though in this case the move to more obviously commercial content is not driven by greedy business owners, but rather a decline in the state's support for artistic endeavour and a desire by performing arts organisations merely to survive.

Hence not-for-profit organisations in the performing arts sector are increasingly examining their traditional business models, with their often over-reliance on diminishing and unpredictable state funding. Most are exploring new ways to generate revenues or better manage costs, often through techniques or management approaches borrowed from for-profit sectors. Some are examining how the spaces they often own as venues or rehearsal space can be adapted and repurposed to become creative and cultural hubs for a local population, encouraging participation in as well as viewing of the cultural heritage of a region or state. For some the re-evaluation is even more fundamental, questioning their core reliance on cultural heritage as a key differentiator in the marketplace, and how meaningful this is to a potential audience with a huge range of different experiences to choose from. Arguably, such new business models may need to focus far more on issues around value, based on a more consumer-centric view of the world. One of the key areas that organisations are exploring in this regard is developments in digital technologies.

3.6.4 Digital opportunities

Technology is already extensively used to enhance live performances. From early developments in the areas of sound and lighting systems, to the use of things like projection technologies and today the potential for applications using digital avatars (see Chapter 9) and virtual reality, technology has long played a key role in ensuring live performances are as engaging and exciting as possible for audiences. The emergence of digital platforms in particular has also changed how performances are marketed, and how communities are built around specific performing arts organisations (e.g. most performing arts organisations will have a Facebook page or something similar), and rather than use things like outdoor advertising, companies are increasingly turning to digital media as the critical platform for their promotional efforts.

But it is perhaps in their ability to reach new audiences and more fully engage with existing ones that digital developments are currently generating most interest. During COVID, many performing arts organisations posted free content online—perhaps sections from a performance, an interview with a 'star' performer or with a stagehand to explain life backstage. Such content was typically provided free to audiences to maintain their interest in the arts and to remind them that the organisation, despite closing its doors during COVID for an extended period, still existed. Such activities incurred significant costs for the relevant organisations, costs that arguably cannot be maintained without some level of new revenue to support them. It is to this issue that much management attention is now turning: how to maximise the value of digital assets.

Viewing performing arts content online appears popular, though perhaps this has been skewed by COVID in recent years to present a rather more optimistic view than may be the case post-COVID. The recording and digitisation of performances can be expensive; hence revenues need to be generated to cover these costs. This is particularly so as viewing of digital content may not generate the same level of additional revenue as attending a concert or performance in person. Such visits in person may also result in the purchase of a programme, merchandise, drinks or food, often relatively high-margin goods compared to ticket sales and crucial to a venue in terms of generating profits. If digital attendance significantly reduces in-person attendance (as predicted by commentators like Soares, 2019), then a very large number of digital tickets will need to be sold to make up for this decline in 'real-world' audiences.

This increase in overall audience size may indeed be possible. Certainly, digital distribution offers the prospect of reaching new younger audiences, audiences in rural areas and even international audiences, traditionally beyond the reach of most of the smaller organisations in the performing arts sector. But if everyone has the same idea, then competition is likely to be intense. And it won't just be competition from another opera or theatre company, but potentially from any of the organisations providing content to viewers. The sheer amount of content available via digital platforms makes securing any audience attention and interest difficult. Hence those in the performing arts sector may find themselves competing directly with highly sophisticated marketing organisations that have grown up online, and who deeply understand how to reach digital audiences and secure their interest and spending.

Digitising and producing content will be just the first step. More challenging will be how this content is marketed and sold to potential audiences. Issues around how the content is designed and presented, how it is priced and promoted, and what platforms it is distributed over will all need careful consideration.

3.7 Conclusions

The performing arts sector, then, is highly diverse, encompassing those organisations that are clearly very focused on generating profits, and those for whom profit is perhaps less of a concern, focused as they are on maintaining the presence and perceived value of traditional and regional cultural content in the minds of the population. Its diversity is further stressed by the broad range of stakeholders involved in its operation, their often very different goals and agendas, but also the sheer range of content that is currently available, from dance to opera, classical music to theatre. But this diversity may be under threat. Whether it be the generally declining level of support for the sector from state authorities or the sheer range of alternative ways to consume content that have emerged in the last 20 years, the sector is arguably challenged as never before.

New approaches to the operation of the sector are required. For those working in performing arts organisations this may involve a re-evaluation of their core business model, how their organisation interacts with consumers, and the types of assets and capabilities they need to build. For those of you considering entering the sector, then, this is a challenging but potentially exciting time. The sector needs new perspectives and ideas as never before, particularly in how it relates to and attracts the attention of younger consumers. Perhaps the best sources of such perspectives are the younger employees who are currently entering the sector, who will understand the competitive environment and potential opportunities offered by digital developments better than most. However, for the sector to prosper and survive, it also needs new employees who understand a business as well as an artistic agenda and who can balance the two in the complex operating environments of performing arts companies.

3.8 Activities

- Visit a live performance. Catalogue the range of factors that contribute to your experience, including the performance itself, tangible service elements and intangible elements of the event.
- Think about how performing arts companies might reach out and secure the interest of younger audience groups. Should they consider changing the nature of performances, lowering prices, finding more appropriate partners and alliances or changing their marketing campaigns?
- Your local theatre intends to run a summer programme of highly commercial productions to attract tourists during the summer holidays. Who are the various stakeholders that this decision might affect? How might each stakeholder group define success in this context? Are there tensions in keeping everyone happy?
- What might a performing arts organisation do to reduce the risk associated with staging a new show? What revenue sources might they seek?

Notes

1 ATG, www.atgentertainment.com.
2 www.georgiantheatreroyal.co.uk.
3 For those of you who might be interested in a finance career in the performing arts, it is worth reviewing the Amans paper (and the references it cites) in some detail.
4 https://www.westendbestfriend.co.uk/news/a-webf-article-risk-and-reward-in-theatre-productions#:~:text=The%20West%20End%20Model&text=A%20musical%20with%20a%20very,70%25%20capacity%20over%2014%20weeks.
5 https://thehustle.co/the-economics-of-broadway-shows#:~:text=The%20upfront%20cost%2C%20known%20on,m%2D%2420m%20for%20musicals.
6 https://thehustle.co/the-economics-of-broadway-shows#:~:text=The%20upfront%20cost%2C%20known%20on,m%2D%2420m%20for%20musicals.
7 https://www.nature.com/articles/d41586-023-04086-z#:~:text=A%20new%20antibiotic%20often%20costs,growing%20threat%20of%20antimicrobial%20resistance.
8 https://www.vulture.com/2013/11/spider-man-leaves-behind-broadways-biggest-bill.html.
9 https://www.bbc.co.uk/news/entertainment-arts-26336382#:~:text=Andrew%20Lloyd%20Webber's%20latest%20musical,March%20after%20sluggish%20ticket%20sales.
10 Mintel report, 2020.
11 Ibid.
12 Ibid.
13 Ibid.
14 The Theatre Communications Group, annual report 2023.
15 *Arts Audiences: Insight,* Arts Council England, 2011.
16 Statista Reports, 2024.

References

Addis, M. and Rurale, A. 2021. *A Call to Revise Cultural Business Management: Managing the Cultural Business.* Routledge.

Amans, O. P., Mazars-Chapelon, A. and Villeseque-Dubus, A. 2015. Budgeting in institutional complexity: The case of performing arts organisation. *Management Accounting Research*, 27, pp. 47–66.

Amorim, D., Jiménez-Caballero, J. and Almeida, P. 2020. The impact of performing arts festivals on tourism development: Analysis of participants' motivation, quality, satisfaction and loyalty. *Tourism & Management Studies*, 16 (4), pp. 45–57.

Baden-Fuller, C. and Morgan, M. 2010. Business models as models. *Long Range Planning*, 43 (2–3), pp. 156–171.
Barringer, B. and Ireland, R. 2016. *Entrepreneurship: Successfully Launching New Ventures.* Pearson.
Bathurst, J. A. and Stein, T. S. 2008. *Performing Arts Management: A Handbook for Professional Practices.* Allworth Press.
Bilton C. 1999. Risky business: The independent production sector in Britain's creative industries. *International Journal of Cultural Policy*, 6 (1), pp. 17–39.
Casadesus-Masanell, R. and Ricart, J. E. 2010. From strategy to business models and onto tactics. *Long Range Planning*, 43, pp. 195–215.
Chen, N. and Dwyer, L. 2017. Residents' place satisfaction and place attachment on destination brand-building behaviours: Conceptual and empirical differentiation. *Journal of Travel Research*, 57 (8), pp. 1026–1041.
Chesbrough, H. 2010. Business model innovation: Opportunities and barriers. *Long Range Planning*, 43 (2–3), pp. 354–363.
Giannini, T. and Bowen, J. P. (eds). 2019. *Museums and Digital Culture.* Springer International Publishing.
Hamel, G. 2000. *Leading the Revolution.* Harvard Business Review Press.
Hernández-Mogollón, J. M., Duarte, P. A. and Folgado-Fernández, J. A. 2018. The contribution of cultural events to the formation of the cognitive and affective images of a tourist destination. *Journal of Destination Marketing & Management*, 8, pp. 170–178.
Hirschman, E. C. and Holbrook, M. B. 1982. Hedonic consumption: Emerging concepts, methods and propositions. *Journal of Marketing*, 46 (3), pp. 92–101.
Holbrook, M. B. and Hirschman, E. C. 1982. The experiential aspects of consumption: Consumer fantasies, feelings, and fun. *Journal of Consumer Research*, 9 (2), pp. 132–140.
Johnson, G., Angwin, D., Whittington, R., Regner, P. and Scholes, K. 2023. *Exploring Strategy: Text and Cases.* Pearson.
Kim, W. C. and Mauborgne, R. 2005. *Blue Ocean Strategy: How To Create Uncontested Market Space and Make The Competition Irrelevant.* Harvard Business Review Press.
Luo, C. Y., Tsai, C. H. (Ken), Su, C. H. (Joan) and Chen, M. H. 2023. From stage to a sense of place: The power of tourism performing arts storytelling for sustainable tourism growth. *Journal of Travel & Tourism Marketing*, 40 (8), pp. 728–743.
Nelson, P. 1974. Advertising as information. *Journal of Political Economy*, (4), pp. 729–754.
Osterwalder, A. and Pigneur, Y. 2010. *Business Model Generation: A Handbook for Visionaries, Game Changers, and Challengers.* New Jersey: Wiley.
Osterwalder, A., Pigneur, Y. and Tucci, C. (2005). Clarifying Business Models: Origins, Present, and Future of the Concept, in *Communications of the Association for Information Systems*, p. 16.
Soares, P. S. 2019. *New business models in the digital economy applied to the smart tourism sector—The case of U.Porto's digital museum app.* Master's thesis, Universidade do Porto, Porto, Portugal.
Teece, D. 2010. Business models, business strategy and innovation. *Long Range planning*, 43 (2–3), pp. 172–194.
Zott, C. and Amit, R. 2010. Designing your future business model: An activity system perspective, *Long Range Planning*, 43, pp. 216–226.

4 Television Broadcasting and Narrowcasting

4.1 Introduction

Broadcasting, in a variety of forms, has been at the heart of home entertainment for over 70 years, during which time it has grown into a global industry worth over $575bn in 2024.[1] During its history, it has evolved into a complex ecosystem of business-to-business and business-to-consumer sectors, and a core vehicle for the development and exploitation of visual content.

In recent years it has evolved beyond its traditional 'broadcast' model of a single message sent to multiple recipients simultaneously, to a model focused on the customised delivery of content to individuals, when and where they require it ('narrowcasting'). In this chapter we will review the evolution of the sector, examine the types of company involved in the value chain and their key roles and processes, assess the implications of the move from a broadcast to narrowcast model, and illustrate a critical change in the basis for business operation evident throughout the entertainment industry, a move from distribution- to attention-based economies.

In doing so we highlight some key themes, including the intimate relationship between broadcasting and technological innovation, the key role of the state in shaping and regulating the market, the proliferation of platforms and fragmentation of audiences and broadcasting's critical role as a brand-building window for products and services. In terms of key business issues, we will review methods of new product / service development, along with the idea of 'open' and 'closed' innovation, before examining the peculiarities of how this operates within the broadcasting / narrowcasting sectors.

We start with some history.

4.2 A brief history

If we define broadcasting as a method of communication, which sends a single message simultaneously to multiple recipients, then its modern history typically begins with experiments in the radio medium. The evolution of radio in a series of breakthroughs in wireless telegraphy through the late 19th and early 20th centuries by researchers like Tesla, Marconi, Popov and Baviera reveals the intimate and highly influential role of technology in the establishment of broadcasting as a medium. Indeed, the growth and commercialisation of both television and radio could only proceed as technical developments were made in delivery platforms and reception equipment, in radio's case from simple AM radios, through digital audio broadcasting to today's multiplatform services. Whilst the establishment of radio as a viable broadcast medium was largely

DOI: 10.4324/9781003498599-4

driven by scientific curiosity and enthusiasm rather than astute commercial acumen, its growth was certainly fuelled by commercial interests. Early stations in the US were typically established by radio manufacturers and department stores to sell radio sets, and by media owners to sell their products—e.g. newspapers. This 'sponsorship' model was subsequently replaced by advertising as the main revenue for commercial stations.

The early history of radio also reveals a clear desire by governments to be intimately involved in operating and regulating the broadcast airwaves. Many early radio services were established by governments as part of a public service remit to serve the nation (e. g. BBC Radio founded in 1922). At the same time commercial stations, focused more on generating profits, were obliged to secure licences from early government-appointed regulators (e.g. the Federal Communications Commission (FCC) in the USA). Equally what could or could not be broadcast, whether in the form of programmes or advertisements, and who could own radio stations, was regulated by government. This model would soon be replicated in the television sector.

The early history of television was again as much driven by the ambitions and curiosity of scientists and engineers as people of commerce. Early experimental work was carried out by Rignoux and Fournier in Paris and Rosing and Zworykin in Russia in the first years of the 20th century. But if television is defined as the contemporaneous transmission of moving, monochromatic images with continuous tonal variation, then it could be argued that John Logie Baird first achieved this privately in the UK on 2 October 1925.

In most territories we can see the evolution of television broadcasting in broad historical phases. In the first phase television typically emerges in the form of government-sponsored initiatives. What is often called 'public service broadcasting' was driven by a desire by governments to establish an influential position in the emerging industry, to encourage the diffusion of the technology but also to build a medium to assist in the social and cultural recovery of countries post-World War One and Two. Whilst the BBC launched experimental broadcasts in 1932, and a regular service (one channel) in 1936, such developments were largely halted during World War Two. The immediate post-war period, however, was characterised by the rapid growth of consumer uptake of television technology, underpinned by the development of public service television channels like ARD (Germany, 1954), RAI (Italy, 1954) and Beijing Television (now China Central Television) in 1958. Such organisations were typically state-run, typically at least partly funded by public money and offered a very limited number of channels providing content to inform, educate and entertain the public rather than generate profits.

Phase two in most territories saw the launch of commercial channels that were free to the public, privately owned and profit-focused. Typically relying on advertising to generate revenue, channels such as ITV in the UK (launched in 1955) were often established in deliberate competition with the existing government-sponsored public service broadcasters. Such services, often known as 'free to air', 'over the air' or 'terrestrial TV', typically required only an aerial and television set to secure access.

This trend towards increased competition would continue in phase three, with the evolution of what were typically called pay-TV services delivered via a variety of emerging technologies, particularly cable infrastructures and satellite delivery, and characterised by a new business model which required the user to pay a subscription fee for access. HBO would launch its first service in the USA in 1972, in the form of encrypted, analogue 'over the air' services, requiring a subscription fee and specialist equipment (a set-top box) to access it, followed by Showtime in 1976. In Europe, pay-TV would first appear in France with Canal+ in 1984, followed by Sky TV in the UK in 1989. In Asia, Star TV (Satellite Television Asia Region) would launch in 1991. Typically privately owned and profit-orientated, such services would be the basis for the next phase of television evolution, the growth of narrowcasting.

Whilst beginning life as analogue services, pay-TV services were relatively quickly converted to digital, allowing their owners to draw on the internet and emerging broadband infrastructure as a new vehicle for the distribution of their services. 'Catch-up' services launched by existing companies, whereby users could stream broadcast content at their convenience, typically via broadband, were soon augmented with new dedicated narrowcast services from organisations like YouTube (founded in 2005), Netflix, Hulu and Amazon Prime, focused on delivering customised content via the internet to individuals and ultimately overturning the traditional broadcast model.

Of course there are significant exceptions to this overall model. The USA evolved in a rather different way, focused from its earliest history on commercial stations, rather than public service broadcasters. Broadcasts began in earnest when CBS's New York City station W2XAB began broadcasting their first regular seven-days-a-week television schedule in the 1930s, alongside NBC (National Broadcasting Company), followed by ABC (American Broadcasting company) in 1943 and (much later—1986) the Fox Network. The country's dedicated public service broadcaster (PBS) only began operation in 1970 and remains a relatively minor player in the overall broadcast market.

Whilst we see mature markets in many territories, other regions are still evolving through these stages, but evolving fast. Television broadcasting in Africa was late to emerge, with the first service (WNTS—the Western Nigeria Television service) launched in 1959 (though radio had a longer history—first introduced into Nigeria in 1932 by the BBC with its 'Empire service'), followed by services in Egypt (1960) and the Congo (1962). Other territories like South Africa, despite being one of the most technologically advanced compared to other countries in Africa, would only see its first television services launched in 1976. Whilst the services originated as analogue-based, free-to-air offers, with significant government support, 1995 saw the launch of the first major pay-TV platform, a satellite delivered service from MultiChoice, followed by Canal Horizons and Nilesat. Digital services would only emerge in 2008, in South Africa, though most services have now migrated to digital.

4.3 Some technical background

As already suggested, most broadcasting services were originally launched on analogue systems, with television signals delivered from a central playout centre, via a series of ground-based (hence 'terrestrial') masts, to an aerial attached to each house, and then to an individual television set. Analogue services could also be delivered via cable and satellite systems. Analogue technology provided relatively little bandwidth, however (imagine a narrow pipe), and hence services were limited in terms of the number of channels of programmes they could accommodate, typically one or two channels per provider. Even early pay-TV platforms could only offer 15–20 channels at maximum using two major infrastructures to deliver content, analogue satellite and cable.

The move to digital infrastructures proved hugely significant for providers. Whilst expensive to develop and launch, they allowed providers to supply content in higher resolutions, launch a new range of interactive services (e.g. home shopping) and, perhaps most significantly, through compression technologies, transmit far more channels within the same frequency band compared to analogue. Sky TV, the major pay-TV operator in the UK, launched its own digital satellite service in 1998 with 140 TV channels and a range of interactive features (e.g. pay per view). Cable companies quickly followed. With improvements in technology, such services are now able to deliver over 300 channels of television along with a range of sophisticated interactive services (e.g. internet web browsing, access to content streaming services). We will return to the further implications of the move to digital later in the chapter.

Digital terrestrial services began to emerge in the 2000s, initially in the UK, Sweden and Germany, often in the form of free-to-air services provided by the pre-existing public service and commercial TV operators, again requiring an aerial but now augmented with a set-top box to decode the digital signals, with enhanced picture quality and yet more channels.

As well as providing a range of new services, the set-top box used to decode television signals also provided something new for providers, a return path, a way for consumers to directly interact with the providers and a critical source of key consumer data, collected and stored through the set-top box. Broadcasting traditionally had no such return path: it was a one-way medium, from broadcaster to viewer, with little opportunity for interaction. Collecting data on viewing habits was time consuming and costly. Set-top boxes (and now increasingly smart TVs and cloud-based services), made the process of interaction (and data collection) far cheaper and more straightforward. The move to digital also provided the opportunity for suppliers to explore the potential benefits of linking the delivery of television services to the emerging broadband internet networks proliferating across the world. Initially merely providing access to internet resources, broadband networks are increasingly used for the delivery of the core television service itself, obviating the need for an aerial, satellite dish or cable connection.

Advances allowed much of this technology to be increasingly integrated into the televisions themselves, removing the need for set-top boxes. As of 2025, most televisions sold have integrated digital decoders for free services, so in the UK come with pre-installed digital terrestrial services Freesat and Freeview, and increasingly allow direct access to dedicated narrowcast services like Amazon, Hulu and Netflix. If a household has access to a reasonably robust broadband network, a wide range of television services are likely to be available. Such services can also be accessed on your games console, PC or mobile phone.

4.4 The structure of the industry

Let's explore some of the types of company involved in this dynamic and evolving sector before looking at their business operations in more detail. Core elements of any television broadcast infrastructure will include a technology platform (e.g. the aforementioned digital terrestrial, cable and satellite systems, internet and broadband networks), channel providers and programme makers. Early broadcasters provided all such elements through a single organisation: they were what is typically called vertically integrated, encapsulating all the elements required to produce and broadcast a television service. Hence the BBC developed the technological broadcast infrastructure, made television programmes through its own internal production facilities (BBC Studios) and collated these programmes into specific BBC channels which were then broadcast to the consumer. Similar models are found in some pay-TV operators—e.g.

Star TV runs a technological infrastructure (for most of its history, satellite-based), makes programmes, and markets and distributes its own channels.

At the same time, some organisations rely on external partners to provide elements of the service. When Channel 4 was launched in the UK in the mid-1980s, partially subsidised by the UK government, but essentially a commercial channel relying on airtime sales of advertising to fund its operation, it was launched without its own programme production division. This was done deliberately, as part of its founding charter, partly to encourage the growth of what are typically called independent programme makers. These companies exist outside vertically integrated television companies, and their sole purpose is to produce television programmes. Before Channel 4, the incumbent broadcasters, BBC and ITV, both had their own production facilities, and hence there were relatively few opportunities for independent companies to flourish. The creation of Channel 4 created further demand for programming, which had to be provided by independent companies. Equally independent channel production companies emerged, who aggregated programmes into channels and supplied them to existing typically pay-TV platforms (e.g. MTV in the USA, Flextech in the UK).

Other key participants in the sector include governments, regulators, technology providers, service companies (e.g. specialist companies offering services like accountancy and legal advice, talent management companies, production services like specialist caterers, camera hire, special effects studios etc.), advertisers and of course the consumer. This creates a complex ecosystem of interacting organisations. Let's look at some key processes through which the ecosystem operates, focusing on how new products are created.

4.5 New product development and programme production

One of the best ways to identify how organisations work together within this ecosystem is by exploring programme production. The creation of new content falls into the business activity known as new product (or service) development. What does academic theory tell us about the process of product and service development more broadly?

Literature on how new products are developed is extensive, covering descriptive analysis and prescriptive guidelines in a wide variety of industries. This is at least partly a result of the significance of the activity to corporations. Along with corporate acquisition (buying or merging with other companies—see Chapter 5), new product development is one of the key ways in which an organisation grows (Kotler, 1988). As the 'nexus of [corporate] competition' (Brown and Eisenhardt, 1995, p. 343), firms who are good at it win in the market. As a mechanism for change in a company it is 'a critical means by which members of organizations diversify, adapt and even reinvent their firms to match evolving market and technical conditions' (Brown and Eisenhardt, 1995, p. 344).

Hence new product development it is an issue that is generally seen as critical by most business organisations, as it has a significant impact on what an organisation is going to look like, think like and act like. Thus 'product development is among the essential processes for success, survival and renewal of organisations, particularly for firms in either fast paced or competitive markets' (Brown and Eisenhardt, 1995, p. 344).

A significant body of empirical study has grown up around new product development (NPD) and, given its importance, the focus is usually on defining characteristics of the product or development process that lead to new product success. One of the best organised approaches to categorising this very significant body of work was developed Brown and Eisenhardt, (1995), who identify three major research streams (where the product development project is the unit of analysis), each building on a pioneering study. Research in each stream focuses on a particular element of product development. These broad streams remain relevant today in that more contemporary research has continued along similar lines of enquiry. The following sections briefly outline these themes.

4.5.1 The rational plan school

Much of the impetus, methodology and aims of the rational plan school of new product development are modelled after research originally conducted by Myers and Marquis (1969). Their focus was on identifying the 'very broad range of determinants of [the] financial performance of the [new] product' (Brown and Eisenhardt, 1995, p. 345). Hence the aim of this and many subsequent studies has been to identify the variables that are correlated with the financial success of new products.

An early subject of much of this research work was the process of new product development itself. A structured 'rational' process became fashionable, after the models proposed by Urban and Hauser (1980) and consulting company Booz Allen Hamilton (1982). They typically outline a set of logical and rational steps, involving sequential hand-offs between functional areas such as research and development (R&D), manufacturing and marketing. They propose formal procedures and formats to help integration of stages and the interaction of different functional groups. It was typically outlined as following a simple path, developing an overall strategy for new product development (do we actually need them, of what kind?), followed by idea generation, idea screening (a first analysis of ideas), detailed business analysis, selection of the final shortlist, development, testing and finally commercialisation (product launch).

The model is very structured, linear and convenient, with one function handing the product idea neatly over to the next when they are finished with their contribution. These processes were often described as stage gate models, with ideas moving through a series of stages (e.g. idea generation or research) and gates (the application of specific criteria to an idea) to select which product ideas should be further developed, and which discarded. Typically, the process begins with the organisation developing an overall view of its own corporate ends and how new products will help it achieve them—that is, strategy setting. This sets the overall guidelines and parameters within which new product development happens. This will usually involve a strategic assessment, which Hax and Majluf (1991) suggest should include a review of the organisation's mission (its reason for existence), external and internal environments and strategic goals. These are synthesised to generate a set of requirements that any new product or service must attain in its development—which are then translated into a set of requirements that each idea must fulfil to pass a particular gate (e.g. it must create profit margins of 10%).

This would be followed, in the rational model, with concept generation, during which large numbers of ideas are generated and screened / selected for further development. A typical market-driven concept-generation process (see for example Bitran and Pedrosa, 1998, p. 174) begins with establishing the overall needs of the company in terms of new product development, establishing the needs of the consumer (typically through market research), identifying product requirements (and typically ranking them), establishing design parameters, generating relevant concepts, selecting the most appropriate and finalising the required design attributes before development.

The objective of the selection / screening process is to 'allocate resources between those projects which have the most likelihood of helping the firm meet its objectives' (Kelly and Storey, 2000, p. 47). De Brentani (1986) suggests that applying a systematic and formal management decision approach to idea screening (e.g. through a stage / gate model) has been closely linked to improved success in the development and launch of new products. Such screening measures can be single- or multi-stage, involve formal and/or informal measures, and will typically use quantitative and qualitative tools. Often when reviewing ideas for new products, relevant information may be in very short supply within an organisation (particularly for radically new ideas) so 'the only information on which to make a decision may be the subjective opinions of the management team' (Kelly and Storey, 2000, p. 47).

4.5.2 New product attributes

Focusing more on the characteristics of products themselves, the NewProd study (Cooper, 1979), examined 102 successful and 93 failed products in 103 industrial firms in Canada to identify the characteristics of successful new products. It sharpened the emergent emphasis on product advantages, market attractiveness and internal organisation of the development process as being key to the potential success of a new product. This was followed by Cooper and Kleinschmit (1987), who examined the hypothesis developed from the NewProd study in a further 125 manufacturing firms. The study revealed relative product advantage as the most important determinant of product success—that is, the intrinsic value of the product, including unique benefits to customers, quality, cost and innovativeness of features relative to existing products.

Subsequent research in the rational approach school has subjected each of these major variables (e.g. process, product attributes) to ever more rigorous examination—e.g. the importance of predevelopment planning (Dwyer and Mellor, 1991), marketing and R&D involvement (Hise et al., 1990), the speed of product development and how to accelerate the process (Cordero, 1991; Gupta and Wilemon, 1990). No doubt this ever more forensic approach will continue but, in summary, researchers suggest that successful product development is the result of rational planning and execution. Specifically:

- Careful attention to planning and selection processes to identify an appropriate product concept.
- Execution of the development plan in an efficient and effective way by a competent and well-coordinated cross-functional team that operate with the blessing of…
- …a supportive senior management team.

The rational school has arguably not taken as much account as it might have of the less overtly 'rational' influences of organisational culture, politics and group decision making in terms of their impact on both product and process. Partly because of this, whilst the school has produced a huge list of 'what to do' prescriptions, it has been relatively less helpful in advising practitioners 'how to do it'.

4.5.3 Communication web

The second major school identified by Brown and Eisenhardt is the communication web approach, which focuses on the 'narrow effects of communication on project performance' (Brown and Eisenhardt, 1995, p. 345). Studies typically focus on only one variable, communication in the product development team, but do so in significant depth. They explore the workings of the new product development project team more closely, with the overall view that communication between project team members and outsiders stimulates the performance of development teams. The more successful the team are at communicating, the better the results of the process will be.

The first major piece of research in the school was conducted by Allen (1971, 1977) and focused on the flow of information in R&D groups. The researchers asked R&D staff to keep track of their communications over time during the development of various new products. Early results suggested the importance of communications between functions (e. g. R&D and the manufacturing or marketing team) during the new product development process and identified gatekeepers (Allen, 1971), high-performing individuals who communicated more than most and with people outside their speciality, bringing information into the organisation and dispersing it to their fellow team members, as being of particular importance in successful projects. Not only did these individuals gather and disseminate external information but they also facilitated the external communication of their fellow team members (Katz and Tushman, 1981). Ultimately the presence of active gatekeepers led to better-performing teams than those without.

Research into the importance of external communication continued with Ancona and Caldwell (1990, 1992). They noted that new product development team members tended to communicate mostly with those in the same functional group outside the team, and hence the more functions represented in the core project team the more external communication took place.

Internal communication between those within individual project teams has also been the subject of intense interest. Studies by Keller (1986) and Ancona and Caldwell (1992) both point to the importance of the quality and quantity of internal communication to the success of a team. Such research suggested that individuals in different functions understood product development in different ways, leading to different interpretations of even the same information. Failed projects were characterised by 'sequential attention by functional groups such that each departmental view dominated a particular phase of the project' (Brown and Eisenhardt 1995, p. 357). Successful projects overcame this by simultaneously combining different perspectives in a highly interactive and iterative fashion.

4.5.4 Disciplined problem solving

The third approach, the disciplined problem-solving school, focuses on the effects of 'product, a development team, its suppliers, and leaders on the actual product development process' (Brown and Eisenhardt, 1995, p. 345), with an emphasis on global industry comparisons. It has largely evolved from studies of highly successful Japanese product development practices in the mid-1980s (Imai et al., 1985; Quinn, 1985). Ultimately, successful product development is seen as a balancing act between the relatively autonomous problem-solving initiatives of the project team and the overarching vision for corporate strategy by top management.

Imai et al. (1985) and Quinn (1985) studied product development projects (typically focused on extensions and improvements to existing products rather than new-to-the-world products) across a variety of industries in Japan, looking for factors that contributed to successful product development. Their findings revealed a more detailed and subtle interpretation of many of the factors identified as being key in the rational plan school. Particularly important to success were:

- The extensive use of supplier networks: that is, strong formal ties between the organisation and external suppliers.
- The use of cross-functional teams, allowing access to a diverse range of information and perspectives.
- The overlap of development phases (to speed up the overall process), but only when supported by constant communication amongst project members.
- Active 'subtle control' by senior management, allowing the project team enough room to 'get on with it', but with parameters in place to ensure the final product fitted in with the overall company strategy and its product portfolio.

This characterised an emerging focus for much of the research in this school, which was to measure speed to market as the key, if not sole, performance measure, perhaps because it was one of the easiest to measure and was relatively objective in a discipline where finding widely agreed-upon objective measures of success had been a challenge. Other factors, less focused on operational planning and speed, such as success in the market, had proved much more difficult to measure objectively and usually relied upon the often-biased views of management. Speed to market emerged as a relatively simple-to-measure factor, and remains so today. Hence new tools have emerged (e.g. the waterfall approach often used in software development) to help speed up product development.

4.5.5 Towards an integrated approach

Brown and Eisenhardt see useful elements in all the approaches, and that they 'focus on both overlapping and complementary sets of constructs' (1995, p. 365). The rational plan approach provides a broad overview of many of the elements required for successful product development, the problem-solving school offers more detail on actual steps in the process and the role of senior management in establishing product and corporate strategy, and the communication web approach focuses on the specific communication that goes on in the process. Brown and Eisenhardt (1995) attempt to integrate all these elements into an overarching model of the factors affecting the success of a new product based on several theoretical foundations. They focus particularly on organisational, process and strategy issues, creating a hugely complicated series of interacting variables that need to be analysed and managed, including the product concept, market potential, potential consumer, nature of the project (e.g. project leader, team composition and organisation), team processes (efficiency, effectiveness, communication, adherence to financial constraints), support of senior management, involvement of suppliers and so on. Without doubt, this is a complex and challenging agenda.

4.5.6 Product development in the service sector

The focus of attention in product development research then shifted to the service sector as its importance grew in the global economy (Oke, 2002), though research on service innovation still lags that in the manufacturing sector (Griffen, 1997). Early attempts to improve new service development (NSD) processes looked to the existing work on new product development for guidance. Whilst overarching processes and approaches were useful, it soon became apparent that there were several significant issues, specifically around service characteristics, that existing approaches to product development did not take account of and that were critical to the success of new services. Services are generally considered to have several characteristics that differentiate them from manufactured products, specifically:

- **Intangibility:** services tend not to be seen or felt (Gadrey, 2000), though their effects or output can last a long time. This makes evaluation and comparison of services prior to purchase and consumption very difficult (Storey and Easingwood, 1998).
- **Inseparability:** services are typically produced and consumed at the same time; they are coproduced (De Bandt, 1995) simultaneously by provider and consumer (e.g. think about a haircut). Hence the provider–client interaction is key, and the user's view of the overall service is influenced heavily by the service delivery system.
- **Variability:** quality standards are highly variable. The quality of service provided by an individual (e.g. a hairdresser) may vary over time and will vary from individual to individual.
- **Perishability:** given the influence of intangibility and inseparability, services typically cannot be stored.

It is notable that services appear to share certain characteristics with cultural products (e.g. the perishability of the value of a ticket to the theatre, the intangibility of a television programme, the inseparability of a performance in a theatre) and we will return to this point throughout the book.

Hill (1997) provides a more subtle differentiation, in that he defines a product in the sense of a change of ownership, and a service in the sense of a change in the condition of an object. Whilst other differences have been suggested and the debate still rages about the precise differences between products and services, the aforementioned characteristics are consistently cited. As Easingwood suggests, however, 'care should be taken not to over claim. Not all services are intangible, produced simultaneously, heterogeneous and perishable, and some manufactured goods may possess one or more of these characteristics' (1986, p. 265).

Studies that have looked at development in the service sector have identified a similar set of factors to studies of manufacturing goods in determining success, notably 'the importance of a proficient and market orientated new product development process, the importance of synergy between the requirements of the new product and the resources of the firm, and the attractiveness of the marketplace' (Storey and Easingwood, 1998, p. 338).

As in the manufacturing sector, there is significant variability in the degree to which service firms use formal and structured systems to develop new services. Easingwood (1986, p. 272) suggested that in the mid-1980s, only 26% of the broad range of firms he surveyed had entirely formal product screening systems, 52% had mixed formal and informal systems and 23% had entirely informal approaches. Similarly, according to research amongst British service firms in 1999, most service companies did not have formal mechanisms with which to generate new ideas, and only 25% of them searched for new ideas on a continual basis (Kelly and Storey, 2000).

In terms of the new service development process itself, like manufactured products, ideas come from many sources, from inside the firm and outside it, from formal and informal search procedures' (Kelly and Storey, 2000, p. 46). However, owing to the ease of copying in some service industries, competitors have typically been identified as a more important source of ideas than customers. Teixeira and Ziskin (1993) found that 80% of banks view their competitors as the main source of new service ideas.

Perhaps most significantly, it has been regularly reported that service companies have been even less successful than manufacturing companies in launching successful new services, and that radical innovations are far less common (Griffen, 1997; Oke, 2002). This is partly explained by the idea that because the client–provider interaction process is an integral part of the service, the development of a new service is usually far more complex, conceptually, than the development of a tangible new product and hence more prone to errors. The typically heavy involvement of humans in service delivery is a huge complication, given that human behaviour is difficult to predict and model.

Moreover, several other studies have suggested that service companies tend to lack a strategic focus on new service developments compared to manufacturing companies (Martin and Horne, 1993; Oke, 2002). Further Bowers (1989), Scheuing and Johnson (1989) and Martin and Horne (1993) have suggested that service companies tend not in general to use a formal process for developing and screening new service ideas. Since the use of such procedures has been found to have a significant impact on the outcome of new product development (Griffen, 1997; Storey and Easingwood, 1998 this is likely to be a major contributor to the lack of success of many new services.

4.5.7 Decision making in new product / service development

There appear to have been relatively few specific attempts to look at the nature of decision making in the process of new product / service development. The focus of research has been on prescriptive guidelines for better practice, particularly around process, organisation and communication. Whilst these have some implications for how decisions happen, few pieces of research have identified decision making as their core focus.

One of the few commentators to specifically look at decision making (Ozer, 2005) suggests four groups of factors that might influence decision making in new product or service development:

- Task-related factors: complexity, importance, information scarcity, task instructions.
- Decision maker-related factors: expertise, diversity, organisation.
- Elicitation-related factors (how options are evaluated): discrete value elicitation, probability distribution elicitation, other relevant criteria.
- Aggregation-related factors (how views are collated): mathematical, behavioural, mixed, electronic meetings, other elements of process.

In reviewing these factors, Ozer notes that new product / service development decision situations tend to be:

1 Complex and uncertain. This encourages tool use to help analysis and reduce risk, and the use of comparable cases to generate data when little relevant information is available. However, we also note that it may encourage a range of less positive decision behaviours (e.g. uncertainty avoidance, ritualistic behaviour, over confidence).

2 Happening in teams, in which a mix of experts and objective participants is required, the latter to mitigate the effects of subjective closeness to a new service (Ozer, 2005). He notes that well-structured teams are good for decision making; they usually improve accuracy, cover a wide range of views and improve group interest in implementing the decision (Davis and Toseland, 1987). However, we also note that teams can have a very negative effect on decision making (e.g. through various manifestations of groupthink, see Janis, 1972).
3 Prone to departmentalism. Differing departments drawn together into the decision-making process place different levels of importance on a new idea, or want to emphasise different elements in its development (Dougherty and Heller, 1994).
4 Sensitive to the availability of relevant information and how information is shared. Departmentalism and political behaviour may lead to team members not sharing relevant information (Adams et al., 1998).
5 Highly sensitive to the clarity of guidance from senior management, a lack of clarity leading to delays, confusion and new products / services that do not fit with corporate requirements.

Krishnan and Ulrich (2001) have undertaken perhaps the most comprehensive and contemporary review of decisions taken during various phases of new product and service development. They provide a framework for identifying these decisions which divides new product and service development-related decisions into two broad categories: decisions taken at the institutional level (e.g. the plan for product development, rules established to guide the process) and single-project decisions (concept development, product design, manufacturing plan etc.). This framework has had some empirical testing and appears to be robust in describing the type of decisions that are typically taken (see Iturriagagoitia and Melón, 2005).

The Krishnan and Ulrich model confirms the importance of a number of factors that have consistently been mentioned throughout the new product / service development literature, specifically issues of process, organisation and strategy and planning. Hence in focusing our review of the cultural industries literature, we will look at these main areas to describe how organisations go about developing new products from an institutional perspective:

1 **Organisation:** how do cultural companies organise to create new products and services? That is, their use of teams, their composition, involvement of senior management, involvement of suppliers and customers etc.? What range of functions is involved?
2 **Rules for the management of the process:** how is the process structured, is it structured in a formal or informal way, what are the stages? What decisions are made and how?
3 **Strategies:** are there specific strategies and tactics associated with product development and how are broader corporate strategies played out through product development?

4.5.8 New product development in the television sector

Perhaps the most fundamental process in the sector involves the production and supply of content—that is, the television programmes themselves. A typical broadcaster will have at least three departments involved in securing and marketing programmes; see Figure 4.1.

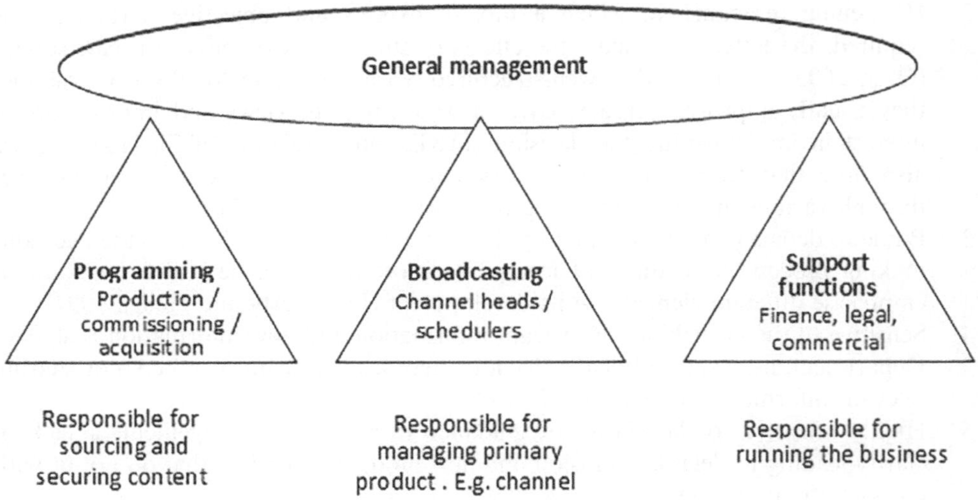

Figure 4.1 Critical functions in television product development
Source: author.

In most broadcasters there will be teams focused on programming—sourcing the programmes (from either internal or external sources), a broadcast team focused on aggregating programmes into channels, distributing them through the technology platform and marketing them to consumers, and a range of support teams (e.g. finance staff, business affairs and legal teams). The process of new product development is typically initiated by those running specific channels or genre departments (e.g. drama, comedy, natural history), who will have particular needs for specific types of programmes (e.g. we need a new drama series for 9pm on a Thursday). These programmes may be supplied in a variety of ways.

- New programme commissioning—the creation of completely new programmes.
  - They may be made by internal production teams.
  - They may be commissioned from external, independent production companies. Broadcasters will typically have commissioning rounds, when their specific requirements are released to potential suppliers, who vie for the opportunity to make the programme. Equally independent producers will also approach broadcasters with their own ideas for new programmes, outside these commissioning rounds.
  - It is worth noting that public service broadcasters usually have strict and overt quotas they must adhere to in terms of how much content is sourced from internal or external sources. For example, ITV and the BBC must adhere to quotas imposed on them by the broadcast regulator Ofcom as part of their public service remit, to source at least 25% of content from independent sources. Typically, these requirements are NOT necessarily extended to all other types of TV company (e.g. private companies, pay-TV companies), creating new programming opportunities.

- Programme acquisition—acquired programming is already made, and often already successful on other channels. In the UK Channel 4 acquires *The Simpsons*, for example, a pre-made programme already successful in the USA on the Fox Network. Such acquisitions usually grant the broadcaster the right to distribute (broadcast) the content in a specific territory, for a specific period. Again, public service broadcasters may have limits imposed on them by regulators in terms of the maximum amount of programmes that can be acquired, rather than made.

Teams within the programming department are typically organised around specific genres, including drama, news, comedy and factual programmes. The typical structure of the programming division of a major broadcaster is shown in Figure 4.2.

Let us consider the steps associated with the identification and selection of a single idea for a programme (its 'commission'). As already suggested, such ideas come into broadcasters from a variety of sources, including internal sources such as internal producers (from an internal production operation when present), genre groups and channel teams. Equally they may be externally generated: ideas are brought to the attention of commissioners by external producers, acting talent, writers or their agents. Ideas may come in a variety of forms, as phone calls, a one-page treatment or a fully worked-out script with talent attached.

In both large and small broadcasters, once an idea comes in to the company, it is typically allocated a 'champion' who is its main advocate and will drive the development process. In all cases very early discussions between the champion and head of a genre or channel head tend to be very informal, made up of an exchange of emails or brief conversations. Decision making tends to be around a broad yes or no to an idea and identifying what more information is required to develop it. After this initial discussion, if an idea is to move forward into development, the process becomes more formalised. A typical commissioning / development process is illustrated in Figure 4.3.

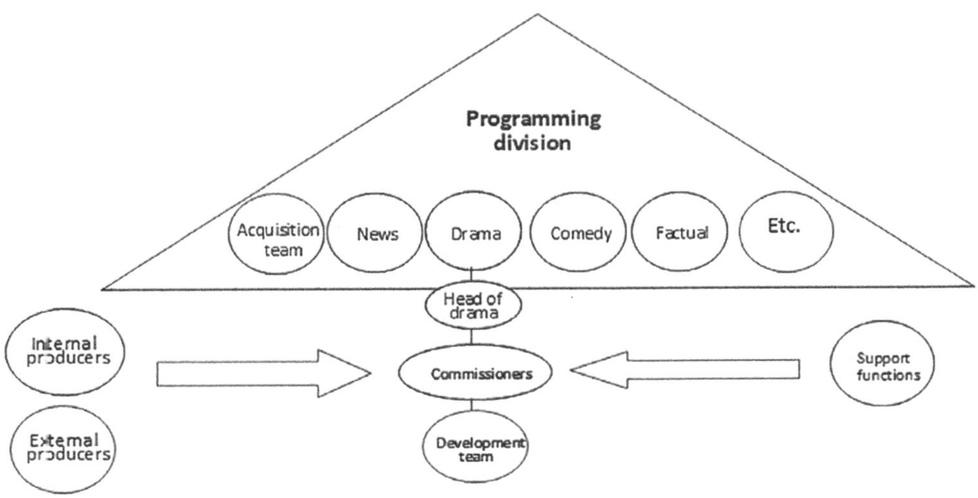

Figure 4.2 The programming team
Source: author.

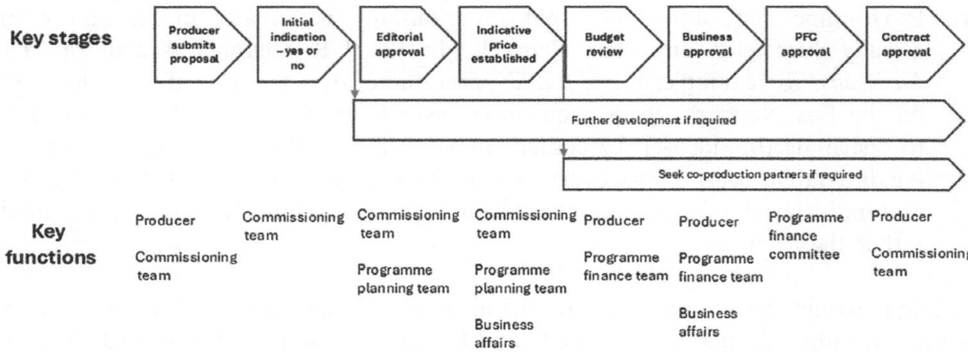

Figure 4.3 Programme commissioning at a major broadcaster
Source: author interviews.

The core commissioning process, then, involves generating and sourcing ideas, refining them (in development) and moving them through a series of organisational hurdles (the 'gates' mentioned in the previous section). It has three major strands of decision making associated with it:

- Creative: approval of creative elements, such as script, talent, overall 'look' etc.
- Business: project elements around the core creative concept—e.g. production budgets, timing, locations etc.
- Underlying these are a series of issues around the idea as product—i.e. target audience, potential place in the schedule, value for money etc. These might be considered creative or commercial depending on how the issues are treated, and who is considering them.

Creative and commercial decision making is brought together in the development process. This process tends to vary by genre, but generally it involves taking an idea that has some indication of internal support and further refining it along with internal or external producers, assessing it more rigorously, and finally pitching it to senior management of the channel or genre. In something like high-budget drama development this is often a very lengthy process, typically focusing on further developing the creative idea, script development, episode development, confirming the interest of talent and exploring in more detail the specific look and feel of the production. Preparations will also be made to pitch the idea to relevant internal audiences (e.g. senior management). All these issues inevitably affect business issues around the project which are also addressed during development (e.g. budget, timescale, fee due to the production company, legal issues around rights etc.). Each potential idea will be worked on as a joint project between producer (internal or external) and commissioner or member of the development team. Other, non-creative staff (e.g. lawyers) are drawn in as and when required.

This process of further defining creative and business issues is institutionalised in broadcasters through series of meetings and documents like 'editorial specification forms', part of the pro forma production contract which lists the writers' and director's brief. It is essentially a contract that articulates the creative ambitions of the production. Given the huge potential for different interpretations of the same creative idea, this is seen as essential in establishing a contractual basis for the assessment of creative fit with ambitions once the programme is made. This process often continues at a later stage through a series of 'tone meetings', where producers and commissioners meet to establish parameters for other creative features—music, design of sets and wardrobe etc. Such a long and involved process may take years, not months.

By contrast, the development process in the factual genre is characterised by being much more rapid. Creative concepts are often based around 'access', to an individual or situation. This access may be very time-dependent, and hence development must often be very rapid to capitalise on an opportunity. The development process often focuses on getting more detail on a situation or story, or the approval of an individual to be included in a programme rather than lengthy script re-writes.

During development, heads of commissioning will maintain ongoing discussion with channel management to update them on progress. There will typically be a creative and business sign-off before presentation to senior management for formal 'green light', the approval to commission the programme and start production. The head of genre and head of commissioning will probably have already signed off the main creative elements—e.g. tone, cast, writer, director—and the director of business affairs will have approved the major project elements (timing, budget etc.).

Once the project idea has been fully developed, it is finally presented to senior staff for sign-off (a green light to commission). This tends to be a two-tick system, with approval required by the head of a genre group and head of the channel for which the programme is being developed. If the project is an internal one, it will also require the sign-off of the head of internal production.

This single process is however wrapped up in a much wider range of processes and systems, including ongoing commissioning and development, planning, broadcasting and scheduling.

4.5.9 The ongoing process, open and closed innovation

A single process of commissioning and development is part of a much larger whole involving multiple organisational processes and functions. Broadly there appear to be four groups of processes in the ongoing life of the broadcaster in relation to commissioning and development:

1 Long- and mid-term planning: establishing goals and parameters in creative, scheduling and budgetary terms for genres, channels and the organisation as a whole.
2 Commissioners dealing with creatives, nurturing ongoing relationships, identifying sources of ideas, developing and shortlisting them.
3 Business affairs involvement in individual projects and ongoing planning and control of genres and channels.
4 Formal commissioning rounds (typically two per year).

Individual commissioning decisions happen within the context of a set of overall genre and channel plans; these creative plans are in turn conditioned by overall corporate plans and strategies. Creative plans, usually made up of channel and genre plans, typically fall into three time periods:

1 Long-term, up to five years. In drama particularly, given the often-long lead times for programming, quite detailed plans are drawn up with a three- to five-year horizon.
2 Mid-term strategic plans (one to three years) provide the more direct context for individual programming decisions around major programmes or initiatives.
3 Short-term / annual: most effort is expended on this level of planning, typically covering the forthcoming 12–18 months. Programme genre budgets are turned into specific commissions, re-commissions, acquisitions and schedule slots. Within that, plans may be adjusted on a quarter-by-quarter basis, or around commissioning rounds. The overall planning process at ITV is typical of this annual planning (see Figure 4.4).

It is probably worth noting at this point the significant reliance that many large broadcasters and narrowcasters have on external sources (e.g. independent television production companies, writers, directors, actors) for ideas for new products. They rely to a degree on external sources for their product innovation. This is typically characterised as an 'open innovation' model, as opposed to a 'closed' model.

So-called 'closed' innovation has characterised the development of new products and services across all major industries for most of the industrial revolution. It relies on several key premises:

- We (the organisation) hire as many smart people as possible as a source of internal innovation. Further, we equip them with appropriate labs, equipment, budgets and training.
- We develop our own ideas, select the most appropriate and fund them. Hence, we own all the intellectual property rights in the idea and final product / service.
- We launch the products / services ourselves, taking care of all marketing and distribution.
- Given that we own all of the intellectual property rights, and have incurred all of the costs in the development of the new product / service, we secure all of the revenues resulting from its sale.

This is a closed model, where a single organisation incurs all the risks and costs of development, but also benefits from all the revenues (should the product / service be successful). Intellectual property ownership is clear, costs and revenues are not shared with anyone, and all development happens within a single organisation (perhaps with the input of a limited number of external suppliers). The boundaries of the

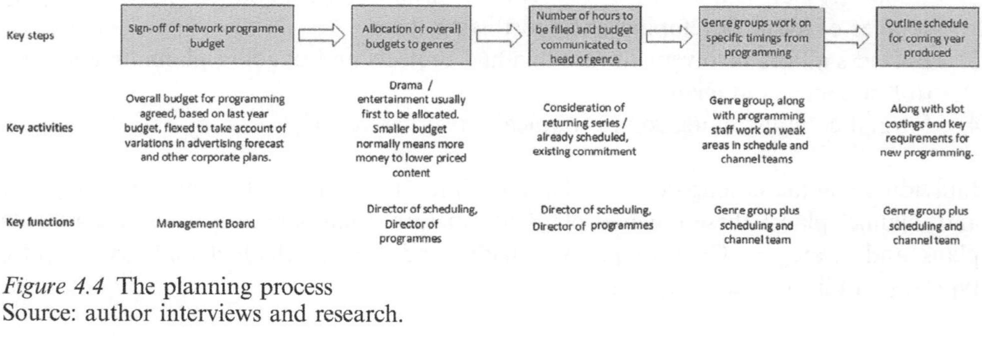

Figure 4.4 The planning process
Source: author interviews and research.

organisation itself are fixed and impermeable. The implications are clear: we need to hire and retain the best talent we can find and equip them with the right resources—the more talented our workforce, the more likely we are to be innovative, and the more we deny our competitors access to this talent. But it is a very high-risk, high-reward model. We incur all the costs, all the risk, but we will benefit from all the revenues should the innovation prove successful.

More recently, particularly since the 1990s, there has been a move to more open models of innovation in many industries, particularly those involved in technology development and pharmaceuticals (where it can cost $15bn and 10 years to develop a new product like an antibiotic). Organisations increasingly realised they could not hire all the smart people, could not afford to shoulder all the costs of product / service development themselves, did not wish to incur all the risk themselves and could offset it by finding the right partners to work with. Increasingly, then, the focus moved to innovation across a network of organisations and individuals, some within a company, some outside it.

In this new 'open innovation' model, the boundaries of the organisation itself become more permeable. Ideas can enter (from external sources) or exit the organisation more easily. Organisations work closely with others to share the costs of product / service development, hence sharing the risk. However, this does throw up a range of challenges compared to traditionally closed innovation organisations. Who are the right partners? How are deals to be structured? Who ultimately owns the intellectual property? How are revenues best divided? How do firms share what might have been considered highly valuable and commercially sensitive information about new research and ideas? Interestingly, for those looking at these issues in other sectors, the cultural industries have had a tradition of following an open innovation model for most of their history.

Most organisations in the cultural industries work with external partners that are neither part of their organisation nor full-time employees. Movie studios rely on external actors, writers and directors. Record labels rely on musicians, song writers, producers and their management, who aren't employees. Game publishers rely on external games development companies for new ideas. Broadcasters and narrowcasters in turn rely on a range of external parties to fulfil their goals, particularly talent (writers, producers, directors, actors and the agencies that represent them), and independent programme production companies. All these external individuals and organisations constitute what has become known as the 'independent sector' and we will return to the issue in more depth in Chapter 7.

But looking at a typical broadcaster, we can see a very 'open' approach to innovation (see Figure 4.5).

As can be seen from the diagram, for a typical broadcaster, some ideas are internally generated (A) and some come from external sources, e.g. independent production companies (B). Some ideas are developed through to completion, others move out of the organisation to be completed by other companies—e.g. another broadcaster (C). Some ideas may be developed without partners, others may be developed with other broadcasters or production companies (in a coproduction—D). Some new products may even be acquired (E), fully finished and perhaps already successful on another broadcast service. The final service is likely to be a combination of all these different types of new product.

We see a similar situation in the music sector, gaming industry and most cultural sectors. These sectors have been working with independent creative agents for many years, establishing how to share costs, risks and revenues. They have worked out how to

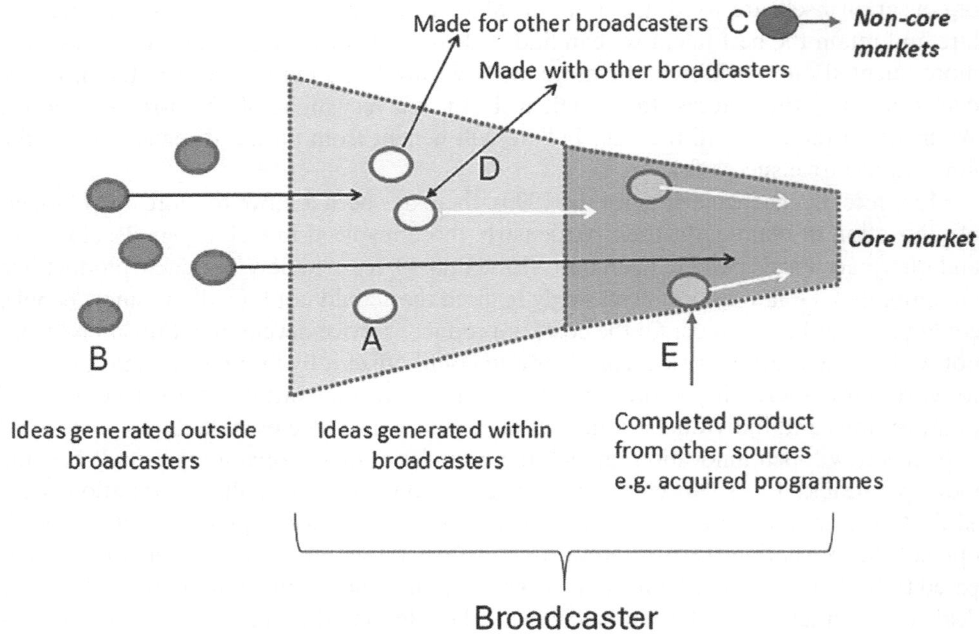

Figure 4.5 Open innovation in a broadcaster
Source: author.

identify and work successfully with key external talent. They have dealt with issues around how to share intellectual property rights and revenues. Hence for any industry sector looking for ways to become more open in their approach to innovation, a close study of how this is handled in the cultural sector may be beneficial.

What we can observe from the previous analysis is that the generation of new content in the television sector is a complex and multifaceted process, involving many different stakeholders, all with potentially differing agendas, goals, time horizons and decision-making criteria (see Figure 4.6).

For a programme to be made, all these agendas must be aligned to some extent, based on a business model that rewards all involved parties.

4.6 Business models

Given the complexity of the broadcasting ecosystem, a wide range of business models have emerged to support its functioning.

The early public sector broadcasters typically did not have a profit agenda, but rather a political, social, cultural and technological one. They sourced revenue and resources from the governments that typically established them. In some territories this was in the form of a licence fee (essentially a tax) collected by the state. Individual consumers had to pay an annual licence fee to access the public broadcaster services. For example, in the UK, to access BBC services (at least legally), consumers still need to purchase an annual TV licence, currently around £175 per year. This revenue is collected by the government, then remitted to the BBC to cover the costs of its operation. Similar licence-based models are evident in many territories, including Germany, Italy (paid via

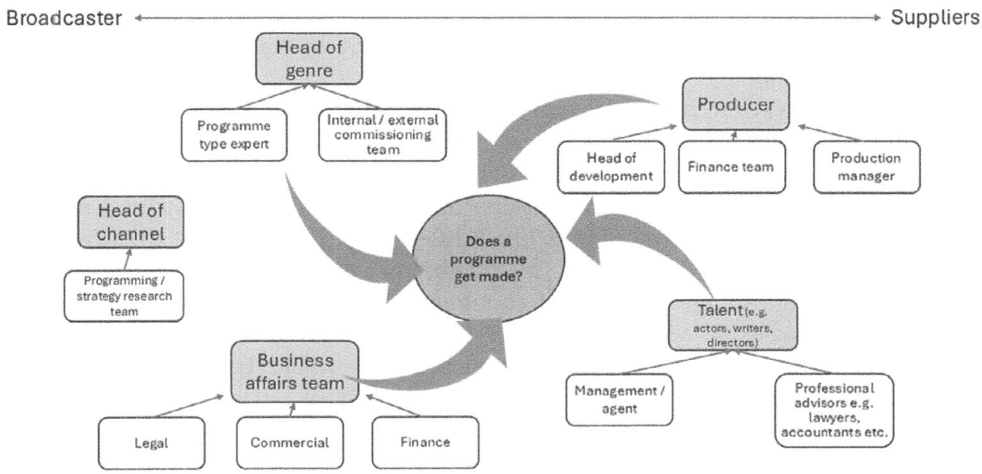

Figure 4.6 Stakeholders in programme commissioning
Source: author.

your electric bill) and Greece. In many other territories, whilst they existed in the early history of broadcasting, such licence fees have now been abolished, including Denmark, France, New Zealand and the Netherlands. No such systems have ever existed in countries like the USA and China.

Commercial broadcasters tended to rely on advertising (airtime sales) to generate their revenues. Broadcasters' channels were 'brand-building windows' that allowed simultaneous access to large audiences, potential consumers who might be interested in the products being sold by advertisers. If Unilever is to launch a new shampoo, or BYD a new car, or Apple a new iPhone, an advertisement placed on one of the major commercial channels can typically guarantee it will be watched by a relatively large number of viewers, and hence potential consumers. Such brands will typically work with an advertising agency to make the advertisement, then buy airtime slots (typically in 15–30-second blocks to produce a required number of 'impressions' or a specific reach) in the broadcaster's channel schedule to broadcast it. The revenue gleaned from such transactions is then used by the broadcaster to run the company, covering, amongst other things, the costs of creating new programmes.

Pay-TV services introduced a new business model, the subscription model (though one might argue this had already been presaged with the licence fee model adopted by many public service broadcasters). To access services, consumers would commit to paying a monthly fee. Pay-TV companies were innovators in exploring other ways in which content might be monetised. Pay-per-view (PPV) offerings typically required a one-off payment to watch a specific programme, aired at a particular time. Sporting events (live boxing matches, live soccer matches) proved particularly popular with viewers. Video on demand (VOD) was another revenue-generating tool, whereby viewers could access specific programmes at whatever time and however often they wished for a fee. The initial focus for this tended to be films, which could be rented (to be watched within a certain timeframe) or indeed bought (typically downloaded to a set-top box, now accessed via the cloud).

Two key issues emerge from this analysis: how such organisations are assessed in terms of performance, and the guidelines (the golden rules) that emerged from this for success in launching a pay-TV service.

In terms of the key measures of success for such a platform, three tend to attract the most attention. **Subscriber acquisition** is key—that is typically how many new users join the service each month (quarter or year). This is the overwhelming focus for most new TV services (particularly the narrowcasters) during the early stages of their development. Whether it is pay-TV providers like HBO or Sky TV, or any of the newer narrowcast services like Netflix or Hulu, the number of new users was the measure most commentators (including the financial community) used to assess the success of the service. After that came **ARPU** (average revenue per user)—that is, what level of revenue is generated by each subscriber. Typically, this would be an additive figure, combing subscription fees, along with any pay-per-view or video-on-demand revenue they generate. Finally, the platform would be assed in terms of **churn**—that is, how many subscribers the service lost each month. Combined (subscriber acquisition, ARPU and churn), these measures offered an overview of how well the service was performing and the amount of revenue it was generating.

Emerging from this came the guidelines for best practice in terms of ensuring the success of such a service. Firstly, barriers to subscriber acquisition needed to be minimised. Asking potential users to pay a (potentially high) subscription fee and buy expensive new equipment to access the service was seen as a key barrier to subscriber acquisition. Hence in most cases, the technology needed to access the service (perhaps a satellite disk and usually a set-top box) was heavily subsidised by the platform provider, in many cases being given away for free. At the same time, channels tended to be packed into bundles or tiers. There would typically be a basic service, with a relatively small number of channels that subscribers could sign up to for a minimal price (again encouraging take-up and high subscriber growth). Other bundles, offering more channels and services, were offered to subscribers if they wished to upgrade their viewing experience (for an increased price, and hence a higher ARPU). Today, viewers of Sky TV can sign up to a basic or 'essentials' package, covering the main Sky TV channels, or the 'ultimate' package covering all the Sky channels and services. Additional sports and movie channels can typically be added for an additional fee.

The second key requirement emerged in the form of 'premium' content. This was essentially content that could not be accessed via any other broadcast or narrowcast service. In most territories this first manifested in the form of premium sports (which essentially, at least in Europe, meant soccer matches) and Hollywood films, which would typically take years to appear on traditional terrestrial services. Hence most pay-TV services launched premium film and sports channels, offering access to content that was not available on any other TV service, in turn launching a bidding war amongst television services for the most valuable content. The rights to show Premier League football matches in the UK are currently owned by Sky Sports—allowing exclusive access by Sky subscribers to live Premier League soccer matches. It cost Sky the eye-watering fee of £6.7bn for the television rights for four years. The BBC, unable to afford the fees for this full service, can only show recorded highlights of the matches.

The final key ingredient was marketing. Up until the arrival of pay-TV in most territories, there was little or no competition for the incumbent TV services (typically a few PBS and commercial channels). The arrival of pay-TV introduced new levels of competition, and new services that needed to be launched to the public. Suddenly, television companies had to shout to be noticed in an increasingly crowded market and began to invest heavily in their marketing efforts. Whilst this was led by the emerging pay-TV companies, public broadcasters and existing commercial channels soon followed and marketing budgets have grown significantly. We will return to how marketing evolved in the sector in Chapter 8.

Hence when examining the performance of pay-TV platforms, we typically focus on subscriber acquisition, ARPU and churn, and in launching such services particular attention is paid to minimising the barriers to subscriber acquisition, offering the technology for free, securing premium content and investing heavily in marketing.

New pay-TV services, particularly in the narrowcasting sector, have broadly followed these guidelines, though for many, their initial plans did not prove as successful as they might have hoped. Most have focused on subscriber acquisition as their main goal, hence investing in premium content, minimising the cost of adoption (typically exploiting existing broadband infrastructure to deliver the service, hence minimising upfront technology costs) and offering a variety of different channel packages and tiers. Overwhelmingly, the focus of commentators has been on subscriber acquisition as the key assessment measure, consistent and ongoing growth in subscriber numbers generally securing positive reviews from the finance community, for example. More recently, however, several providers, particularly those focused on content from one particular source (e.g. Disney+ drawing on the Disney back catalogue and content, Paramount+ on the Paramount library), have found themselves with growing subscriber numbers, but relatively low levels of revenue per subscriber (ARPU).

Services were launched with very low initial subscriber charges to encourage take-up. This was contrasted with significant set-up costs for the service provider. A lack of significant, profitable revenues meant that many accumulated substantial costs as a result. According to some estimates, Disney+ would invest over $11bn in its operation before starting to make a profit (which it began to do in 2024, having launched the service in 2019). Subscription fees and various video-on-demand offers were simply not sufficient to cover costs and generate substantial profits. As a result, business models were revised in many cases, with advertising being introduced as a second significant revenue source. Hence the most basic tiers of many narrowcaster services (including Disney+, Netflix and Amazon Prime) are now based on channels which carry advertising. The viewer pays a subscription fee, and their viewing experience is interrupted by advertisements. Only if the subscriber opts for a higher tariff tier can they avoid watching advertisements.

We have reviewed licence fees, advertising, subscriptions and pay-per-view as key revenue drivers for broadcasters and narrowcasters alike. But there are other sources of income. Once a programme is made, it can be exploited in a variety of ways. If the programme is successful, other broadcasters, often in foreign markets, may also want to show it (as acquired programming). Hence, we have seen the emergence of a growing market in international programme sales between broadcasters to generate additional revenues. Channel 4 reportedly paid 20th Century Fox around £15m for the rights to show new episodes of *The Simpsons*, for example.

For much of the latter half of 20th century, packaged media also proved a lucrative source of profits, with programmes released on VHS or Betamax tapes, DVDs or Blu-ray disks. Indeed, for some types of content (e.g. Hollywood films) this would provide to be the most profitable revenue source when compared to theatrical release or sales to broadcasters. Should a programme be successful it might also be suitable for exploitation via merchandising, with programme-related toys, games, books and other memorabilia generating significant revenues—though typically only for the most successful programmes. Some broadcasters would also be involved in setting up TV-based home shopping services and may in turn secure a share of the revenue from products sold.

We will return to the methods by which content might be exploited later in the chapter.

4.7 Windowing

Business models in the broadcasting and narrowcasting sectors are heavily influenced by windowing. Windowing is a term derived from the film industry, referring to the sequence in which a film (or increasingly any programme) and its associated products are released to the public. Figure 4.7 shows a typical release schedule for a Hollywood film in the 1980s.

Most Hollywood films would typically be launched in American cinemas initially, before being released in other territories. There were a number of good reasons for this. Firstly, it helped manage risk. The performance of a film could be first assessed in the USA before a decision was made about the most suitable level of investment required to launch it in other territories. A highly successful film in the USA would warrant a significant effort in terms of marketing and the production of many copies (prints) of the film for the rest of the world. A poorly performing film might lead to a much smaller level of subsequent investment and support; essentially studios could cut their losses if initial demand proved to be low, minimising the number of film prints and their subsequent spend on marketing.

The release of the film in the USA might also benefit its rollout in other territories. Word of mouth and positive reviews might spread globally, building potential demand for the film in other territories before any marketing spend. The appearance of popular merchandising in the USA would equally spur demand for such products in the rest of the world. Merchandising for the first *Star Wars* film (1977) was already being imported (through what is known as the grey market—hence semi-legal) into Europe before the film had been released in European cinemas.

A strong theatrical performance would also put the film distributor in a strong position when negotiating tariffs for the sale of the film to TV companies. Pay-TV companies were quick to take advantage of opportunities to show films closer to their

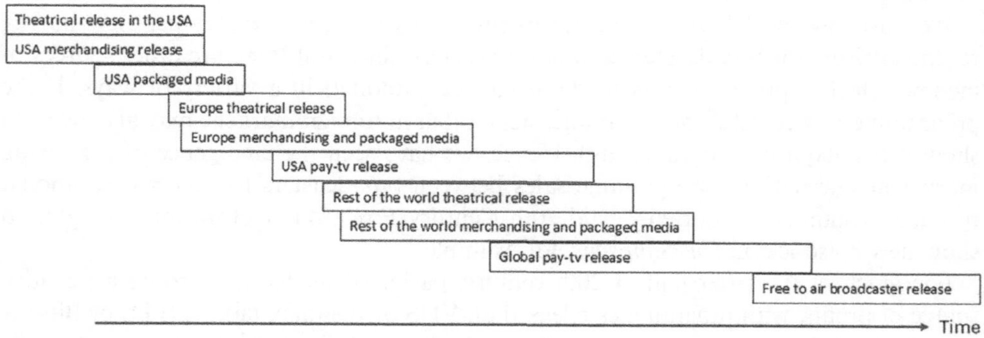

Figure 4.7 Traditional windowing patterns
Source: author.

theatrical release as part of their new service offering. Before the advent of pay-TV, viewers of terrestrial TV could wait many years before the film was available for broadcast. Pay-TV channels could offer the film within months of its cinema release (and more recently, on narrowcast services, within days of their release in cinemas), through video-on-demand services, and subsequently on dedicated film channels.

In recent years, this windowing approach has changed radically, as can be seen in Figure 4.8.

Increasingly, with the removal of the constraint of having to produce large quantities of physical copies of a film to send to cinemas (most films now being digitally distributed to cinemas), film distributors have opted to release films globally from launch (also known as 'day and date' releasing). Some of these films may also be released on premium pay-TV services within days (and sometimes on the same day) as their appearance in cinemas. The fee to watch the film typically equates to the cost of buying the film on packaged media. On the one hand, this appears to be a rather foolhardy approach. For a start it's highly risky, as marketing budgets must be large and spent simultaneously around the world. There is little opportunity to test-market the film in a single territory first. Territories don't benefit from word of mouth before the film is launched. What this approach does ensure, however, is that the maximum amount of revenue is generated as quickly as possible.

Film companies can now expect to generate the vast proportion of financial returns within months of the film's release. This is key as films become ever more expensive to make, and investors want to secure a rapid return on investment. Further, the previous 'long tail' approach, wherein film companies might have to manage the film over the course of years, rather than months, was also associated with high levels of piracy, and a grey market in merchandising and packaged media. Also, pay-TV companies will pay a significant premium to be able to show the film within days of its release in cinemas.

Broadcasters and production companies in the television sector have also begun to experiment with more sophisticated windowing strategies to maximise the size of the market and potential revenue for individual television programmes. Typically, up until the emergence of the streaming services, windowing in television was relatively simple and limited. A completed programme would normally have an exclusive window being broadcast on the channel of the commissioning broadcaster. After that it was typically sold to other international broadcasters. A final window might emerge if the programmes were then repeated on those channels at a future date (re-runs) or sold to other parts of the same broadcasting company (e.g. syndication to local stations in the

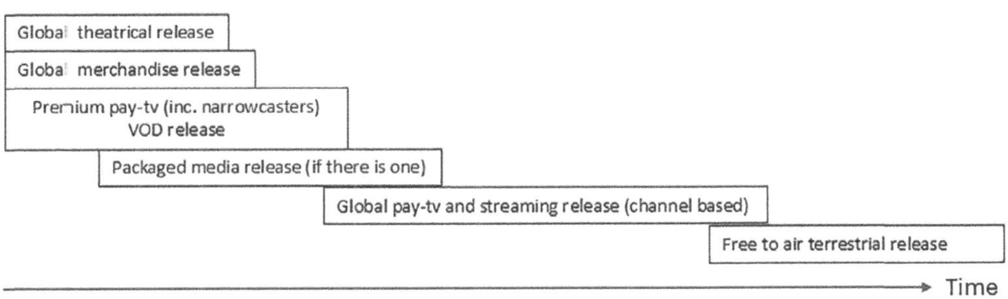

Figure 4.8 Emergent windowing patterns
Source: author.

USA). More successful programmes might have a packaged media and merchandising release, but this was typically limited to a very few—only the most successful programmes might benefit from these opportunities.

One variation of this model emerged with the growth of 'formats'. Formats are essentially the blueprint for a show, often in the quiz / competition show or comedy genres—e.g. *Big Brother*, whereby a successful show's major elements (its format, competition rules, style, sets etc.) would be packaged and sold to a foreign broadcaster, who would then remake the show with local presenting talent and participants, adapted to the region's tastes and preferences. Hence a successful show may have multiple lives in different territories, and examples include *The Office* (initially successful in the UK, subsequently remade in the USA and Australia) and *The Traitors* (an All3Media International format which has secured format sale deals in Korea, India, Africa, Romania, Spain and Central and Eastern Europe), which have been sold globally as 'formats'.

Streaming services introduced new windowing opportunities. Films may go directly to the streaming service and have no theatrical release (in cinemas) at all. Programmes might have an exclusive run on a broadcaster's channel, before being sold to a streaming platform and then local broadcasters in foreign territories. For a streaming company's self-made 'marquee' programmes (those that had the highest cost, with the best talent and highest profile), a period of exclusivity on the streaming service might then be followed by sales to other streaming services, sales to more traditional pay-TV companies and finally to local broadcasters. Hence a major series like *Foundation* might first have an extensive period of exclusivity on the Apple TV service (Apple was the commissioning organisation), before featuring on one of the generalist streaming services (e.g. Amazon Prime), then appearing on a major pay-TV operator channel (e.g. Sky One in the UK), before finally appearing on a local broadcaster's channel (e.g. BBC One).

In each case, windowing aims to maximise the audience for a programme and exploit every possible revenue stream. With the evolution of new ways in which content can be distributed, and the continued rise in costs of programme production, providers continue to experiment with different windowing approaches to maximise profits and minimise risks, a point we will return to when we discuss the potential role of AI in Chapter 9.

4.8 From distribution to attention economies: the changing fortunes of broadcasters

In this section we begin to explore perhaps the most fundamental shift in the cultural industries in the last 30 years: the move from distribution- to attention-based economies, using television as a case study. For much of the history of broadcasting, those organisations that controlled distribution of services to consumers assumed positions of significant power. Early broadcasters faced relatively little competition. Up until 1986 (with the launch of Channel 4), residents in the UK only had access to three television channels, two provided by the BBC and one provided by commercial broadcaster, ITV.

Consumers had very little choice in what to watch at 8pm on any given day, with only three programmes to choose from. Hence audiences for any single programme or channel tended to be large—for those choosing to watch TV, all the audience's attention was focused on the three channels. This placed the two broadcasters in a strong position in negotiations with their partners. On the one hand, if an advertiser wanted to advertise on television, it only had a limited range of channels to choose from (indeed, in the UK this was initially limited to one commercial channel—ITV; the BBC does not carry advertising). Hence commercial broadcasters were in a strong position to negotiate high airtime rates from those advertisers.

Equally, broadcasters were in a strong position when negotiating with external programme suppliers. For an independent production company in the UK in 1980, there were only two companies who might be approached with that idea, the BBC and ITV; there were limited slots in which that new programme might appear and significant competition for those slots, not least from the broadcasters' own internal production facilities. Hence if the BBC and ITV both passed on the idea, there was very little chance of the programme being made and distributed; the independent company relied on funds from the broadcaster to make the programme (the 'production budget'). In such a scenario, broadcasters could set the rates they paid to production companies, who relied on funds from broadcasters to make the production and make a profit—usually called a 'production fee'.

There were some upsides as well as significant downsides for independent producers in such a scenario. On the one hand, should the production be greenlighted by the broadcaster, the production company was assured of the funds to cover its production (plus a profit margin). Further, when the programme was broadcast, given the relatively low level of competition it could be assured of relatively high viewing figures from significant audiences, particularly if the programme was aired in prime time, the critical broadcast hours when audiences were largest, typically between 6pm and 10pm.

However, there were potential downsides. Most significantly, broadcasters would often leverage their powerful positions to secure all the rights in a programme. Whilst they only, in theory, needed the home territory broadcast rights to distribute the programme, they would often also insist on securing international programme sales rights, format rights, merchandising, image and packaged media rights. Hence independent companies were left with nothing when a programme was completed: they did not build a library of rights for further exploitation (these belonged to the broadcaster). Initially this did not pose a problem for the production companies, as such markets were relatively small and needed expensive sales teams to exploit them. Production companies appeared relatively willing to include these rights alongside broadcasting rights.

Hence, by controlling distribution (and access to large audiences), broadcasters remained as the most important and powerful organisations in the ecosystem. Distribution was hard to secure, but if it was accomplished (i.e. the programme was broadcast), audiences tended to be large given the lack of competition and choice.

Things would change, however.

In most territories, new competitors would arrive, typically in the form of new commercial channels, then pay-TV services and, subsequently, particularly with the evolution of digital infrastructures, narrowcast services. The launch of digital services allowed more channels to be offered to consumers by incumbents. New companies arrived with their own channels and services. By the 1990s, consumers had multiple television providers to choose from and literally hundreds of channels from which to select a programme to watch at any given time of the day.

All these new services needed programming to fill their channels. Hence demand for new content increased. At the same time, the expanded range of distribution providers put independent companies in a better position to negotiate the best production fees. If the BBC and ITV did not want to commission the programme, then maybe Channel 4,

Channel 5, Sky TV, Netflix or Amazon might do so. Best of all would be a bidding war where multiple providers wanted to commission the programme, driving up the fees due to the production company. It also put independent companies in a better position to negotiate on rights. Whilst the BBC might insist on acquiring all rights in a programme, new entrants like Channel 4 would prove to be more flexible, allowing independent companies to retain certain key rights. More and more production companies focused on retaining rights in the programmes they made, and as the international programme sales, packaged media and merchandising markets grew in value, this would prove to be key in production companies accumulating a library of valuable rights that might be exploited to generate significant future revenues.

The television sector has seen enormous growth in levels of competition compared to its early, more oligopolistic phase. This has had enormous implications for viewing habits. When only three or four channels exist, all the audience's attention is focused on them, and audiences tend to be large. When 300 channels are available, across multiple platforms and devices, audience attention is smeared across all of them. Getting distribution is no longer the key challenge—indeed, getting distribution is relatively easy; someone amongst those 300 channels is likely to want to commission your idea for a programme. But whilst distribution is easier, getting anyone's attention is now incredibly hard.

There is now a huge amount of consumer choice in the television sector, but the absolute number of viewers, and their viewing hours, have not kept pace with the growth in choice. Those large audiences secured by the early broadcasters are relatively static in size, but are now shared over countless providers, channels, programmes and platforms. With such a wide range of offerings, how do you secure the audience's attention, how do you get them to watch your service, channel or programme? This is particularly so when audiences have a range of other home entertainment activities they can indulge in, from streaming music, watching TikTok videos on mobile devices or using the television or portable devices to play electronic games. This is the new critical challenge in broadcasting: securing audience attention in a hugely crowded market. The previously powerful positions of the major broadcasters are increasingly diminished, as distribution becomes easier to access.

So who are the new powerful figures in the television sector? Well, essentially, those that can command and direct audience attention. Whether that be talent (e.g. actors, presenters, writers, directors), production companies with a reputation for developing successful programmes in a specific genre (e.g. reality TV), internet influencers who moderate and direct audience attention to specific content, or indeed the algorithms that advise consumers on their next choice of content based on their previous viewing behaviour, power now resides with those who can marshal consumer attention and direct it to a specific service, channel, programme or clip.

This is particularly troublesome for larger commercial broadcasters, who have relied on providing access to large simultaneous audiences to brands to secure advertising revenues. Those large audiences have been dwindling, with their viewing time and attention increasingly spread across services from a wide variety of providers. At the same time, early indications are that some of the most valuable segments of the viewing audience—younger age groups—are increasingly moving to non-traditional platforms to consume their content, particularly narrowcast services like Netflix, YouTube and TikTok. Ofcom (the UK's broadcast regulator) point to significant changes: reports in 2021[2] and 2022[3] suggests viewers aged 16–24 spent 53 minutes per day on average watching broadcast TV. This is compared to 158 minutes for an average viewer (a figure that has declined every year since 2010). Younger viewers, the reports claim, are increasingly shifting their time and attention to streaming services, creating a significant divide between younger and older audiences. When audiences move, so do advertisers. Hence some of the advertising budgets previously allocated to large broadcasters are increasingly moving to their new narrowcast competitors (who have increasingly introduced advertising-supported channels and services).

At the same time, broadcasters have had to invest in new technologies to keep pace with their new rivals. From launching new digital channels to building catch-up services (e.g. the BBC's iPlayer, ITV's X service), remaining accessible and relevant in the market is increasingly challenging, and costly. Combined with the rising costs of programme production, broadcasters face the prospect of diminishing audiences (and hence revenues) and increasing costs. Arguably, this is not a scenario that can continue for ever.

So what are broadcasters trying to do to address these issues? Five strategies stand out.

Firstly, as already noted, incumbent broadcasters have been forced to launch new services to compete with their emerging competition. They initially launched new channels, and internet-based catch-up services—allowing access to programmes outside the normal broadcast schedule (e.g. BBC iPlayer). Subsequently many broadcasters have united to launch new packages of content. In the UK, Freely is a new free streaming service, launched jointly by the major terrestrial broadcasters (BBC, ITV, Channel 4, Channel 5), drawing together all of their content, with access via the internet and typically built into televisions from Hisense, Panasonic, Bush and Toshiba amongst others. All of this has proved expensive in terms of investment in technology, new content and marketing.

If broadcasting budgets are under pressure, it makes sense to focus funds and attention on the most valuable parts of the broadcast schedule. For virtually all broadcasters, this means prime time, that period of the day when most viewers spend most of their time watching television. This is typically considered to be the period between 6pm and 10pm. For commercial broadcasters, these hours are the most attractive to advertisers, given that they generate a large proportion of all viewing. Hence for US television networks, prime time is likely to generate 70–80% of all advertising revenue.

In the context of limited programming budgets, it makes sense for broadcasters to focus their attention and funds on this part of the day. Other parts of the schedule (e.g. the schedule from midnight to 6am) might be populated with 'filler' content, cheaply acquired content from other broadcasters or re-runs of existing programmes. But for the prime-time slot, broadcasters are likely to invest in significant programmes. Such programmes are often referred to as marquee programmes—those that are likely to be the most expensive to produce but have the greatest prospect of securing the highest viewing figures. Often these are programmes that are designed to work across platforms, with programmes like *Big Brother* or *America's Got Talent* exploited across terrestrial TV services, multichannel pay-TV operations, the internet and mobile. Television programmes on a single broadcast channel might be augmented with pre-launch coverage on another channel, late-night round-up shows and special features on other channels. Online services might include news events, results updates, games and voting. Mobile apps might be developed to allow viewers to interact with the show directly.

Such marquee programmes might be in any genre (though reality shows proved disproportionately popular in the 2020s), from drama to the natural world. They are likely to be the most expensive programmes to produce and run, and hence come with the highest risk. To offset this risk they are likely to appear in valuable prime-time slots to maximise potential audiences and hence it is critical that they generate significant viewing and revenues.

Broadcasters have been criticised, however, for failing to take full advantage of these opportunities—that is, they have been slow to build ancillary revenues beyond advertising. But they are increasingly focused on this agenda given the emerging threats to the core advertising model. Hence significant planning is usually now involved in developing these marquee programmes, with particular attention paid to how new sources of revenue might be exploited. For a BBC programme like *Walking with Dinosaurs*, a high-cost, high-profile marquee programme, a vast array of revenue-generating opportunities were explored and exploited, from programme sales to merchandising and games.

The *Walking with Dinosaurs* series was a huge success in the UK, and ultimately sold to broadcasters in over 40 countries. In the USA it became one of the most watched documentary series on cable TV. The series produced 11 books, translated into 14 languages, with over 1.5m units sold worldwide. Over a million copies of the series on DVD were sold. Hence broadcasters have had to diversity their scope of operation, interfacing with a variety of other business sectors (the toy industry, publishing, events) to maximise revenues from any single program.

Finally, given the importance of securing new revenue sources and cost cutting, some broadcasters have responded by allowing themselves to become part of larger entertainment conglomerates, with expertise in these new markets. This is best demonstrated by the American broadcast networks. ABC is part of Disney, NBC is part of NBC/Universal (which in turn is owned by major telecoms and entertainment company Comcast), the Fox network is part of the Fox Corporation, and CBS is part of Paramount Global. If we look at ABC's situation, we see it is part of the Disney corporation, which also has ownership stakes in film and television production studios, controls significant content brands (Marvel, Pixar, Lucas Films etc.), has its own pay-TV channels, has a dedicated packaged media division and its own merchandising operation, and is engaged in a range of other activities—e.g. theme parks and retail. Hence its core broadcast television operation can benefit from preferential access to key content and can rely on expertise in pay-TV, packaged media sales and merchandising, without having to go to external parties. Losses in the broadcasting division can be offset by profits in others.

Other broadcasters have resisted such integration but made other moves to secure their position. One of their major strategies has been to buy independent production companies. Ensuring a flow of viable content is proving to be a crucial challenge for many, and buying a production company can help ensure this flow is consistent. In the UK, ITV has in recent years bought Eagle Eye Drama, Hartswood Films, and a majority stake in Moonage Pictures. Other notable acquisitions include Mammoth Screen, Twofour Group, World Productions, Big Talk Productions, Tetra Media Studio and Leftfield Entertainment. Such acquisitions help deny talent and ideas to other broadcasters and help to diversity the broadcaster's own production capabilities into new genres. Warner Bros, an American conglomerate, has also been active in buying UK production companies (e.g. Shed Media, Wall to Wall Productions, Ricochet, Twenty Twenty). Narrowcasters have followed this approach to some degree, with Amazon purchasing the content library and production capabilities of MGM, and even Netflix, who tend to commission and acquire content from external sources, invested in a major production studio in 2018 (Albuquerque Studios).

In each case, it is evident that broadcasters are attempting to re-aggregate the large audiences they have lost to new competitors, defend their positions as brand-building windows for advertisers, control the flow of new content and develop new sources of revenue. The critical question of course is will it be enough? Being a stand-alone broadcaster, outside a large integrated entertainment company, appears to be a more and more vulnerable and risky option for many. Few stand-alone broadcasters can compete with the development and production budgets being spent by many of their narrowcast competitors. In 2025, Netflix planned to spend approximately $18bn on content production, according to BroadcastPro ME[4], with the company's chief financial officer, Spencer Neumann, stating that they are far from reaching a ceiling on their content investment. Apple TV has plans to spend over $7bn, Amazon $9bn, and for large integrated companies like Warner Bros., the spend is even higher, at over $19bn. This compares with the typical £1.5bn that the biggest commercial operator in the UK, ITV, spends on production every year. Perhaps the future for ITV reflects the future of many older broadcasters, as part of larger, integrated entertainment conglomerates, or as partners with other broadcasters in joint service provision (e.g. the Freely example cited earlier).

Narrowcasters are not free of challenges. Increased competition has put a damper on constant growth in subscriber acquisition numbers. Low subscription fees provide an ongoing challenge to revenue generation, so most narrowcast providers have subsequently put their subscription fees up every year, though they can't go too far. Customers appear willing to jump to new services as they appear, producing potentially high levels of churn. Free services like YouTube and TikTok provide a ready alternative to expensive subscriptions. The fight for premium content consistently raises their costs of operation. Their relatively huge programming budgets require constant growth in revenues and profits.

Established narrowcasters also face challenges from a new breed of provider. Often launched by consumer electronics companies and built into their products, so-called FAST (free advertising-supported streaming television) services are now emerging across the world. Typically free and supported by advertising, they often resemble a traditional TV-like experience (unlike the user-generated content on YouTube and TikTok), with viewers tuning in to scheduled programmes, though some offer ad-supported video on demand (AVOD) as well. First launched by Pluto TV, and followed by Roku, many TV manufacturers are now developing their own services, and pre-installing them into the televisions they produce, providing a dedicated button on their TV remote controls to access the service—e.g. services from LG and Samsung. The dedicated button ensures prominence. Such services increase levels of audience fragmentation and heighten the battle for content, audience attention and advertising budgets. In an age of ever-increasing (and potentially confusing) choice, for some consumers opting for a service already built into a television may be the simplest and cheapest option.

4.9 Conclusions

The television sector then has witnessed profound changes over the last 30 years, driven by vastly increasingly levels of commercial rivalry and the digitisation of content and infrastructures. Companies traditionally dominant in a distribution-based economy have seen their power diminish and often now face existential crisis. Other companies have emerged to dominate the space based on new, and still evolving, business models.

Consumer choice has blossomed, but their attention is now smeared over a huge range of providers, services, platforms and devices. Securing their attention has become the new strategic high ground, and it is still unclear at this point which organisations will emerge as best positioned to secure and guide the audience's viewing experience in the future.

Whilst these enormous changes have proven very challenging for some organisations (e.g. the traditional terrestrial broadcasters), for others, including independent production companies, significant new opportunities to create and retain value have arisen. In many ways the television sector is in a transitionary stage, and many questions remain to be answered. Can the traditional broadcasters manage this phase in their development and emerge as viable providers in the future (or will they have to merge with large entertainment conglomerates to retain their position)? Can they still be 'all things to all people' or will they have to focus and specialise (on specific parts of the day, audience segments or genres, for example). Can the market continue to support an unrelenting flow of new streaming-based services, and what is the most appropriate business model for them? How will the war for content play out? Can programming budgets continue to rise in the spectacular way they have in recent years? How are windowing strategies likely to develop (particularly once AI is introduced into the mix)? How will the inflow of consumer data affect what is being made and how it is distributed?

These are challenging and significant questions and for those of you intent on entering the business, they create a complex and evolving set of both opportunities and threats that you will need to engage with during your careers.

4.10 Activities

- Watch a TV programme. Who was involved in its production? Find out the production company. Was it an independent company, or the broadcaster? Was it a coproduction? Who else was involved in funding / producing the programme? Identify the flow of funds.
- Look at a piece of older television content and track its distribution and windowing. When and on what platform was it first released? How long did it stay on the platform? What was the next window? And the next?
- Develop your own idea for a 'marquee' television programme. What revenue streams might you hope to develop for it?

Notes

1 Business Research Insights, 2025.
2 Ofcom, 2021, *Online Nation* report.
3 Ofcom, 2022, *Media Nations* report.
4 https://www.broadcastprome.com/news/netflix-plans-18bn-content-investment-for-2025.

References

Adams, M. E., Day, G. S. and Dougherty, D., 1998. Enhancing new product development performance: An organisational learning perspective. *Journal of Product Innovation Management*, 15, pp. 403–422.

Allen, T. J. 1971. Communications, technology transfer and the role of the technical gatekeeper. *R&D Management*, 1, pp. 14–21.

Allen, T. J. 1977. *Managing the Flow of Technology*. Cambridge MA: MIT Press.

Ancona, D. G. and Caldwell, D. F. 1990. Beyond boundary spanning: Managing external dependence in product development teams. *Journal of High Technology Management Research*, 1, pp. 119–135.

Ancona, D. G. and Caldwell, D. F. 1992. Bridging the boundary: External process and performance in organisational teams. *Administrative Science Quarterly*, 37, pp. 634–665.

Bitran, G. and Pedrosa, L. 1998. A structured product development perspective for service operations. *European Management Journal*, 16 (2), pp. 169–189.

Booz Allen Hamilton. 1982. *New Product Management for the 1980s*. New York: Booz Allen Hamilton.

Bowers, M. R. 1989. Developing new services, improving the process makes it better. *Journal of Services Marketing*, 3 (winter), pp. 15–20.

Brown, S. and Eisenhardt, K. M. 1995. Product development: Past research, present findings and future directions. *Academy of Management Review*, 20 (2), pp. 343–376.

Cooper, R. G. 1979. The dimensions of industrial new product successes and failures. *Journal of Marketing*, 43, pp. 93–103.

Cooper, R. G. and Kleinschmit, E. J. 1987. New products: What separates winners from losers? *Journal of Product Innovation Management*, 4, pp. 169–184.

Cordero, R. 1991. Managing speed to avoid product obsolescence: A survey of techniques. *Journal of Product Innovation Management*, 8, pp. 283–294.

Davis, L. and Toseland, R. W. 1987Group vs. individual decision making: An experimental analysis. *Social Work with Groups*, 10, pp. 95–110.

De Bandt, J. 1995. *Services aux Entreprises: Informations, Produits, Richesses*. Paris: Economica.

de Brentani, U. 1986. Do firms need a custom-designed new product screening model? *Journal of Product Innovation Management*, 3 (2 (June)), pp. 108–119.

Dougherty, D. and Heller, T. 1994. The illegitimacy of successful product innovation in established firms. *Organisation Science*, 5 (2), pp. 200–218.

Dwyer, L. and Mellor, R. 1991. Organisational environment, new product process activities and project outcomes. *Journal of Product Innovation Management*, 8, pp. 39–48.

Easingwood, C. J. 1986. New product development for service companies. *Journal of Product Innovation Management*, 4, pp. 264–275.

Gadrey, J. 2000. The characterisation of goods and services: An alternative approach. *Review of Income and Wealth*, 46 (3), pp. 369–387.

Griffen, A. 1997. PDMA research on new product development practices: Updating trends and benchmarking best practices. *Journal of Product Innovation Managemen*t, 14, pp. 429–458.

Gupta, A. K. and Wilemon, D. L. 1990. Accelerating the development of technology based new products. *California Management Review*, 32 (2), pp. 24–44.

Hax, A. and Majluf, N. 1991. *The Strategy Concept and Process: A Pragmatic Approach*. Prentice Hall.

Hill, P. 1997. On goods and services. *The Review of Income and Wealth*, 23 (4), pp. 315–338.

Hise R. T., O'Neal, L., Parasuraman, A. and McNeal, J. U. 1990. Marketing / R&D interaction in new product development: Implications for new product success rates. *Journal of Product Innovation Management*, 7, pp. 142–155.

Imai, K., Ikujiro, N. and Takeuchi, H. 1985. Managing the new product development process: How Japanese companies learn and unlearn, in Hayes, R. H., Clark, K. and Lorenz, C. (eds). *The Uneasy Alliance: Managing the Productivity-Technology Dilemma*. Boston: Harvard Business School Press.

Iturriagagoitia, J. M. Z. and Melón, M. G. 2005. *Analysis Of the Decision Making Processes in NPD Projects Within Innovative Companies: An Empirical Study in The Valencian Region (Spain)*. Urban/Regional 0507006, University Library of Munich, Germany.

Janis, I. L. 1972. *Victims of Groupthink: A Psychological Study of Foreign Policy Decisions and Fiascos*. Boston: Houghton Mifflin.

Katz, R. and Tushman, M. L. 1981. An investigation into the managerial roles and careers of gatekeepers and project supervisors in a major R&D facility. *R&D Management*, 11, pp. 103–110.

Kelly, D. and Storey C. 2000. New service development: Initiation strategies. *International Journal of Service Industry Management*, 11 (1), pp. 45–62.

Keller, R. T. 1986. Predictors of the performance of project groups in R&D organisations. *Academy of Management Journal*, 29, pp. 715–726.

Kotler, P. 1988. *Marketing Management*. Prentice Hall.

Krishnan, V. and Ulrich, K. T. 2001. Product development decisions: A review of the literature. *Management Science*, 47 (1), pp. 1–21.

Martin, C. R. and Horne D. A. 1993. Services innovation: Successful verses unsuccessful firms. *International Journal of Service Industry Management*, 4, pp. 48–64.

Myers, S. and Marquis, D. G. 1969. *Successful Industrial Innovations.* Washington DC: National Science Foundation.

Oke, A. 2002. Making it happen, how to improve, innovation capability in a service company. *Journal of Change Management*, 2 (3), pp. 272–281.

Ozer, M. 2005. Factors which influence decision making in new product evaluation. *European Journal of Operational Research*, 163 (3), pp. 784–801.

Quinn, J. B. 1985. Managing innovation: Controlled chaos. *Harvard Business Review*, 63 (3), pp. 73–84.

Scheuing, E. E and Johnson, E. M. 1989. New product development and management in financial institutions. *International Journal of Bank Marketing*, 7 (2), pp. 17–21.

Storey, C. and Easingwood, C. 1998. The augmented service offering: A conceptualisation and study of its impact on new service success. *Journal of Product Management Innovation*, 15, pp. 335–351.

Teixeira, D. and Ziskin, J. 1993. Achieving quality with customer in mind. *Bankers Magazine*, January and February, pp. 29–35.

Urban, G. L. and Hauser J. R. 1980. *Design and Marketing of New Products.* Prentice Hall.

5 Electronic Gaming

5.1 Introduction

We have been playing games for a long time; indeed some historians, tracing evidence of gaming back nearly 8000 years, argue that humans were gaming before we invented the wheel. The earliest generally recognised evidence of gaming was unearthed in the Sumerian city-state of Ur (now southern Iraq) where, as long ago as 4000 BCE, two players would engage in the *Royal Game of Ur* on a custom-made clay tablet board composed of 20 squares. In 2200 BCE, the early inhabitants of China were playing a form of *Wei Qi* (what we might call *Go* today) on a square board called a Go-Ban. In Egypt in 1500 BCE, players were competing in *Senet*, a variation of which is still played today. Scandinavia gave us *Hnefatafl*, the Indian sub-continent *Chaturanga*. Why has gaming proven to be such an enduring, consistent and evident form of human interaction? Well, it certainly appears to fulfil several critical human needs. From the need for achievement, the need for self-discovery, for reward and recognition, to the need for escape from the mundanity (or indeed the inherent threats) of everyday life, to the need for social interaction, games can fulfil a wide variety of human needs and wishes.

Play is a complex construct, hence even defining a 'game' can be challenging. Few definitions capture all of gaming's complex implications, though some common elements include the requirement for it to be voluntary (hence there is some agency or free will involved) and that it typically involves overcoming what might be considered unnecessary obstacles. Typically, the principle point of the game will not be a learning outcome or to make money, though these can follow from the game and indeed some games may have had their origins in learning—the beginnings of well-known board game *Snakes and Ladders* can be traced to an early Indian variant that taught the right approach to developing positive karma. Certainly, we can learn a lot about ourselves and others through the gaming experience. Generally, however, the main aim of most games is to achieve a fun and enjoyable use of one's time through the creation of a separate world and timeline to 'normal' life, in which mundane day-to-day activities can be ignored in favour of more interesting and exciting endeavours. These alternate worlds do however need guidelines for participants; hence the final aspect that seems common in most definitions is that games typically have rules, a set of instructions and guidelines for how the new 'world' operates and functions, creating a safe space for participants to enjoy different activities.

Games are the subject of interest from a wide variety of different disciplines, with 15 Nobel Prizes for economics having been awarded to mathematicians studying games (in the discipline of 'game theory', the most famous probably being Professor John Nash

DOI: 10.4324/9781003498599-5

Jr. and the Nash Equilibrium theory). In this chapter we will explore gaming's most recent manifestation, in the form of electronic games. Emerging in the 1970s, electronic gaming has proven to be one of the fastest-growing and most dynamic sectors of the cultural industries, far outstripping the growth rate and ultimate size of sectors such as music and cinema in just 50 years. But this dynamism and volatility has brought its own share of challenges for organisations in the sector.

Generally, perhaps given its relative youth, the games sector has suffered from a lack of attention from academics and commentators when compared to other cultural industry sectors, so there is a relative 'paucity of studies addressing and investigating issues and challenges faced by businesses operating within this industry' (Cabras et al., 2017, p. 306). In this chapter we will aim to draw on a variety of different sources including academic studies, market reports and input from industry commentators to understand these challenges further and in particular how organisations have innovated to identify and exploit industry developments.

5.2 A brief history

The very earliest forms of electronic games emerged during the mid-20th century, largely in the form of experiments by early computer scientists designed to test the capabilities of newly developed computer hardware. As with the earliest developments in television and radio broadcasting, initial innovation in the electronic gaming sector was very much the domain of scientists and researchers. As early as the 1950s computers were used to play *Noughts and Crosses* (or 'tic-tac-toe'). *Tennis for Two* (the inspiration for *Pong*) emerged towards the end of the decade, followed by the first forays into the science fiction and fantasy genre with *Spacewar!* (developed partly by researchers at MIT) in the early 1960s. *Game of Life* was the first to utilise ASCII (the American Standard Code for Information Interchange) in the 1970s.

It was during the 1970s that electronic gaming first began to move out of the laboratory and into the consumer space as gaming arcades began to emerge. Japanese company Atari led the charge as a front runner in the supply of coin-operated arcade-based machines, combining hardware and software in a single dedicated device, with *Pong* an early success, followed by *Space Invaders* (from another Japanese company, Taito) and *Asteroid* (again from Atari) towards the end of the 1970s.

Electronic gaming continued its march out of the laboratory with the launch of the first domestic gaming console in 1972—the Magnavox Odyssey—which would go on to sell an impressive 300,000 units, aided by the fact that at least for its early history the console had no significant competition in terms of the domestic American market. This could not last, however; success in any business sector tends to attract envious attention and inevitably competition, initially from a new gaming console produced by Atari (the 2600 cartridge system which went on to sell 30m units) and subsequently from the Apple II home computer that could also be used to play games. This latter initiative would be picked up by other hardware manufacturers focused on the production of early domestic PCs that could also play games, with products from Commodore (the VIC 20 and later C64), Acorn Atom, the Sinclair ZX Spectrum and Amstrad CPC 464. Critically these devices allowed home users to play a variety of different games on the same hardware device by simply swapping software, and perhaps even create a game themselves.

The rapid diffusion of gaming hardware (dedicated consoles and home PCs) in the domestic setting and increasing consumer demand for new gaming experiences also created the market conditions for the proliferation of independent games developers, charged with innovating new ideas for games and building them, often with the support of larger funding- and distribution-based companies, this latter group increasingly known as 'publishers' (Newman, 2013). The barriers to entry for games developers were relatively low at this stage, just requiring a PC, some programming knowledge and a good idea, and the sector saw a proliferation of 'bedroom' programmers developing games ideas on domestic PCs.

Unfortunately, the quality of games from these newly emerging developers varied greatly, and in 1983–1984 the infant games industry faced a major problem, prompted by an oversupply of relatively low-quality games, with poor playability and riddled with coding bugs (perhaps the most notorious being 1982's *E.T. the Extra-Terrestrial* from Atari), leading to a significant decline in demand and retail prices. Even lower prices failed to restore consumer confidence in the software sector, and demand for games continued to decline, leaving retailers with shelves stacked with poor-quality games they simply could not sell. Many early suppliers in the games sector exited the industry as a result (e.g. Mattel and Coleco) and even successful companies like Atari faced significant challenges with its then owner Warner Communications attempting to sell off or reduce the size of major parts of the company.

It would take Nintendo, with its particular attention to the quality control of games, partly through an initial focus on the use of its own in-house development division rather than relying on independent games developers, careful control of cartridge manufacturing, eye for character (early releases including *Super Mario Brothers* and *Donkey Kong*, games that had already been successful in the arcade context) and reliable and resilient hardware (e.g. the Game Boy and subsequently the Switch) to restore consumer confidence and begin to rebuild the industry. Interestingly this apparent need to control the production process and utilise proven technologies (e.g. the cartridge-based system) would later work to Nintendo's disadvantage given its reluctance to embrace the emerging digital technology of the 1990s, the CD-ROM, allowing Microsoft and Sony, who did embrace the new technology, to pull ahead in the race for market dominance.

By the end of the 1980s games consoles and PCs on which games might be played were a regular sight in many homes, but the woes of the industry would continue. Problems emerged in the hardware market, which was arguably oversupplied by different console and PC options. With demand spread over a large range of different and incompatible devices, manufacturers struggled to sell sufficient hardware units to cover their costs and generate reasonable profits. As a result, many hardware manufacturers left the sector to focus on other initiatives and the number of suppliers shrank significantly, leaving only a handful (including Sega, Nintendo, Sony, 3DO and Atari) by the end of the 1990s. The modern shape of the electronic games hardware sector finally began to emerge, ultimately dominated by three major console manufacturers, Sony with the PlayStation, Microsoft with the Xbox and Nintendo with the Wii. With the market largely divided up between three major players, each could secure sufficient market share to make their operations potentially profitable though, as we will see, the market could still be a challenging one.

Up until this point the dominant commercial logic focused on the sale of hardware (consoles, PCs) and physical copies of games via physical retailers. For a typical €50 game, the retailer was likely to secure €14 (around 28%), the distributor €6 (12%), the developer / publisher €20 (40%) and the console manufacturer €10 (20%) based on a licence fee on every game sold for their console (Rutter and Bryce, 2006). Such games would often have a relatively short product life cycle, quickly being removed from retailers' shelves if demand was declining, to be replaced on valuable retail shelf space by new releases.

An alternative model emerged with the development of mini games that were typically played on PCs, built using pre-existing programming software like HTML and Flash. This is perhaps best exemplified by the efforts of Miniclip, a company established in 2001 to distribute simple, easy games, often with a satirical edge, that required relatively little hardware processing power. Games could be developed quickly, and with modest budgets. Games could be given away for free, with subsequent charges to consumers for upgrades and more content (the freemium model). The Miniclip site hosted many hundreds of such games, most initially designed to be played on home PCs. Whilst Miniclip started as a developer, it quickly developed into a major publisher of these simple, inexpensive games, working with over 300 independent developers. Whilst most commentators now agree that the golden age of Flash-based mini games played on PCs is largely over, it did prove that small, simple games could be the source of significant consumer demand and in many ways laid the foundation for the next and possibly most significant development in the evolution of the gaming industry, the move to mobile.

Whilst early examples could be traced back to the 1970s, there was an explosion of interest in mobile gaming in the 1980s and the launch of a variety of dedicated handheld, cartridge-based devices, led chiefly by Nintendo but closely followed by Japanese company NEC. Nintendo would lay its claim to dominance in the sector in 1989 with the launch of its Game Boy device, later cemented when the platform was used as the launch pad for the *Pokémon* game franchise. Other notable suppliers included Atari with the Lynx system, the Neo Geo Pocket and Bandai's WonderSwan. The major console manufacturers would also try their luck in the mobile space with Sony's launch of the PlayStation Portable (PSP) in 2004.

But perhaps the biggest revolution in the mobile gaming sector (and perhaps the electronic gaming sector as a whole) was not driven by the games hardware manufacturers themselves, but by their compatriots in the mobile telephony sector. As mobile phones became pervasive, phone manufacturers sought ways of differentiating their new phones from those of competitors and providing pre-installed games (e.g. *Snake* on the Nokia 6110) proved to be a very successful idea. Some phone manufacturers even took this further with the launch of their own devices dedicated to gaming (e.g. the Nokia N-Gage and Ericsson Xperia Play), though few lasted more than a few years.

Mobile phone-based gaming created new opportunities for gamers to extend their gaming experience beyond the home. Previously tied to bedrooms and living rooms, requiring dedicated hardware and typically a reasonably sized screen, gamers could now game on the move, creating new opportunities to fill their time (e.g. downtime when travelling) with gaming opportunities. The mobile phone also significantly expanded the gaming demographic, previously dominated by young males, to potentially include anyone who owned a compatible phone, meaning older and younger demographics and women. It created increased demand for new, simpler games that did not require the processing power or graphics of the typical console (e.g. puzzle, trivia, card and word games), building on practices established in the era of PC-based Flash games, encouraging developers and publishers like Miniclip to refocus on mobile phones and prompting the entrance of new developers into the market.

With technical developments in the phone sector like touch screens, improved storage, better graphics, processing and networking capabilities, dedicated mobile gaming devices increasingly seemed expensive and unnecessary, particularly for the casual gamer. As such we have seen an explosion of gaming on mobile phones, based initially on simple, addictive franchises such as *Candy Crush* and *Angry Birds*. The ‘freemium’ business model became firmly established, with such games free to download and play, further lowering the barriers to adoption, subsequently generating revenue from optional in-app purchases (e.g. player cosmetics, loot boxes, additional downloadable content) or associated advertising. The typical demographic of gamers also broadened as a result to include more ‘casual gamers’, more than 40% of whom are women (Srinivasan & Venkatraman, 2010). As mobile phones increasingly match the capabilities of domestic PCs, mobile games have become more sophisticated and complex, often drawing on a social context to attract and retain users. Hence a highly complex, action-packed mobile game like Tencent’s *Honor of Kings*, a multiplayer online battle arena (MOBA), first launched on mobile phones in 2015, can consistently draw 100m active daily users.

Exploiting this ubiquitous mobile technology, the electronic games market has rapidly grown to dwarf many other cultural industry sectors, reaching a global size (if we include advertising) of approximately $347bn in 2022.[1] Of that total, mobile gaming accounts for nearly $248bn, or 71%. This extraordinary growth rate is typically forecast to continue, albeit at a somewhat slower rate, with some estimates suggesting a global electronic gaming market worth over $650bn (Statista) by the end of the decade. As we might expect, much of this is likely to be driven by developments in the mobile sector, particularly with the widespread launch of 5G and 6G networks over the coming years as telecoms operators search for ever more engaging applications to fill the vastly expanded bandwidth.

We are now in an environment where electronic games often play a vital role in the exploitation of other cultural franchises including books, films and television programmes. As packaged media versions of film content (e.g. DVD and Blu-ray copies of films, typically the most profitable element of their entire release schedule) decline in popularity with the rise of streaming services, new sources of revenue need to be developed to fill the gap, and gaming has often proven to be a vital ingredient in the economics of planning a new content franchise. It is an attractive prospect, particularly as new blockbuster games can generate billions of dollars very quickly after launch, exemplified by *Grand Theft Auto V,* which generated $1bn of sales within three days of its release.[2] Even the biggest Hollywood films can take weeks or months to reach such enormous levels of revenue.

In other cases, games are driving the development of new film and TV content, with successful cross-overs like *The Angry Birds Movie, The Super Mario Bros. Movie* and *Tomb Raider* emerging as successful film franchises based on their earlier successes as games. *Halo* and *The Last of Us* become relatively successful TV franchises. Following this trend, television streaming companies like Netflix have already established gaming divisions to capitalise on the intellectual property (IP) of the TV programmes they develop through things like its *Netflix Stories* application and, at the time of writing, YouTube was also experimenting with playable games through its *Playables* service. Equally successful electronic games are a vital ingredient in other entertainment fields like the toy sector: *Minecraft* can now be played in the 'real world' thanks to the efforts of toy company Lego, whilst other games can generate significant revenues in terms of action figures and associated merchandise.

Ultimately the electronic games sector has evolved relatively quickly into a critical part of the overall cultural ecosystem, both as a source of content and as a key tool for those in other sectors to maximise the value of their investments in franchise creation and content exploitation. Whilst this presents those in the industry with significant opportunities, it also poses major challenges. No longer can ambitious developers and publishers concern themselves solely with electronic games. To fully maximise their investment in content development they need to understand how other industry sectors like film, TV, advertising and toys function, they need skills in building and maintaining alliances, they need to navigate complex legal and intellectual property issues, they need to understand how a variety of technologies are evolving, all the while maintaining an intimate knowledge of and relationship with the consumers they hope to serve.

Perhaps the most significant recent development in the gaming sector was the global pandemic, the COVID-19 outbreak of 2020–2022. Lockdowns and the enforced closure of most out-of-home activities kept consumers in their homes, and many turned to gaming (in all its forms) to help fill their time. Demand for electronic games hardware and software increased dramatically (as did demand for things like television streaming services), and games firms went on a major recruitment and investment drive to help service this increased demand. But the boom could not last, and once COVID was over, and as an economic recession bit in many countries, demand returned to pre-COVID levels, with most of the same gaming companies announcing significant job cuts and the closure of gaming projects—e.g. highly successful companies like Epic Games (maker of *Fortnite*) laid off 16% of its workforce—there were significant redundancies in established companies like Ubisoft and Niantic (makers of *Pokémon Go*) and Amazon closed its gaming channel. Ongoing difficulties in the industry saw major developers like Bungie, once owned by Microsoft (though subsequently becoming independent again in 2007), look for a major company to help it with its economic woes, finding a partner in Sony, who acquired the company in 2022. Of the then approximately 1200 Bungie employees, nearly 25% would subsequently be made redundant to manage costs in the combined company.

5.3 Mergers and acquisitions

The organisational dynamics of the electronic games sector are often driven by such mergers and acquisitions (M&A). M&A is one of the key ways in which a company grows: it is often referred to as an external method of growth, compared to internal growth—e.g. adding a new product line, also called organic growth. M&A is a common method of growth throughout all business sectors; indeed, some sectors like professional services (accounting firms, lawyers, management consultancies) are characterised by their use of this particular method. A merger is typically when two companies come together on relatively equal terms; an acquisition is when one company (typically the larger or more dominant company) buys another. The process of M&A is typically long, involved, complex and expensive. Partly this expense is due to the fact that deals will typically require the support of expensive external experts to execute them (investment banks, lawyers, accountants etc.). The process involves searching for appropriate targets, contacting them, performing a valuation (how much is the company worth), negotiation, due diligence (a more detailed review of the internal workings of the target company), purchase and then post-deal integration.

M&A is often driven by the search for what are called synergies, extra value that is realised by bringing two companies together (often called the 1+1=3 principle). The argument is typically that by bringing two companies together, you might create more value than that which could be created by each company on its own, hence the combined value is greater than the sum of its parts. Such synergies might for example emerge in the form of sales synergies, or more typically cost synergies—e.g. we are bringing together two companies, each with a headquarters building, but we don't need two headquarters for the newly merged company, so we can shut one, thus decreasing our combined costs. Costs might also be reduced through things like economies of scale in purchasing. It is notable that in the case of Sony's acquisition of Bungie, mentioned earlier, one of the first things Sony did was to cut significant costs at Bungie, largely in the form of laying off Bungie staff.

M&A is incredibly common and popular amongst companies as a method of growth. Often M&A becomes a recipe for growth that all firms are expected to pursue—e.g. the mergers of retail and investment banks in the UK in the 1980s. Yet, in most cases, M&A does NOT work: it destroys value in both companies. According to some researchers, 50% of all M&A destroys value[3]; others suggest that this figure might be closer to 70%!

Why? This seems extraordinary. One of the most well-established methods of corporate growth typically results in value destruction! Well, there are a number of reasons why most M&A fails to create value. Some authors have suggested that organisations tend to pay too much for the companies they acquire (Fernandes, 2019). For others, the synergies upon which the deal was based fail to materialise, or take much longer to develop than expected, and cost far more to realise. More often than not, however, the root of the problem, for both mergers and acquisitions, lies in a lack of attention paid to the human capital elements, and the dangers of a clash of cultures between the two organisations. The process of M&A tends to be driven by the deal, its legality and financial considerations (e.g. how much do we pay, how much can we realise?), with less attention paid to the post-deal integration and the ongoing operations of the combined companies. This tends to be the real challenge of M&A.

We don't have to look far to find a good example in the cultural industries. In 2001, the then leading provider of internet access in the USA, AOL (America Online), acquired Time Warner for approximately $164bn, the largest acquisition / merger in US history at the time. When the deal was announced the combined value of the companies (what is typically called their market capitalisation) was just over $350bn. In many ways the deal made a lot of sense. AOL could provide distribution (access to its subscribers), and Time Warner could provide content (from its film, music and publishing divisions). Warner had attempted to develop its own online presence but had failed, and AOL was desperate to acquire content that it could deliver to its users.

But the acquisition failed, and by the time of the demerger (the splitting up of the two companies) in 2010, AOL, which had made up the majority of the total valuation (contributing around $250bn to the total of $350bn) was worth approximately $3.6bn. It was subsequently sold to Verizon Communications for $4.4bn. What happened? How could such a good idea lead to such disastrous outcomes?

Given his involvement in the deal, the author can attest to the huge amount of attention that was paid to the deal itself, the financial, legal and regulatory elements particularly. Far less attention was paid to the cultures of the two companies, and if and how they would work together. They did not; their respective cultures clashed. The AOL leadership was young, brash, vocal and, to some, arrogant. They were the new royalty in the business world. They took up the majority of the senior positions in the newly merged company. The team at Time Warner were older, more conservative, more risk-averse and seemed willing to take a back seat in the operation of the new company. They came from a company that was seen to be old-fashioned and in decline. There was relatively little integration of the two companies, the cultures collided, the synergies failed to emerge—indeed, negative synergies emerged which began to damage both companies. They did not really understand each other's businesses and made little effort to develop an understanding. The combined company had four chief financial officers in three years, never a good sign.

It is sometimes described as the worst deal of all time; Nina Munk's book *Fools Rush In* provides a fascinating commentary on the deal for those interested in going further, but her conclusion is clear. For her, the deal was not motivated by logic or strategy but by egos, the ego of the then ascendant chief executive of AOL (Steve Case) and particularly that of Gerry Levin, the chief executive of Time Warner who was about to retire. He wanted to leave with a flourish, and a legacy. Whilst relatively common, ego is rarely a good reason for M&A.

The two reasons most cited for the general failure of M&A to create anticipated levels of value are cultural friction between the two companies and a lack of post-acquisition integration planning[4], and this proved to be a perfect example of these forces at work. The cultural industries have been rife with M&A for the last 20 years, particularly in the fields of electronic gaming, broadcasting (with broadcasters acquiring independent programme production companies) and of course in the popular music sector, with the merger of a number of major record companies. The research has yet to be done on whether these deals created the value that was hoped or destroyed it.

5.4 Structure and dynamics

The gaming sector has evolved into one of the most dynamic, exciting, fastest-growing but also most turbulent sectors of the cultural industries, characterised by waves of dramatic innovation and seemingly inexhaustible expansion, combined with major setbacks, retrenchments and recessions. We will now explore the drivers behind these trends in more detail.

In exploring the structure of the electronic games industry, we can conveniently separate it into two broad parts: hardware and software. The hardware (often called 'platform') sector of the industry concentrates on the development and marketing of specific gaming devices, consoles and their handheld portable equivalents. A cyclical evolutionary process has emerged, with major upgrades in speed and graphics in existing devices emerging every three to five years, driving a hardware-based console war, with each major manufacturer attempting to outdo their competition through improvements in graphics processing, storage and networking capabilities. As a result of this constant investment and innovation, even with relatively high prices for new consoles, manufacturers typically derive relatively little profit from the sale of the devices themselves, often losing money on the sale of each and every one sold. Profits are driven by the subsequent sale of software—the games themselves—with the console manufacturer deriving income from the sale of every game licensed to the console.

This in turn created a 'network' effect at the heart of the competitive struggle between hardware manufacturers. Having the bestselling console attracts games developers to create games for that platform (maximising the developer's chances of securing a significant return on their new game). This ongoing supply of new games (particularly those that are 'exclusive', at least initially, to a specific console—e.g. *Halo* on Microsoft Xbox) in turn makes the console the most attractive to consumers. Growing numbers of consumers using the platform maintains the interest of developers in creating games for the platform, encouraging more consumers and so on. A very positive virtuous circle emerges.

Nintendo were the first major manufacturer to buck this trend towards ever more powerful and capable consoles (as mentioned in Chapter 2). Given the relatively limited hardware performance, at least compared to the rivals from Sony and Microsoft, of its Wii console, and focus on family-based games that required comparatively low levels of graphics and processing power, Nintendo were not in an expensive race to constantly research, develop and deploy leading-edge technologies, so their costs were lower and they were in the enviable position of generating profits on the sale of the consoles as well as the games themselves. Despite this break from the norm, the console market remains one with relatively high barriers to entry, requiring significant resources to develop the hardware platform and regularly update it, as well as market and distribute it. The relative failure of numerous 'new' platforms (such as the crowdfunded *Ouya* micro platform, introduced in 2013, which only sold a total of 200,000 units) attests to the difficulties of entering the market and surviving its challenging economics.

Subsequently the early dominance of consoles and dedicated handheld devices in the electronics games market has been overtaken by the emergence of more generalist hardware, PCs and mobile phones that can now cater to the demands of even the most hard-core gaming fans as well as undertake a range of other entertainment, productivity and communications tasks.

Hardware requires software to operate, of course, and as far as consumers are concerned, that software is in the form of the game itself, though this is in turn dependent upon another critical piece of software, the gaming 'engine', which is worth mentioning here. The game engine is a complex piece of software used by games developers in the creation of electronic games. Essentially it acts as an overall platform and set of software tools to help speed up and simplify the game building process. Such engines are often developed for specific games or platforms, though over time they are often shared across games, platforms and indeed companies. Whilst many engines are available, a number have emerged as dominant in the sector, including the Unreal Engine developed initially by the founder of Epic Games, Tim Sweeney in the early 1990s. Two alternatives are Frostbite, developed by games company DICE for its *Battlefield* series, which went on to be used in such games as *Mass Effect*, and Source, developed by Valve and utilised in games including *Counter Strike, Half Life 2* and *Portal*. Developers in the mobile space have also drawn on engines such as the Flare3D Engine used to develop *Farmville* by Zynga Games and the increasingly ubiquitous Unity Engine (now in its fifth generation) developed by Unity Technologies.

For most consumers, however, software means games, and the software sector is now dominated by a relatively small number of major hardware manufacturers with software development capabilities (e.g. Sony Interactive Entertainment, Microsoft Gaming, Nintendo) and large publishers and games developers (e.g. Tencent Interactive Entertainment, NetEase, Electronic Arts, Epic Games etc.). These are complemented by a very large number of smaller developers encouraged into the industry by relatively low market entry barriers, particularly in the mobile gaming sector. Indeed, in terms of sheer numbers, electronic gaming, like many other sectors of the cultural industries, tends to be dominated by SMEs (small and medium-sized enterprises). Of the nearly 2000 games firms in the UK, 95% are SMEs according to research conducted by The Association for UK Interactive Entertainment in 2015.[5] They also note that it is a relatively 'youthful' industry in terms of the age of these companies, with 64% of gaming SMEs launched in the previous five years. A similar profile exists in most other developed countries, though obviously the sheer number of firms will vary significantly—e.g. there were an estimated 47,000 games firms operating in the USA in 2023.[6]

We can start to understand the dynamics of the industry and the interaction of organisations within it by looking at its value chain and network.

Hardware manufacturers have similar internal value chains (see Figure 2.5 in Chapter 2) to most other consumer electronics manufacturing companies, beginning with research and development, design, followed by procurement (sourcing raw materials and components), assembly, quality control and testing, distribution and after-sales service. Another critical activity will be establishing and managing relationships with third party software developers, hence the value network extends to companies supplying manufacturers (e.g. with software or components) and finally the retail sector.

The software network is typically based on three major activities: game development, game publishing and retail. Game development is the province of a wide range of organisations, from tiny one-person bands working in bedrooms to medium and large organisations with hundreds of employees. Whilst these companies are focused on developing games, they are typically reliant on bigger publishers for two critical activities: funding game development and marketing and distribution of the final product. The value network, then, relies on retailers in a variety of forms to provide the final product to the consumer.

Given their often relatively small size and the significant costs involved in developing a game (mainly a labour cost at this stage), developers tend to only work on one or two major projects at a time (though this number might increase if they are working on smaller mobile-based games). Hence each major project is a significant risk for the developer, and should things go wrong in the development process it can have catastrophic implications for the company as whole. This is particularly so if the work is being done for a publisher, who may have a change of heart and want to stop investing in a game's development, make a major change to narrative, characters or gameplay or release the game earlier than initially planned, requiring the developer to rapidly redeploy existing staff, lay some staff off or find new staff. This requirement for flexibility in turn requires an intimate knowledge of and good relationships with the network of freelancers working in game development, and flexible and agile game development processes.

Within this categorisation of the software sector there is significant blurring of boundaries. Larger games developers with some successful titles and franchises behind them often become publishers (e.g. Electronic Arts and Tencent) helping to fund and market the games of other developers. Equally, publishers will typically own their own dedicated games development teams and companies. Indeed, there has been a significant trend in the last 20 years for larger publishers to buy up developers and smaller publishers—e.g. over time Microsoft has bought or had significant shares in FASA Interactive, Bungie, Digital Anvil, Ensemble Studios, Rare, Lionhead Studios, Mojang and most recently Activision Blizzard. Some organisations like Microsoft and Sony may fulfil the roles of suppliers of hardware, games development, publishing and (thanks to the growth of digital distribution of games) even direct-to-consumer retailing via portals such as Xbox Live and PS Direct. Companies will often experiment with new initiatives at different stages of the value chain, developers may experiment with being a publisher, publishers may try out the role of retailer. Success will typically lead to a permanent change in the structure and scope of the organisation; failure typically leads to a retrenchment to earlier organisational forms based around a proven product / market scope and ways of working. Hence the sector is in a constant state of change and flux.

Let's look at each of these categories in a little more detail to find out what you might be doing if you actually worked for one of these companies.

5.4.1 The software sector

Games developers are typically involved in a variety of activities, from developing games concepts to designing the games and gameplay (thinking through issues like characters, the structure of the game, its narrative or story and its overall look) and using games engines to code the games for various platforms. For a detailed review of the game development process see Morisawa (2015).

Within this process there will be teams working on artwork, game play, graphics, audio and back-end software engineers dealing with those vital elements of the game that consumers typically don't see. Games development will call on the skills of designers, artists, musicians and writers, supported by a range of internal support staff involved in managing hardware issues and testing and localisation teams who work on adapting the game for the requirements of different geographic territories. Companies will often draw on external freelancers to work on specific projects for activities like scriptwriting, graphic design, music, artwork and voice work. Unless this work is funded by the game developer itself (perhaps with the aim of self-publishing the final game), it is typically considered 'work for hire', funded by a major publisher who will own the intellectual property in the resultant game. Games developers will attempt to develop close and ongoing relationships with major publishers. These relationships can be crucial, and a poor relationship may lead to cancelled projects and even bankruptcy for the developer, as was the case for the Swedish games developer Grin, which went out of business in 2009 after disagreements emerged with their publisher over payments for a games project (see Sandqvist, 2012).

Publishers take care of everything else—from identifying promising ideas, funding the process of game development, helping to manage the development and production process (publishers typically assign producers for each game development project, who focus on keeping the project on track and solving problems) to finally marketing and distributing the finished product. Broadly we might consider three different types of publishers: those that are part of a hardware platform supplier (e.g. Sony), software publishers with significant internal capabilities in all aspects of game development (e.g. Square) and publishers that act mainly as coordinators / producers for a range of third party suppliers, who essentially outsource most of the activities of game development (e.g. Enix).

Given the difficulties of predicting the success of a new game, publishers will aim to develop a 'slate' (a range) of new games projects, in different genres, aimed at different demographics and user groups, to maximise the potential for success of at least a few of their new releases. This can and does often cause tensions within publishers and larger developers, as teams are moved from one game project to another to address emergent problems, to meet tough deadlines or to focus on the development of a particularly crucial or large-scale (often called 'AAA') title. At the time of writing, Bungie, having been acquired by Sony, moved the majority of its team involved in developing and running the very successful (but increasingly aged at almost 10 years since launch) *Destiny* franchise to other projects (specifically their new project *Marathon*), vastly reducing the amount of future content planned to be released under the *Destiny* banner, and ultimately ensuring its ultimate decline.

Developing a range of different games simultaneously offers the best chance of producing at least one game that makes it to profitability, offsetting losses from the majority of games released that typically fail to attract significant consumer attention and spending and hence don't cover their costs. This lack of success for most games is partly explained by the sheer number of electronic games being released at any one time. One estimate suggests 30 new games were launched on Steam (one of the dominant PC-based games distribution platforms established by Valve in 2003) *every day* in 2021 (but with up to 30% of them selling less than 100 units), rising to 40 new games per day in 2023 according to Steam analytics site SteamDB.[7] Due to this generous supply of new games, consumers have a huge range of choice in the market and significant buyer power. Given its importance in attracting consumer attention, marketing is key to ensure the visibility of the game and remains a critical function for publishers.

This is particularly so in the mobile sector, with widely differing estimates suggesting an average of 300–400, or even as high as 2000, new games released globally each day.[8] Visibility and prominence on major application distribution and retail platforms (e.g. Google Play, the Apple App Store, Tencent MyApp store) is thus critical to a mobile game's prospects, though such prominence comes at a cost, with Apple retaining up to 30% of the retail price of a game. To achieve visibility in a hugely crowded market, major mobile games publishers are also likely to spend significant funds on marketing themselves and their games, and, for some firms, the numbers can be huge; according to their annual report, King Digital Entertainment (the company behind *Candy Crush Saga*) spend nearly $500m per year on marketing activities, and to compete Supercell, another major developer / publisher, spend on average $1m on marketing per day.

Some games developers decide to self-publish, avoiding the involvement of external publishers, and hence undertake all of these activities themselves (in some cases producing surprising breakout hits like *Stardew Valley* and *Vampire Survivors*). Generally, however, marketing and distribution require significant funds and are hugely risky, with the failure of a single self-published title potentially meaning the end of a small developer. Hence most developers rely on larger publishers for these services, particularly when major new games (AAA titles) are the focus. Such games can have huge development budgets (estimates suggest it cost over $400m for Bungie and its publisher Activision Blizzard to develop and market the aforementioned *Destiny* franchise), far beyond the resources of most independent game developers. In return for funding, the publisher will command a large share of the profits from the retail of the game, and in most cases retain the intellectual property rights in the resulting game (in a similar way to a record company owning the intellectual property rights of an album whose recording it has funded). Historically (and to some extent today) publishers would also arrange the physical distribution of the final product to the ultimate stage in the value network, retailers, though this role has diminished in many territories with the rise of digital distribution over the internet.

Such retailers might include dedicated games retailers with real-world stores, or (just as likely) large general stores and supermarkets. Whilst publishers would not necessarily have the physical assets to undertake such distribution (warehouses, trucks etc.), they would work closely with specialist distribution companies who did. Increasingly, however, the sale of electronic games is achieved through online stores, either the sales of physical games (CDs in packaging) or digital versions to be downloaded to hardware-based storage devices. Indeed, some consoles are now being sold without any method of reading physical media (e.g. Xbox series S launched in 2020), relying completely on digital downloads to provide the necessary software to play games. For some publishers this has allowed them to focus on their own retail and distribution operations and lessen their reliance on external retailers. Mobile games typically rely on major application retailing sites, like the Apple App Store or Google Play or specialist gaming sites like MiniReview for distribution. Some mobile game developers and publishers will also sell directly to consumers via their own online sites—e.g. Playdigious.

5.4.2 Hardware

In terms of the hardware sector, companies are typically involved in research and development, manufacturing, distribution and marketing. Unlike more traditional consumer electronics, success in the electronic game market appears to be more volatile, unpredictable and subject to rapidly changing fashions (resembling demand in the film, TV and music sectors). This perhaps explains the number of failures of more traditional consumer electronics companies like Matsushita (through an alliance with Electronic Arts) and Toshiba (through a proposed alliance with Apple) to successfully enter the games market. Successful hardware manufacturers need to be masters of research and development, manufacturing, distribution and marketing to be considered competitive. Equally they need strong relationships with content companies (the games developers and publishers) to ensure that the hardware is supplied with a regular flow of high-quality software. This is a tough agenda for most companies.

Perhaps this partly explains Sony's relative success in the market—significant expertise in manufacturing and marketing of consumer electronics, combined with expertise in working with content suppliers and managing these often-turbulent relationships (partly due to the broad range of companies within the Sony Corp. group itself, including film and TV companies). Certainly, the decision by major software developers and publishers to work with Sony and produce versions of their games for the PlayStation platform (including Square, the producers of the *Final Fantasy* series, and Enix with *Dragon Quest*) proved to be crucial in establishing Sony's legitimacy and credibility in the marketplace. Sony's ability to develop and maintain these relationships is illustrated by evidence that as early as 2000 (only five years after the launch of the very first iteration of the PlayStation), they were already dealing with 540 external software developers and publishers worldwide (Dentsu Soken, 1999).

Difficulties are exacerbated by the ongoing console 'wars' mentioned earlier as manufacturers compete for dominance. Such competition typically revolves around the technical capabilities of hardware—hence there is a constant incentive to upgrade existing technology for the next generation of consoles. This in turn requires significant investments in research and development and the utilisation of leading-edge components such as chips, storage devices, network architecture etc. Further, new launches are typically backed with extensive (and expensive) marketing campaigns. If all these costs were reflected in the retail price of the new hardware it would probably be so expensive that widespread adoption of the new console would be highly unlikely, ultimately limiting sales of the software (games) that manufacturers rely on for the majority of their profits. Manufacturers will therefore typically sell their consoles with razor-thin profit margins or even at a loss[9] to ensure that retail prices are low enough to encourage mass consumer adoption of the hardware. Should prices rise too much, consumers may feel it more sensible to invest in a PC, able to play games and undertake a range of other useful activities (communication, productivity etc.) rather than invest in a dedicated games console.

Once a console is launched and starts to sell large quantities, the cost of components tends to fall (partly through the experience curve effect mentioned in a previous chapter). This then allows the manufacturer to introduce console variants and lower retail prices, encouraging further take-up later in the product's life cycle (perhaps moving from the early to the late majority—see the adoption / diffusion model in Chapter 8). It still means, however, that profits are rare on the sale of hardware alone. As already suggested hardware manufacturers are only likely to see major profits on the sale of successful games that they have licensed to their platform.

5.4.3 Porter's 5 forces model applied to the electronic games sector

Imagine you are working for a company that is thinking of entering the games market. Should it do so? Is it an attractive market? We might consider using one of the tools mentioned in Chapter 2 to analyse the industry, something like Porter's 5 forces (P5F). The tool asks us to consider issues of buyer and supplier power, threat of substitutes, threat of new entrants (i.e. barriers to entry) and competitive rivalry to assess the overall attractiveness of an industry. As with most of the tools already described in Chapter 2, the basic idea of the model is relatively straightforward and easy to understand; this simplicity is probably why tools like P5F, SWOT and PESTLE are so commonly utilised in business analysis. You don't need an MBA to understand how the tool was constructed or its major principles. But it is in how such tools are actually used in analysis that mistakes are usually made by users.

The first mistake we might make in using P5F would be to undertake an analysis for the industry as a whole. Doing it at this 'macro' level would produce many contradictory results—for example, in terms of barriers to entry. Barriers to entry for games developers, particularly in the mobile sector, are typically relatively low—entrants only need some minimal programming equipment (e.g. a PC and some generic software) and a really good idea (hence the early growth of 'bedroom' programmers mentioned earlier). For organisations wishing to become major hardware manufacturers, however, the barriers are almost impossibly high, necessitating world-class capabilities in manufacturing, marketing, distribution and alliance management combined with significant financial resources to invest in new technologies.

When considering supplier power, we might suggest that suppliers of the most technologically advanced components (chips, storage devices etc.) to the major console manufacturers are in a relatively strong position, able to charge high prices and dictate the negotiations. Suppliers to major publishers, on the other hand (e.g. games development companies), have much lower power to determine prices as there are so many games developers. If a publisher cannot agree terms with one supplier, they can always turn to another to develop a game.

At some levels of analysis, when exploring customer power, we might suggest it is very strong—e.g. end consumers have considerable power when buying (particularly mobile) games given the vast range of new games available. When buying consoles, however, the end user typically has less power as there are only a few variants to choose from. At another level in the industry, we might consider customers as the publishing companies, in that they are often the customers of games developers. Here we would have a different set of dynamics to consider when deciding if customers or suppliers have the most power.

Hence it is often necessary, particularly when using P5F, to focus on a particular type of company or a particular part or level of the industry to extract useful insights. Using it at too broad a level (this is also very true for the PESTLE tool) will not produce useful insights and may in fact confuse rather than help the decision maker. Ensuring you are clear about your unit of analysis (e.g. are we looking at the manufacturing sector, games developers, the end user or an earlier part of the supply chain?), carefully defining your terms and working at a relatively granular rather than macro level will help ensure that your analysis is consistent, detailed and provides useful insights for decision making.

It is also dangerous to rely on one tool or technique alone. In assessing if we should enter the games market, then, we would carefully use a variety of different tools to explore the environment (P5F, PESTLE, life cycle analysis, adoption / diffusion models, competitor analysis, benchmarking) combined with a detailed review of our internal assets and capabilities, before considering what we might achieve in this new market.

5.5 Current developments and trends

5.5.1 Crowdfunding

As is the case in other sectors of the cultural industries (see Chapter 10), new methods are emerging to fund content development. Rather than relying on major publishers (who will fund a game's development in return for a significant share of the retail price and who are likely to own any resulting intellectual property in the game), or relying on personal sources of funds (e.g. borrowing from a bank), developers can now turn to gamers themselves, through general crowdfunding sites like Kickstarter or more specialised sites like Gamefound (https://gamefound.com/en). Potential consumers are turned into potential investors as they are invited to invest relatively small amounts of money in the development and launch of a new game. In return they receive rewards based on the level of their investment, though typically this will include a copy of the game when it is completed, ongoing updates and potentially merchandise.

Whilst there are examples of successful games funded in this way (e.g. Double Fine Production's adventure game *Broken Age*, which raised over $3m in funds), there is little prospect of such funding sources being used to develop major AAA titles given their huge budgets and complex development challenges. The method is perhaps more promising when it is focused on reviving classic gaming titles that may no longer be available but for which there is an existing consumer market (e.g. one of the earliest PC games, *Elite*, gathered a fanatical group of consumers for its initial release and was reincarnated nearly 20 years later as *Elite Dangerous* after a successful crowdfunding campaign) or for smaller mobile or PC-based games. Whatever the genre or hardware platform, games have typically become one of the most popular categories on most general crowdfunding sites, with Kickstarter claiming it had enabled the funding of over 40,000 games projects by 2024.

5.5.2 AI

As with just about every other major industry, gaming companies are currently wrestling with the role of AI in their evolution. Whilst AI in a more primitive form has had a relatively long history in the electronic gaming sector, particularly in its use in procedurally generated games, recent developments (particularly in generative AI) have propelled it to being seen as a fundamental enabling technology for the future. Much of the focus is on its potential to 'hyper personalise' a gamer's experience, with 'smarter' individual enemies (or indeed any non-player character) responding directly to an individual player's specific actions (or indeed voice prompts) and evolving their behaviour over time. These interactions will be tracked by developers and publishers, using AI in data mining on user behaviour, allowing them to track how games are being played by users and make rapid changes to gameplay if required. The further integration of AI into existing game engines would enable such changes to be made with relatively little involvement from the developer's staff. Given that labour costs are typically the highest costs in the development of a game and its operation, such initiatives could radically reshape the economics of the games development sector.

AI is also likely to emerge in opportunities for gamers to 'mod' (modify) their games. Modding is already a well-established activity for many gamers, taking off with modding of *Doom* (a 'first-person shooter' game or FPS), but now expanded to include popular games such as *Minecraft, GTA V* and *Elder Scrolls V: Skyrim*. Such mods may range from simple changes in player character cosmetics to more grand efforts to completely alter the game world environment, either in terms of appearance or gameplay. Specific mods for a particular game can become popular with many gamers, and in some cases they are even adopted by the game's developer themselves (e.g. the 'capture the flag' variant for FPS *Quake* was originally developed by users before subsequently being included in official versions of the game).

Whilst this began as a very unofficial activity, not necessarily approved of by the game's supplier, companies will now often release specific software tools to encourage users to modify their experience of the game—e.g. players of *Elder Scrolls V* have access to an official game editor made available by the developer, whilst games studio Maxis released modding tools for their game *The Sims*, even before the game was officially launched. Valve, which publishes games online, typically for play on PC, have a 'workshop' service allowing mods to be downloaded in supported games.

Certainly, mods can help support player engagement with a game, offering a chance for self-expression and creativity, and potentially extend a game's shelf life, though concerns swirl around legal and intellectual property issues and the degree to which modders should be allowed access to core elements of technology in which games companies may have invested heavily, an investment they will want to protect in terms of its commercialisation. Attempts by companies like Valve to monetise modding (introducing a paid mod feature into its platform Steam) have so far been generally unsuccessful, drawing a very vocal and negative response from some elements of the gaming community.

AI and particularly generative AI will almost certainly make it easier than ever before for modders to generate new content; indeed AI can now offer these modders the chance to create their own games in entirety, thanks to developments like the Rosebud AI Gamemaker, an AI-based platform that can generate games through simple text instructions. With 48% of 16–34-year-old mobile gamers suggesting they like to create their own content in mobile games, according to research conducted in the UK by Mintel in 2024[10], modding is unlikely to disappear any time soon and may blossom with the further integration of AI.

5.5.3 Adaptation to changing gaming demographics

For much of its history the demographics of the gaming sector was dominated by younger to middle-aged males. New consoles (e.g. the Nintendo Wii) and mobile gaming enabled an expansion to older and younger age groups, and the inclusion of more women and other family members. These (relatively) new gaming segments are typically less likely to own a console and less likely to make in-app game purchases[11], hence games companies are on a constant search for new ways to monetise them by addressing their specific interests and preferences. One key area of focus is on in-game socialisation, considered by up to 52% of gamers in the UK to be the most appealing aspect of gaming[12], particularly in non-traditional gaming segments. Hence, we might forecast ever closer links to social networking sites, the owners of which may become the new gatekeepers to mass gaming audiences.

Given the lack of interest in owning consoles in many growing gaming segments, some companies are exploring further opportunities in cloud-based gaming, with games hosted on remote servers, typically streamed to devices (including mobile phones and PCs but also, critically, 'smart' televisions), meaning that potential gamers may already have, in essence, all of the hardware they need to game (perhaps with the exclusion of an optional dedicated games controller, which could be purchased for a relatively low price, for those for whom the television remote control proves frustrating). Such cloud-based platforms include NVIDIA GeForce, EA Play, Shadow, Amazon Luna and Antstream (aimed at fans of 'retro' games from the 1980s and 1990s).

The major console manufacturers also appear to have begun a turn towards a more subscription-based cloud-enabled business model. Services such as Xbox's Game Pass (or Sony's PlayStation Plus) allow users to access a variety of games (which the user can play, but does not ultimately own), streamed from central servers to multiple devices (consoles, PCs and mobile devices), for a monthly fee. These subscriptions are already often a requirement for console gamers who wish to engage in multiplayer activities (e.g. player vs. player games, PVP). Their continued evolution in turn relies on further consumer take-up, which in turn relies on the regular supply of new cloud-enabled games and, for many territories (see the later section on gaming in Africa), ongoing improvements in the quality of internet access, with speed requirements typically at least 5Mbps for basic games and ideally upwards of 20Mbps for more complex games.

The mobile sector is likely to continue its growth and ultimate dominance of the gaming market in terms of hardware platforms. With the rollout of 5G networks, and the inevitable move to 6G networks, telecoms operators need to find compelling applications to utilise the significantly increased bandwidth available, and mobile games of increasing sophistication, delivered via the cloud, are likely to remain an attractive option, particularly as phone hardware continues to improve in terms of functionality. As early as 2023 with the launch of the iPhone 15, Apple claimed its ability to handle the processing and graphics demands of even the most sophisticated AAA titles, once only playable on dedicated, high-end consoles. We can also expect further experiments in the mobile space by the major console manufacturers.

Another area for further initiatives to attract and monetise growing gaming segments is likely to be virtual reality (VR) and augmented reality (AR). Once forecast as the future of gaming, to date it has rather disappointed forecasters, remaining a relatively small niche of gaming activity, with ownership of VR / AR equipment in the UK relatively low in 2023, at approx. 7% of gamers (Kantar, 2023). Many forecasters predict a very rapid upturn in its use in gaming, however, suggesting that 216m gamers are likely to be regularly using AR / VR as part of their gaming experience by 2025.[13] For this to happen the price of AR / VR hardware will need to decline, it will almost certainly need the support of major hardware providers to further integrate the technology and finally games developers / publishers will need to take on the very risky (and expensive) proposition of launching major games franchises that utilise AR / VR as part of the core gaming experience. We will return to this issue in Chapter 9.

Commercially, in addition to revenue derived from the sale of hardware and software, which is likely to be minimal amongst emergent consumer segments, we are also likely to see the growth of advertising (around-game and in-game) as a key revenue stream, particularly for brands that are relevant to emergent segments and that might somehow be integrated in a meaningful way into the games themselves. Imagine visiting a restaurant as part of an action / adventure game, but then being able to order from it, with the food arriving at your door half an hour later (the in-game takeaway), and getting a reward for it in the gameplay, or buying a new cosmetic 'skin' for your player and being able to order the same outfit from a major fashion brand. Whilst the freemium model so evident in the mobile gaming sector is useful for driving adoption of games, by definition it does not generate direct revenue, relying on in-game purchases to do so. Yet emerging segments appear less willing to make such purchases, and hence companies are turning to advertising as a vital revenue source. But in-game advertisements can produce very different responses from gamers, with most accepting it as a necessary evil (though typically choosing to ignore it) and others, particularly those using PCs and consoles, often actively disliking it, suggesting that too much in-game advertising might put them off engaging with a game.

Hence gaming companies will need to be bold and clever in experimenting with fresh advertising ideas, from product placement, sponsorship and in-game but background advertising to advertisements that tie in closely with in-game rewards. A further potential revenue generator which games companies may seek to secure a portion of in the future may be attendance at and betting around competitions and tournaments in the esports area.

5.5.4 Esports

Along with mobile gaming, another major trend to have changed the electronic gaming landscape since 2010 has been the emergence of esports. Whilst the sector is still searching for a clear definition of itself, it is broadly concerned with consumers spectating at electronic games tournaments and competitions. As early as 2013, 70m people were recorded as watched esports.[14] Whilst debate continues as to whether electronic games tournaments genuinely qualify as sports (as opposed to merely competitions), audience demand for the opportunity to watch events continues to grow. A partial proxy for this growth is revealed by examining Twitch viewing figures. Twitch is an American video streaming service focused on live gaming events. Launched in 2011, by 2012 it delivered around 100k average concurrent viewers for its streams. This has now grown to 2.3m concurrent views in 2024[15] with 98,000 channels of content streamed simultaneously.

Initially very much the province of amateurs (in its first incarnation in 1972 competitors were students from Stanford University playing *Spacewar!)*, competitions and tournaments are now dominated, at least at high levels, by professional players, particularly in multiplayer teams. Major teams such as FaZe Clan (USA), Fnatic (global), Newbee (China) Team Spirit (Serbia) and Natus Vincere (Ukraine) all have websites where their adoring fans can look at player profiles, follow news and buy associated merchandise.

The leagues, competitions and tournaments themselves are typically organised by major games publishers and developers (e.g. Riot Games organise the *League of Legends* World Championship, Valve Corporation run The International for *Dota 2*, Blizzard runs the *Overwatch* League etc.), though some specialist organisations have emerged focused on organising events (e.g. ESL—the Electronic Sports League—and Major League Gaming). These organisations in turn rely on sponsors to help fund the events, as they would in more traditional sports. The largest current sponsors in esports include technology firms like Intel, drinks companies like Red Bull, Monster Energy and Coca-Cola and financial services companies like Mastercard and HSBC.

Thanks to these sponsors, prizes can be significant, with *Dota 2*'s 2021 tournament, The International 10, offering total prizes of over $40m and with the winning team taking home a prize of $18m. As well as tournament prize money, players in the more successful and well-established teams can also expect an individual salary between tournament events.

Popular game genres in esports include MOBAs, FPSs, fighting games, sports games and real-time strategy games, hence popular titles at tournaments include *League of Legends, Dota 2 (Defenders of the Ancients), Overwatch, FIFA World Cup* and *Valorant*. Some tournaments are focused on a specific game—e.g. *The League of Legends* World Championship, *Dota 2* International and *Fortnite* World Cup finals—whilst others have emerged which include a variety of different games including Cyber World Games, the Evolution Championship series and Intel Extreme Masters. Whilst major events can command airtime on specialist TV channels (e.g. South Korea's OGN), the focus is typically on delivery of viewing opportunities via the internet (through applications like Twitch), though tickets are also sold to attend tournaments in person, with 45,000 sectators attending a venue for the PES 2016 UEFA Euro tournament in Paris in 2016, beating the previous record of 40,000 for the 2014 *League of Legends* tournament in South Korea.

Complementing physical sports, esports are now generating significant betting revenues, with some estimates suggesting the betting market was worth $2.5bn in 2024.[16] Many traditional betting operators (e.g. William Hill, Ladbrokes and Bet365) now offer the opportunity to bet on esport events. The overall growth in the sector is generally forecast to continue, with estimates of the total size of the esports audience at around 577m viewers in 2024.[17]

Given this ongoing growth in demand and developments in the gaming ecosystem, it appears increasingly possible for gamers to have a professional esports career based on participation in various tournaments and competitions. For those with even loftier aspirations, esports are being actively considered for inclusion in the Olympic Games, and whilst they did not appear in the Paris 2024 games, their inclusion in subsequent games seems a possibility, with an inaugural event in Saudi Arabia planned for 2025, though the event was subsequently moved to 2026 and ultimately cancelled by the International Olympic Committee (IOC).

5.5.5 Gaming in emerging territories

For most of the history of the electronic games industry, the majority of games content and hardware manufacture has tended to originate in the USA, Europe, Japan and more recently China. However, new games companies are emerging from developing countries to challenge this dominance, at least for local gamers. Let us look at the environment in Africa as an example. The vast majority of gaming in Africa takes place on mobile phones, owned by approximately 45% of the population in sub-Saharan Africa in 2022[18], though given its relatively youthful population, this ownership is forecast to increase significantly in the next five years. With console and PC games priced at $50–70, relatively high data fees and costs for subscription services, dedicated games consoles often costing at least $500, and gamer-focused PCs even more, the usual PC gaming and console set-up so evident in the Global West is typically beyond the means of most gamers in Africa. Gaming cafes which offer access to this high-end hardware are an emerging alternative to ownership (though at the time of writing there was only one such café in Kenya offering access to high-end PC games), but the focus of the emergent games industry in Africa is predominantly on delivery of games to devices that are already in the hands of a large proportion of the potential consumer base—mobile phones.

According to a GeoPoll and PAGG 2024[19] report, 92% of the estimated 200m gamers in sub-Saharan Africa choose to do so primarily or exclusively on their mobile phones. The same report also noted that up to 70% of these gamers spend less than $5 per month to support their gaming habit. According to the Newzoo Global Games Market Report (2023)[20], co-produced with Nigerian based games developer Maliyo Games, the average African gamer will only spend $6 per year on games (this spend being on in-app purchases in typically free-to-play mobile games), although some territories reach higher figures (e.g. $12 per year in South Africa).

This focus on games delivered to mobile phones has also allowed the growth of domestic developers[21], who can enter the market relatively easily (when compared to developing a major AAA title for a console or PC), many of whom have chosen to focus on developing what they consider more relevant cultural content, including Leti Arts' *Africa Legends* project or Dimension 11's *Legends of Orisha*. The GeoPoll and PAGG 2024 research suggests that 44% of African gamers feel that most games from outside Africa lack cultural relevance and would like to see an increase in games with characters that look like them and reflect their history, culture and daily lives. Interestingly according to the same study, 56% of respondents were unaware of any games made in Africa or domestic games developers, suggesting the need for domestic suppliers to increase their visibility to local gamers. To this extent there appears to be an as yet largely untapped market for local content creation.

One interesting question emerges around the degree to which Africa, and indeed other developing markets (like south-east Asia), will play 'catch-up' with their more developed peers, or if they will leapfrog technologies. In a catch-up scenario we would see the further growth of console and PC gaming, ultimately approaching the penetration and usage levels found in more developed territories. However, there have been numerous research papers exploring technological evolution in emerging markets suggesting that rather than 'catching up' with peers, territories often leapfrog them (Lee and Lim, 2001), essentially skipping one or several stages in the evolution of technology. In this latter scenario, Africa may never develop a significant console / PC-based electronic gaming infrastructure; rather, with ongoing improvements in the capabilities of mobile devices, and price pressure minimising the widespread adoption of consoles and gaming PCs, it will be the mobile market that will continue to dominate in terms of how electronic games are distributed and consumed.

Despite this, existing hardware providers and major publishers remain interested in developing their business in Africa. Microsoft for example have built a team to scout the continent (along with other territories like Latin America and the Middle East) for the best games development talent with which to work, offering help in funding, mentorship and developing technical capabilities. Such initiatives are often supported by local governments hoping to increase inward investment into the country. Africa Games Week, supported by the South African government, hosted an event in 2024 where 120 local developers could meet potential international investors, including major hardware providers and software developers.

Whilst significant obstacles remain for gaming in Africa, including an unpredictable and unstable power infrastructure, patchy internet connectivity and unaffordable internet access, price barriers to the purchase of gaming hardware and a lack of local, relatable content, the market is forecast to grow to top $1bn in value in 2024 (GeoPoll and PAGG, 2024). But the industry remains relatively unproven, particularly in any attempt to develop content with broad international appeal beyond the continent (and even content that will work across all 54 countries within the continent itself); hence it is still perceived as a relatively attractive but high-risk territory in which to invest, and a difficult one in which to build a domestic career in gaming. Over the next few years, it will be interesting to monitor if this forecast growth is built on global or much more locally originated technology and content.

5.5.6 Gaming in new sectors

Gaming is stretching its boundaries to include new sectors. Given that game engines can be used to render high-quality visuals (often in real time), they are already being used by Hollywood in the film and TV production process. From landscapes, to mass armies and even individual characters (e.g. the droid character K-2SO in the movie *Rogue One*), game engines like Unreal Engine are now being used to create a wide variety of different content. Indeed, some games companies themselves are already experimenting with the use of games engines to make their own TV and film content, *Lumen in the Land of Nanite*, created by Epic Games using the Unreal Engine, being a very good example.

Beyond the entertainment industry, game mechanics are increasingly being used in the development of other software and applications, a process known as 'gamification'. Whilst academic research on gamification is still at a relatively early stage, research that has been conducted tends to focus on its fit with human motivation (see for example the Octalysis gamification framework developed by Chou, 2015), drawing on various game mechanics to encourage user motivation and involvement.

Game mechanics to measure progress (like points systems, leaderboards, rewards like badges or tokens) appear particularly relevant in encouraging interaction and engagement with a variety of systems. Educational settings and the workplace are key locations for such initiatives, utilising gaming elements that encourage competition or cooperation in team building applications (e.g. getting staff to work together to complete a specific mission or level) or online training that can benefit from clear measures of progress, regular feedback and the introduction of 'fun' elements to encourage learning.

Gamification initiatives have been trialled by organisations like the US Army as a recruitment and training tool, in corporations to aid marketing efforts, in the health sector to encourage users to exercise and even in the political and government sector to encourage positive behaviour amongst citizens (e.g. the Social Credit System application initiated by the Chinese government). It will be fascinating to monitor the growth and development of gamification and its application in an increasingly diverse range of sectors in the next 5–10 years.

5.6 Conclusions

From relatively humble beginnings as a way to test the capabilities of computer hardware, electronic gaming has come a long way, very quickly. Its evolution into one of the largest parts of the cultural industry has been beset by problems and setbacks, but its potential for further growth marks it out as one of the most attractive sectors for investment by incumbent companies and new entrants. As it evolves, its influence on other cultural industry sectors, both as a source of new content and as a key part of the economics of exploiting existing or planned content, is only likely to increase.

The consumer market appears well established, with a relatively small proportion of hard-core gamers, who buy multiple high-price AAA titles and are willing to invest in leading-edge consoles on which to play them, supported by a far larger group of more casual gamers, happy to play on their mobile phones, generating relatively little revenue from the games themselves, but driving growth in ancillary revenues like advertising. Perhaps one of the biggest debates for the major console manufacturers, who as we have already seen often lose money on each console they sell, will be the degree to which they continue to support the console sector, launching ever more sophisticated (and potentially expensive) devices to support hard-core gamers who demand the best graphics, fastest response times and most immersive game play. Will the move to subscription services, cloud-based delivery and the increasing sophistication of mobile phones and smart TVs render the console irrelevant? If so, which of the major firms will be the first to take the brave step of admitting defeat, and close their console business?

Equally, the future of the console sector may be secured by ongoing innovation in the sector. Consoles have always based their appeal on being the most technically sophisticated dedicated gaming devices, providing an experience that could not be matched on other devices. As we have noted, these devices (e.g. PCs and mobile phones particularly) have caught up. To maintain their place in the market, consoles need to prove their technical advantages again, and perhaps the most obvious route might be VR- and AR-based games, services and features, requiring significant local processing, networking and storage capabilities. Certainly, they are likely to have a window when such services might only be run on a powerful, dedicated gaming device like a console, though it's likely that PCs will catch up relatively quickly. Indeed, should these enhanced VR services first emerge on PCs, and gain a hold there, then console manufacturers may struggle to justify their existence in the evolving gaming market. We will return to this discussion in Chapter 9.

What appears certain is that electronic gaming has taken its place as a critical and core part of the cultural industries and that this is likely to remain the case into the future, however games are delivered and consumed.

5.7 Activities

- Develop an idea for a mobile game. What are the critical aspects of gameplay? How will you distribute and retail the final game? What will be its business model? How are you going to make it stand out?
- Undertake some market research. How many of your friends game? On what platforms? What are their primary reasons for doing so? How many have bought in-app cosmetics or loot boxes?
- Look at a major merger or acquisition in the sector from five years ago. Are the companies still working together? What have been the major benefits of the merger / acquisition? Have there been problems or difficulties in identifying and extracting synergies?

Notes

1 Statista Reports, 2022.
2 https://deadline.com/2013/09/grand-theft-auto-v-hits-record-breaking-800m-in-first-day-sales-590366/.
3 https://www.valuationresearch.com/insights/avoiding-failed-ma-deals.
4 http://www.milnerltd.com/news/new-milner-white-paper-on-10-steps-to-success-in-mergers-and-acquisitions.
5 https://static1.squarespace.com/static/5f7708077cf66e15c7de89ee/t/60283967bb46d144f7cdcf87/1613248887749/Ukie-Blueprint-for-growth.pdf.
6 Statista Reports, 2023.
7 https://www.videogameschronicle.com/news/a-record-14000-games-were-released-on-steam-in-2023/.
8 Quora, 2024.
9 This long-established rumour in the games industry was confirmed during the Epic vs. Apple trial in the USA in 2021; when asked how much profit margin Microsoft makes on sales of its Xbox console, the then head of business development at Xbox suggested 'we don't [make a profit]; we sell the consoles at a loss'. https://www.theverge.com/2021/5/6/22422691/microsoft-xbox-consoles-profit-software-services-revenue-apple-epic-games-trial.
10 Mintel, Future of Gaming report, 2024.
11 Kantar Profiles/Mintel, August 2023, UK.
12 Ibid.
13 Global Newswire, 2023.
14 https://www.researchgate.net/deref/http%3A%2F%2Fwww.redbull.com%2Fen%2Fesports%2Fstories%2F1331644628389%2Fesports-in-numbers-five-mind-blowing-stats?_tp=eyJjb250ZXh0Ijp7ImZpcnN0UGFnZSI6InB1YmxpY2F0aW9uIiwicGFnZSI6InB1YmxpY2F0aW9uIn19.
15 https://twitchtracker.com/statistics.
16 Statista Reports, 2024.
17 IntentaDigital, 2024.
18 GSMA, 2023.
19 GeoPoll and PAGG. 2024. Gaming in Africa Report. https://www.geopoll.com/resources/gaming-africa-report/.
20 https://newzoo.com/resources/trend-reports/newzoo-global-games-market-report-2023-free-version.
21 E.g. Leti Arts (http://letiarts.com), Maliyo games (https://www.maliyo.com), Dimension 11 (https://www.dimension11studios.com) and publishers like Carry1st (https://www.carry1st.com).

References

Cabras, I., Goumagias, N. D., Fernandes, K., Cowling, P., Li, F., Kudenko, D., Devlin, A. and Nucciarelli, A. 2017. Exploring survival rates of companies in the UK video-games industry: An empirical study. *Technological Forecasting & Social Change*, 117, pp. 305–314.

Chou, Yu-kai. 2015. *Actionable Gamification: Beyond Points, Badges and Leaderboards.* Octalysis Media. ISBN 978-1511744041.

Dentsu Soken (Dentsu Institute for Human Studies). 1999. *Joho Media Hakusho (Databook of the Communications and Media Industries*). Tokyo: Dentsu.

Fernandes, N. 2019. *The Value Killers: How Mergers and Acquisitions Cost Companies Billions—And How to Prevent It.* Palgrave Macmillan.

Lee, K. and Lim, C. 2001. Technological regimes, catching up and leapfrogging: Findings from the Korean industries. *Research Policy*, 30 (3), pp. 459–483.

Morisawa, T. 2015. Managing the unmanageable: Emotional labour and creative hierarchy in the Japanese animation industry. *Ethnography*, 16 (2), pp. 262–284.

Munk, N. 2004. *Fools Rush In.* HarperCollins.

Newman, J. 2013. *Videogames.* Abingdon: Routledge.

Rutter, J. and Bryce, J. 2006. *Understanding Digital Games.* London: Sage.

Sandqvist, U. 2012. The development of the Swedish game industry: A true success story? pp. 134–156, in Zackariasson, P. and Wilson, T. (eds). *The Video Game Industry: Formation, Present State, and Future.* Routledge.

Srinivasan, A. and Venkatraman, N. 2010. Indirect network effects and platform dominance in the video game industry: A network perspective. *IEEE Transactions on Engineering Management*, 57 (4), pp. 661–673.

6 The Popular Music Sector

6.1 Introduction

Perhaps more than any other sector that we explore in this book, the popular music sector has been on a roller coaster ride over the last 30 years. From being one of the most predictably profitable sectors of the cultural industries for much of its existence, the effects of the emergence of a digital economy in music would radically alter the prospects for those large corporations that had flourished in the previous decades, forcing many of them to downsize, merge or leave the industry entirely. Digital developments fundamentally challenged a previously highly successful and profitable business model that had been the foundation for the success and dominance of a small number of large-scale, global record companies. As we will see, the popular music sector as a whole only began to emerge from this period of downturn and disruption towards the middle of the 2010s, and it did so with a new set of major music companies in the ascendant, based on a new business model, and a significantly diminished number of traditional incumbents.

So, what happened?

In this chapter we will review how the popular music sector evolved, its structure and operation, the effects of the emergence of digital formats, how major incumbent companies responded to these new challenges, which as we will see is essentially a lesson in how not to respond to technological innovation, and how the sector has evolved subsequently. In doing so we focus particularly on the recorded popular music sector, detouring into the live popular music sector when appropriate.

From a business perspective, we focus particularly on the issue of corporate strategy, and it is there that we will start the chapter.

6.2 Strategy: an introduction

Corporate strategy typically revolves around creating a future vision for an organisation and developing a plan to get there. It usually encapsulates all of the activities of an organisation, from what products and services are sold, to how they are created, distributed and marketed. It also covers what assets and capabilities (see Chapter 2) the organisation needs to develop, and what contribution is required from the workforce. Given this scope, and the importance of getting it right, it is typically one of the most significant and difficult challenges facing the senior management team who are tasked with developing it. Whilst there are many different views of how to think about business strategy, and how to do it well, continuing on from our analysis in Chapter 2, we

DOI: 10.4324/9781003498599-6

focus on two major approaches: the 'environmental fit' perspective and the 'resource-based' perspective. We will focus particularly on the resource-based view, given its popularity today amongst academics and practitioners.

One approach argues that a good business strategy creates the right fit between an organisation and its environment. Drawing on Darwinian theories, it suggests that successful organisations (or animal species in Darwin's original work) are those that are most well adapted to their environment. Those species are able to find an ecological niche, a gap, where competition (for food, resources, mates) is minimised. This is equally true, it is argued, for organisations: only in the least competitive market spaces can the most profit be generated. Hence organisations need to fit with their environment.

These environments are not static, however. As the environment changes, so too must the species. It must adapt to fit with the changed environment. Failure to do so means extinction, becoming a dinosaur (and we all know what happened to them). The same is true, it is argued, for organisations. Unless the organisation constantly adapts to its changing environment, it is likely to become extinct. How did this play out in the case of the major record companies, faced with a relatively small, but fundamental change to their business environment? We shall see.

Early 'industrial analysis' approaches—typified by Porter (1979) and Shapiro (1989), focusing on company positioning and 'fit'—were criticised for being too static, too focused on product / market position as a defining factor, for ignoring path dependencies (the impact of previous strategic decisions) and potential cooperation as critical influences on firm strategy (Teece et al., 1997). The subsequent impetus amongst management academics to focus on firm capabilities and resources to explore strategy emerged partly from this frustration with existing theories to explain the antecedents and character of sustainable competitive advantage, particularly in fast-changing industries and markets.

Hence a new perspective on business strategy emerged, the resource-based view (RBV), and began to gain ground in the 1980s. With its early origins in the work of Schumpeter (1934) and Penrose (1959), the theory envisages firms as bundles of tangible and intangible resources and capabilities, heterogeneously distributed and persistent over time (Penrose 1959). Sustainable advantage emerges when firms create strategies to develop VRIN (valuable, rare, inimitable and non-substitutable) resources (Barney, 1991; Conner and Prahalad, 1996; Nelson, 1991). Over time such resources and the way in which they are managed emerge in the form of organisational competencies or capabilities (essentially what the firm is good at doing)—enduring qualities of the organisation that confer competitive advantage.

A further extension of the study of capabilities, and one which is currently the subject of significant interest amongst academics, is the idea of 'dynamic' capabilities (first mentioned in Chapter 2). This perspective emerges initially and most comprehensively in the work of Teece et al. (1997) and is particularly relevant to our study of the music sector. The theory focuses on the ability of firms to develop new capabilities and competencies in more dynamic markets through organisational processes aimed at coordination and integration, learning and the reconfiguration of resources. Subsequent work in the field has provided a clearer understanding of the function of dynamic capabilities in high-velocity markets (Eisenhardt and Martin, 2000), the vital role of organisational learning (Zolo and Winter, 2002) and capabilities as 'best practice' (Eisenhardt and Martin, 2000).

A preliminary model devised by Teece (2007) outlines the most significant dynamic capabilities for companies going through periods of significant change in their environment. Teece points to three critical capabilities: **sensing** new opportunities and threats, focused on 'scanning, creation, learning and interpretive' activities (2007, p. 1322), **seizing** opportunities through the development of new products and services, and **managing threats / transforming**—essentially the ability to maintain ongoing change in the organisation in an attempt to address emergent threats and opportunities. This later point perhaps moves us as close as we may get to the idea of a genuinely 'dynamic' capability, as it implies a constant initiative to avoid the traps of path-dependent, historically conditioned thinking and engrained routines that may often accompany success in the marketplace.

We will draw on both the resource-based view and fit-based perspectives in our analysis of the music sector, and the major record companies in particular.

6.3 The industrialisation of music

The early history of the popular music sector is replete with technological innovations. Early efforts at the end of the 19th century produced music players like Edison's phonograph and graphophone, initially marketed to fairs and travelling shows as coin-operated novelty 'entertainment' machines. At the same time Emile Berliner was developing his own gramophone, played using wax disks, a combination he saw as more applicable to the user's home environment. His company (the United States Gramophone Company) would also go on to build the first dedicated commercial recording studio in 1897. Subsequent years saw both boom (the 1920s) and bust (the 1930s due to an economic slump) in the fortunes of the recorded music industry, but by 1950, the shape and function of the modern industry was largely established.

So, what did this shape look like?

For most of its history the popular music industry has been dominated by a relatively small number of large, global organisations, typically called the 'majors'. Before the emergence of streaming, five or six major record companies typically commanded over 80% of sales in the global popular music market, the other 20% being made up of sales by the far smaller 'independent' companies. Every year, sales would typically be dominated by the same set of large, global companies, usually including Polygram, BMG, EMI, Sony Music, Universal Music and Warner Music. The companies all stuck to a similar business model, driven by the sale of physical, analogue sound carriers (like vinyl disks or cassettes), which were relatively cheap to reproduce, and highly profitable once the break-even point was achieved.

Early on these organisations make two crucial discoveries. The first was that spending money on promotion and marketing tended to have a direct and relatively visible impact on sales—the bigger the marketing budget and spend, the more sales of packaged media could be expected. Secondly, once the demand for a song had been created through marketing, the demand had to be fulfilled, and ensuring the vinyl disk (and later cassette, CD etc.) was available in as many retail outlets as possible through significant distribution capabilities again maximised the chances of significant profits on their investment in an artist. Hence control of promotion, marketing and distribution emerged as the critical levers for strategic advantage, and the emergent record companies invested hugely in developing their marketing and physical distribution assets and capabilities. Again, we might characterise this as a distribution-based economy. The organisations that controlled distribution (in this case the distribution of physical sound carriers) were essentially gatekeepers for access to the popular music market. If a musician aspired to become a global star, and address a mass consumer market, they had to deal with the major record companies as the gateway to global audiences.

The profitability of this simple model, and the funds that record companies accumulated over time as a result, allowed the companies to embrace their other key role in the music sector, that of talent spotters and speculative investors. This role saw record companies scouring the music sector for new talent through the activities of what came to be known as the A&R (artists and repertoire) function, teams focused on finding and selecting artists and bands with potential and then investing in them, typically in the form of a recording contract. The recording contract itself essentially paid for the artist or band to record material, often in a record company-owned studio.

It's probably worth mentioning here that when an artist does record material, two distinct products emerge. Firstly, the master tape: the specific recording that the artist made. Because the record company typically paid for the recording, they own and control the copyright and the right (typically called 'mechanical right') to reproduce the music and duplicate and distribute the sound recording. It is this recording that then finds its way onto the sound carriers (e.g. CDs) that are distributed by the company.

The second key output is the underlying music itself: the melody and lyrics (often written down), which is typically owned by what is known as a publishing company (often a division of a major record company). The job of the publishing company is to take this underlying music score and exploit it, and this might be done by licensing it to another artist or band so that they might make a recording of it, or the music might be licensed for use in things like films, TV programmes and television commercials (a popular use for J- and K-pop content). Whilst artists do not have to align themselves with the publishing company associated with the record company (and increasingly today artists are setting up their own publishing companies), this was often the case, ultimately allowing the record and publishing company to own and control all of the outputs of a signed artist.

Hence record companies quickly established themselves as having two key roles in the industry, as talent spotters and developers and as distributors and marketers. These were both activities that required significant funds, so barriers to entry in the industry were high, allowing a relatively small number of companies to emerge, and remain globally dominant.

Having said that, the actual act of finding new talent did not need to be that expensive. Having a small team of staff visiting live music venues or trawling through 'demo' tapes sent in by aspiring artists does not require huge levels of funding. Hence small 'independent' record companies (e.g. Factory Records in the UK) could enter the market, focused on spotting new talent and developing it to some extent. Many often focused on specific genres (e.g. the hard rock label Neat) or audience groups and often claimed to have better relationships with the artists they signed, and closer relationships with the final consumer. However, they did not tend to have the resources to market and distribute content on a global scale and typically relied on the larger global record companies to provide these facilities. Hence an artist might first be spotted and developed by an independent record label, only to be handed over to one of the majors when it looked like their career might take off globally.

Analysis of the popular music value chain reveals another critical stakeholder in the market: the retailer. Record companies did not to sell directly to the consumer (other than in a very small way through mail-order record clubs—a tiny part of their business). Their product, the physical sound carrier, would be sold to a retailer, who would then sell the product to the final consumer. Hence the customer of the record company was NOT the music consumer, it was the retailer (and to some extent the artists themselves). For the publishing company the customer might be another artist or band (or more likely their management team), an advertising agency or TV company. In both cases, the organisations might have relatively little direct contact with the end consumer, something that would become critical during the digital revolution of the 1990s. Figure 6.1 outlines the broad structure of the recorded music value chain.

6.4 Riding waves of technology

New physical formats for sound carriers have been regularly introduced, each offering new functionality or enhanced quality. Vinyl (in various forms—e.g. 45s, long players) gave way to the tape format (again in various forms—e.g. reel-to-reel, eight-track, cassettes) and finally to the CD. At each point, this offered the chance for record companies to do two things. One, reach new audiences—e.g. the development of cassettes and hardware to play them like the Sony Walkman allowed record companies to reach the 'music on the move' consumer, and two, to re-sell their libraries of content to existing audiences. Having bought a song on vinyl, the consumer might buy it again on cassette to facilitate listening on the move, and yet again when the CD version was released, with the promise of far higher audio quality. At this point the record company might have already recovered its initial investment in an artist (the cost of recording the original music)—that is, they had reached the 'break-even' point, through sales of the existing format. Hence any sales on a new format would be highly profitable. Users replacing their existing music libraries with the same music on a new format proved highly lucrative for the record companies.

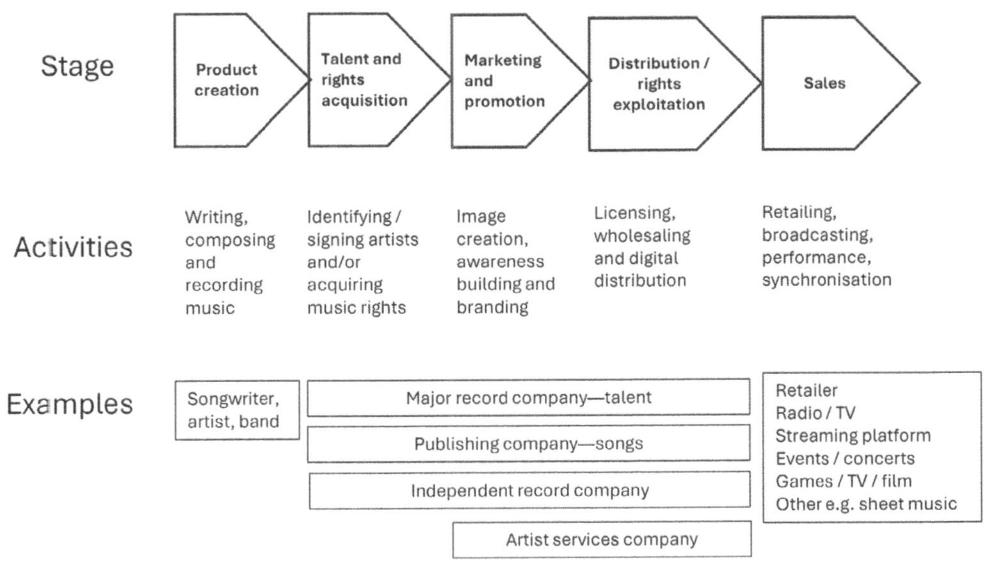

Figure 6.1 The popular music value chain
Source: author.

A critical point here is that up until the introduction of the CD, sound carriers were based on analogue technologies. Such analogue technologies had one major advantage: what might be called built-in copyright control. Let's delve into the mirky world of music piracy briefly at this point to explore the implications of this. Music piracy is essentially the illegal copying and distribution of music content. It is broadly divided into commercial and non-commercial piracy.

Commercial piracy is the large-scale copying and distribution of illegal copies of a piece of content for profit. Typically the province of criminal gangs, it had a built-in bottleneck: the need for expensive equipment. Having secured a copy of the original content, perhaps on a cassette tape, cassettes would need to be duplicated to a relatively high quality (requiring specialist high-volume duplication equipment), then cases would need to be produced, covers copied, blank cassettes would need to be bought, the final cassettes would need to be distributed, all the equipment would need manpower to run and maintain it, etc. Ultimately it was an expensive business, which limited its attractiveness even to criminal gangs, who could often find cheaper and quicker ways to turn an illegal profit.

The second form of piracy is what is called non-commercial. During the dominance of analogue formats this was considered far less threatening than commercial piracy. Essentially the illegal copying and sharing of content, but without a commercial imperative, it was not done for profit. It was often done between friends—songs could be copied onto cassette tapes and given to acquaintances for free. A particularly popular variation was the 'mix tape', a compilation of tracks from different artists, often curated by the 'pirate' for a boyfriend or girlfriend. Whilst essentially illegal (so-called 'fair use' legislation typically only allowed the production of a single copy of owned music as a 'backup'), and with the potential to limit the sales of a particular song, it again had a built-in bottleneck, in this case based on the analogue nature of the medium, as every time the cassette was copied, subsequent copies would decline in quality, introducing unwanted hiss and noise to the point where the copied track would be largely unrecognisable (see Figure 6.2).

The analogue nature of the formats, then, helped control the level of non-commercial piracy in the market. With the advent of digital formats, things were about to change dramatically, however.

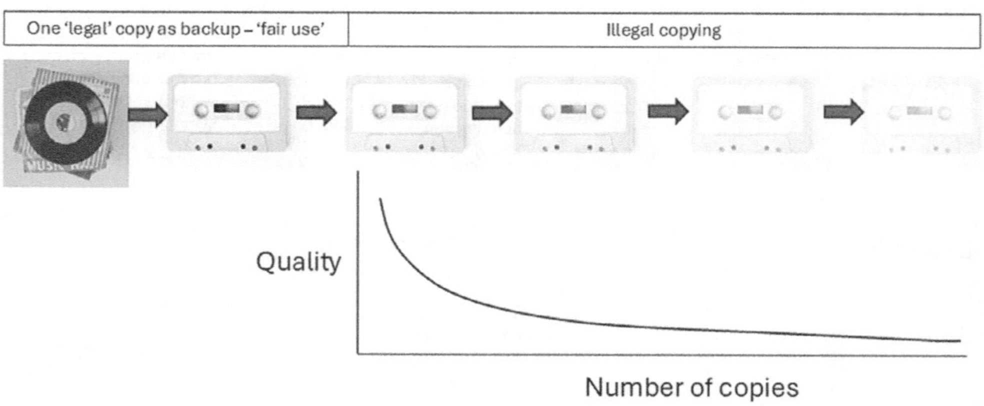

Figure 6.2 The analogue bottleneck: built-in self-destruct
Source: author.

6.4.1 The CD revolution: the perfect storm

The introduction of the CD digital format in 1982 by Philips and Sony would initially prove hugely valuable to the record companies. Within 10 years it had surpassed previous analogue formats (vinyl records and cassettes) as the dominant physical audio format. Consumers rushed to replace their existing music libraries, with higher-quality (and higher-cost) copies, and the turnover and profits of record companies exploded (see Figure 6.3).

Yet in the very characteristics of this new format lay the ingredients of a perfect storm that would radically reshape the industry, and plunge the major record companies into the biggest crisis they had ever faced. Four points are particularly critical. Firstly, in distributing CDs, it is important to realise that the record companies were distributing digitally perfect copies of the music content. This is not a problem, as long as consumers don't have a way to extract the digital copies from the CD, as was certainly the case when CDs were first launched. Unfortunately for the record companies, consumers would quickly find ways of doing exactly this.

So-called 'ripping' software quickly emerged, allowing consumers to copy songs from CDs, creating individual computer files from each song. Developed by technically literate consumers, and typically open source and often free, early examples of ripping software included EAC and CDex. Initially the province of technology 'geeks' and requiring a variety of different software working seamlessly together, programmes quickly proliferated, each easier to use than the last. But there was a further problem for our prospective digital pirate. Each file was huge, typically at least 40mb per song. A full CD might be 500–600mb in total size. Given the limited size of domestic PC hard disks and portable storage mediums (e.g. USB sticks, physical disks) at the time, this inevitably limited how much content could be ripped. Our pirate was even more limited in any attempt to distribute the ripped file. Domestic broadband networks were still a dream of the future, with many computer users relying on 56k modems to connect to the internet. Hence sending a copy of a single ripped music file to a friend would take most of a day. The record companies felt they could relax; piracy was still a challenging task.

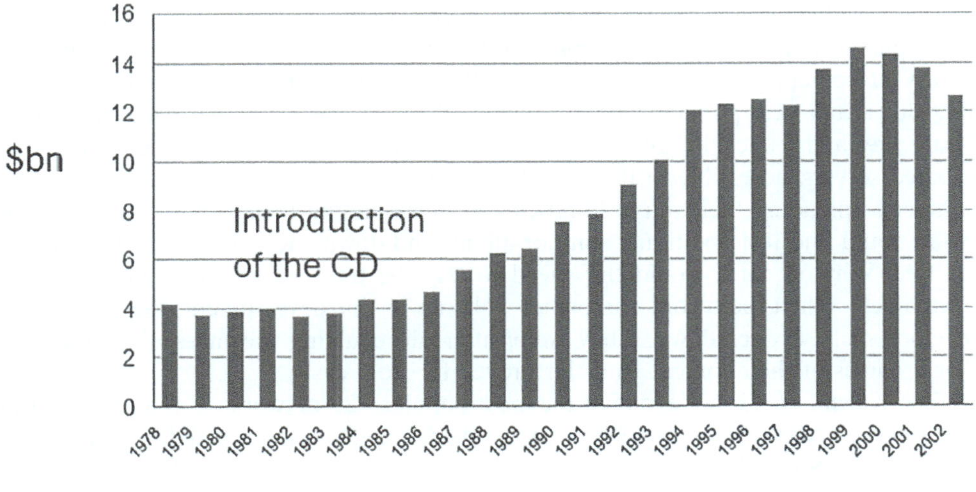

Figure 6.3 Recorded music industry revenues in the USA ($bn)
Source: RIAA Year-End Industry Shipment and Revenue Statistics, reports 1990–2003.

But again, the industry underestimated the ingenuity of the music consumer. The origin of this next development was unexpected. A young German PhD student, Karlheinz Brandenburg, was researching how people perceive recorded music. His subsequent postdoctoral work at AT&T Bell Labs and the Fraunhofer Institute for Integrated Circuits would lead to the development of a relatively small piece of coding that allowed digital music files to be compressed—that is, reduced in size—without fundamentally impacting the audio quality (at least to the human ear). It would eventually become the basis for MP3, a compression algorithm that could shrink the size of ripped files from 40mb to 4mb without dramatically affecting the perceived quality of the music. Quickly adopted by those same technically literate music consumers who had developed ripping software, the combination of ripping and compression software would start to solve some of the early problems of the potential digital music pirate. Tracks could now be copied from CD and compressed to a practical size, using relatively user-friendly and typically free software. Even in the limited world of 56k modems, sending a copy of a music file to a friend was suddenly a whole lot easier and quicker.

Here we should mention a critical point in the difference between analogue and digital formats. We have already noted that analogue formats have, to some degree, built-in copyright protection, in that as subsequent copies are made, quality tends to decrease, to the point where the music is unrecognisable, or at least fairly unpleasant to listen to. Critically, in a digital environment, this bottleneck disappears. Unlimited copies of a digital music file can be made, without any decline in quality. The consumer could send a copy to a friend, who would then send it to five other friends, who could then send it to 50 other friends, then on to 1000 more, and at no point does the quality of the copies deteriorate. 'Super-distribution', as it would be termed, held the potential to allow digitally perfect copies of a music file to be distributed as many times as the consumer wished.

Again, at the time, record companies appeared relatively relaxed. Non-commercial piracy of digital music remained the province of technically sophisticated fans, who found it difficult to distribute their pirated content over existing networks; super-distribution would hardly be an issue with an infrastructure based on 56k modems and without some form of enabling technology to share content on a mass scale.

Again, sadly for the record companies, events would rapidly overtake them. The emergence of online file-sharing hubs would provide a technological infrastructure and library of content through peer-to-peer (P2P)-based networks that proved difficult to shut down and very popular with consumers. Services like Napster, Kazaa, mp3.com, Pirate Bay and LimeWire allowed users to upload their library of music files to distributed servers, accessible to the rest of the fan population. And fans did so in large numbers, uploading their music libraries and downloading their new favourite tracks. A fan could find just about any song or album and download it in reasonable quality, for free. Why on earth would they need to buy the track or album from the record companies? When the record companies woke up to this development, they attempted to close such services down. They were, after all, enabling the mass distribution of illegal copies of their content. But this proved far from easy.

Take Kazaa, for example, one of the most popular P2P networks in the early part of the 1990s. It was owned by Sharman Networks, and incorporated in Vanuatu, an island in the South Pacific. The operation of the company was based in an office in Sydney, Australia, whilst employees were hired as contractors through another company, LEF Interactive. Their servers were initially located in Denmark, the software developers were believed to be based in the Netherlands and the original source code emerged from Estonia. The problem in terms of shutting them down? Where to send the sheriff. Lawsuits against Kazaa (or parts / affiliates thereof) had to be initiated in Estonia, Australia, Vanuatu, Denmark, Sweden, the Netherlands and the West Indies—a complex and expensive undertaking. And of course, if you shut them down in one territory, they could quickly set up in a new country, the distributed nature of the technology allowing relatively easy relocation of critical servers to keep the service live. Closing illegal file-sharing services proved far more taxing and time-consuming than had been assumed.

The final nail in the coffin for the record companies was the emergence of broadband networks, and their rapid rollout and adoption amongst consumers. Suddenly bandwidth limitations were less of an issue. It was easier than ever to upload and download content. Files that might have taken many hours to download via a 56k modem could now be acquired in minutes, or even (certainly today) seconds.

Here then we have all of the ingredients of a perfect storm for the major record companies. The mass distribution of digital masters of music via CD, the emergence of accessible and easy-to-use ripping and compression software, the appearance of file-sharing hubs that proved almost impossible to shut down, and finally the growth of consumer broadband networks. From being the least of their worries, the huge growth of non-commercial piracy amongst music fans emerged as the greatest threat that the record companies had ever faced.

6.4.2 How did the majors react?

For the major record companies, the emergence of digitised music file distribution over networks was initially ignored, then resisted, addressed very much as a threat rather than an opportunity. Their initial response involved various attempts to slow and ideally stop uncontrolled (that is, consumer-led) developments in digital distribution. Record companies, more specifically their publishing arms, did not license new, premium content to the growing number of legitimate (as in they charged for the content and remitted part of the revenue back to the music company) online services, licensing only older or more obscure artists or back catalogue. In turn this led to a lack of premium content which, perversely for the industry, further encouraged the spread of illegal file-sharing.

Significant time, management attention and resources were expended through institutions like the Secure Digital Music Initiative (SDMI) on developing new and enhanced copy protection formats for digital music files and CDs (e.g. Sony BMG's XCP—Extended Copy Protection system). At the same time, record companies attempted to relaunch the CD in the form of the SACD (Super Audio CD) in 1999, designed to offer even higher-quality audio and attract music fans back to physical sound carriers (arguably a classic case of over-serving the existing market, as highlighted by Bower and Christensen, 1999). Inevitably copy protection systems were quickly hacked (sometimes within days of their launch), SACD failed to develop into a significant market and customers continued to get premium content from file-sharers copying new CDs and posting the files on peer-to-peer sites such as Gnutella and Napster. Nothing, it appeared, could stop the growth of consumer-led digital distribution.

With this in mind, the next major response of the majors was to directly address the market with their own offerings, specifically by setting up their own online music file sales and distribution sites. Initially such sites were typically label- and company-specific and often combined with a wider range of company content—e.g. TV and film content, hence Sony's launch of Uville.com and Time Warner's Entertaindom. EMI, the only major record company without significant non-music content assets, sought to buy an existing service that it could control, acquiring a significant stake in new site Musicmaker.com. For others, the best strategy appeared to be cooperation, with Universal and BMG choosing to joint venture in the creation of Getmusic.com. Cooperative ventures proved increasingly popular (partly to ensure that a wide variety of music content was available from different labels), and in addition to Getmusic.com the majors would subsequently invest in further major online initiatives to serve music customers directly, MusicNet (a joint venture between Real Networks, Time Warner, BMG and EMI) and Duet (Sony and Vivendi Universal).

These early attempts to directly address the consumer market met with very limited success, most closing within three to five years of their debut and none returning significant profits to the host company. As has already been suggested, the record companies were not expert in dealing directly with music consumers (their direct customers had been the retailers) and services were often poorly designed and difficult to use, particularly when compared to the illegal file-sharing sites, which had been designed and developed by music fans, for music fans. More fundamentally, why would consumers visit a record label site and pay to download a file, when exactly the same file might be available on Napster or Pirate Bay for free?

Hence the next strategy adopted by the record majors was to cut. Cut prices and cut costs. The first step was to remove MAP (minimum advertised price) practices in the USA with a view to cutting the costs to consumers of packaged media. Universal Music followed this up with a decision in 2004 to cut its CD wholesale and recommended retail price by up to 30% in the hope that retailers would pass on price reductions to consumers and that they would be tempted back to the purchase of physical sound carriers. Unfortunately, the cut had limited success (other than cutting the profit margins available to the record companies themselves) because they also chose to cut volume discounts to retailers and cooperative promotional budgets, so little of the price cut was actually passed onto the consumer.

Finally, all of the majors went on major internal cost-cutting exercises. Universal Music cut 11% of its global workforce in 2003. Universal's competitors had already undergone painful cuts of their own. Sony Music Entertainment laid off 1000 people, or 10% of its global workforce in March 2003 and EMI had already eliminated about 1900 jobs, or about 19% of its total workforce, since late 2001. In all, nearly 8000 jobs, approximately one in five, disappeared from the six major record companies during the period 2000–2003.

The record companies' failed attempts to close file-sharing services, launch their own services or create new technical barriers to piracy left them with only two further options. Firstly, an emotional appeal directly to the consumers themselves. Record companies launched extensive PR and advertising campaigns to make the consumer feel guilty about what they were doing. Drawing on a wide range of artists, from Metallica to Madonna, music magazines were suddenly full of quotes from pop stars describing how the emerging wave of non-commercial piracy was literally stealing money from their pockets and devaluing their efforts to make music. Artists were encouraged to fight back against the pirates. Metallica (one of the highest-profile and most popular heavy metal bands of the period) initiated legal action against Napster after discovering that an unreleased track had been illegally uploaded to Napster and was circulating around various radio stations in the USA.[1] The band not only pursued $10m in damages, but provided Napster with a list of over 335,000 usernames of their own fans (indeed, some of their biggest fans) who had downloaded their songs, successfully petitioning to have their accounts blocked from the platform. Despite arguing that Napster's actions were morally and legally wrong, Metallica faced a significant backlash, as many consumers perceived the band's actions as an out-of-touch attack on their core fans rather than profit-orientated criminals.

When this failed to have any significant impact, the record companies turned to the courts, prosecuting individual users of file-sharing sites (having already tried to prosecute the site owners themselves, largely unsuccessfully) and deployed teams of lawyers to work on potential new legislation—e.g. the proposed 2005 Berman Bill, which would have further limited how consumers could use digital media and allowed new technology to be deployed to limit digital functionality.

Sadly, at least for the record companies, none of their initiatives worked, and non-commercial music piracy continued to spiral out of control. In many ways, the record companies went through two phases as file-sharing began to emerge. Initially, ignoring it, convincing themselves that it was not a significant threat and that it would eventually go away or come under their control. It did not. Their second approach was to try and kill it, put the MP3 genie back in its bottle and introduce as many barriers to file-sharing as possible.

What characterises all of these efforts is an apparent disregard for the emergence of digital file-based music as a major opportunity, and any assessment by the record majors of the new assets and capabilities they might need to take advantage of it and maintain their position in the value chain. The major record companies had limited experience of working together, yet they quickly joined forces to address the threat through the SDMI programme. But they had a tradition of being competitors, and arguably did not 'play well together', so they found it difficult to cooperate and agree on the right approach, slowing their decision making. This almost guaranteed an end to any prospect of a rapid and coordinated response to new market or technical developments. The majors had relatively little expertise in rapidly identifying and integrating new technologies into the core operation of their business. Individual major changes in technology could be accommodated (the move from vinyl to cassettes to CD) but the rapid identification, trialling and implementation of many new smaller technologies appeared beyond them. And finally, and perhaps most crucially, they all opted to launch consumer-facing propositions whilst lacking any significant competence in dealing directly with music consumers.

The natural constituencies of the record companies for most of their history were artists and music retailers; the end consumer was always at a distance. Arguably as a result the record companies' corporate and label brands were some of the least significant and powerful in attracting attention in the music sector. Whilst you might be a fan of Blackpink or BTS, do you know which record company label they are signed to? Probably not. Equally, music companies appeared to demonstrate fundamentally flawed views of the needs and wishes of online music consumers during this early, critical period. They saw them either as passively content to wait and eventually be led by whatever solution the majors decided upon, or as eagerly awaiting the opportunity to access legitimate music and therefore be willing to pay money, part with valuable personal information and, at least initially, endure endless technical headaches and usage restrictions to access the same content that was available elsewhere for free. The reality was very different as consumers rapidly went about redesigning their own value equation for music as one of unlimited choice, free access and flexible use.

Fundamentally, the record majors assumed that they could launch successful consumer services, without having built capabilities in understanding changing consumer usage of music and how technology was allowing consumers to establish their own terms for use, and their continued insistence on strict usage conditions and subscription-based models did much to alienate them from the early generation of online music users. Assuming that such competencies could be rapidly built, whilst mired in complex joint venture agreements with traditional competitors (e.g. the SDMI initiative) was clearly erroneous. By partnering with each other, rather than with well-developed consumer-facing organisations, they ensured their failure. None of the early customer-facing initiatives mentioned survived the end of the decade. Whilst they were investing heavily in ultimately unsuccessful ventures and anti-piracy technologies, prices were being cut on CDs to attract consumers back to physical media, significantly impacting the profitability of the physical media business model. It was, indeed, a perfect storm.

The implications of the major record companies' failure to properly address changes in their business environment and to build new assets and capabilities were clear for all to see. In 1999 there were six large, extremely profitable global record companies: Warner Music Group, EMI, Sony (known as CBS Records until January 1991, then known as Sony Music thereafter), BMG, Universal Music Group and Polygram. By 2004 there were five (with Polygram merging with Universal). By 2008 there were four, with BMG and Sony Music merging to create a single joint venture. By 2012, there were only three: Universal Music Group (having absorbed EMI's recorded music division), Sony Music Entertainment (BMG had been fully absorbed into Sony, which had then absorbed EMI's publishing division) and Warner Music (which picked up the remaining elements of EMI in July 2013). From six dominant, hugely profitable companies to three, struggling to attain any significant level of profitability.

Figure 6.3 showed the rapid growth of the music sector in the USA up to 2000 thanks to the launch and growth of the CD. Alternative data from the IFPI[2] suggests total global recorded music revenues of around $21bn in 2000, almost all (i.e. about 98%) of which was derived from the sale of physical sound carriers (with a very small proportion from performance and synchronisation rights). Subsequent years would be dire for the entire industry, with over a decade of constant declines in turnover and profit, reaching its lowest level in 2013–2014 with global revenues of only $12.8bn (IFPI Global Music Report 2025). According to the same data source, by 2024 total industry revenues had recovered to around $29.6bn, with streaming accounting for around 70% of that revenue and sales of physical sound carriers accounting for only 16%. Downloading (rather than streaming) accounted for around $880m in sales in 2024, having reached a peak between 2010 and 2015 with around $2.5bn in sales, but subsequently declining significantly with the rise of streaming. Performance and synchronisation rights exploitation and other revenues accounted for approximately $3bn in sales in 2024.

In many ways, the emergence of a new disruptive technology in the popular music sector in the form of digital music files is a lesson in how incumbent companies should not respond to environmental disruption, how a failure to adapt and 'fit' could be disastrous. The companies failed to anticipate the scale of the impact of new developments. As they became aware, they chose to ignore them, then put all of their efforts into stopping them through the law courts and technical solutions, alienating the most die-hard music fans, in some cases by putting them in prison.

As the value of their existing assets and capabilities (e.g. the global physical sound carrier distribution network they had built) continued to diminish, they failed to understand what new capabilities and assets might be required to flourish in the new environment (e.g. consumer relationship management). All of this in turn seemed to be wrapped up in a good degree of hubris and a feeling that 'it can't happen to us—we are too big and too powerful'. Hence, according to the theory of dynamic capabilities described earlier, they failed to sense the change, seize the commercial opportunity it presented and reconfigure their asset and capability base to suit the newly emergent environment. So, what might the major record companies have done differently?

Business theory tells us that organisations need robust planning systems, part of which should be an environmental scanning process whereby data is regularly collected on changes in the external environment (e.g. market changes, innovative technologies, competitor activity), which is then fed into the annual business planning process. The process typically includes reaching out to external stakeholders (e.g. suppliers, partners, customers, consultants) to assess their view of the changing environment. On a more regular basis, the organisation as a whole should be constantly monitoring its environment for changes—this should be part of everyone's job, and time should be allocated for this to happen. Arguably, the record companies failed in this regard.

A further challenge emerges, however, when changes are sensed. The information needs to move throughout the organisation to the relevant parties. But in many ways, the hierarchies that organisations are structured around are not that good at moving information around. They are often complex, with multiple levels and departments. Who needs the information? How do we get the information to the relevant person? This is particularly so when information is collected at the bottom of the organisation, by those, often at the lowest formal levels, who are closest to the market, who perhaps understand how it is changing better than anyone. The information needs to move rapidly up the organisation. In some ways hierarchies are structured so that the movement of information upwards is deliberately limited. Senior leaders do not want to be bothered by daily problems. Layers of staff are installed to deal with these problems before they get to the top. Hence information often stalls when it reaches middle levels as middle management attempt to deal with the problems themselves—after all, that's what they are paid for. This can lead to potentially critical issues and information being stuck at this middle level, with staff who have neither the resources nor the strategic perspective to properly deal with the issues. Perhaps the record companies might have benefitted from flatter organisational structures?

When changes are sensed, opportunities need to be identified. Arguably this is a question of the mindset of the organisation. Is it ready to change? Does it feel it really needs to? Or is it, like the record companies, being forced to consider walking away from a position in the market and a business model that had proved hugely successful and profitable for it in the past? Successful companies find it hard to change and will typically resist it with all their might. This is exactly how the record companies responded. The senior management who had built their very successful (and lucrative) careers based on their command of a specific business model and market structure did all they could to protect that historical position, and hence saw digital file distribution almost exclusively as a threat to the old order, rather than an opportunity to be exploited. All of their time and effort went into shutting down digital distribution, rather than building the appropriate resources and capabilities to exploit it.

And what might those assets and capabilities be? How should the companies have reconfigured their operation to take advantage of this disruptive but potentially lucrative opportunity? Perhaps the first and most significant issue was to realise that the huge investments they had made in creating physical distribution networks would become less and less valuable in the new environment. Equally, with developments like the set-top box and the internet the promotional platforms they had utilised in the past would become far more powerful. As well as being shop windows, they could become shops and were likely to take the opportunity to benefit from the attention that music content could create by generating and selling music content themselves. Equally, in an environment of ever more content, and ways to consume music, promotional platforms that could command audience attention and direct their focus and interest would become even more powerful.

Certainly, the record companies might have started to develop their capabilities in building direct relationships with consumers, perhaps through partnerships and alliances with consumer-facing brands, or consumer-facing promotional platforms (e.g. television). They needed to develop skills in collecting, managing and using consumer data. Identifying where revenue might be generated in the future would be crucial—less in the sales of physical sound carriers and more through developing and curating relationships with consumers (perhaps via subscription models) and monetising the attention that music can generate. They certainly needed to protect their position as 'the best way for musicians to make it', through alliances with emergent organisations like Live Nation. They needed to strengthen their control over key brands and exploit every relevant revenue-generating opportunity (which they did to some extent through the development of 360-degree deals—see section 6.6).

Ultimately, they were largely unsuccessful in most of these initiatives and paid the price of nearly 20 years of decline and disruption.

6.4.3 The emergent industry and a new business model

Whilst the major incumbent companies in the music sector spent all their time and resources in dealing with what they saw as a threat, trying to kill file-based music distribution, other companies embraced the huge opportunity to redefine the shape, structure and operation of the popular music sector.

Initially, the focus was on digital downloads. Emulating the 'buy to own' model of physical sound carriers, legitimate sites emerged selling file-based copies of music tracks for download. Some of these were the previously illegal sites, as they attempted to develop a legitimate position in the new value chain. Hence Napster, once the scourge of the record companies, and having been shut down in 2001, relaunched itself as a legitimate downloading site, and quickly thereafter as a subscription-based service, but struggled to gain content licences from the inevitably suspicious record companies and publishers. Without major record label support, Napster's fate was settled, and it went bankrupt in 2002. The name and brand were subsequently traded to a variety of companies (Roxio, Best Buy, Melody VR and finally Infinite Reality in 2025) but ultimately it has failed to re-acquire its formerly significant position in the post-CD music sector.

Other new companies proved to be more successful. Apple, facing increasing pressure in the business-to-business computer sector that it had built its early success on, had decided to pivot to more consumer-focused businesses. Having considered a variety of options (including digital cameras and gaming consoles), they opted for the music sector, as Steve Jobs noted at the time: 'We did iTunes because we all love music.'[3]

Apple would launch the iPod in 2001 (an idea that was first presented to Philips Electronics by its then chief technology officer Tony Faddel, though they passed on the idea, leading him to join Apple), followed by the iTunes Store in 2003 selling songs and albums; indeed, it was the only legal digital catalogue of music to offer songs from all of the major record labels at the time. Again, the initial model was download to own, rather than streaming (which would only be launched via Apply Music in 2015). The downloaded content could only be played via the iTunes application or on the iPod. Given its ability to offer content from all of the major record labels, iTunes quickly became the largest music vendor in the USA (by 2008) and by 2010, at least according to its own figures, it was the largest music vendor in the world.[4]

Whilst Apple focused its efforts on a 'downloading to own' model, other companies were beginning to establish streaming and the subscription model as a viable alternative. Founded in 2006 and launched commercially in some European territories in 2009 (before being launched in the USA in 2011), Spotify adopted a streaming model, based on monthly subscriptions, combined with an advertising-based freemium model with access to a basic service freely available to users but with some associated usage restrictions—e.g. no access to content in offline mode. The paid subscription tier allowed users to access content without advertising or usage restrictions. This was a radical change to previous music business models, as at no point did the consumer 'own' the content; rather, they essentially rented it. Consumers only have access to content whilst they pay the monthly subscription fee. Once they stop paying and their subscription ends, no matter how many months they have paid for, they can no longer access any content (other than through the freemium tier, which often limits the use of playlists). Interestingly in 2009 Spotify itself introduced a downloading option, though this option was then removed in 2013.

Inevitably Spotify began with relatively inexpensive subscription fees in order to attract as many users as possible. But as a result, it would only achieve profitability in 2024, with a net profit of $1.1bn based on revenues of $15.7bn. Despite this, a significant number of companies were attracted into the streaming sector: Saavn in India in 2007 (now JioSaavn since its merger with Jio in 2018), Google (Google Play Music launched in 2013), Tidal (2015), YouTube Music (2015), a variety of offerings from China's Tencent Music Entertainment Group (including QQ Music, KuGou and WeSing) and Amazon Music (launched in 2016). Streaming has generally been viewed as the saviour of the popular music industry, helping it recover from the post-CD slump, and overtaking physical sound carrier sales in 2019.

To some degree, we have returned to the relative equilibrium of the pre-streaming industry, with a small number of very different large companies dominating a global music market. Yet significant if subtle changes have been wrought by the move to a streaming-based music economy, many of which are the subject of current academic research, outlined in section 6.5.

6.5 Emerging themes and academic research

Significant debate has emerged around how streaming has affected the way in which content creators are remunerated in the new digital music economy. Commentators and indeed artists have been busy making their voices heard in the press and media, complaining about the unfairness and opacity of the emerging model and the very low rates of pay that they receive when their content is streamed. Some artists have gone as far as removing their content from selected sites in protest (e.g. the removal of the album *Atoms for Peace* by Radiohead's Thom Yorke from Spotify in 2013). Academics have been exploring this issue for some time (see Sinnreich, 2016; Marshall, 2015; and more recently Hesmondhalgh, 2021). Particular attention is paid to the low per-stream rates that artists secure from the main streaming sites. Figures such as $0.00331 per stream paid by Spotify, or $0.00495 per stream paid by iTunes, are regularly mentioned as illustrating how even in this new economy, artists are still being exploited by large corporations (indeed with such figures the current system seems even more exploitative than life in the days of CDs).

The picture is rather more complex than that, however, with the calculation of revenues due to any specific artist for any specific track being rather more intricate and involved, with total payouts to artists having only a limited amount to do with the much-discussed per-stream rates and much more to do with bargaining positions and brand power. Certainly, the data is complex and often highly confidential and commercially sensitive. Detailed evidence that might be used to compare the streaming environment to the physical media environment (and hence whether things have generally got better or worse for artists and content creators) is difficult to come by and hotly debated, but a balanced view of the debate can be found in the Hesmondhalgh (2021) paper mentioned earlier, for those interested in the issue and particularly for those aspiring performers who want to work out how they might be remunerated by the major streaming platforms. Research will continue in the area, artists will probably continue to complain, the streaming platforms themselves will continue to bemoan the huge amount of their revenue (typically estimated at around 70%) that is remitted back to rights holders. Perhaps the only hope for some resolution is a greater level of clarity and publicity in how such calculations are made by all parties.

A second major stream of research focuses on how consumer attitudes to consuming music have changed as a result of the emergence of streaming. Whilst a significant amount of attention is paid to things like the decline in album sales compared to the growth in popularity of single tracks, perhaps more significant is the issue of consumers' attitudes to the value of music itself, particularly that the move from physical sound carriers to digital files and streaming has somehow affected consumers' feelings of ownership and indeed the very relationship they have with music (see for example Bartmanski and Woodward, 2015). Whilst there are antecedents for a non-ownership model (e.g. music has been distributed by radio and television, lent via libraries), packaged media, for most of its history, had been distributed to consumers based on an ownership model (in the same way we might own a watch, a piece of furniture or domestic appliance). Streaming has changed this model, leading to what some commentators (e.g. Belk, 1988, 2014) have called 'a post-ownership economy' and a dematerialisation of music (Sinclair and Tinson, 2017).

Research into the psychology of ownership (see the aforementioned Sinclair and Tinson, 2017 paper) suggests that consumers can have a sense of ownership for even immaterial objects and services like streaming, a feeling of ownership that contributes to an enhanced sense of self identity. Why is this important? Jussila et al. (2015) argue that a sense of psychological ownership can lead to very significant business outcomes, including greater levels of consumer loyalty, enhanced feelings of satisfaction and higher levels of word-of-mouth promotion.

Initial research in the area during the period when downloading of songs as discrete music files dominated, suggested great similarities between the previous ownership model and the emergent downloading environment in terms of consumer attitudes. Subsequent research, into the increasingly dominant streaming market (where no file is necessarily downloaded to a device, though this is possible to enable offline listening, a service typically offered in higher-cost tiers by providers), does indicate that even in a dematerialised environment consumers do develop a sense of ownership with the music they consume via streaming services thanks to functionality that enables high levels of 'control, choice, mobility and the manipulability of music streaming applications' and the consumer's ability to share music and interact across social media platforms (Sinclair and Tinson, 2017, p. 7). Whilst significant further research is required before we have any definitive sense of whether streaming is fundamentally affecting how consumers view the value of the music they consume, early research would suggest that consumers still have a very intimate, emotional and significant relationship with streamed music and are still using it as a way to help define and announce their sense of self identity, even if that is within a business model that does not allow the consumer to legally own the music they consume at any point.

A third issue, piracy, perhaps inevitably, remains a critical issue for the industry and focus of research by academics. As we have seen, non-commercial piracy by consumers emerged as perhaps the most disruptive element of the move away from physical sound carriers to file downloading in the 1990s and 2000s. To some extent, streaming was seen as the solution to the situation as for most streaming consumers, at least in theory, they would never actually have access to a digital file that they could pirate. Equally, with low subscription fees for many services at launch, why would the consumer even need to pirate—by paying a small fee they had access to a 'jukebox in the sky', that gave them as much content as they could consume, whenever they liked, on just about any network-enabled device.

But piracy has continued, though in a rather different form; indeed to some extent the way in which streaming is often sold (the freemium model, where the service is available for free as a basic tier, but with significant usage and access limitations) has for some academics encouraged a resurgence of piracy. Freemium streaming services have been characterised for consumers 'as a means of discovering…new track releases, and thereafter [they] acquire these tracks illegally' (Borja and Dieringer, 2016, p. 86). According to research in 2018, over a third of music consumers still committed acts of music piracy, and between 2016 and 2019 piracy through the method of stream-ripping saw a 1400% growth, making it one of the most widespread forms of music piracy today.[5]

Rather than the overwhelming focus on illegal copying and sharing of individual music files that characterised the 'Napster' era, studies of piracy have advanced to focus on how the streams themselves might be recorded, copied and distributed. Stream-ripping can be defined as 'the process of obtaining a persistent copy of streamed content without permission, and therefore illegally, from third party streaming services' (PRS for Music, 2020[6], p. 7). This process typically involves downloading or extracting audio or video content from streaming platforms without permission, using software such as YouTube-DL.[7] Permanent copies of audio and visual content can be recorded: in the case of audio content, typically in the form of MP3 files, which are then usable by the 'pirate', even after their subscription to the service is cancelled. Equally such content can be easily shared with other, non-subscribers. Research by Incopro and Kantar Media identified YouTube as the leading source of content for stream-ripping, followed by Spotify, SoundCloud and Deezer.[8] By 2020, Johnson[9] suggests that 23% of internet users globally had accessed illegal stream-ripping websites.

A second major form of piracy has emerged (in the music and television / film sectors) through password-sharing; indeed, this appears to be the current focus of attention for providers in addressing the growing volume of content piracy. Broadly defined as 'sharing login credentials with other people so they also have access to your account'[10], password-sharing is often regarded as something of a 'grey area' in digital music consumption, partly because it is credited with helping the streaming industry's initial explosive growth (Jackson, 2022)[11] by some commentators.

Indeed, password-sharing's classification as a criminal offence 'will probably come as quite a shock to most people', particularly given how normal the practice has become (Jackson, 2022). Despite popular streaming platforms like Spotify explicitly prohibiting password-sharing in their terms and conditions (Spotify, 2024), the platforms' enforcement attempts, to date at least, have been relatively minimal. Whether motivated by peer pressure, economic factors or the lack of perceived punishment methods (i.e. there are few perceived consequences), piracy continues to be a challenge to the industry in maximising its returns on investment in content creation. Certainty new anti-piracy technologies and regulation will be introduced, but if we have learnt anything from the previous decades, it is that consumers can be highly resourceful and innovative when faced with a new challenge to overcome.

Two further issues emerge from our examination of the implications of the emerging streaming economy for organisations in the sector.

We have already seen a variety of new organisations emerging as powerful actors in the new music value chain, particularly streaming platforms which are often backed up by major technology companies (e.g. Apple, Tencent). But even in terms of the core activities of the major record companies, new competitors are emerging. So-called 'artists services' companies are now offering their facilities directly to artists. Companies such as CD Baby, TuneCore, Too Lost and AWAL have deconstructed the role of the record company into its constituent parts, offering marketing, distribution, reproduction and publishing services to order. Rather than relying on an all-inclusive and -encompassing 'record deal' from a major label, artists can now contract with individual companies for the specific service they require. Need help promoting your new band, need your latest recording replicated on CD and distributed, need help developing your career, need access to a digital distribution platform, there are now a range of companies willing to offer their services on a contract-by-contract basis and ultimately the artist only pays for what they need. Whilst this probably does require more effort and organisational skill on behalf of the artist, it certainly fits with an emerging view of the modern music artists as rather more business savvy and organised than artists in previous years, actively managing their own brand and business and drawing on a range of facilities and suppliers as and when they are needed. Will the major record company disappear as a result? Probably not—they are highly experienced in these areas, after all—but the emergence of such alternatives does help to weaken the record company's previous position as 'the only place to go' if you want a successful long-term musical career.

The final and potentially most significant issue we will cover in this chapter is the increasing importance of the live music sector.

6.6 The live music sector

For most of its long history, artists in the music sector have distributed their content and derived their primary income through live performance. Indeed, before the development of music stored on packaged media (initially wax cylinders, then vinyl, cassettes etc.) and radio in the 20th century, it was the only way in which artists might develop an audience and hence a career. With the emerge of new distribution methods (e.g. packaged media), the role of the live performance in the popular music sector began to change. Rather than an end in itself it was increasingly seen by the emerging industry as a means to an end—that is, as a promotional tool to sell packaged media.

Live tours, then, were essentially a marketing initiative and, in most cases, a marketing cost. Tours were an expensive business and there was little prospect of a significant profit being made based on ticket sales and merchandising. What would be expected was a consequent rise in package media sales during and after a tour. Hence with the recording of a new single or album, artists were expected to tour, playing at a series of live events wherein the new content would be exhibited to potential packaged media consumers.

The major record companies themselves were only involved to a limited extent in the tours. Typically, they would be called on by the artist and their management to advance money for touring expenses (perhaps hiring additional musicians, booking hotel rooms, securing transportation, paying for food and drinks etc.), an advance that would be ultimately repaid to the record company by the artist. They might also provide a tour manager to deal with the band and touring logistics. Well-organised record companies might also be involved in supporting local promotion for the tour itself, arranging appearances by the artist on local radio and TV, or in local music retail stores. But rarely were such investments seen as a source of significant potential profits for the record companies, other than through their effects on the sales of physical sound carriers.

Hence tours were largely considered a promotional expense, and direct touring profits (a rare thing indeed at the time) were arguably less important than potential increases in the profile and fan base for the artist, to be monetised by increased package media sales. Often modest sales of merchandising tended to be the province of the artist, their management and the other organisations involved in delivering the tour.

The live tour introduces a range of new actors and organisations into our consideration of the major elements of the popular music value chain (see Figure 6.4).

Artists' managers tend to be in overall charge of an artist's career (aided typically by the A&R team from a record company), and their primary role is as a coordinator between the various organisations involved with the artist—record company, music publisher, agent, promoter and potentially even corporate sponsor. **The agent** is typically more focused on the artist's live career, helping to arrange and organise tours. Hence, they are likely to be involved in planning the tour (how many concerts, where, and when they are played), potentially arranging logistics, helping identify venues, arranging contracts and budgeting the tour, often focused on a specific territory.

Promoters are perhaps the most critical element of the live music value chain after artists and consumers. Promoters are involved in securing appropriate venues, scheduling the tour, detailed logistics and budgeting. They will also typically be onsite

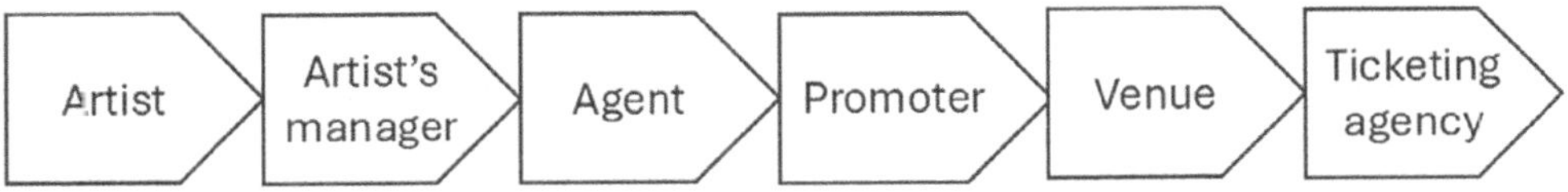

Figure 6.4 The live music value chain
Source: author.

through preparations for a performance and the performance itself, solving last-minute problems. As their name implies, they tend to particularly heavily involved in the promotion and marketing of the event. In many ways, then, given their responsibly for hiring venues (concert halls, arenas) and taking on the burden of promoting the event, they are the major risk-takers in the live music value chain. They must fund the initial investment in the tour and take on the majority of financial risk. Hence promoters need significant financial resources (or indeed a range of potential sponsorship deals) to support their activities. Live Nation has emerged as one of the most powerful tour promoters in the world. Despite the challenges of COVID, their revenue in 2024 was $23.16bn, they employed over 16,000 staff and provided their services to over 50,000 events. A large company, then, with very significant resources.

Significantly, Live Nation has consolidated the industry vertically. It now owns and operates venues and has stakes in critical music festivals (e.g. Brazil's Rock in Rio festival). In 2009 it merged with Ticketmaster, one of the largest ticketing firms in the world. It is also increasingly seen as a viable alternative in helping to manage and support an artist's career (through its Live Nation Concerts division), hence taking on elements of what an artist's manager, agent and record company might usually be expected to fulfil.

From being considered largely a cost to be endured, the tour and the live music sector generally has become the fastest-growing part of the music industry in terms of revenues. This shift was inevitably compounded by the growth of content piracy in the CD era, and the effects of this piracy on the pricing of packaged media, with retail prices being regularly cut to attract digital 'pirates' back to the legitimate purchase of physical sound carriers. This meant that packaged media was no longer the source of super profits it had been for the record industry in the past. Live music became the sector that might compensate for these declines in profit.

This became particularly so as the music merchandising market, again traditionally a sector driven by live events and touring, began to explode. By 2023 it had reached $13.4bn (Billboard), with estimates suggesting it might reach over $16bn by 2030 (MIDiA Research). Hence estimates of the total size of the live music market suggest an attractive market, with strong growth potential. Estimates suggest a total market value of $38.6bn in 2025 (including ticket sales, sponsorship and merchandising, licensing fees for live TV broadcasts and streaming events), expected to grow to over $63bn by 2034.[12]

Individual tours can generate significant returns. Taylor Swift's 2024–2025 Eras Tour generated over $2.1bn in ticket sales, and $200m in merchandising sales[13], playing to over 10m spectators in 149 concerts across five continents. On a slightly smaller scale, Elton John's Farewell Yellow Brick Road tour generated $939m, and U2's 360° tour generated ticket sales of $768m.[14]

Individual sectors of the live events market have seen particular growth. The festivals market, for example, has grown significantly, reaching a value of around $3bn in 2025 and forecast to witness huge growth to $24bn by 2033.[15] An increased number of events and level of diversity in the festival sector (with festivals for individual musical genres and differing consumer segments—e.g. older fans, families), combined with the growth of music tourism, and increased revenues from the provision of diverse services (art, food, wellness activities and luxury accommodation) has combined to propel festivals forward as a critical part of the live music sector.

Festivals are increasingly focused on regional artists and musical genres, often celebrating a particular area or region's cultural heritage—e.g. festivals like IMP's (an India-based social networking community) X-Festival help to highlight homegrown and local talent like Indian Ocean and Agnee. IMP intend to roll out the festival to other major cities across India to spotlight talent in each city. This focus on local content has in turn helped to build the demand for music tourism. The music tourism sector, with attendees often travelling long distances to attend festivals such as the UK's Glastonbury or Coachella in the USA, was estimated to be worth $7.8bn in 2025, growing to $14bn by 2032.[16] The success of major festivals has encouraged smaller cities and countries to host their own festivals, often promoting the rich cultural heritage of the location more generally (e.g. the Paleo Festival in Switzerland, or the Sziget event in Hungary). Such festivals can provide a huge boost to local tourism, with attendees often planning longer holidays in the region around the events themselves.

Sponsorship has played a particularly significant role in the growth of the festival market, significantly outpacing growth in ticket or ancillary revenues. Indeed, according to some research, sponsorship will typically generate up to 70% of revenues for festival organisers.[17] From retail banks to major cosmetic companies, footwear brands, electronic games publishers, soft (and hard) drinks companies and consumer electronics companies, all are queuing up to find the right festival to sponsor, potentially allowing them to deepen their relationship with their consumers.

Perhaps inevitably, then, the record companies have turned their attention to the live music sector with a level of scrutiny they had not in previous years. As suggested earlier, the live tour has not been the core province of the record company in terms of profits, focused as they were on packaged media sales. Hence record companies might be involved in advancing touring support funds, but the role of the tour was ultimately promotional, rather than direct profit generation. Today, however, things have changed.

With the growth of live music compared to sales of packaged content, record companies decided they needed to get more involved. What are typically called 360-degree deals began to emerge in the 1990s. Under this arrangement, the record company is involved in all aspects of the artist's career and can hope to benefit from all resultant revenue streams, taking a share of touring revenues, merchandising sales, image rights and of course packaged media and streaming sales. Artists including Korn, Robbie Williams and Jay-Z have struck such deals with their record companies. Universal Music, Taylor Swift's record label, secured a deal wherein they too benefitted from a portion of the merchandising revenues generated from her tour.

Interestingly, similar style deals are also increasingly common in deals with major promoters like Live Nation. Artists (including Madonna and U2) have concluded deals with them that include a share of merchandising revenues to be shared between the artist and promoter. Madonna also included a share of potential record sales in return for an advance on the recording of three new albums and a share of licensing fees in her deal with Live Nation. To an extent, then, Live Nation is taking on an increasing number of the roles and responsibilities provided by record companies in previous decades.

All major record companies today tend to want to sign 360-degree deals with their artists, and the logic is clear. The recorded content they fund the production of is a critical part of building the artist's brand, and the record companies, in the context of declining profits from the sale of content via packaged media and streaming, want to benefit from all of the revenue that brand might generate. Whilst the prevalence of the 360 deal is likely to remain, the interesting question for the record companies is whether artists are willing to continue to strike such deals with them, or if they prefer to sign such arrangements, given the growing importance of live revenues, with increasingly powerful promoters (or even ultimately the major brands that sponsor tours and festivals).

Of course, not every part of the live music scene has grown to the same extent as that of festivals and arena tours. Indeed, some sectors have seen significant challenges and resultant declines. Perhaps the most significant for emerging artists has been the decline in small venues. Small venues, including clubs and bars, are traditionally where emerging artists learn their performance skills. Not only honing their musical 'chops', they learn the importance of audience interaction. They have often been the venues where A&R representatives are sent to discover the 'next big thing', whether it be Coldplay performing in a small London pub called the Laurel Tree, or Oasis at the Joiners Pub in Southampton (with tickets priced at £3). Hence, they have played a vital part in the popular music value chain. But with rising rents, utilities costs, staff costs and insurance premiums, the prospects for small venues have been under threat for some time and, for many, COVID was the final nail in the coffin, forcing them to completely shut down for long periods. Many did not re-open. The economic downturn sparked by the COVID pandemic has also prompted music fans to become more selective in how they spend their leisure funds, in general preferring to opt for attending a smaller number of large-scale events, instead of more regular attendance at their local club or bar (Economics Observatory, 2025).

The UK's MVT (Music Venue Trust) estimates that 35% of smaller venues (often termed 'grassroots' venues) have closed over the last 20 years in the UK, with an average of two venues per week leaving the industry in 2023. Some venues find it easier to stop hosting live events, some to sell up completely, with many being converted to residential accommodation or food and drink outlets. In some cases, the building of residential housing in local areas surrounding venues has led local residents to complain about noise levels, leading local councils to limit the granting of live music licences or imposing early curfews on loud music. Similar trends have been noticed in major cities throughout the world.

Without such venues it is argued that it will be harder than ever for new talent to emerge. Learning to perform in front of a web camera is not the same as standing eye to eye with an expectant audience hoping to be impressed. Without a pipeline of new talent, who can perform at live events as well as in the studio, the future of the popular music industry looks challenging. We return to this issue when we discuss the use of digital avatars at live events in Chapter 9.

6.7 Conclusions

The popular music sector, then, has witnessed profound changes in the last 30 years. From being one of the most consistently profitable sectors of the cultural industries, to one that shrank in size for nearly 20 years, forcing major changes in its power structure and ecosystem, it is in many ways a lesson in how large, successful incumbent companies can struggle to adapt to changes in their environment. Again, we see an industry in which control of distribution (in this case the physical distribution of sound carriers) allowed a small number of large firms to become dominant. However, the value of physical distribution infrastructures has diminished, and we are now in an environment in which it is easier and easier to get distribution, but harder and harder to attract audience attention to your specific piece of content.

Success can be a powerful deterrent to change, as organisations cling on to business structures and business models that have allowed them to become profitable and powerful in the past. Perhaps more than any other sector, this proved to be the case for the major record labels, who struggled to adapt to their changing business environment, allowing other firms to emerge and develop their own successful business models and change the 'rules of the game'.

We have also seen how much influence technology can have in disrupting a previously stable and profitable business model and ecosystem. Technology continues to disrupt the industry in a variety of ways, with AI potentially redrawing the boundaries between artist and fan in the future. We will return to the sector and explore how technology may affect its evolution over the coming decades, in Chapter 9.

6.8 Activities

- You are working for a major record company and have been asked to develop a new idea for a product / service to generate revenues. What is it? Think about exploiting the attention that music generates, rather than the music itself.
- Take your favourite artist. What record label are they signed to? What publishing company? Are they signed to different companies in different regions? Do they have deals with other types of company (artist services, promoters etc.)? Have they struck 360-degree deals?
- Read David Byrne's outstanding book *How Music Works*, 2013, Canongate Books. Byrne was the frontman of *Talking Heads*, before developing his solo career. From a performer's perspective, how have their lives changed in the last 20 years?

Notes

1 West, T. 2025. Metallica and Napster—were they right all along? Crunch. https://www.crunch.co.uk/knowledge/article/were-metallica-right-napster.
2 IFPI Global Music Report 2025.
3 Interview with Steve Jobs, 2008, *Fortune*, March 7.
4 iTunes Store Tops 10 billion Songs Sold (Press release). Apple Inc., February 25, 2010.
5 Walraven-Freeling, M. 2021. The value of piracy: Future back thinking, MUSIC x. https://www.musicxtechxfuture.com/2021/04/07/the-value-of-piracy-future-back-thinking/ (Accessed: February 3, 2025).
6 https://www.prsformusic.com/-/media/files/prs-for-music/research/full-stream-ripping-research-report-2020.pdf (Accessed: May 2, 2025).
7 Bayley, J. 2023. Record companies in Germany take successful action against hosting provider of stream ripping software, YouTube-DL, IFPI. Available at: https://www.ifpi.org/record-companies-in-germany-take-successful-action-against-hosting-provider-of-stream-ripping-software-youtube-dl/ (Accessed: May 2, 2025).
8 Awbi, A. 2017. In focus: Stream-ripping, PRS for Music: royalties, music copyright and licensing. Available at: https://www.prsformusic.com/m-magazine/features/focus-stream-ripping (Accessed: May 8, 2025).
9 Johnson, A. 2020. 22 years after the DMCA, online piracy is still a widespread problem. RSS. Available at: https://itif.org/publications/2020/02/07/22-years-after-dmca-online-piracy-still-widespread-problem/ (Accessed: May 8, 2025).
10 Trevino, A., Guccione, D. and Cutler, A. 2023. What is password sharing? Keeper Security Blog—Cybersecurity News & Product Updates. Available at: https://www.keepersecurity.com/blog/2023/04/24/what-is-password-sharing/ (Accessed: May 9, 2025).
11 Jackson, M. 2022. UK gov says password sharing on streaming services is illegal Update2. ISPreview UK. Available at: https://www.ispreview.co.uk/index.php/2022/12/uk-gov-says-password-sharing-on-streaming-services-is-illegal.html (Accessed: May 9, 2025).
12 Dataintelo research, 2025.

13 Pollstar, 2025.
14 Ibid.
15 The Business Research Company, 2024.
16 Coherent Marketing Insights, 2025.
17 Cognitive Market Research, 2025.

References

Barney, J. 1991. Firm resources and sustained competitive advantage. *Journal of Management*, 17 (1), pp. 99–120.

Bartmanski, D. and Woodward, I. 2015. *Vinyl: The Analogue Record in the Digital Age*. Bloomsbury Publishing.

Belk, R. 1988. Possessions and the extended self. *Journal of Consumer Research*, 15 (1), pp. 139–168.

Belk, R. 2014. You are what you can access: Sharing and collaborative consumption online. *Journal of Business Research*, 67, pp. 1595–1600.

Borja, K. and Dieringer, S. 2016. Streaming or stealing? The complementary features between music streaming and music piracy. *Journal of Retailing and Consumer Services*, 32, pp. 86–95.

Bower, J. L. and Christensen, C. M. 1999. *Disruptive Technologies: Catching the Wave. The Entrepreneurial Venture: Selected Readings*. Harvard Business School Press, pp. 506–520.

Conner, K. R. and Prahalad, C. K. 1996. A resource-based theory of the firm: Knowledge vs. opportunism. *Organization Science*, 7, pp. 477–501.

Eisenhardt, K. M. and Martin, J. A. 2000. Dynamic capabilities: What are they? *Strategic Management Journal*, 21 (10/11), pp. 1105–1121.

Hesmondhalgh, D. 2021. Is music streaming bad for musicians? Problems of evidence and argument. *New Media & Society*, 23 (12), pp. 3593–3615.

Jussila, L., Tarkiainen, A., Sarstedt, M. and Hair, J. F. 2015. Individual psychological ownership: Concepts, evidence and implications for research in marketing. *Journal of Marketing Theory and Practice*, 23 (2), pp. 121–139.

Marshall, L. 2015. Let's keep music special. F—Spotify: On-demand streaming and the controversy over artist royalties. *Creative Industries Journal*, 8 (2), pp. 177–189.

Nelson, R. R. 1991. Why do firms differ, and does it matter? *Strategic Management Journal*, 12 (52), pp. 61–74.

Penrose, E. 1959. *The Theory of the Growth of the Firm*. Oxford: Basil Blackwell.

Porter, M. 1979. How competitive forces shape strategy. *Harvard Business Review*, 57 (2).

Schumpeter, J. A. 1934(2008). *The Theory of Economic Development: An Inquiry into Profits, Capital, Credit, Interest and the Business Cycle*. Transaction Publishers London.

Shapiro, C. 1989. The theory of business strategy. *The RAND Journal of Economics*, 20 (1), pp. 125–137.

Sinclair, G. and Tinson, J. 2017. Psychological ownership and music streaming consumption. *Journal of Business Research*, 71, pp. 1–9.

Sinnreich, A. 2016. Slicing the pie: The search for an equitable recorded music industry. in Wikstrom, P. and DeFillippi, R. (eds). *Business and Innovation and Disruption in the Music Industry*. Cheltenham: Edward Elgar, pp. 153–174.

Teece, D. J. 2007. Explicating dynamic capabilities: The nature and micro foundations of (sustainable) enterprise performance. *Strategic Management Journal*, 28 (13), pp. 1319–1350.

Teece, D. J., Pisano, G. and Shuen, A. 1997. Dynamic capabilities and strategic management. *Strategic Management Journal*, 18 (7), pp. 509–533.

Zollo, M. and Winter, S. 2002. Deliberate learning and the evolution of dynamic capabilities. *Organization Science*, 13 (3), pp. 339–351.

7 Organisation and Labour in the Cultural Industries

7.1 Introduction

Having reviewed several key sectors in the cultural industries in previous chapters, you should now have a better sense of how such sectors are structured, the types of company which inhabit their ecosystems, some of their major processes and the changes that have been wrought in the industry in recent decades, typically driven by digitisation. In the next set of chapters, we will review some enduring themes in academic research into these sectors, from how they are structured to how they utilise specific business functions like marketing. We will also explore how the industry is likely to evolve over the next decade in Chapter 9.

To begin, we look at issues of organisation and labour and ask some fundamental questions. Are organisations in the cultural industries structured in a fundamentally different way to other business sectors? How do workers in the industry view the work that they do? Are there specific challenges for leaders and managers in the sector that we don't encounter in other business sectors? What can those in the cultural industries learn from approaches to leadership and management in other business sectors, and can other sectors learn from the cultural industries?

We have already reviewed the basics of how business organisations are typically structured in Chapter 2. We noted the dominance of hierarchical forms, the specialisation of roles and responsibilities into functions and layers, coordinational forms such as the matrix / project structure and the processes that normally operate within companies (e.g. planning). How do these play out in the cultural industries? We will also explore some of the long-held beliefs, emerging from academic commentors, about how the sector operates on a practical basis, beliefs that have in many ways become established, dogmatic and largely unquestioned. We will challenge some of these views with empirical evidence that in some cases directly contradicts these established 'truths', suggesting the industry may operate in a rather different manner to the depictions in many academic commentaries.

Hence, we will explore how organisations are structured, the role of projects and genres, the role of conflict and constraint, the presence of the independent sector and corporate intermediaries and the well-documented 'creative / commercial split' in cultural industry organisations. From a business studies perspective we will explore some of the core concepts that tend to occupy the attention of the human resources department, along with those in management and leadership positions. Specifically, we will explore ideas like employee engagement, organisation as collective action and what motivates employees to undertake their roles.

DOI: 10.4324/9781003498599-7

7.2 Organisational forms in the cultural industries

Academics who have explored the issue are keen to point out that the cultural industries are characterised by quite specific organisational forms, that don't necessarily occur in other business sectors. This difference is driven by the character of the product and the process of its creation (Garnham, 1990; Ryan, 1992; Björkegren, 1996); it is driven by the specific history of the industry and how it's evolved over time (Williams, 1981; Hesmondhalgh, 2006) and indeed extends to how the industry as a whole is organised (Björkegren, 1996)—that is, its ecosystem. Organisations in the cultural industries have novel functions that you don't find elsewhere (Negus, 1992; Bourdieu, 1984) and novel roles, like creative management (Ryan, 1992; Negus, 1992; Bourdieu, 1984; DiMaggio, 1977). Further the presence and role of the artist and other creative personnel or symbol creators (Ryan, 1992; Tonybee, 2000) mark the industry out as 'different'. We will explore each of these issues in subsequent sections.

Attempts have been made to characterise cultural organisations more broadly, such as the model proposed by Davis and Scase (2000). They characterise organisations based on two criteria: how organisations coordinate activity, and their mechanisms for control. Coordination can be explicit, enshrined in organisational structures and processes, often written down as sets of organisational rules and guidelines, or can be far more informal and tacit, rarely written down but understood and shared by all as part of the organisational culture. Equally control can be exercised in a formal and hierarchical way, explicitly describing how roles and responsibilities are allocated, who reports to whom and about what, what performance is expected from individuals, groups and the organisation as a whole, or it can be far more informal and collegial, with little overt hierarchy, few explicit performance targets and a blurrier allocation of roles and responsibilities. According to this framework, then, the cultural industries are populated by organisations in four broad categories:

- Commercial bureaucracy—typically large organisations, well established, professionally run by businesspeople, focused on making profits, with a clear and highly structured formal organisation: e.g. Canal+ in the pay-TV sector, major record companies like Universal Music and games publishers like Tencent etc.
- Traditional / charismatic—these are typically smaller organisations, with operations based on a set of shared values, often with more of a focus on lifestyle and creative ambitions rather than profits, often run by owner-managers who have typically set the organisation up, are involved in the ongoing management of the company and play a key role in establishing its culture. Many independent games developers or television production companies might fall into this category.
- Cultural bureaucracies—often operating under a public service remit or some level of government control: typically these are large-scale organisations with lots of formalised rules and regulations, complex structures with significant hierarchies, autonomous departments and typically multiple agendas which can lead to internal clashes over meeting commercial pressures verses public service goals: e.g. public service broadcasters, government bodies involved in funding performing arts.
- Network organisations—typically very small or micro companies, often with less than five employees or sole traders, with virtually no formal structures or control measures, typically operating in networks with other companies, often doing outsourced work: e.g. the thousands of individual freelance animators and directors in the Tokyo area that support the Japanese animation industry.

Whilst this is a fairly clear and easy to comprehend model, it's not particularly helpful in answering one of our core questions: are organisations in the cultural industries really that different to those in other sectors? The above categories are essentially so broad that they cover organisations in just about any business sector. We can find commercial bureaucracies everywhere (e.g. most large organisations in the fast-moving consumer goods sector, most banks, most large technology companies etc.). Cultural bureaucracies can be found in most sectors where there might be some level of government interest or oversight, in NGOs, in the third sector (charities) and so on. Companies in the traditional / charismatic sector describe just about any start-up or SME firm developed under the auspices of a charismatic founder or entrepreneur. Equally most business sectors have a range of micro companies and sole traders that often service larger companies in the sector. Such broad characterisations, then, are not that helpful. Perhaps we need to look at a more granular level at the structure and operation of organisations if we want to identify potential differences.

In terms of their composition, certainly we see many functions present in cultural organisations that are found in other types of business: finance departments, marketing teams, HR staff and so on. Whilst their specific areas of focus and practice might be somewhat different to those in other sectors (e.g. there are certain technical financial issues that the finance manager of a television production company needs to understand about the process of production), their overall aims and goals tend to be similar to their peers' in non-cultural sectors: a finance team in a record company are as likely to be focused on monitoring and managing costs and revenues as those in a consumer electronics company. Those in charge of marketing in a pay-TV company are as likely to be obsessed with the consumer as those in a retail bank.

We may come across a few functions that are unusual and perhaps unique, however. In no other industry are we likely to encounter A&R teams, or commissioning departments, or a team in charge of props, costume or makeup. Inevitably the sector has thrown up a range of unusual and very specific functions, that typically play a critical role in developing the specific products that emerge from the cultural economy. But again, this is not particularly unusual. Each major business sector contains organisations that have evolved specific functions to service the production and sale of their products, from the pharmacy vigilance department of a major pharmaceutical company to the syndicated lending team in a corporate bank. So, whilst their specific characteristics and operation may be interesting and unusual, their mere presence does not mark out the cultural industry as particularly different.

Perhaps there is more that is unusual in how these functions tend to be organised and operate. Something that is certainly not unusual is the use of the project form and matrix structures as critical organisational devices. The idea that creative businesses are essentially project-based businesses (Castañer and Campos, 2002) has a long history, and numerous studies have highlighted the project as the main organisational form for cultural production (Elliot, 1972; DeFillippi and Arthur, 1998; Ryan, 1992). But again, this is hardly unusual; there is unlikely to be a single business sector that does not make use of projects as an organisational device, or that has not experimented with matrix structures to integrate project and day-to-day work activities.

One organisational method that does emerge as somewhat unusual is the use of genre. Negus (1999) points out the use of genre (along with the project team) as the major organisational form in the music sector. A brief review of other cultural sector organisations suggests a similar project- / genre-based structure in television (for example, the existence of drama, factual, comedy and entertainment genre departments), electronic games and the publishing sectors. Drawing on work by Frith (1996), Negus highlights genre's role in the music industry as a way of linking the question of music and what it sounds like to the question of the market and who will buy it. Hence 'record companies are not unified businesses, but collections of units organised according to musical genre' (Negus, 1999, p. 49).

He also notes (1999, p. 28) that 'genres are formally codified into specific organisational departments, narrow assumptions about markets, and "targeted" promotional practices'. Hence not only do they guide organisational practices, but also how workers 'see', understand and interact with the market. They are the core unit of management for record company leaders and are a device through which resources are allocated 'to some types of music and not to others' (ibid). Hence, they are critical in helping the organisation structure and organise work, address its market and enact important choices about resource investment and strategic direction (i.e. corporate strategy; see Chapter 2). Neale (1980, p. 19) describes genres more broadly as 'systems of orientations, expectations and conventions that circulate between industry, text [content] and subject'. Hence, he sees them as ways in which industries organisations are structured, as influential on what content is produced and how audiences interact and interpret it.

Firms may operate across a variety of different genres (a 'portfolio' of genres, covering a variety of different parts of the market in order to spread risk) or they may focus on a specific one. Independent companies, whether in television production or record labels, will often focus on one specific genre (e.g. in the television industry a production company focusing on natural history, or comedy or drama, for example); indeed we also see this in some television channel companies—e.g. Discovery's initial focus on natural history channels. Larger publishing-focused companies will typically try to incorporate a variety of genres into their offering to maximise coverage of the marketplace.

But again, we might question if the idea of organisation by genre is really that unusual. If one were to examine a large consumer products multinational like Unilever, we would see multiple divisions with different cultures, products and ways of working as a result of their focus on different parts of the market. The division producing beauty and wellbeing products is likely to operate in quite a different way to the home care or foods divisions. Each will have different markets, approaches to product development, promotional tools and ways of working. The type of staff that might be recruited for one division might not work well in another. We might equally see a variety of different divisions in an organisation like Apple or Hisense. Ultimately whether it's called genre, division or SBU (strategic business unit), these are all variations of organisational tools that help organisations divide up and allocate work and think about and address their marketplace. Perhaps it is in the way that genre connects commercial and artistic issues that marks it out as at least a little different, particularly in the context of the activities of suits and creatives.

7.3 Suits verses creatives

Another perspective on how organisations function in the cultural sector is the much-discussed (but unfortunately rather less debated) idea of the creative / commercial split evident in such organisations. This 'split' is a theme of research established by the influential work of Adorno and Horkheimer (1944 / 1977) as a result of their rather theoretical analysis of post-World War Two American culture and the commodification of entertainment products by large business conglomerates.

This view of organisations in the cultural sector characterises organisations as being divided into two rival camps: those involved on the creative side, and those involved in the administrative, business aspects (the 'suits'). For writers such as Adorno and Horkheimer, this division was seen as intrinsic, and the basis for conflict. The conflict emerges from the desire of creative artists to create content, and the desire of business interests to make profits from the resulting product. Further they would argue that business interests were ultimately dominant (given their control over funding and distribution), were focused on maintaining this unequal power relationship, of always promoting a commercial agenda and ultimately crushing genuine artistic endeavours in the quest for ever higher profits. In many ways, this view has become part of the canon of research intro the creative industries, particularly as part of the sociological stream of research.

Throughout the work that has followed in this vein several findings have emerged so consistently that they have almost taken on the status of dogma. Because of this 'split', content production is field of struggle (Bourdieu, 1993), an ongoing conflict between creative and business agendas in cultural organisations (Elliot, 1972; DiMaggio, 1977; Stratton, 1982a; Stratton, 1982b; Cohen, 1991; Ryan, 1992). As a result of this conflict, and unequal power relations, the creative ambitions of artists are consistently curbed in favour of the commercial interests of the organisations for which they have to work (DiMaggio, 1977; Ettema and Whitney, 1985; Ryan, 1992). This conflict, it is suggested, arises from fundamental differences in the needs of the artist, to create art and culture, and the needs of large-scale entertainment companies to consistently create profits and control the artists that serve them.

DiMaggio characterises these differing goals as 'the aspirations of artists for creative expression and the desires of management to be able to predict and control' (1977, p. 443). Throughout such commentaries there appears to be an in-built assumption that these aspirations are antithetical, that they cannot exist simultaneously without creating significant organisational conflict. This is partly explained by the nature of the processes by which these aspirations are pursued. On the one hand there exists a set of artistic processes wherein 'the arbitrariness of creation defies reduction to precise universal operating rules' (Ryan, 1992, p. 110). Management and business processes on the other hand are characterised as relying on rules and clear processes to ensure certainty and control of creative aspirations (hence as a constraint), with the aim not of product diversity or consistently developing high-quality cultural content 'but to higher profits' (Cantor and Cantor, 1992, p. 60).

There are some (very few) examples of research which does contradict this rather stark and arguably oversimplified conclusion. The author's own experience of first working in, then researching, the industry (see Roberts, 2010 and 2011) based on interviews with a variety of creative staff and senior business management in the television sector revealed a rather more blurred and less clear-cut situation. He notes that in many of the large-scale entertainment companies he examined, management decision making often starts with a creative rather than commercial agenda. He describes meeting senior business executives who emerged as hugely creative individuals, and indeed artists / creatives who demonstrated enormous commercial and business acumen. Hence, from an individual perspective, the boundaries and attitudes of the various 'suits and creatives' he met seemed rather more blurred than previous research suggested. Individuals demonstrated different orientations and concerns depending on the situation and context and moved between the roles of creative and suit accordingly.

In attempting to explain this variation, he notes that in many previous studies, research has tended to focus on and draw on the opinions of creative staff, to the exclusion of other constituencies—it has largely ignored the views of the 'suits' themselves. Interviews are conducted with the creative teams and individuals, and when other (non-creative) functions are discussed, it is from their perspective alone. The business affairs teams, legal teams and finance function are rarely included in such rounds of research interviews. This has helped build a very one-sided view of the functioning of cultural organisations and has tended to characterise business functions merely as constraints on the aspirations of the creative staff, as bullies, always happy to put profit before artistic endeavour, though one wonders if this emerges more from the agenda of the researchers rather than the interviewees themselves. Indeed, other academics and commentators have gone as far as to characterise business functions as the 'humdrum' interests (Caves, 2000, p. 1), so boring and predicable in their outlook that they are hardly worth considering at all.

Hence, in much of the research you are likely to review when reading academic papers exploring the operation of the cultural industries, particularly in the field of content production, business functions and the business agenda are seen in an almost exclusively negative way, as a constraint on artistic and creative endeavour and little else. Non-creative functions, then, are ascribed the role of a constraint on the 'professional autonomy or creative freedom of individuals' (Ettema and Whitney, 1985, p. 8). Early studies of the production of news introduced concepts of constraint in the form of filters, flows and gatekeepers to the research vocabulary of those studying media production (Negus, 2002). Paul Hirsch (1972) focuses on a specific tier of corporate intermediaries in constraining and filtering the creative outputs of artists (see section 7.4). In the music sector, Negus and Frith identify the strict financial parameters set by senior management on the activities of creative staff and other functions (Negus, 1992; Frith, 1983) as a key constraint. More recently Berkeley's 2003 research identifies constraints working at a variety of levels in the television industry in the UK at the industry, market and organisational levels. Constraints might also exist in the form of the formats (Ryan, 1992) that artists are forced to adhere to by funders, blueprints for what content (a K-pop album, a TV game show) should look or sound like.

Hence business interests represent the 'bad guys', as there is an implied suggestion that all constraint (on artistic endeavours) is a bad thing. But is it? Very occasionally another view is expressed, wherein constraints can have a positive effect on creative endeavour. Ettema, in a case study of the development of a television programme for the PBS television network in the USA, describes how professional values, organisational routines and organisational conflict all imposed constraints 'but also guided and energised the creative activity of the executive producer' (Ettema and Whitney, 1985, p. 103). Constraint here establishes guidelines and parameters within which the artist has to be creative—indeed, in some cases, having to be even more creative to overcome potential constraints and barriers. The fact that the producers of a film did not have millions of dollars to spend on location-based filming forced the creative team to find ways around this constraint. Limited budgets can indeed force creative solutions to emerge.

Gareth Edwards, now a prominent film director, made his first major film, *Monsters*, for under $500,000 using prosumer-level equipment (e.g. digital video cameras rather than 35mm film), using non-professional extras who happened to be at the filming location when the film was being shot, with footage downloaded onto memory sticks each day (and emptied each evening ready for filming the next day) with special effects largely produced on his home PC using programmes like Adobe. Arguably this is film making in its most 'constrained' form. The film would go onto gross $4.2m in worldwide ticket sales[1] and receive a variety of industry awards (e.g. Best British Film at the 16th Empire Awards in the UK). In this case, the very constraints within which Edwards had to work arguably forced him to new levels of creativity. He would go on to direct such well-known successes as *The Creator* and *Jurassic World Rebirth*.

Imagine yourself being asked to write a joke. A joke about absolutely anything, of any length, in any genre. It's difficult to know where to start with absolutely no constraints on your creativity. Being asked to write one about a specific subject, with a specific timescale, to be delivered to a specific audience, to achieve a specific end, by a specific comedian (all ultimately constraints and limitations), can be much more inspiring.

So even if we accept that the business functions involved in cultural organisations do indeed always act as a constraint (though the evidence is far from comprehensive or conclusive), perhaps that is not always the negative thing it is portrayed as by academic commentators on the cultural industries—perhaps it can be a positive, or even a necessary ingredient for creativity. The other key output of this perhaps over-stressed division between those on the creative and business sides of the organisations we are exploring is the idea that the functioning of these organisations is necessarily characterised by conflict (between the two groups) and, again, that this conflict tends to have inevitably negative consequences. There are two critical points that might be made here.

Firstly, that conflict, at some level, features in the operation of just about every organisation that has ever existed. No organisation is entirely homogeneous. They are typically made up of diverse individuals, with differing agendas, goals, interests and aims. Individuals are divided up into different functions and levels, again with different measures and definitions of success. Resources (be they talent, funding, equipment etc.) are typically scarce, even for the largest organisations, and different parts of organisations will fight to secure what they feel they need. A marketing team may want a huge injection of funds to launch a new promotional campaign, whilst the operations team want to invest those funds in a new set of equipment on the shop floor. The IT team want to upgrade everyone's PCs, whilst the HR team want to spend the money on training everyone in the use of AI. Members of staff and management will disagree over the best strategy for the organisation, whether a new product should be invested in or if an office should be opened in a new country. The functioning of every part of every organisation is to some extent beset by disagreements and conflicts. It's the job of management to manage these conflicts and trade-offs to the benefit of the organisation as a whole. Hence the mere existence of conflict in the production of cultural content, or in the operation of cultural organisations, and the fact that some functions don't get on with others, is in no way unusual, unexpected or specific to the sector.

Secondly, as was our observation about constraints, why should we assume that conflict is always a negative thing? Indeed, sometimes it appears absolutely necessary for the production of outstanding cultural content. The fact that according to many commentators John Lennon fought constantly over musical direction with Paul McCartney produced content that would change the very nature of popular music. David Lee Roth and Eddie Van Halen disagreed violently on occasion, yet their joint efforts to lead Van Halen redefined the hard rock genre and guitar playing for an entire generation. The brothers behind the British band Oasis have had numerous very public fallings-out. There are many stories of film actors setting the screen alight with their performances, whilst hating each other off-screen (Indian Bollywood stars Salman Khan and Shahrukh Khan had a particularly significant 'bust up' in 2007). Film directors James Cameron, Werner Herzog and Alfred Hitchcock all had heated relationships with their key actors yet produced astonishing performances from them.

Removing conflict from the operation of organisations is probably impossible and, in many ways, perhaps more significantly, may be ultimately undesirable. Conflict can be fruitful, as long as it is managed, which is ultimately the role of the senior leaders and managers in an organisation. It is when it is not managed, when it is not clear and overt, when it runs unchecked, that it becomes problematic. Its existence in the cultural industries, then, hardly marks them out as in any way different to any other business sector. Perhaps it is in how managers and leaders in the industry deal with this conflict that problems do emerge. We will return to further examine the nature and characteristics of conflict in section 7.6.

7.4 Organisational intermediaries and the independent sector

Perhaps where we do see some more significant differences between the cultural industries and other business sectors is in its overall structure and ecosystem, particularly the existence of what has come to be called the 'independent' sector. In every industry we tend to see the existence of large and small organisations, but rarely do we find the nature of the relationship between the two that we find in the cultural industries.

In many parts of the cultural industries, we see the existence of large-scale organisations that focus on funding product creation, distribution and marketing—let's call this the 'publishing' role. The major record companies, electronic games publishers and broadcasters all fulfil these functions. Equally all rely at least partially on a series of external organisations and individuals as sources of innovation. Major record companies rely on smaller independent record labels to find and partially develop new artists (as well as having their own tier of A&R executives). Games publishers regularly rely on external games developers to create new ideas for games, Broadcasters rely on independent production companies and external individuals (e.g. writers, actors, directors) to propose ideas for new programmes. Perhaps in no other sector are large incumbent companies quite so reliant on smaller external organisations as a source of product innovation. A major bank, clothing brand or consumer electronics company will typically have its own internal innovation resources (e.g. a research and development department). For many, innovation and developing new products and services is too important and commercially sensitive to rely on a range of external companies to provide it. As we have seen (Chapter 4), a more 'closed' model of innovation has traditionally been the almost universal approach wherein ideas are generated and funded internally within a company, development leads onto product launch, with all of the resultant revenues accruing to the company. Sharing good ideas with external agencies was seen as commercially dangerous, having partners can complicate and extend the development process, and who wants to share the revenues? Hence a 'closed' model of innovation has been dominant.

But this is not the case in the cultural industries, as we began to note in Chapter 4. For all of their history, organisations in these industries have relied on external agents to produce, develop and deliver their products, from the actors involved in producing a play, directors who are hired to direct films or record producers to help record an album. Traditionally, these external agents are not employees of the publishing organisation. They are hired, temporarily, to complete a project (e.g. create a piece of content). Thereafter, they are free agents again. This causes some complications given that ultimately 'artists necessarily occupy a position of structural independence within the capitalist commodity producing process which places them beyond the organisational disciplines to which waged labour is subjected: they are assigned creative licence in the very heart of production' (Ryan, 1992, p. 46).

As cultural sectors industrialised, this model expanded to include external organisations that might take on a similar role to individuals in developing and producing content. Independent record companies, television production companies and games developers emerged, remaining independent of the large organisations they might be working for on a project. They liked their independence. Once a project was completed, they were free to pitch ideas to other large (often competing) organisations and they did not have to work to the ongoing and strict rules governing the operation of the far larger publishing companies they served.

This reliance on external agents for innovation is partly a result of the need for a constant flow of new products. Most new products struggle to return the funds invested in them (they barely 'break even'). A significant proportion lose money. A very few are hits. In such an environment, and with the difficulties of predicting the performance of a piece of cultural content, it is vital to continually launch new products into the marketplace in the hope that the next one will be the big hit, that pays for all the losses. Whilst many large publishers do have their own internal innovation and product teams (e.g. a broadcaster like the BBC has its own production division, BBC studios; Tencent has its own game development team), they do not generate a sufficient number of new ideas to satisfy either management or the market. Hence publishers consistently rely on external agents and companies to provide even more ideas.

Perhaps inevitably, then, these large 'publishing' organisations manage their relationships with the independent sector vary carefully, in an attempt to ensure that they work with the best external talent, and their competitors do not. Over time, specific roles have emerged in these organisations to address this challenge—that is, intermediaries—working on the boundary between the organisation and the independent sector, whose job it is to identify and secure the best independent talent.

According to DiMaggio, then, virtually all 'culture producing organisations include brokers who mediate between the aspirations of artists for creative expression and the desires of management to be able to predict and control' (1977, p. 443). For other academics, these 'brokers' are called intermediaries, whose role it is to 'bind working artists to the organisation's mode of rationality' (Ryan, 1992, p. 117). Hirsch (1972) suggest that they have a boundary-spanning role, existing at the edge of organisations, constantly monitoring the external environment in the hunt for new ideas and talent. At other points he calls them 'contact men' and 'talent scouts', noting that 'in the production sector, the technical [creative] and managerial levels of organisation are linked by boundary spanning talent scouts, for example, acquisition editors...located on the input boundary of the focal organisation' (ibid, p. 644).

Turow (1985) notes that, within the major television networks in the USA, 'special departments are formed [to facilitate the task of finding new product]' (in Ettema and Whitney, 1985, p. 109). At a more general level, Bielby and Bielby note the activities of television network programme executives who 'mediate the business relationship between creative personnel employed by independent production companies and advertisers who bear the costs of distribution' (1994, p. 1291). Other examples might include a manga editor in the publishing industry, or the A&R team in a major record label.

There are two key roles implied here. One is a monitoring role, scanning and exploring the external environment for the best talent. The second key role is securing it and then establishing the ground rules for the organisations to work together effectively. In this latter role, these intermediaries have also been called the creative management strata, a tier of managers within the publishing organisation that understand both the aspirations of creative talent and the needs of the organisation to generate revenue and profits. Members of the creative management strata need to be able to discuss a creative issue with an artist, and moments later have a detailed discussion with a finance director about the implications of a particular decision. To be effective, they need to have a deep understanding of both the artist's and corporation's agendas, they need to understand the language each group uses and be persuasive and authoritative in discussions with both. They need to be able to demonstrate artistic and creative insight, combined with business knowledge and skills. Their role is highly significant and important, as according to some commentators they often operate with high levels of autonomy, and in conjunction with artists they are 'delegated the responsibility of producing marketable creations, with little or no interference from the front office [senior management] beyond the setting of budgetary limits' (Hirsch 1972, p. 644). Hence, they are a rare, and highly prized, group of employees. For some of you reading this book, perhaps with performance in your own background, this may be an exciting potential opportunity to consider when planning the next steps in your career (see Chapter 10).

7.5 A diversion into organisational behaviour and the work of the HR team

With this suggestion in mind, that the reader may see themselves in the future in a leadership or management role in the cultural industries, it is probably worth diverting our attention at this point to consider the role and function of a management team more broadly, and to do this we need to consider some basic tenets of organisational behaviour and the role and functioning of the HR team. We do so at a time when innovative organisational forms are evolving in every business sector. As the external environment for organisations has changed and evolved in recent years, so has the internal environment that managers and leaders have to navigate and manage.

The industrial revolution (and it could be argued even longer-term institutions like the military and organised religion) left significant organisational legacies in most countries. Business organisations were built like machines, designed to be stable and predictable. Organisations took on the form of permanent hierarchies, with centralised, top-down decision making and stable, specialised roles for employees. Work processes were routinised and standardised and the workforce itself was relatively homogenised. Ultimately, employees were replaceable cogs in enduring organisational machines. In recent years, however, this has begun to change significantly, partly in response to an increasingly chaotic and unpredictable external environment (often termed the VUCA environment, given its volatility, unpredictability, complexity and the ambiguity of changes).

In today's business environment change is rapid, unpredictable and often driven by global forces such as geopolitics. To cope with this uncertainty, organisations have moved toward more decentralised structures. Work is increasingly carried out by temporary, project-based teams, where responsibilities are fluid and boundaries between roles are less clear. Processes are more flexible and improvised, shaped by a workforce that is becoming more diverse in background and skills. These shifts have drawn growing attention from both academics and practitioners, especially around the question of how organisations can remain 'healthy' and productive in such a turbulent context.

Research consistently shows that organisational performance is strongly influenced by the human side of work, typically the province of the HR (human resources) department. The way people collaborate, the quality of workplace relationships, how jobs are designed, how people are rewarded and the attributes of employees themselves are all critical. Studies such as those by Nohria, Joyce and Roberson (2003) and Fulmer et al. (2003) demonstrate that the difference between successful and unsuccessful firms is often explained less by strategy or structure, and more by how effectively people and processes are managed.

A central theme in this research is **employee engagement**. Although the term is broad, it essentially refers to the attitudes of employees toward their organisation, and the quality of the employer–employee relationship. The UK's Engage for Success[2] project illustrates this importance clearly. Its research shows that organisations with high employee engagement enjoy better outcomes: higher revenues and profits, stronger customer satisfaction, greater productivity, more innovation and lower staff turnover.

The evidence therefore suggests that leadership, management, job design and workplace culture are not peripheral concerns but central drivers of performance. As Schneider (1987) argues (see his Attraction–Selection–Attrition model), people make the place. Organisations should not be seen as abstract entities but as the collective actions and behaviours of those who work within them. Writers such as Jim Collins (2001) expanded on this perspective, offering practical guidance for leaders on how to build effective organisations by focusing on people first.

Within this debate, one of the most widely studied topics is **employee motivation**, often viewed as a core component of engagement. Motivation can be defined as the psychological force that initiates, directs and sustains behaviour at work. Latham and Ernst (2006, p. 181) describe it as 'a set of energetic forces that originate within as well as beyond an individual's being…resulting from the reciprocal interaction between the individual and the environment'. Several key points emerge: motivation is shaped by the context of work; it is not directly visible but inferred from behaviour; and it involves three dimensions—choice (whether and how to act), effort (the energy put into action) and persistence (how long effort is maintained). Motivation research falls into two main traditions: **content theories** (which examine *what* motivates people) and **process theories** (which examine *how* motivation operates).

Content theories emphasise needs, values and job characteristics. Maslow's Hierarchy of Needs (1987) suggests that people are motivated by a sequence of needs, from basic survival (warmth, food etc.), through the need for socialisation, to self-fulfilment. The implication for managers is straightforward: without fair pay and security, employees will not engage with higher-level goals such as personal growth or innovation McClelland and Burnham (1976) highlighted the role of achievement, affiliation and power needs, especially for managers. Herzberg's Job Characteristics Model (1968) focused on job design, arguing that motivation can be improved by altering how work is structured—through task variety, autonomy and meaningful responsibilities—rather than simply hiring or firing people.

Process theories, by contrast, examine the dynamics of motivation. They address questions such as how much effort people expend and why motivation rises or falls.

Three areas are particularly influential: perceptions of fairness, goal setting and expectations of success. First, fairness is crucial. Employees must feel they are in a fair exchange with their organisation, that they are appropriately rewarded for their efforts. Perceptions of injustice—whether from unequal pay, poor treatment or lack of recognition—undermine trust and reduce commitment. Since fairness is experienced subjectively, leaders must actively assess and manage how policies and practices are perceived.

Second, goal setting is a powerful motivational tool. Locke and Latham's (1990) goal-setting theory suggests that specific, challenging (but realistic) goals drive higher performance. However, two conditions are critical: feedback must be provided so employees can track progress, and individuals must be committed to the goals. Without these, even well-crafted goals will fail to motivate.

Finally, expectations matter. The concept of **self-efficacy**—a person's belief in their ability to succeed—strongly shapes motivation. Research shows that employees with high self-efficacy are more willing to accept challenges, persist in the face of setbacks, and adapt behaviour when obstacles arise. As Marcus Buckingham (2005) notes, self-efficacy is context-specific: people may feel highly capable in one domain but not in another. Creating environments that build confidence can therefore enhance both motivation and performance.

In summary, the study of employee engagement highlights that organisational success depends not just on structures or strategies, but on people—their needs, perceptions and attitudes. Whether through fair treatment, effective goal setting or building confidence, motivating employees is central to building resilient and high-performing organisations in today's unpredictable business world.

Having the knowledge and insight needed to actively and positively shape these aspects of people and behaviour is essential for those who wish to optimise their ability to lead and contribute to an organisation's success. But do they apply universally to all business sectors? What about the cultural industries? What motivates those who work in a record company or games developer? What are overall levels of employee engagement like in the industry? Is the industry populated by 'healthy' companies? Does it train its managers and leaders in appropriate interpersonal skills?

Perhaps a brief word of warning here. Academic papers in this research theme—that is, the study of creative labour and work—are very much dominated by sociologists, tend towards the academic (rather than practical) and often read more like papers on political philosophy rather than the operation of companies. This is typical of much research into the cultural industries and is an important intellectual contribution to our understanding of the sector, but it's not necessarily that helpful for practitioners (e.g. you in your job as the head of HR) trying to improve the performance of their organisations. Hence, we have been selective in this review, trying to highlight those pieces of research with more practical relevance, but with pointers to more academic work where appropriate.

In reviewing the research that has been conducted into these ideas in the cultural sector, a number of themes and terms arise consistently, particularly terms such as 'emotional labour' and themes around the unusually precarious nature of employment. There are regular references to the increasing 'casualisation' of employment. Casualisation refers to a perceived decline in the number of full-time jobs in the cultural industries, and a turn to part-time, ad-hoc roles and a reliance by companies on freelancers.

Ursell (2000) argues for example that 'the size of permanent staffs with terrestrial producer-broadcasters has diminished, casualisation of the labour force has increased, entry to the industry is more difficult and less well rewarded or supported, average earnings have dropped and working terms and conditions have deteriorated' (2000, p. 805). The implication here is that this casualisation, which emerges partly out of a desire by large companies to cut staff costs and improve flexibility of operation, has led to declining wages and worsening working conditions. These observations about the television sector are confirmed by other academics (see Sparks, 1994 or Born, 2004) and those exploring other cultural sectors (see for example McRobbie, 1998 on fashion, Blair and Rainnie, 2000 on film and Tonybee, 2000 on music).

Interestingly, part of the reason for this may also be the rather privileged position that creative talent might be seen to occupy according to some academics. Miège (see 1979 and 1987) argues that creative talent is privileged in that those with it are afforded far more autonomy than other types of worker: the constraining and controlling organisational rules that apply to the latter just don't apply to the former. We saw similar arguments from Ryan (1992) earlier in this chapter. As a result of this 'privileged' position, combined with a certain amount of glamour, many people want to work in the industry, hence there is a massive oversupply of labour for creative jobs, explaining why artists ultimately tend to suffer from underemployment and insecurity (Miège, 1987, pp. 82–83). It's an interesting dichotomy, as on the one hand someone with creative talent is potentially hugely privileged, and on the other, as a result, they can't get a job, and when and if they do, are likely to be underpaid compared to other business sectors for the short period of time they have it. For those of you hoping for a career in the cultural industries, the literature suggests you may have a tough time (see Chapter 10 for more on this).

Other commentators have voiced an even more overtly negative perspective, suggesting that the difficulties many find in securing cultural work has more to do with traditional social structures that are essentially exclusionary in nature. Issues of gender, ethnic background, caste and class position all contribute to limiting access to cultural jobs to a privileged few, many of whom already have family connections in the industry. Self-exploitation emerges as a by-product, wherein those without a privileged position are forced to exploit themselves, offering their labour free or at a low level of remuneration in exchange for the opportunity to build a network of contacts and establish their position in the industry (McRobbie, 1998). Working for free as an intern in the mail room of a record company or as an unpaid runner on a television production may be the only routes into the industry for some.

Should you secure a role, what's the likely nature of the work and how do workers relate to it? Well, for many, it's literally a labour of love. Lee (2013, p. 8), in his useful review of research in the area, suggests that 'what emerges consistently from creative labour research is the pleasure which cultural workers derive from their work and the enthusiasm with which they launch themselves into their chosen careers'. Hence 'work for these cultural producers has become a venue for "self-fulfilment, autonomy, independence"' (ibid). If we draw on the model of motivation mentioned earlier, Maslow's Hierarchy of Needs, cultural work is indeed a place where workers can strive for the 'self-actualisation' described as the ultimate layer of the hierarchy.

Cultural industries are a venue for 'emotional labour', an idea originally developed by Hochschild (1983) whereby workers draw deeply on elements of their emotional lives as part of the labour process. At a granular level, this early work focused particularly on how workers had to manage their own emotions to create appropriate and beneficial interactions with other workers and customers. He notes the development of 'feeling rules' that help to guide interactions between individuals. Hochschild's original conception of this had rather negative connotations, suggesting that such a relationship between the worker and their work allowed organisations to extend even greater levels of control over their employees, a level of control that extended to non-work areas, fusing 'a sense of personal satisfaction with a sense of company well-being and identity' (1983, p. 132). Hence it is perhaps a venue for what Florida might call 'soft control' (2002, p. 13).

As a result we are faced with a situation in which workers in the cultural industries appear to be willing to accept poorly paid, insecure roles (indeed, even roles without any pay at all given the importance of the volunteer role for many performing arts companies), with poor working conditions (e.g. long working hours), and in which organisations potentially manipulate emotions to exploit workers, but also one in which there is the potential for them to invest their physical and emotional life in a potentially self-actualising career.

Hence 'questions of identity, subjectivity and affect [emotion] are vital in understanding the macro-structures of creative labour' (Lee, 2013, p. 7). For those interested in the subject, Banks' review of the characteristics of creative labour, *The Politics of Cultural Work* (2007), would be a logical place to start your further research.

7.6 Implications for managers and leaders

What, then, are the implications of everything we have discussed so far for those of you who might aim for a management or leadership role in the creative industries in the future? If we are to believe much of the academic research we have reviewed in this chapter, your first step would be to make a choice: do you want to be a suit or a creative? We are told that these are two distinct groups, with very different agendas and working practices who generally don't get on, so you had better choose your side and stick to it as each group has certain behaviours and values they are expected to practise, and that should be adhered to if you want your career to develop.

A rather more nuanced exploration would suggest that these divisions are not quite so clear-cut and fixed as has been suggested in the literature. Suits can be creative; creatives can be very business-like. Indeed, there appears to be a tier of workers in many organisations, the creative management strata, who need to understand and be able to interact with both constituencies if they are to fulfil their function. They need to be able to interact and understand the creative agenda, and the type of working conditions that are likely to satisfy a creative individual or team, whilst at the same time being able to have a very business-like discussion with the business affairs team, CEO or finance director.

A key question we might ask here is whether current organisations in the cultural industries are set up to help employees develop this breadth of knowledge or if they are set up to channel individuals down one path or another? What are the opportunities for someone in the business management team to interact and work with more creative staff? Are these opportunities built into development and training programmes? Is this cross-fertilisation something that is encouraged? Surely, it's a good idea: we want creative staff who understand the business agenda, and business staff who are sensitive to the needs of the creative community. Dealing with conflict between the two can only be easier if each understand the other's perspectives.

Unfortunately, as organisations get bigger and more complex, they tend to become more hierarchical, with clearly separated levels and functions, and ever greater levels of specialisation and clearly delineated career paths. Employees may be forced down one route or another. Smaller companies tend to be generally less hierarchical, with more flexibility in how roles are defined and developed. Perhaps it is this latter type of company, then, that offers the greatest potential for more junior staff to develop a broad overview of the operation of both creative and business-orientated functions. Rather than pitching your CV to a major game publisher, record company or broadcaster, perhaps a better place to start your career might be one of the smaller companies that serve them. Start-ups can be even more fluid and are often highly dynamic in how work is defined and allocated, and roles are typically multifaceted. Certainly, the founder of a start-up often finds themself having to deal with creatives, customers, suppliers and financiers. They need to be the head of marketing, product development, operations and the head of finance. Perhaps this, then, is a better environment for our future creative managers to start to build their careers.

Whatever your career path, as a future manager or leader, you are likely to spend a great deal of your time dealing with conflict. Indeed, many of those writing about the cultural industries suggest it is the core characteristic of the operation of organisations in the sector, specifically the ongoing conflict between creatives and suits. Whether we agree with this idea, that the cultural industries are the venue for particularly high levels of conflict between different functions, conflict is an inevitable and emergent characteristic of the functioning of most organisations, and it's the job of the management team, well, to manage it.

The term conflict does come with strong negative connotations, however. Conflict is generally seen as a bad thing, as something that happens when things go wrong. People instantly start to look for someone (else) to blame. But it does not have to be, as we have already seen in this chapter—some very productive creative relationships have thrived on conflict. Indeed, it can be a strong force for good and the positive development of both cultural content and organisations. But managers and leaders do need to understand it and establish when it might be damaging an organisation and its employees, rather than helping to develop it.

Let's explore two issues in this regard, one the nature of conflict and, two, what can be done about it.

Conflict, in organisational terms, typically refers to '…perceived incompatibilities in the interests, beliefs, or views held by one or more [people]' (Salas et al., 2014, p. 605). In a business context, conflict tends to emerge most commonly in three areas: task-based conflict (differing viewpoints or opinions about how to best execute tasks), relationship-based conflict (interpersonal differences that spark annoyance or tension) and process-based conflict (how to divide and delegate tasks among people). Conflict can also emerge around issues of resource allocation—who gets the biggest share of financial or skills-based resources. In whatever form it emerges, it seems to be a core characteristic of the functioning of most organisations.

Arguably it is the fear of conflict that can be most damaging. Arising from the mindset that all conflict is dysfunctional and a symptom of problems and mistakes, conflict is typically seen as something to be avoided. This in turn may lead to individuals not expressing themselves, not disagreeing (particularly with the boss), not challenging inherited ways of doing business, not proposing new ideas for innovative approaches, not challenging the status quo. The aim is to avoid overt conflict at all costs. In the VUCA environment we discussed earlier, this can be fatal for a company (as it nearly was for the major record companies). In such a dynamic and changeable business environment, we need new perspectives, we need challenging new ideas, we need conflict!

What are the implications for the practising leader or manager? Well perhaps the worst thing they can do is to try and hide conflict or dismiss it as unimportant, particularly in a context of 'emotional labour', with employees pouring their hearts and souls into their jobs. Conflict needs to be made overt and obvious to all, recognised as important and then dealt with. Certainly, the reaction of managers and leaders when conflict does arise is likely to influence the nature and duration of its impact.

The idea of **psychological safety** can be helpful here. Psychological safety is a mutual belief and confidence amongst employees that it is perfectly acceptable to speak openly about ideas, concerns, fears and / or mistakes within the organisation and that doing so will not have negative consequences for the speaker such as being punished, rejected or diminished in status within the group. Conflict then is allowed, even welcomed. The evidence suggests that the extent to which teams and organisations are psychologically safe is positively related to performance. Hence one of the core concerns of the leader or manager is to create a psychologically safe environment for their workers.

Whilst a full discussion of psychological safety and how to create it might fill an entire book, we can outline a few issues that help to support it. Leaders and managers need to focus particularly on shaping the organisational context and ways of working. The organisation needs a sound structure that actively supports cooperation and allows different opinions to emerge, and within this context, two issues stand out: good task design and developing appropriate organisational norms.

If task- and process-based conflict is the source of significant potential conflict in an organisation, then it is incumbent upon the management and leadership team to focus particularly on how work is devised, divided up and allocated (task design). Role clarity, for example, is a key foundation for coordinated action in an organisation. Ambiguity and confusion around who is responsible for what is a primary source of conflict which may be avoided or at least minimised by ongoing attention to making very explicit the expected contributions of each organisational member, and re-establishing this clarity as conditions change, as they inevitably will. Leaders need to work with the HR team and other functional leadership to ensure this is an ongoing process.

'Norms' are particularly significant in this context. Norms are essentially rules of conduct that govern how the members of an organisation work together and what they can expect from each other. They describe what is considered good and acceptable behaviour and what is not. There may be norms around how employees are expected to communicate with each other, how employees are assessed and rewarded (or punished) or how conflict and disagreement will be managed. These norms may be enshrined in written documents (an employee handbook), or processes and procedures (e.g. HR systems around dispute resolution), but they are at their most powerful when they are consistently demonstrated and lived by the management team themselves.

The issue of **authentic leadership** has attracted much attention in recent years and is relevant here. Academics have been trying to identify the best approaches to organisational leadership for many years. Models of command and control, transactional versus transformational leadership, charismatic leadership and Level 5 leadership have all been explored and proposed as a solution to the dilemma of finding and developing good leaders. More recently, there has been a turn to the idea of authentic leaders. Relying principally on inspiring standards, not inspiring charisma to motivate followers, authentic leaders have a clear set of values that they live by and demonstrate to employees every day. These values become manifest in the form of behavioural norms. In a move away from the typical image of the heroic, loud, charismatic leader architype, Gardner et al. (2005, p. 344) 'are struck by the uplifting effects of lower profile but genuine leaders who lead by example in fostering heathy ethical climates characterised by transparency, trust, integrity and high moral standards. We call such leaders authentic leaders'. Ultimately authentic leaders are role models for the rest of the organisation. They embody required norms of behaviour. If a leader wants the operation of the organisation to be based on a set of values and norms that encourage cooperation and support psychological safety, they need to demonstrate these norms every day. How does the leader respond when conflict emerges, how do they respond when employees disagree with them publicly? Their subsequent behaviour will send significant cues and guidelines to the rest of the organisation as to what is considered acceptable behaviour and what is not.

Interestingly, where we find the highest levels of psychological safety, we may find the highest levels of overt conflict. People are happy to disagree and argue. They know they can do so without it damaging their careers. Hence in some ways leaders and managers must strive to achieve a position where conflict, argument and disagreement is an expected and acceptable state of affairs. Whilst we might continue to discuss the benefits and antecedents of psychological safety and the nature of conflict, we have other issues to discuss, so our commentary has to be cut short. For those of you interested in diving deeper into these issues, we would recommend anything by Amy C. Edmondson (e.g. *The Fearless Organisation*, 2018) as a good place to start.

Much of this, then, points to the importance of people management as a core function of leadership and management teams and the HR function. It is ultimately their responsibility to ensure that the organisation has the right mix of skills and capabilities to achieve its goals. They are responsible for finding talent, securing it, developing it and retaining it. They divide up work and allocate it in a fair and equitable way. They help create a positive and supportive culture within the organisation. This inevitably extends to the cultural industries. It seems intuitive and obvious, the cultural industries (at least until the emergence of AI—see Chapter 9) have been entirely reliant on people to generate ideas, and to develop and sell them. They are above all else 'people businesses'. But for some commentators, the cultural industries are, compared to other businesses, relatively poor at managing people.

In an interesting overview of the media sector, two unusual commentators, Annet Aris and Jacques Bughin (unusual as they were practising strategy consultants working for a company called McKinsey in the early parts of their careers, rather than lifelong academics), suggest that for many media companies, 'their people management processes do not ensure systematic, high-quality output' (2009, p. 338). Indeed, media and cultural businesses seem to be well behind the wave of best practice when it comes to the human resources function. The authors see the function of HR in many cultural companies as more focused 'around administration and union negotiations than strategic people management' (ibid). Whilst much of their evidence appears anecdotal, rather than the result of rigorous academic research, the writers have worked with a significant number of major organisations in the cultural industries for one of the leading management consultancies in the world, and perhaps as such, we should take note. According to their research, few human resources departments in the cultural industries see their role as particularly strategic, employee roles and job descriptions are often unclear, and there is rarely systematic mentorship and development of individuals with high potential.

Ultimately, they suggest that whilst companies may exert significant efforts in finding and hiring talent, whether this be talent on the creative or business sides, they are not good at developing and retaining it. Roles and performance measures are not defined sufficiently, and development feedback is patchy and inconsistent. Compensation is often lower than that in other sectors, unless the individual reaches the very highest levels of management or develops a high-profile creative reputation (in which case their compensation can far exceed those in other functions and at other levels and appears to some workers to be disproportionately high compared to their own). The overall impression is of career paths that resemble tournaments in which luck plays a hugely significant role and in which most people will fail to win the ultimate prize of a successful and enduring career in the industry.

Their insights are useful, practical and a welcome alternative commentary to much of the academic work available on the sector. Their book, *Managing Media Companies*, is to be recommended to the reader, but perhaps best reviewed only after a few years of practical experience, and perhaps having undertaken an MBA.

7.7 Conclusions

We set out in this chapter to answer the fundamental question of if and how organisations in the cultural industries differ from those in other business sectors. Many commentators have suggested that they do, based on their historical evolution, the nature of the workforce and the types of products and services they provide. But perhaps in our review we have found more things in common with other sectors than things which make it different. Certainly, we see the presence of hierarchies as a predominant organisational form, along with the presence of specialised functions and roles. We see extensive use of the project and matrix forms of organisation, common throughout all business sectors. We do see the presence of certain organisational functions which don't exist elsewhere (e.g. the A&R team), but again this specialisation is characteristic of most business sectors. We see the presence of functions dominated by those with a more creative outlook, and those better placed to fulfil more administrative roles but, again, this is little different to most other types of business.

We find conflict at every turn but argue that conflict appears to be inherent in the operation of all organisations given their heterogeneous composition. There is nothing particularly unusual about the conflict that tends to emerge in cultural organisations. Perhaps, however, it is not managed as well as it is in other industries, and perhaps this comes down partly to how the cultural industries train its leaders.

One area that does provoke some interesting discussion is the nature of the ecosystem that surrounds the organisations themselves, and their particular reliance on an 'independent sector' as a source of creativity and innovation. The presence of intermediaries and creative management emerges as a result, and perhaps in this we see one of the key ways in which the cultural industries are different. Organisations in the cultural industries have been managing this characteristic of the sector for most of their history. In many ways they are at the leading edge of what has emerged as the idea of 'open innovation'—that is, coproduction of innovation across networks. Perhaps other industries might benefit from examining practices in the sector and learning how cultural organisations manage across organisational boundaries. Equally it would appear that the cultural industries have a lot to learn from other sectors in terms of adopting a more strategic perspective in the HR function, and how to best find, nurture and retain talent.

7.8 Activities

- Review your own plan for finding a job in the cultural industries. What sectors are you targeting, for what type of role? What are your key assets and capabilities in attempting to secure this role? Critically, what is your plan B?
- Review the context for conflict you have encountered in your own working life to date. This might be in a part-time job or even working with other students on a group project. What was the source of the conflict and how was it resolved? What might you do differently next time?
- How are businesses in other sectors dealing with the issue of open innovation? What challenges are they facing? How are they dealing with them? What can organisations in the cultural industries learn from their approaches?

Notes

1 Box Office Mojo, 2014.
2 See https://engageforsuccess.org for further detail.

References

Adorno, T. and Horkheimer, M. 1977/1944. The culture industry: Enlightenments as mass deception, in Curren, J., Gurevitch, M. and Wollacot, J. (eds). *Mass Communication and Society*. London: Edward Arnold.

Aris, A. and Bughin, J. 2009. *Managing Media Companies*. Wiley.

Banks, M. 2007. *The Politics of Cultural Work*. London: Palgrave Macmillan.

Berkeley, D. 2003. Creativity and economic transactions in television drama production, in Beck, A. (ed.). *Cultural Work: Understanding the Cultural Industries*. Routledge.

Bielby, W. T. and Bielby, D. D. 1994. All hits are flukes: Institutional decision making and the rhetoric of prime-time network programme development. *American Journal of Sociology*, 99, pp. 1287–1313.

Björkegren, D. 1996. *The Culture Business*. London: Routledge.

Blair, H. and Rainnie, A. 2000. Flexible films? *Media, Culture and Society*, 22 (2), pp. 187–204.

Born, G. 2004. *Uncertain Vision: Birt, Dyke and the Reinvention of the BBC*. London: Secker and Warburg.

Bourdieu, P. 1984. *Distinction*. Cambridge Massachusetts: Harvard University Press.

Bourdieu, P. 1993. *The Field of Cultural Production*. Cambridge: Polity Press.

Buckingham, M. 2005. What great managers do. *Harvard Business Review*, Mar 83 (3), pp. 70–79.

Cantor, M. G. and Cantor, J. M. 1992. *Prime Time Television: Content and Control*. Second edition. Newbury Park: Sage.

Castañer, X. and Campos, L. 2002. The determinants of artistic innovation: Bringing in the role of organizations. *Journal of Cultural Economics*, 26, pp. 29–52.

Caves, R. E. 2000. *Creative Industries*. Harvard University Press.

Cohen, S. 1991. *Rock Culture in Liverpool: Popular Music in the Making*. Clarendon Press.

Collins, J. 2001. *Good To Great: Why Some Companies Make the Leap…and Others Don't*. Random House Business.

Davis, H. and Scase, R. 2000. *Managing Creativity*. Open University Press.

DeFillippi, R. and Arthur, A. 1998. Paradox in project-based enterprises: The case of film marketing. *California Management Review*, 40 (2), pp. 5–139.

DiMaggio, P. J. 1977. Market structure, the creative process and popular culture: Toward an organisational reinterpretation of mass culture theory. *Journal of Popular Culture*, 11, pp. 433–452.

Elliot, P. 1972. *The Making of a Television Series: A Case Study in the Sociology of Culture*, London: Constable.
Ettema, J. S. and Whitney, D. C. (eds.) 1985. Introduction in individuals in mass media organisations. *Sage Annual Review of Communication Research*, 10.
Frith, S. 1983. *Sound Effects: Youth, Leisure and the Politics of Rock and Roll.* Constable.
Frith, S. 1996. *Performing Rites.* Oxford: Oxford University Press.
Florida, R. 2002. *The Rise of the Creative Class: And How it's Transforming Work, Leisure, Community and Everyday Life.* New York: Basic Books.
Fulmer, I. S., Gerhart, B. and Scott, K. S. 2003. Are the 100 best better? An empirical investigation of the relationship between being a 'great place to work' and firm performance. *Personnel Psychology*, 56 (4), pp. 965–993.
Gardner, W. L., Avolio, B. J., Luthans, F., May, D. and Walumbwa, F. 2005. 'Can you see the real me?' A self-based model of authentic leader and follower development. *The Leadership Quarterly*, 16 (3), pp. 343–337.
Garnham, N. 1990. *Capitalism and Communication.* London: Sage.
Herzberg, F. 1968. *One More Time: How Do You Motivate Employees?Harvard Business Review*, 46, pp. 53–62.
Hesmondhalgh, D. 2006. *The Culture Industries.* London: Sage.
Hirsch, P. 1972. Processing fads and fashions: An organization-set analysis of cultural industry system. *American Journal of Sociology*, 77 (4), pp. 639–659.
Hochschild, A. R. 1983. *The Managed Heart: Commercialization of Human Feeling*. Berkeley: University of California Press.
Latham, G. P. and Ernst, C. T. 2006. Keys to motivating tomorrow's workforce. *Human Resource Management Review*, 16 (2), pp. 181–198.
Lee, D. 2013. Creative labour in the cultural industries. sociopedia.isa.
Locke, E. A. and Latham, G. P. 1990. *A Theory of Goal Setting & Task Performance.* Prentice-Hall Inc.
Maslow, A. H. 1987. *Motivation and Personality.* Third edition. Pearson Education.
McClelland, D. C. and Burnham, D. 1976. Power is the great motivator. *Harvard Business Review*, 54 (100–110), pp. 159–166.
McRobbie, A. 1998. *British Fashion Design: Rag Trade or Image Industry?*London: Routledge.
Miège, B. 1979. The cultural commodity. *Media Culture and Society*, 1, pp. 297–311.
Miège, B. 1987. The logics at work in the new cultural industries. *Media, Culture and Society*, 9, pp. 273–298.
Neale, S. 1980. *Genre.* London: BFI.
Negus, K. 1992. *Producing Pop.* London: Edward Arnold.
Negus, K. 1999. *Music Genres and Corporate Cultures.* London: Routledge.
Negus, K. 2002. The work of cultural intermediaries and the enduring distance between production and consumption. *Cultural Studies*, 16 (4), pp. 501–515.
Nohria, N.Joyce, W. and Roberson, B. 2003. What really works. *Harvard Business Review*, 81 (7), pp. 42–52.
Roberts, J. 2010. Revisiting the creative/commercial clash: Decision making during product development in the television industry. *Media Culture & Society*, 32 (51), pp. 761–780.
Roberts, J. 2011. Producers' decision-making during product development in the television industry: Addressing the cognitive gap. *International Journal of Media Management*, 4, pp. 277–295.
Ryan, Bill. 1992. *Making Capital from Culture.* De Gruyter.
Salas, E., Shuffler, M., Thayer, A., Bedwell, W. and Lazzara, E. 2014. Understanding and improving teamwork in organizations: A scientifically based practical guide. *Human Resource Management*, 54 (4), pp. 599–622.
Schneider, B. 1987. The people make the place. *Personnel Psychology*, 40, pp. 437–453.
Sparks, C. 1994. Independent production: Unions and casualisation, in Hood, S. (ed.). *Behind the Screens: The Structure of British Television in the Nineties.* London: Lawrence and Wishart.

Stratton, J. 1982a. Reconciling contradictions: The role of the artist and repertoire person in the British music industry. *Popular Music and Society*, 8 (2), pp. 90–100.
Stratton, J. 1982b. Between two worlds, art and commercialism in the record industry. *Sociological Review*, 30, pp. 267–285.
Tonybee, J. 2000. *Making Popular Music*. London: Arnold.
Turrow, J. 1985. Unconventional programmes on commercial television. In Ettema, J. S. and Whitney D. C. (eds), *Individuals in Mass media organisations, Sage Annual Review of Communication Research*, 10.
Ursell, G. 2000. Television production: Issues of exploitation, commodification and subjectivity in UK television labour markets. *Media, Culture and Society*, 22 (6), pp. 805–827.
Williams, R. 1981. *Culture*. London: Fontana.

8 The Consumer, Content and Marketing

8.1 Introduction

In this chapter we will trace the evolution of the cultural consumer, and how organisations have had to develop their content propositions and marketing capabilities to keep pace. In doing so we review some the core concepts of modern 'business-to-consumer' marketing, including the marketing mix (the four Ps), market segmentation and the use of market research.

The evolving discipline of marketing has had a mixed reception in the cultural industries. On the one hand, it is sometimes seen as something to be avoided by artists who wish to express their own very personal perspectives and artistic imperatives, irrespective of the immediate demands of the marketplace. Marketing is often seen as the main driver of the 'dumbing down' of culture, proposed by Adorno and Horkheimer in the 1940s. Equally, as we will see, given the high levels of cost and risk associated with the development of most cultural products, and their very high failure rates, it offers the potential to help create products that respond to specific consumer demands and hence improve their chances of success.

Whatever our view, it is certainly the case that it is taking on an ever more important role in the functioning of the industry as a whole, and the organisations within it.

8.2 The evolving consumer

For much of the history of the cultural industries, the consumer has been a relatively passive receiver of the industry's output. Whilst they might have had an overall effect on the types of content that was being produced, based on their response to previous products (e.g. detective shows on television might go through a period of particular popularity, a specific genre of music might emerge as fashionable amongst consumers, hence encouraging the industry to produce more of the same), their direct input into the characteristics and features of specific productions was limited. Market research techniques were relatively basic and appeared ill fitted to the peculiarities of the cultural product. Whilst in other industries, protypes and early versions of new products might be market tested amongst consumers before significant investment was made in further refining and developing the product, this is difficult if not impossible to do in the cultural industries.

Most cultural products needed to be developed to an almost fully finished state before being shown to potential consumers. Television programmes and films would need to be finished before being exhibited, music albums needed to be fully recorded

DOI: 10.4324/9781003498599-8

and mixed before they were heard by the audience. Whilst a certain amount of pre-testing might be possible (e.g. focus groups reviewing finished films, preview performances of new plays), by this point the vast majority of the product's development budget has typically already been spent and only relatively limited changes to the final product are possible. Indeed, many such initiatives are focused more on making final changes to the marketing campaign or release schedule for the product, rather than making changes to the product itself. Hence consumers were relatively limited in their involvement in product development.

Market research tools and techniques were relatively expensive to deploy, took time, effort and skill to arrange, and generated data with only limited use, given that the product was typically almost fully finished. Further, many in the industry were reluctant to fully embrace a more market- / consumer-driven approach. Individual content creators might feel they had a unique and innovative view that it was their prerogative to portray in the content they created. Who was the consumer to tell them how to portray their vision? What did they know? Listening too closely to the 'voice of the consumer' might indeed lead to a general 'dumbing down' of cultural content.

Further, given a lack of competition, consumers were relatively passive in their consumption patterns. They might have only two channels of television programming to choose from, on a single technological platform. To see a particular programme, they needed to watch the television at a very specific time on a specific day of the week—there was little choice involved. For the recorded music fan, they might only be able to choose between one or two formats (e.g. cassette or vinyl) and would ultimately be limited to their own content library. The radio might be an alternative, but this was programmed by someone else, and you were not guaranteed to hear the content you hoped to. For the live music fan, they might be forced to wait for a specific tour, at a specific venue, if they wished to see their favourite musician perform.

Ultimately, consumers were forced to take a back seat in the operation of the industry as recipients, rather than active participants in its operation. But things would change, driven by increasing competition and technological evolution in the industry.

Technical developments would initially allow the development of greater levels of competition in sectors like the television industry with the emergence of pay-TV platforms, and cable and satellite delivery. Subsequent developments including the growth of digital networks would encourage even more competition in the television space. From an environment in which, in the UK for example, up until the early 1980s consumers only had a choice between three channels on an analogue terrestrial network, consumers now have a large range of television providers to choose from. Digital terrestrial broadcasters remain (e.g. the BBC and ITV) but now complemented by a range of additional digital terrestrial channels (e.g. Channels 4 and 5), a variety of traditional pay-TV providers (e.g. Sky and Virgin), now accompanied by a range of streaming services from aggregators like Amazon and Netflix, and specialised providers like Disney and Paramount. This in turn is complemented by consumer-driven video on demand (VOD) services like YouTube or TikTok. Each service needs to announce its presence and advantages over competition.

Consumers can now view up to 300 channels of content. They can view programming when and where they want it thanks to 'catch-up' services like iPlayer and ITVX delivered via broadband networks. They can consume content on their (increasingly smart) TVs, mobile phones, computers or games consoles. This may happen in the home, or when travelling. As such, perhaps as never before, consumers can, if they choose, take an active role in determining their multifaceted viewing experience. At the same time, these devices and platforms are actively collecting consumer data about what we are watching and how we are watching it. Indeed, for some of the new providers in the television space (e.g. Netflix), consumer data and its application are at the heart of their strategic plans.

In other sectors, consumers have demonstrated that they too wanted greater control over their cultural experiences. In the popular music sector, dissatisfaction with the traditional business model led the consumer to develop new ways of acquiring and consuming music content. For much of its history, music had predominantly been distributed in the form of relatively expensive packaged media. The album format (e.g. 10 or 12 songs packaged together) came in for particular criticism, often with a few standout singles bundled together with lower-quality, 'filler' material. In other cases, even in the newly emerging digital sector, strict usage conditions meant that content purchased via one platform (e.g. iTunes) could only be played back on associated hardware (e.g. the iPod or iPhone).

In many ways the growth of non-commercial piracy (see Chapter 6) was a direct reaction against this restrictive traditional model and how the value of music was perceived. Consumers increasingly wanted specific content (e.g. not necessarily albums), available via a variety of different platforms, that could be played on any device, when and where they wanted it. Ideally, they wanted it for free and they also wanted to share it with their friends. They found ways to circumvent attempts by the major record companies to limit this. The evolution of ripping and compression software and its packaging into easy-to-use applications was very much driven by the consumer and active, technically literate consumer groups. Free-to-use software was regularly released, updated and posted to consumer forums. File-sharing services (e.g. Kazaa) evolved, supported by consumers who were willing to share the content they stored on their hard drives. Consumers were fighting (back) for their right to party.

Finally, consumers found they could take content creation into their own hands. From the growth and popularity of services such as YouTube, Instagram and TikTok, or Roposo and Moj in India (after the banning of TikTok), the emergence of pro-quality music creation software that could be run on home computers (e.g. GarageBand, Apple Pro Tools), combined with the emergence of distribution platforms like SoundCloud and Substack, to developments in digital cameras, digital video recorders and microphones, consumers found they could create and distribute their own content, and in some cases even make a living from it. Whilst we might debate whether the true democratisation of content creation has really come to pass as many early advocates of the internet proposed and hoped for (even the sparce anecdotal data that is available on user-generated content suggests that the vast majority of online content is created by a tiny proportion of internet users—the 1% rule, whereby it is claimed that 99% of online user-generated content is created by only 1% of users, with the rest merely consuming rather than creating it), the co-creation of content between active internet users and more traditional content companies is already a hot topic in the industry.

Of course, many consumers don't want to take quite such an active role in managing their cultural experiences. Choice can be chaos, it can be tiring and it can be expensive. For some the alternatives offered by one or two content providers on a single platform will remain their consumption model of choice. They are happy for someone else to go to the trouble of finding good content, curating and programming it, building it into a satisfying schedule of watching or listening. But without question, technical and competitive developments in the last 20 years have put the consumer in a far more powerful and potentially active position when it comes to interactions with content and its providers.

So how have providers responded? One response has been the provision of ever more content. New distribution platforms need new consumer-facing services: in the TV sector, new services need channels, channels needed programming. New music streaming services need a constant supply of new music. New games consoles need new games to demonstrate and exploit their technical sophistication. Yet the prospects for new content are not always positive.

8.3 The content wave

It is a hard fact of the cultural industries that most content fails to generate sufficient revenue to cover the cost of producing it.

This is not unusual in any way. Whilst precise proportions tend to vary with industry sector (higher in consumer goods, lower in health care), and some estimates of between 80% to 90% failure rates were common in academic papers in the 2010s, more recent and rigorous research suggest that between 40% and 50% of all new products fail to meet their objectives, and in some product categories like baby products and baked goods the failure rate of new products does reach towards 80% (see Rutkowski, 2022). Most new products are likely to fail, then.

The position seems equally pessimistic in the cultural industries. Again, estimates tend to vary significantly and have to be drawn from a variety of sources, but for example Steam, the PC game distribution platform, has noted that 80% of games released on the platform fail to reach $5000 in revenue in the first two weeks of sales.[1] In a similar vein, some estimates suggest only 20% of electronic games achieve profitability.[2] A report by SuperScale Research and GamesIndustry.biz[3] found that 83% of launched mobile games fail (are withdrawn) within three years. The same report goes onto suggest that 43% of games are cancelled during development. A similar situation is evident in other sectors, with anecdotal estimates suggesting even in the pre-pandemic boom times, only 20–30% of Broadway theatrical productions fully paid back their investors[4] (though the precise proportion is likely to vary with the genre—e.g. musical, play etc.). Anecdotal evidence[5] would suggest a similar situation in the film industry, with 80% of films failing to recoup their investment.

Many different views are expressed as to why this might be the case, but three issues are worth focusing on: the effect of the oversupply of content, the cost of content development and the difficulties of predicting the performance of new content.

According to the WIPO (the World Intellectual Property Organization), over 9511 films were produced in 2023[6], with India leading the way with over 2500 films. The overall growth in numbers was particularly driven by China, more than doubling its output to 792 films in 2023. The USA, traditionally a powerhouse of film production, ranked only fourth with 510 films. In other sectors we see equally large flows of content; we have already noted in Chapter 5 that some estimates suggest as many as 2000 new mobile games (though estimates vary widely) are released globally each day (Quora, 2024). The idol recruitment process developed by Johnny Kitagawa in Japan produces hundreds of new J and K-Pop acts every year. Other estimates, cited by both the CEOs of Warner Music and Universal Music at industry events in 2022, suggest that up to 100,000 tracks of music are uploaded to SoundCloud, Spotify, Apple and their peers every day.[7]

Of course, all of this pales into insignificance when we consider the volume of content being uploaded to social media and video platforms like YouTube by 'consumers' every day. According to Tubefilter[8], 500 hours of video content are uploaded to YouTube every minute, equating to 720,000 hours of new content each day, or according to YouTube's own corporate source, 20 million videos per day.

If we add this to pre-existing content libraries, the result is a huge volume of content available to consumers, with more and more content added every day. Yet the audience for content is not expanding significantly, nor the number of daily hours they are spending listening, viewing or playing content. These latter measures appear relatively static. In this increasingly crowded content market, then, it is more and more difficult for content providers to alert consumers to their specific piece of content, to encourage them to consume it, to monetise it in some form and hence to generate sufficient revenues to make profits.

The second element of this equation is of course the costs of content creation, as profits are only likely to emerge once costs have been recouped. Whilst the average cost to make a Western feature film is around £100m[9], including production and marketing costs, in some cases this is far exceeded. Estimates suggest that *Pirates of the Caribbean: On Stranger Tides* cost over £380m, *Avatar: The Way of Water*'s budget was $350m and *Spider-Man 2* cost $280m. Such high costs can also be found in the television sector: whilst the first series of *Game of Thrones* cost a mere $6m per episode, by the final series this had spiralled to over $15m per episode.[10] But even this seems moderate compared to the Amazon show *Rings of Power*, costing upwards of $60m per episode. Netflix spent $233.1m (£193.8m) on making *3 Body Problem.*[11] Even non-fantasy genre series, with limited sets and no special effects, can be expensive: single episodes of *Friends* or *The Big Bang Theory* typically cost around $10m.[12]

We have already noted the high costs of staging and running a West End or Broadway show in the performing arts sector (see Chapter 3), with staging costs (before a single ticket is sold) starting at around $1m for the most modest production, up to $50m for the most ambitious productions, and running costs typically in the $250k–$500k range per week.

Games too can consume huge production and marketing budgets. *Grand Theft Auto V*'s development budget exceeded $137.5m (representing a team of 250 people working on the project for five years), excluding marketing and promotion costs, according to one analyst.[13] For Bungie's *Destiny* the development and marketing budget was estimated to be around $400m. In a 2023 report by the UK Competition and Markets Authority it was stated that AAA games that were greenlit for a potential global release in 2024 and 2025 received an average development budget of $200m, up from $150m in 2018.[14] Court documents presented in a case focused on games publisher Activision revealed that the total budgets (including development and marketing) for three *Call of Duty* games released between 2015 and 2020 varied between $450m and $750m.[15]

Given these high production and marketing costs, perhaps it is inevitable that content can struggle to make a profit. The final, and perhaps most challenging, issue is that 'no-one knows anything'! It has long been argued that predicting the performance and success of new cultural content is difficult if not impossible. Even the most successful actors, directors, producers and musicians, with long track records of success, can suddenly find themselves producing flops.

We have already noted Andrew Lloyd Webber's 2014 struggles with a new production, *Stephen Ward*, having invested nearly £2.5m staging the new production, only for it to close in a mere four months (see Chapter 3). In a similar vein, in 2002, Eddie Murphy, a hugely successful multi-award-winning American comedian and actor, having starred in a string of highly profitable films, launched his latest film, *The Adventures of Pluto Nash*, which had a $100m budget, but only managed to generate total global cinema revenues of around $7m.

In the popular music sector, Fleetwood Mac produced one of the bestselling albums of all time with their 1977 *Rumours* album, selling a total of 40m copies worldwide. Their follow-up album, *Tusk*, would go on to sell around 4m copies. The list of 'one-hit wonders', artists who have only a single successful song in their entire careers, is enormous.[16] Immediate success in the cultural industries, then, does not guarantee continued success. Tastes and fashions change, consumers move on and their thirst for new and innovative content usually appears to outweigh their loyalty to specific artists or franchises. Predicting these often-rapid changes in taste and fashion appears to be particularly difficult.

So why on earth would anyone bother? Content is expensive and typically difficult to produce, it is generally considered difficult to predict in terms of its likely performance and ultimately unlikely to generate a return on investment. That's not good business practice. Well, there is another outcome, of course, but it is rare. The spectacular success, the blockbuster, the big hit.

Successful films, games and music content can generate huge returns, very quickly. The movie *Avatar* (2009) had a very high budget, of $237m. But the movie grossed well over $2.9bn in cinemas alone, not including merchandising sales, packaged media sales or sales to television (we might estimate that this could add at least an additional $500m to the total). *Ne Zha 2* (China, 2025), costing a relatively modest $80m to create, has already generated cinema revenues of $2.2bn, even before a version dubbed into English was released in the USA.

Not only can successful content generate huge revenues and profits, but it can also do so incredibly quickly. *Grand Theft Auto V* achieved retail sales of $1bn within three days of its launch. Estimates suggest it sold 11m copies in its first day of release, and 29m copies within six weeks of launch. *Black Myth: Wukong* sold 10m copies in its first three days of launch, and *Zelda: Tears of the Kingdom* sold a similar number in its launch weekend.

Even in the unpredictable world of performing arts, some content can generate significant returns. Estimates suggest that the Broadway production of *The Lion King* has generated sales of over $2bn based on over 10,000 performances. The musical *Wicked* has generated sales of $1.7bn. *The Phantom of the Opera* (one of Andrew Lloyd Webber's successes) has generated $1.3bn. These are just revenues generated on Broadway in the USA. If we include worldwide revenues, then estimates suggest *The Lion King* has generated over $8bn, and *Phantom of the Opera* over $6bn.

The ultimate blockbuster is the piece of content (typically called a franchise) that can work on multiple platforms—that is, it can be successfully exploited across different sectors of the cultural industries. Estimates suggest that the *Pokémon* franchise has generated over $113bn in revenues since 1996, including $100bn in retail sales, $9bn in mobile games sales and $1.1bn in cinema ticket sales. It has even managed to generate $3m in aircraft livery sales. A franchise like *Star Wars* has also been successful on multiple platforms, generating over $10bn in cinema tickets, $30bn in merchandising sales, $4bn in video games sales and $1.8bn in book sales. The *Harry Potter* franchise, worth an estimated $34bn, has been exploited as a film, book, in merchandise, video game, studio tours, a stage play and is about to become a major TV series.

In some areas of content, the focus is particularly on finding relatively unknown talent and hoping for an unexpected break-out hit. Alanis Morissette was a relatively unknown music artist who had two relatively unsuccessful albums before her breakout hit album, *Jagged Little Pill.* Her relative lack of global success up to this point (though she was well known in Canada) meant that the record company could fund a relatively cheap album in terms of recording and production costs and could sign a contract with the artist in which the record company would secure the vast proportion of revenues and profits should the album be successful. Emergent artists are not in a strong position when negotiating with a powerful record company. The album went on to sell over 33m copies globally, a hugely profitable endeavour for the record company. It would subsequently be the basis for a theatre adaptation.

Hence the business model can work, but it's highly unpredictable, and without the emergence of breakout blockbuster hits to compensate for the vast majority of content that is loss-making, it is ultimately unsustainable for a company.

8.4 Managing risk

The list of successful content we have just described tells us a great deal about how practitioners in the industry have traditionally tried to deal with these high levels of risk and uncertainty.

Producers are likely to draw on existing, well-known and culturally significant characters; *Ne Zha* is a good example, and we might also cite the Disney Princess franchise, drawing on traditional Western fairy and folk tales. Further, producers will be particularly interested in content that has already been successful in one part of the cultural industries. Hence *Harry Potter* was a hugely successful literary franchise before it was considered as a potential feature film. The Avengers were successful as comic book characters, before the Marvel Cinematic Universe was ever considered. Many successful manga titles have had continued success as feature films or TV series (e.g. *Naruto, Attack on Titan, Sailor Moon*) based on their initial success as manga. Success in one area means that there are already likely to be a significant group of potential consumers for new types of content based on the franchise, significantly reducing risk.

Producers are also likely to be interested in follow-ups of successful content in the same genre or media. The early success of *Avengers Assemble* has led to another 37 films being released, with eight more at various stages of development as of 2025. *Avatar* has up to six films planned to follow up on the success of the 2009 original.

Another way in which risk can be reduced is in the use of well-known artists in the creation of content. For film and TV this may mean actors, writers or directors. In the music sector it's likely to include musicians, but also music producers and remixers. In an orchestral environment, this might mean specific conductors or featured soloists. This can even extend to the use of particularly well-known artists and designers in the games sector—e.g. Shigeru Miyamoto (*Mario* and *Zelda*), Yoji Shinkawa (*Metal Gear Solid* series) or Yoshitaka Amano, whose design skills have been integral to the *Final Fantasy* franchise. In each case the use of well-known and established talent, whether in front or behind the camera, reassures both investors that they are likely to make a return on their investment and audiences that they are likely to enjoy the experience of consuming the content.

From a corporate point of view, one of the key strategies of most large content providers is content diversity. If it is difficult to predict if a specific piece of content will be a hit, it's seen to be best to spread risk by producing a variety of different content (a 'slate' or portfolio of content). Hence major record companies will have different labels catering to different genres and audience groups. Movie studios will have production divisions focused on different genres, audience groups or working within specific budget parameters. Walt Disney Corp. for example houses Walt Disney Studios, Disney Animation, Pixar, Marvel Studios, Lucasfilm, Searchlight Pictures, 20th Century Studios and FX. Major television production companies are likely to have production operations for different genres (entertainment, comedy, documentary etc.). In each case the overall aim of the organisation will be to produce a broad range of content, in different genres, covering as much of their target audience as possible in the hope at least one blockbuster hit will emerge.

Even within the broad categories of J-pop and K-pop, subgenres have emerged, allowing providers to target specific parts of the market. Combining elements of pop, hip-hop, rock, R&B and electronic music in different ways, artists and bands can be developed to service specific sub-groups of consumers with particular musical wants and needs, allowing companies to present a diverse range of content to the marketplace in the hope that one particular song or group might catch a cultural or fashion wave and emerge as a major hit.

The final strategy utilised by providers to help offset the high risks associated with product development and launch, and to maximise the chances of a reasonable return on investment, has already been mentioned: the deployment of significant marketing budgets to support the release of the new product. This might be in the form of promotional campaigns, or pre-release testing. Combined with traditional windowing strategies, the performance of a new piece of content in one territory or media allowed companies to set marketing budgets at appropriate levels for subsequent rollout of the product in other markets. A film that was a significant hit in the USA was likely to attract significant marketing spend in other international territories. For those that performed poorly, the company might wish to cut its losses and limit subsequent investment in marketing. Hence traditional approaches to windowing allowed a certain degree of market testing.

These businesses are highly 'hit-driven', then. Organisations rely on the major hits to make up for the losses they make on the majority of content they produce that does not make a significant return on investment, that does not cover its costs and hence is ultimately loss-making. Producing a broad range of content, aimed at different parts of the overall market, supporting this content with significant marketing budgets, and the use of 'star' talent with a high public profile have emerged as the key strategies for most providers.

But when we discuss marketing in this context, do we mean the same thing as marketing in other business sectors? What exactly are we describing? Before analysing the specifics of marketing in the cultural industries further, a brief overview of the core tenets of the marketing function might be useful.

8.5 Marketing 101

Whilst we cannot hope to cover all of the critical components of marketing here, we can highlight some of its core elements as the basis for your further study. As suggested in Chapter 2, the marketing function typically represents 'the voice of the customer or consumer' in an organisation and is particularly focused on understanding the customer / consumer, and guiding the organisation through the process of developing appropriate products and services for them. Once developed, marketing is then critical to how these new products are promoted to the customer: they need to be aware of the new product or service to begin to generate an interest in it, before ultimately buying it. Three critical elements of marketing are worth discussing here: the use of market research, market segmentation and the marketing mix (or the four Ps).

8.5.1 Market research and segmentation

If you work in the marketing function of any organisation you are likely to spend a good deal of your time researching the marketplace. Such research will typically have two particular areas of focus: developing a deep understanding of the customer / consumer and understanding broader changes in the business landscape. When looking at customers / consumers we are typically interested in their characteristics, their needs and wants and their behaviour as buyers. For business-to-consumer-based organisations, we are likely to explore things like consumer demographics (gender, income, location, job, education level), psychographics (their motivations and desires) and behavioural characteristics (how they buy products, how they use and assess them). An enormous range of tools and techniques have emerged to help us explore these areas, including surveys, focus groups, concept testing, usage testing studies and customer interviews. Many of these were developed first in the fast-moving consumer goods sector (FMCG), hence they are utilised by companies like Unilever, P&G and PepsiCo on a daily basis. Organisations in the business-to-business sector tend to focus more on understanding the functioning of complex decision-making groups and how and why organisations as a whole make their purchase decisions, hence they are likely to focus more on customer visits, lead user analysis and tools like QFD (Quality Function Deployment).

As market researchers you may also be charged with looking at the business environment more broadly using a variety of alternative tools. What are the major changes in the social environment, how is technology evolving, how might economic trends impact our business (e.g. the imposition of tariffs by the Trump administration in 2025), are there new regulatory or legislative initiatives that may impact our business? Tools like the PESTLE model already mentioned in Chapter 2 can be useful in this regard. You will almost certainly be researching your competitors and examining their work practices and product range (through things like benchmarking). You might also be exploring the attractiveness of new markets by using tools such as Porter's 5 Forces. You might want to consider what level of maturity a market has achieved, using product life cycle models, or the degree to which a product, service or technology has penetrated a marketplace using Roger's adoption / diffusion model (2003), described in section 8.5.2.

Our focus as marketers is very much outwards, aimed at developing a clear understanding of the functioning of the market, particularly from a customer point of view, and how that market is likely to evolve. One tool that is often used to capture the diversity of the market is the idea of market segmentation. It's an analytical and organising device that helps marketers analyse market data and reduce it to useful pointers in terms of specific marketing strategies (e.g. around product development, promotion or pricing).

A market segment is a group of customers who have similar needs that are different from customer needs in other parts of the market. Where these customer groups are relatively small, such market segments are often called 'niches'. Segments might evolve around differing customer needs or wants, different demographics, different purchasing behaviours, different sensitivities to price, different parts of the global market and so on. Rather than attempting to produce a single product or service to address an entire market, most companies attempt to differentiate themselves by providing products for specific parts or segments of the market.

Hence an organisation producing hair shampoo might have a portfolio of shampoos for different consumers—a range for consumers who want a cheap product, an expensive one, a highly scented one, one without scent, one focused on dealing with medical conditions like dry scalp, another with strong green credentials, one for the French market, another for the Asian market and so on. In a similar vein car producers will have a variety of models targeting the first-time buyer, the company car owner, the off-road fan, the luxury car buyer and so on. Segmentation can be a useful tool to understand existing consumers (who may differ in the reasons they purchase a particular product or service) and to identify new market segments that might be addressed (see Figure 8.1).

For example, assuming that all visitors to an opera performance share the same needs, wants and desires can be very misleading. The attendees at a specific opera performance are likely to be divided up into those that attend because they love opera, those that just want a night out, those who like to dress up, those who like particular genres of opera, fans of particular composers, fans of particular performers, some who received a heavily discounted ticket price, some who paid full price, some who live next to the opera house, some who may have travelled long distances, some who think the provision of high-quality support services (the bar, toilets, parking etc.) is of critical

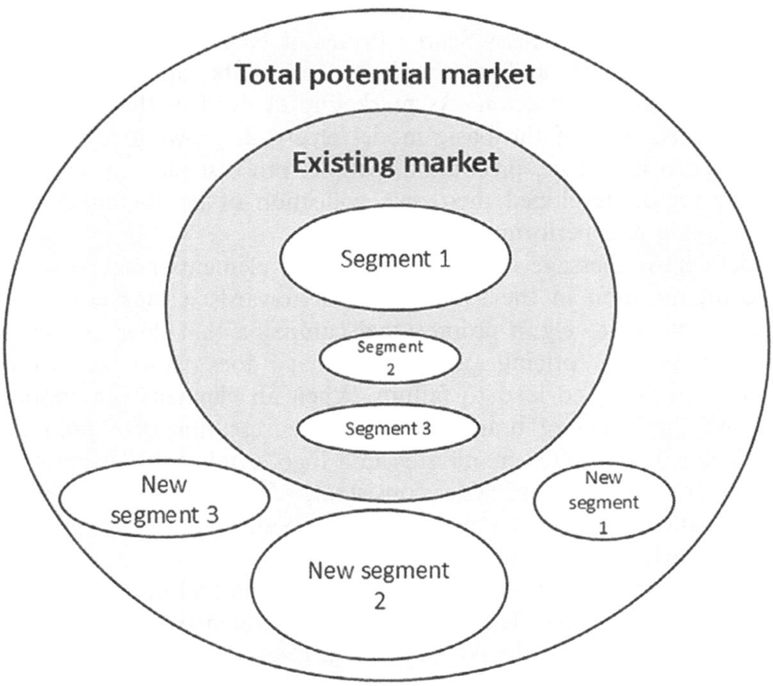

Figure 8.1 Segmenting a market
Source: author.

importance to the overall experience, others who are likely to ignore these issues completely and are just focused on the performance, some who visit every week, some who might visit once a year. The point being that even for something as apparently homogeneous as an audience for an opera, there may be many different motivations and assessment criteria for a positive experience working under the surface. The aim of segmentation analysis is to assess and understand these different drivers, identify the most attractive segments and adapt products and services accordingly to more closely meet their requirements.

Marketers are often intent on finding valuable new segments that might be the source of further demand and hence revenues and profits. Certainly, in the opera sector, most providers feel that they need to focus on younger audience segments as a potentially untapped source of future demand. Not all untapped new segments will be attractive, however; some may be too small to be attractive, too difficult to address (e.g. the company may need to develop significant new assets and capabilities to service the segment) or already serviced by a dominant competitor. Hence again it is likely to be the role of the marketing team to analyse potential new segments in terms of economic viability and attractiveness.

8.5.2 The marketing mix or four Ps

Having decided on a set of targets (e.g. market segments), what tools and techniques can marketers call on to devise new marketing strategies? Most activities are focused on what have become called the marketing mix or four Ps of marketing: that is, product, place (or distribution), price and promotion. The idea originated in McCarthy's 1960 book *Basic Marketing: A Managerial Approach*, drawing on the earlier work of Harvard Business School Professor Neil H. Borden. It was a simple and self-explanatory idea, and its simplicity helped its rapid adoption by practitioners in the marketing function. As marketing evolved in the second half of the 20th century, variations of the basic model emerged, growing to seven Ps in one model (product, price, place, promotion, people, process, physical evidence). Those in the service sector developed their own collection of Ps, including people, positioning, packaging and performance.

The model's basic message is that each of these elements need to work together, pulling the organisation in the same direction towards a marketing goal. Inconsistency in any element—e.g. a promotional campaign that does not support a distribution strategy, a pricing approach that does not fit with product characteristics—is likely to lead to failure. When all elements are supporting each other, we have the basics of brand marketing, the creation of a product / service, with a particular image (often manifested in a logo, symbol or design characteristic) whose characteristics are identifiable, consistent, self-supporting and help to differentiate the product or service from those of competitors (e.g. the Apple brand).

Let's look at each in a little more detail.

Product: marketers are regularly involved in designing and developing the look and feel of products and services. This might be from scratch or might be based on the work of other departments in the company—e.g. research and development (R&D) or engineering teams. Their input might cover such issues as what does it look or feel like, how does it function, what are its usage conditions, and particularly what are its key advantages over existing competitor products (sometimes called its USP or unique selling proposition)? This might also include how existing products or services might be improved or upgraded (often called incremental product innovation). In making their recommendations, the marketing team are likely to have reviewed existing products and suppliers in the marketplace, drawing on primary (e.g. focus groups, customer surveys) or secondary (e.g. competitors' product brochures) sources. They might also draw on tools like product life cycle, adoption / diffusion or product portfolio models.

Life cycle models are relatively straightforward, in that they suggest products and services go through various stages of sales (and particularly sales growth) as they evolve, from introduction, through rapid growth, maturity (when sales growth plateaus) and eventual decline. At each stage various elements of the marketing mix, including product characteristics or promotional strategy, might need to be modified to maximise performance. Of particular concern tends to be maturity, when sales growth tends to stall, often as a result of new competitive products entering the market. At such points the marketing team may need to think about how to modify the product or service to promote a new surge in sales growth, or they may decide to allow the product to go into decline, particularly if the costs of maintaining it are too high, or if because of technological developments it would be better to design an entirely new product.

A second perspective can be drawn from **adoption / diffusion models** such as that first described by Rogers in his 1962 (see the 2003 updated version) book *Diffusion of Innovations.*

The model argues that the total potential market for any new product or service can be divided up into different sub-segments, each with different consumer characteristics. Radically new products tend to be first adopted by innovators and early adopters (typically around 16% of the total market) with a relatively high appetite for risk. They like new ideas, are willing to engage with complex product descriptions and often require a lot of technical information to make their purchase choice. They are typically relatively well off and very sociable; they are likely to spend a lot of their time talking to friends and colleagues about their new acquisition. They are followed by the slightly more risk-averse early majority (around 34% of the market). This compares to a group like the late majority (again around 34% of the market), with a low risk appetite and little patience for overly long technical descriptions of the product; indeed they are only likely to adopt a new product if it's recommended to them by one of the early majority. They tend to have lower financial resources and are much less likely to proselytise about their new acquisition. Finally, the product is adopted by laggards (around 16% of the market). For each of the major segments there may need to be changes to elements of the marketing mix, including product characteristics, pricing and the promotional campaign. For example, a key aim of any early promotional campaign is likely to be to turn innovators and early adopters into vocal opinion leaders, encouraging them to spread the word to other parts of the market about the new innovation; hence it may rely heavily on social media.

Further Rogers outlined characteristics that potential consumers tend to evaluate when deciding whether to adopt an innovation, including compatibility (how well does this innovation fit with existing values, patterns of behaviour or products?), trialability (can you try it before you buy it?), relative advantage (in what way is this innovation better than the alternatives?), observability (are its benefits noticeable?) and simplicity / complexity (the easier it is to learn or use, the faster it diffuses).

Another product-related issue that marketers are often involved in includes ensuring the right mix of products is being developed and offered. We mentioned this as being particularly important in the cultural industries, with organisations producing a wide range of different products to address multiple parts of the overall market. **Product portfolio analysis tools** have emerged in other sectors to assist the marketer in this regard. Such tools are typically used to assess the range of products currently supplied by an organisation in terms of their importance and potential. The aim typically is to create a balanced portfolio of products which deliver profits today and have the potential to deliver profits in the future.

A typical model is the Boston Consulting Group product portfolio model. This model categorises products according to their relative market share (their potential to generate profits today, typically characterised as high or low) and their growth potential (the potential to generate profits in the future, again typically characterised as high or low market growth rates). Different products will be at different stages of their life cycle and hence will have different prospects. Cash cows are vital—they are likely to deliver strong profits today. This is based on the fact that such products have a high level of relative market share (they are very popular with consumers), but the market is not growing dramatically (low industry growth rate). Fast-growing markets tend to be expensive to compete in. There are often a significant number of competitors (everyone is attracted to a fast-growing market), so significant funds are spent on things like promotional campaigns. As such, costs are high, and profits relatively limited. However, when industry growth slows, competitors often leave markets, promotional and product development budgets can be cut, and ultimately higher profits secured. This is the case for cash cows.

Profits are typically then invested in 'stars', products with high market share and high industry growth prospects. Whilst these are critical products for the future of the company, their high industry growth rates typically mean high levels of competition, and hence limited profits. But they offer the prospect of becoming cash cows, once industry growth rates slow.

Further 'question mark' products offer the prospect of high growth potential, but with limited potential to generate revenues due to low relative market share—that is, products from other providers are more popular. However, it might be that with changes to a product's characteristics or function (e.g. improving a camera on a mobile phone), or with better distribution, bigger promotional budgets etc., then more market share might be obtained. Hence, they may require further investment to become successful 'stars'. Finally, dogs are products that are generally in decline (low market share, low industry growth rates) and probably should no longer be supported with significant investments in things like product development and promotion. Arguably they should probably be discontinued.

The aim of using the model is to ensure that an organisation has a balanced range of products and services in each of the key categories (particularly stars and cash cows) and that dogs are identified and killed off. A variety of models have emerged to complement the BCG approach, including the GE-McKinsey directional policy matrix and the Parenting Matrix proposed by Goold et al. (2006).

Price: in making pricing decisions, marketing staff will often find themselves working with other key functions—perhaps the operations team who are involved in the manufacture or delivery of the product, and almost certainly the finance team whose role it is to monitor costs, revenues and profits. With its origin in the bargaining between buyers and sellers, pricing now fulfils a role far broader than merely identifying what a consumer has to pay, helping to manage demand and customer expectations and hence impacting on the satisfaction that a customer gets from consuming a product or service. Certainly, there is significant evidence that many consumers use price as a critical indicator of product / service quality.

How do companies usually set prices? Well, as Kotler et al. (2009) note, the decision is likely to be partly driven by the organisation's immediate objectives for the product / service. Is the aim to maximise the market share of the new product? If so, a lower price might be set than competitive products to drive market penetration. The end game for such a strategy is usually related to developing an advantageous cost structure, given that as market share increases, the volume of products produced will increase, and the company will start to benefit from the 'experience curve' (the more you make of a product, the better you get at it, potentially cutting production costs) and potentially benefitting from volume discounts from suppliers (further cutting costs). Both mean lower costs, and potentially higher profits than competitors.

The focus may be more on maximising current profits (e.g. for a cash cow), in which case a higher price point might be selected. Some might choose Sony's typical approach of 'market skimming' (Kotler et al., 2009)—starting with a high price and reducing it over time: e.g. whilst current 8K televisions command a huge price premium (potentially only attractive to innovators and early adopters), consumers in the early majority segment are well aware that the price of such new technology is likely to decline over time.

Some organisations choose to adopt a cost-plus model, based on a detailed analysis of the costs of production, then adding in a required profit margin to generate a specific return on investment (often termed target return pricing). Others will fix prices driven by what competitors are charging for similar products. The image of the product as a luxury or mere necessity good is also likely to play a highly significant role in price setting. In each case, an overriding concern for the marketing team is to ensure that whatever price is set, it is supported by the rest of the marketing mix—e.g. it fits with the product's characteristics, takes into account how the product will be distributed (e.g. additional stages in the distribution chain are likely to add additional costs) and fits with its image and the way in which the product / service is promoted.

Whilst the marketing team might be very involved in setting initial prices, they may be even more active in decisions around specific promotional pricing initiatives. From special event pricing to 'buy one get one free' campaigns, cash rebates or low-interest financing (for major purchases like cars) there are a huge range of ways in which the marketing team may temporarily adjust standard pricing to encourage purchase. The area of dynamic pricing is of particular interest to many business sectors, enabled by technological developments that allow prices of products and services to be rapidly changed on an hour by hour, or even minute by minute, basis, even in a 'live' retail environment. Yet it is fair to say that such initiatives do not always produce intended outcomes—a 'buy one get one free' campaign may lead to future sales being cannibalised, or changing the price of one product in your portfolio may affect how other products are perceived in a negative way. A promotional offer on one type of product may lead to increases or declines in sales of other products.

Whilst such promotional pricing campaigns were applied with relatively little analysis in the past, leading to often unexpected and unfavourable outcomes, the art of promotional pricing has now become a science, driven by complex mathematical models of likely consumer behaviour. At the heart of many such models lie assumptions around price elasticities and likely demand curves. Price elasticity measures the sensitivity of consumers to price changes. If a slight change in price leads to a very significant change in demand, then demand is elastic. If a similar change in price leads to only a small change in demand, it is described as inelastic. Different products have different price elasticities, and these will further change depending on promotional pricing initiatives. Combined with historical sales data, extremely complex models can be built that allow accurate forecasts of consumer responses to price changes to be developed, an area of marketing that has been particularly driven by the retail and FMCG sectors. This is representative of the way in most marketing decision making is now highly analytical, driven by huge volumes of consumer data, built into complex, typically computer-based, models. This is an interesting and significant change as for much of its history, marketing was the function you went into if you were more creative and visual, and perhaps less confident in areas like numerical analysis and model building. This is no longer the case. To fulfil the potential of marketing today, marketeers need strong numerical and analytical skills to maximise the value of the consumer data they increasingly have access to.

Place: organisations often sit within complex webs of suppliers and distributors; they are part of what have become known as supply chains (also called value chains—see Chapter 2). Whilst such supply chain management tends to be thought of as the province of the operations or purchasing teams within an organisation, marketers often get involved in decision making around distribution or retail channel management and in analysing the impact of such decisions on the ultimate consumer. In an era of globalisation, supply chains have taken on new importance as the drivers of competitive advantage in some sectors; indeed well-known marketing academics (see Achrol and Kotler, 1999) have gone as far as to suggest that in our increasingly networked global environment, competition is now between supply networks, often stretched across distant territories, rather than individual companies.

Such supply chains will often include manufacturing companies, suppliers of components and raw materials, wholesalers, retailers, distributors, trading companies, transport companies, warehouses and so on. A broad range of organisations, then, often with different agendas, aims and goals, processes and priorities. Hence the chain needs careful management, and indeed we have seen the emergence of supply chain management (SCM) as a distinct and important function in many companies, particularly those like Apple, P&G and Coca-Cola who rely on complex manufacturing and distribution chains spread across the globe. The challenge is a difficult one, as different agendas, systems and processes need to be coordinated and synchronised across many different organisations (and potentially territories) if the consumer is to receive the product in an appropriate final form, when they need it, at a cost they can afford.

Two factors have driven the focus on supply chain management in particular. The first is cost. According to some estimates, distribution costs can account for up to 30–40% of all product costs (Kotler et al., 2009), so finding cost savings in how the product is distributed can reap significant rewards in terms of potential profit margins. Manufacturing makes up another significant proportion of costs and finding suppliers who can manufacture components, supply raw materials and assemble finished goods at the lowest cost has become a critical commercial lever for many organisations. Conversely, getting these decisions wrong can add hugely to a company's costs and limit its flexibility, ultimately ensuring that it is never commercially competitive, and unlikely to make a significant profit.

A second major factor has been the increasing focus on the need for organisational speed and agility. Working with a range of different suppliers, in different parts of the globe, with different specialisms can add to an organisation's flexibility and ability to respond to frequent and fast-moving market changes. The ability to rapidly change from one supplier to another, and to quickly reconfigure the supply chain, without having to fundamentally redesign one's own organisation, offers significant speed advantages. Equally, again, getting this wrong can be disastrous. Apple's reliance on external chip suppliers and Chinese manufacturing capabilities proved to be a significant challenge during the COVID-19 epidemic, and during the geopolitical instability of the early 2020s. Apple's move to broaden its supplier base and lessen its reliance on China as a manufacturing base (partly as a result of President Tump's global tariff policy) has meant a greater focus on other territories (including India and the USA itself) as core parts of its global supply chain.

Choosing the right route to market, and the appropriate type and level of intermediaries and suppliers, and developing the appropriate systems and processes to ensure a unified approach to serving the ultimate consumer remains a critical strategic challenge for many organisations and is at the centre of many digital transformation projects. For marketers, such decisions must be intimately integrated with choices about product, promotion and pricing. Further, typically all such decisions are now made within an 'omni-channel' context—that is, a business environment in which companies may use a variety of different channels to reach the consumer, including websites, mobile apps, mail order, television, physical stores and social media, in an integrated approach in which each channel contributes to and feeds off the functioning of others. Further, new technologies like drone delivery, autonomous vehicles and the application of AI to manage complex global systems offer the potential to radically enhance or disrupt existing approaches to supply chain management (as the internet did when it first emerged). This creates a hugely complex decision-making context.

In all such cases it is marketing's role to prioritise the consumer and customer, rather than focusing entirely on their own company in decision making. A supply chain may be hugely efficient and effective from an internal perspective (e.g. in terms of managing costs), but unless it is getting the right product to the right consumer at the right time and price, no amount of internal efficiency will secure long-term competitive advantage. This is particularly so if supply chain management also includes elements of customer relationship management and customer service, as it increasingly does. Customer enquiries about the progress of an order, or indeed complaints about the products they have received or requests to return a product, may be the only personal contact a customer has with the organisation (other than placing the order) and hence it is vital the exchanges are handled carefully with a view to maximising customer satisfaction. Such exchanges can turn regular, brand-loyal consumers into active advocates against the organisation, or convert first-time users into regular shoppers.

Ultimately many highly successful firms have built their entire business model and strategy on how well they manage their supply chain, including Unilever, Coca-Cola, Ikea, Toyota and Apple, and in the business-to-business sector, companies like Alibaba, and it remains a critical element of the marketing mix, with growing importance in terms of its influence on profitability and the nature of the organisational / consumer relationship.

Promotion: this is perhaps the element of the marketing mix most associated with the core marketing function; indeed, as we will subsequently see, in some sectors marketing means promotion and little else. Even a brief overview of the field could fill an entire book, so we can only skim the surface of the subject in this section. Generally classified under the term marketing communications, it is essentially the way in which organisations attempt to reach out to consumers or customers to inform, persuade or remind them about their products and services.

Marketing communications are typically divided up into broad categories including:

1 Advertising—that is, paid-for promotion, often on television, radio, online or in newspapers, including variants like outdoor advertising and billboards.
2 Sales promotion—that is, short-term promotional campaigns, often intended to prompt trial of a product or increase usage. The 'buy one get one free' approach suggested earlier is a good example. Point of sale promotions are also regularly used in retail outlets. They might also be in the form of contests and games.
3 Public relations and publicity, typically designed to improve a company's image, often in the form of coverage which is not paid for in newspapers (e.g. articles) or on television. Marketing tools might include press kits, speeches and annual reports or sponsorship deals.
4 Direct marketing—communications aimed at specific consumers, often personalised, delivered via a variety of routes (traditionally by post, but increasingly via interactive TV or via emails or texts).
5 Word of mouth—communication aimed at encouraging consumers to discuss and 'spread the word' about a specific product or service, often used in online chatrooms, or through blogs.
6 Personal selling, of the type often used in mobile phone shops or car dealerships.

Such tools are typically used to build awareness of a product, service or brand, encourage take-up and trial of new products, increase product usage or promote a positive image for an organisation as whole. The focus therefore might be on providing key points of information to persuade a consumer, to create an overall brand image to engage with the consumer's emotions, or to try and encourage the consumer to take action (make a decision, make a purchase).

The overall aim of any marketing communication is likely to be specifically linked to the immediate aims or goals for a specific product or service—e.g. building awareness of a new product or reminding consumers of a brand they may not have used in a while. This will then be reflected in the various elements of communication design—e.g. what is the core **message**, what is the **creative strategy** (what the message should look and sound like), what is the most appropriate **media strategy** to deliver the message (e.g. what channels should be used—TV, cinema, radio, magazine, online etc.). In considering the latter issue, data and estimates of reach (how many different people will be reached), frequency (how often people are likely to see the message) and impact (how likely the specific media chosen is to have an effect on the consumer) are likely to be considered.

Different communication media tend to be associated with different overall communication goals. Television, for example, is generally seen as best at creating awareness and building an overall positive consumer view of a product or service. It is good at reaching large potential audiences simultaneously. It is less good at providing large amounts of specific data to specific groups of consumers, but very good at creating an overall image and emotional response. Magazine advertising (and print advertising more generally), on the other hand, can provide much more data and detail, and is often used to complement television advertising, focused on a specific part of the market. Direct marketing tends to be useful for customising messages, and providing a call to action, perhaps an incentive or discount that will turn consumer interest and intention into action (a purchase). Public relations tends to be useful for building the image of a product or organisation but tends to be less useful for calls to action. Hence each major form of media has different characteristics and is likely to be used in different ways to achieve different goals. Such decisions are likely to be further influenced by the characteristics of the target market (e.g. what they tend to read or watch, how they tend to make decisions, how ready are they to act), stage of the product life cycle, availability of marketing budgets (television advertising tends to be expensive, after all), competitive actions and the skills and capabilities of the marketing team.

The overall aim of most promotional campaigns is to integrate activities across a variety of media, using different tools and techniques to achieve strategic and tactical (shorter-term) goals, generally with a view to moving the consumer along the purchase process from awareness (A), through interest (I) and desire (D), to action (A), the AIDA model.

A particular focus in recent years has been on attempting to get better at assessing and measuring the impact of specific communication programmes, something that has proven elusive in the past given the difficulties of separating out the effects of the communication campaign itself from other marketing variables and changes in the business environment. Did consumer demand increase because of a new marketing message, or because of competitive actions, a price cut, a product reformulation or merely because of changing consumer tastes and fashions, for example? Significant data and computing power is now being deployed to answer such questions.

As has already been noted, the four Ps are core elements of the marketing mix, but others have been suggested. In the service sector, the P of People takes on a particular significance given the often-critical role of people in delivering a service. The P of Process also emerges as significant, in terms of the design of the service delivery systems and managing the consumer experience. The discussion amongst practitioners, however, tends to be less around whether these issues are important (they clearly are) and more to do with the degree to which they should fall under the auspices of the marketing department, or whether such issues would be better managed by other teams—e.g. if people are that significant, should their involvement be managed by the HR team, if process is so critical, should the operations team be responsible for developing and running key processes, if place is critical, what should be the role of the supply chain team?

Having briefly reviewed the key levers that marketers shift in order to manage the marketing mix, what can we say about how marketing tends to manifest itself in the cultural industries?

8.6 Marketing in the cultural industries

8.6.1 The brand-building window

When reviewing this subject, we need to take two perspectives into account: the cultural industries as a promotional platform for products and services (the brand-building window), and the specific marketing techniques that tend to be used by the industry itself. The modern cultural industries, particularly television, radio and publishing, create brand-building windows: they are the media that companies in every type of business use to promote their products and services and build their brands. If Unilever wants to launch a new shampoo, they are likely to use TV and radio advertising, magazine advertising and a variety of other resources. If BMW want to remind everyone what high-quality cars they produce, you are likely to see an advertisement on TV or on a billboard.

Hence the cultural industries create the opportunities (the shop window) for suppliers to interact with and influence their buyers. In the television sector, the valuable commodity is airtime, the 'ad break', time between programmes that can be sold in typically 30- or 15-second slots. For magazine publishers it is space on a page that can be filled with an advertisement.

In return for these opportunities, television and radio companies, magazine and newspaper publishers and cinemas are paid fees by the advertisers. These fees are a critical revenue source, and indeed the primary revenue sources for many companies in the cultural industries—e.g. a commercial television channel or a commercial radio station. In some cases, these fees can be huge; to buy a 30-second airtime slot during the American Football Superbowl (and this is before the cost of making the advertisement is taken into account) was likely to cost the advertiser $7–$8m, or about $250,000 per second in 2025! However, it's worth remembering that given the Superbowl's popularity, the advertisement could be reaching over 100m potential consumers simultaneously.

Until relatively recently advertising was generally seen as the most predictable and profitable source of revenues for many in the cultural industries, particularly when compared to things like subscription revenues or ticket sales. The early success of many television streaming platforms was based on relatively inexpensive subscription fees. Yet these fees, whilst encouraging take-up of the service, did little to generate significant profits. It is notable that in the last few years, many such services (Netflix, Amazon, Disney+) have now introduced advertising-funded tiers whereby potential viewers can sign up to the service for free or a relatively low subscription fee (encouraging take-up), but must endure having their viewing experience interrupted by advertisements that provide the revenues for the company to run the service and make a profit. Consumers are given the option to purchase a more expensive service tier if they want to avoid these advertisements (e.g. catch-up services from UK broadcasters ITV and Channel 4, Netflix, Amazon Prime etc.).

Yet the media landscape is dynamic, and as it changes, so do the prospects of major media platforms. Certainly, the emergence of the internet, and particularly social media platforms, has led many in the commercial television industry to worry about their future, as advertising budgets are increasingly spent with new competitors like YouTube or TikTok, rather than with traditional broadcasters. This shift was seen as particularly significant given the apparent propensity for younger viewers (an attractive target market for advertisers) to shift their media usage from traditional incumbent platforms like broadcasters, to VOD online platforms like YouTube, TikTok or Instagram. Fewer than half of 16–24-year-olds now watch broadcast TV from traditional providers weekly in the UK according to a recent survey by the television regulatory Ofcom.[17] New platforms might also offer advertisers new opportunities to interact with consumers in a way they could not with traditional broadcast model platforms. Online platforms have proven useful in addressing each element of the stages involved in moving consumers through the purchase process, from creating awareness to enabling purchase. They have strong community-building potential. They can easily collect consumer data. Hence they are seen as being far more flexible than more traditional promotional platforms.

This perceived shift did much to encourage broadcasters and traditional media owners to attempt to create their own valuable real estate in the new online space in an attempt to re-aggregate the large audiences they had traditionally sold to advertisers. Hence most have developed significant online presences, though none can compete with the reach and depth of platforms like YouTube or Facebook.

As brand-building windows, organisations in the cultural industries are also building their own brands, of course. The airtime they sell to other brands can also be used to promote their own programmes and services—e.g. a significant amount of airtime on the UK's commercial channel ITV1 is used to advertise the company itself, its current and future programmes and services like ITVX (its online catch-up service). An interesting debate ensues: when is it better to sell the airtime to an advertiser, and when is it better to forgo the revenue in return for access to valuable airtime to sell your own products and brands?

8.6.2 The marketing function

The next perspective we might explore in this chapter is how marketing is used by companies within the cultural industries. For most of its history, marketing meant only one thing in the cultural industries: promotion. Its involvement in decision making around things like product, price and distribution, and use of market research, was limited if it existed at all. Whilst there is a little clear evidence as to why this might be the case, we can speculate.

Throughout its history, those in the sector who could create popular content and present it to audiences in an appealing way were seen as special. Whether they be an artist, composer, writer or producer / promoter, individuals who could in some way anticipate audience demands, create new markets and deliver consistently popular content were singled out for praise, promotion and rewards. Often this 'connection' with the marketplace was instinctual, a product of gut feeling, or of an artistic agenda and drive. Continued success marked the individual out as special, different and the possessor of a valuable and rare gift. Certainly, until relatively recently, market research tools did not exist to test these assumptions, so that gut instinct (and involving the individual who had it) would be the only source of assurance that the content might be successful.

When market research tools did begin to emerge perhaps it was inevitable then that certain parts of the industry might resist their use. Essentially, they offered the promise of laying bare this mysterious creative talent, reducing 'gut instinct' to a series of data points that would allow anyone (in theory) to devise and develop successful content. Of course, this proved not to be the case; even the most sophisticated market research and forecasting tools cannot 100% guarantee the success of a new product, but its potential to de-mystify a highly instinctual, complex and valuable skill was the first step in devaluing the rare individuals who possessed it, cutting short careers and reducing their social standing, prestige and ultimately wealth. Perhaps it was inevitable that it would be resisted by some in the cultural industries.

The very idea that businesses in the cultural sector should slavishly listen to the voice of the consumer and respond to their needs and wants was also questioned. Whilst it became a central tenet of marketing in virtually every other business sector, in the cultural industries the idea was looked on with suspicion. How many of the audience had been to art school, had studied what makes 'good' television or films, had learnt the skills of music composition and performance? Was the audience composed of skilled writers and producers? Were they better placed to make judgements about what made good content than the artists and producers who created it? The argument emerged that surely such issues should be left to the individuals who had studied these disciplines and invested their careers in producing content of the best quality.

This anti-marketing feeling was compounded by commentary from academics like Adorno and Horkheimer and the numerous academics who subsequently followed their argument, who saw the growing 'dominance' of the management tier in cultural corporations and the use of modern business techniques like market research (and listening too closely to the demands of audiences) as contributing to the 'dumbing down' and homogenisation of cultural content they noted in the 1940s. It was argued that relying on the audience to determine what content was made would ultimately lead to a reduction in the richness and variety of available content and its intrinsic artistic value.

For others, market research offered little hope of improving the lot of those working in the industry. As already noted, typically, cultural products have to be completed before they can be shown to audiences: it's difficult to test out a film concept in any real detail. Asking people if they would like to see a thriller with a big-name star in it is not really that helpful, compared to showing them a clip of Tom Cruise in the latest *Mission Impossible* film, jumping off a cliff. As such, the costs of producing the content have largely been incurred and hence market research at this point has little to offer in terms of changing the core characteristics of the product. It might lead to a few re-shoots, perhaps a change in the ending, but it's probably more useful in guiding subsequent promotional campaigns than anything else. Add to this the significant cost and time involved in setting up a rigorous market research programme and, certainly up until recently, the relative unsophistication of the market research tools at their disposal, and you can see how much more comfortable it might have been for those in the industry to rely on the skills of a particular individual who seemed to have an instinctive gift for creating content that people like.

For others, the issue was more about distance to the final consumer and the challenges of understanding them. Record companies did not sell directly to consumers, they sold to retailers. Whilst they understood retailers, their knowledge of consumers, their buying habits and behaviour was inevitably more limited (perhaps contributing to the initial lack of success of their direct-to-consumer file distribution services in the 1990s). Film studios sold films to distributors who then sold to exhibitors (the cinemas themselves). Games developers sell to games publishers who then sell to retailers. Book publishers sell to retailers etc. In each case, the organisation collecting the data on consumer behaviour is not the company supplying the content, but rather an intermediary. It is the intermediary that develops the deep understanding of consumer behaviour, their likes and wants. Perhaps it is inevitable, then, that content supply companies did not develop skills and capabilities in analysing consumer markets, given their focus and reliance on business-to-business markets. Whilst in these B2B markets they know what data to collect and how to analyse it (often relying on a sales force), they were less skilled in interacting directly with the consumer and interpreting their desires.

Other organisations, particularly in the performing arts sector, could rely on grants from government and the state to cover their costs, and hence simply did not need to develop the same level of marketing skills to survive as companies in other sectors.

Irrespective of how many tickets were sold, the organisation might still secure sufficient funds from organisations like the Arts Council in the UK to keep functioning. Those days have gone, however, as declining funds from most governments for cultural activities (along with a steady increase in competition) have forced organisations in the performing arts to focus far more on understanding their audiences and providing content that they will wish to see or hear in significant numbers. Most are now investing much more actively in building their marketing capabilities, focusing particularly on the use of social media to develop closer relationships with their consumers and build online communities of fans.

In some parts of the industry, we find marketing activities that don't necessarily get called marketing. Arguably the hiring of the staff who will serve as the ushers in a theatre, work in the ticket office or sell programmes and merchandising, or the staff that serve in the theatre's restaurant or bar, is a critical marketing decision. They will be the main point of contact with the customer, and their attitude and demeanour can have a huge effect on how the consumer judges the overall experience. Get this wrong and no matter how good the performance, some customers may be disappointed. This is more likely to be a decision made by the human resources team, rather than marketing staff, however. Ticket pricing and budgeting decisions may be made by the finance team, in combination with the artistic director, rather than being dictated by the marketing team (though they may have an influence). Choosing which ideas are made into TV programmes are decisions made by the commissioning and channel management team, not marketing staff in the typical television broadcaster. Selecting talent to form the next major boy band at a record label is likely to be a decision made by A&R rather than marketing executives.

Hence it could be argued that a significant amount of marketing activity across all elements of the marketing mix is undertaken in many cultural organisations; it's just not called marketing, and it is typically not centralised under the control of a single marketing department or team. Its influence, then, is significant but diffuse, but also, as we noted earlier, the source of some suspicion. One thing that typically can be relied upon to be at the heart of most marketing departments in the cultural industries, however, are decisions around promotion and publicity. Indeed, promotion and publicity has arguably reached something of a zenith in the cultural industries. Promotional campaigns often cost as much as if not more than the cost of producing the content it promotes, particularly in the film sector. Television companies have become expert in promoting their channels and programmes. Games companies spend huge amounts on 'marketing' (i.e. promotion) to keep pace with their competitors and in launching new games. But this is a narrow definition of marketing.

8.6.3 Current 'best' (and worst) practice?

Perhaps if we want to explore a part of the cultural industries that seems to be exploiting marketing to its fullest, we need to look at Japan and South Korea and their approach to marketing popular music. J-pop and K-pop have emerged as global music genres, generating huge amounts of profits for the organisations behind their key artists. J-pop emerged in the 1980s, taking off in the early 1990s thanks partly to the efforts of Tokyo-based radio station J-Wave, the term being used in its efforts to differentiate the emergent heavily westernised form of pop music it played from traditional enka (Japanese music). This was complemented with the rise of typically female 'idol' singers, seen as models of good behaviour as well as artistic ability.

It is perhaps in the relationship between these idols and their fans that we see marketing at its best (and worst). The idol industry has become a core part of the functioning of the J- and K-pop markets. Perhaps best typified by Johnny Kitagawa (the now discredited founder of Johnny & Associates) and Yasushi Akimoto (producer of AKB48), the *jimusho* (performer management companies) system functions based on the recruitment of large numbers of potential future idols, signing them to long-term contracts (typically 5–10 years) and training them ruthlessly to be singers, dancers and actors. Whilst most don't make it to their initial debut (first appearance on television), or beyond the 'rookie' stage, the companies have large numbers of aspiring artists with different talents (some may be better singers, or dancers or rappers, some may have more of a pop sensibility, or be better at urban R&B) to choose from. They can assemble bands to order in response to changing music tastes and the bands can be relatively large—indeed one of the first and best examples of this, AKB48, founded in 2005, was so called partly because it was planned to have 48 members. What does this mean for the fans?

Firstly, there is a constant supply of new bands and artists to choose from. Idol companies are constantly running auditions (which are often hugely oversubscribed) for new talent, selecting the best talent, developing it and launching new concert tours and content. The original audition for AKB48, for example, was attended by 7924 aspirants, all focused on getting one of 24 positions as first-generation members of the band.[18] Hence companies have a vast and seemingly never-ending talent pool to choose from, and have industrialised the process of finding it.

Secondly, the bands and artists are typically highly accessible to fans. Whilst in the Western model, a U2 fan may follow the band around the world, attending concerts every few years, they are very unlikely to ever meet them in person (there are only four of them, after all!). Having 48 members in the band means that there is always a fresh team available to perform as many live shows as are requested by the audience. Indeed, the AKB48 model takes live performance to a new level. Rather than waiting for an annual or biennial tour, with a limited number of concerts in selected cities, AKB48 fans can see the band perform virtually every day, in their dedicated venue in the Don Quijote store in Akihabara (Akihabara represents the other part of the band's name, AKB), Tokyo. Other members of the band might appear in other venues, concerts and festivals across the country at the same time.

Having such a large band means there are always likely to be some members who are available to appear as guests on radio or television shows or appear at the many 'meet and greet' events that are organised. The band members share the responsibilities and workload and hence are less likely to become 'burnt out' by the constant pressures of touring, music production, doing interviews and meeting fans. As such, in a very positive way, the aim is to break down the traditional barriers between performer and fan and make the band more accessible to the consumer, but in a way that does not exhaust the artist.

This deep involvement between the fan and the artist even extends to the composition of the band itself. By buying CDs of the band's music, AKB48 fans earn the right to vote on their favourite members (in events like the annual *senbatsu sosenkyo*), who might then appear in live performances, feature prominently in music videos or perform on particular tracks. Record purchases may also come with invitations to fan group meetings and artist meet and greet events. Such incentives encourage fans to buy multiple copies of the same CD, maintaining the prevalence of the CD in the Japanese music market, and driving its growth. Dedicated fans are also likely to purchase the same songs on packaged media and via streaming services.

The AKB48 model has worked in many ways—certainly they have sold more records than any other female act in Japanese history[19] and are the seventh-bestselling girl group worldwide according to some estimates, with sales of over 60 million records.[20] Their scope has been extended to include 'sister' groups in China, Indonesia, Thailand, Malaysia, India and Taiwan (the AKB48 Group).

The idol model has been replicated extensively in Japan and was adopted in Korea as the basis for the subsequent K-pop movement, with companies like SM Entertainment embracing the idol production model after researching Japanese companies. K-pop has been significant for broadening the global horizons for its content, however. Whilst Japanese companies seemed content to focus on a mainly domestic audience, K-pop acts are often targeted at a global audience. Hence acts such as Blackpink, BTS, EXO and TWICE have managed to sell significant numbers of records and tour successfully across the world. K-pop acts and their management also seem more willing to cooperate with overseas artists and composers (e.g. Suga of BTS collaboration with Ryuichi Sakamoto, Blackpink's collaboration with American singer songwriter Bruno Mars), and have bands made up of performers from different countries (e.g. TWICE are made up of performers from Korea, Japan and Taiwan). K-pop has actively striven to include English-language lyrics (or at least English-language words) into its songs, particularly its titles. K-pop has also appeared to move away from packaged media to streaming as its main distribution medium: by 2015 84.3%[21] of all music sales in South Korea were streamed, allowing an easier move to global rather than purely local distribution of content. It is also arguable that K-pop has benefitted from the rise of other Korean content in the global market (e.g. K-dramas and horror films). Indeed, perhaps the most significant breakout content in 2025 was the Sony Pictures Animation film *K-pop Demon Hunters*, whose K-pop-inspired soundtrack produced a number of singles that reached top positions on Billboard US and Spotify US charts.

Perhaps inevitably there is a darker side to some of the marketing techniques used to support the J- and K-pop phenomena. The idol system itself can appear to be the ultimate manifestation of the industrialised nature of the modern cultural sector, a machine that takes young talent and ruthlessly selects and rejects it according to prevailing consumer taste. Even for the lucky few that make it through the auditions, they are faced with a gruelling life of constant rehearsals and training and often poor working conditions. Diets and appearance will be controlled, along with social lives. Most 'trainees' will subsequently be rejected before their debut. Even for artists and bands that do debut on television, most are unlikely to secure a long-term career in the industry as companies respond to constant changes in music fashion and tastes by forming, dissolving and reforming bands.

Meet and greet events have even allowed fans to get too close to artists, and when combined with lax approaches to security have resulted in band members being attacked by obsessed fans (members of AKB48 were attacked by a fan at a meet and greet session in 2014). The sexual abuse of trainees has also been the subject of investigation and in some cases legal action. Indeed, one of the founders of the idol model, Johnny Kitagawa was revealed to have abused hundreds of male trainees, leading to his company Johnny & Associates being closed.

The emotional control mentioned in Chapter 7 reaches its zenith in the J- and K-pop system. Artists and group members are typically not allowed to publicly date. This is particularly so for female idols, where a dating ban is typically established to 'win the support of male fans'.[22] Idols must be seen to be well behaved in public; swearing, drunkenness and smoking are typically not allowed. They might even be required to seek the permission of their management company before marrying. Breaking these rules can lead to demotion, expulsion from the group or the requirement to produce a very public apology video (see that posted by AKB48 member Minami Minegishi after being accused of hiding a date with a member of another idol band from her management company[23]).

Whatever our view of the good or bad elements of this approach to marketing, it does reflect a comprehensive attempt to address each of the key elements of the marketing mix. Products are carefully created in line with market expectations, with different products (bands and individual artists) targeted at different parts of the segmented pop market. New products are constantly launched, and declining products (less popular artists) are removed. Attention to place and distribution are carefully planned, both in terms of concerts, touring and events like meet and greets and signing sessions. Sufficient incentives are offered to encourage consumers to buy relatively high-priced packaged media, the CD (and indeed in some cases to buy multiple copies). Promotion is extensive, covering all major forms of media. Brand loyalty is encouraged by allowing the audience to interact closely with their idols. For a very good overview of the distinctive characteristics of K- and J-pop, see a very useful paper by Dal Yong Jin (2020). Clearly, then, the J- and K-pop industries have embraced marketing in its broadest sense, for better or worse.

8.6.4 The data-driven approach

In other parts of the cultural industries, consumer data is being used to craft new types of product. In the field of television programme production, the difficulties of creating content that will work internationally has long been appreciated. Content is typically developed for domestic markets and, if the producer is fortunate, that content might also be popular in one or two additional international territories (ideally including the USA). But content that genuinely works internationally across a range of different countries has been very rare.

A central element of Netflix's global strategy is the creation of content that can be successful across different territories. A core component of this is the data generated through the consumer's interaction with the content they view on the platform. Data is being collected not just in terms of what is being watched, but how it is being watched. Does the viewer pause their viewing at any point, do they stop watching a programme, in which case at what point, what was happening on the screen when viewers switched off? Are elements of the programme watched repeatedly? What other content are they watching? How did viewers react to the actors on screen? How are consumers responding to different prompts and recommendations? How does behaviour change in different territories? What 'works' in Korea, or India, or the UK?

All of this data is being collected by Netflix with a view to producing its own content that can work globally, though early attempts (e.g. the very expensive and relatively unsuccessful *Marco Polo* series) have yet to prove the basis for the approach. Netflix has been more successful at taking content that has first been very popular in one territory (e.g. *Squid Games* in South Korea, *Money Heist* in Spain) and promoting it in foreign countries, which appears to be remarkably close to the traditional model of international distribution.

Again, there is some resistance to this apparently data-driven approach to programme making, particularly if we add in the abilities of AI not only to analyse data, but increasingly to generate music, images and text with minimum human involvement. Is this a way to democratise content creation, making it available to all, or to cut out the expensive, unpredictable and 'difficult' element of human involvement? We will continue this discussion as we explore the future role of AI in the next chapter.

8.7 Conclusions

As a manager in any cultural industry, you are increasingly likely to encounter and have to work with a variety of marketing ideas and concepts. We have discussed a few briefly in this chapter, including segmentation, the marketing mix, market research and ideas like product life cycles and product portfolios. But we have only scratched the surface, and we would suggest reviewing one of the many textbooks on marketing that have been written for further insights into these key ideas. Just about anything written by Phillip Kotler is a good place to start.

Marketing has had a complex and debated role in the growth of the cultural industries. On the one hand it is seen as a saviour, drawing on the huge amount of consumer data that is now available, to help offset the significant risks and uncertainties involved in content creation, offering investors and the audience reassurance that their investment of money and time will be worthwhile. Certainly, with the tsunami of content that is now hitting the consumer, marketing plays an increasingly significant role in ensuring that their attention is driven to specific pieces of content.

Yet there still seems to be an enduring, grumbling suspicion amongst many in the industry that relying too much on the voice of the consumer (and the market research tools that record it) to guide what content is produced may be dangerous and may already be having a damaging effect on the cultural diversity and artistic value and integrity of the content sector.

In many ways marketing has not evolved as fully in the cultural industries as it has in other sectors (e.g. the fast-moving consumer goods industry, luxury goods). Perhaps this is a good thing. What is clear, however, is that companies in the cultural industries are increasingly investing in developing their marketing skills and capabilities. Arguably there is something of a lack of marketing talent in the sector because of this increase in demand. As such it promises to be a fruitful place to think about starting your career. To be successful, however, you will increasingly have to combine your creative and imaginative skills with capabilities in gathering, analysing and using data in your decision making. Further, to maximise the potential of the discipline, you will often need to advocate for marketing to have a broader role than merely promotion, expanding it into discussions of product, price, distribution and people. Whilst this may be a challenging agenda, it's almost certainly going to be an interesting one.

8.8 Activities

- Choose a film that has been successful in your territory in the last year. How was it marketed? What were the creative and media strategy elements of the promotional campaign? How much did the company spend? Who was it trying to reach?

- How might you develop the social media presence of an opera company? How might you use social media to enrich its relationships with younger audiences?
- Review your own media consumption habits. How do you watch television, or listen to music? Do you attend live events, of what types and how often? What about your immediate friends or colleagues? Add up and break down your total content spending; you may be surprised by the results.
- If you are a performer, upload a piece of your own content to a video-sharing site like YouTube or TikTok, or music distribution site. How are you going to get the word out and promote it? How many views / listens did you get? Who were you competing against?

Notes

1 Orland, K. April 7, 2020. 'Ars analysis: ~80% of Steam games earn under $5K in first two weeks'.
2 Video Game Makers Go Hollywood. Uh-Oh. Archived May 28, 2015, at the Wayback Machine from *The New York Times.*
3 https://www.gamesindustry.biz/report-83-of-mobile-games-fail-in-the-three-years-after-launch.
4 https://www.economist.com/business/2016/06/16/no-business-like-show-business.
5 'Most Films Lose Money!' Schuyler Moore, Partner at Greenberg Glusker, *Forbes*, January 3, 2019.
6 WIPO, Global Innovation Index, 2025.
7 https://www.musicbusinessworldwide.com/its-happened-100000-tracks-are-now-being-uploaded/.
8 https://www.tubefilter.com/2019/05/07/number-hours-video-uploaded-to-youtube-per-minute/.
9 https://www.studiobinder.com/blog/average-movie-budget/.
10 CNBC, 2024.
11 https://www.forbes.com/sites/carolinereid/2025/01/09/netflix-number-one-show-3-body-problem-cost-more-than-estimated-at-2331-million/.
12 https://www.buzzfeed.com/noradominick/tv-shows-episode-costs-budget.
13 Sterne Agee's Arvind Bhatia.
14 Zollner, Amelia (April 28, 2023). 'Major Publishers Report AAA Games Can Cost Over a Billion to Make'. IGN. Retrieved April 30, 2023.
15 Saed, Sherif (January 7, 2025). 'Court documents reveal just how much more expensive Call of Duty games are to make compared to even PlayStation's biggest exclusives'.
16 See *One-Hit Wonders*, 2008, by music journalist Wayne Jancik.
17 https://www.ofcom.org.uk/media-use-and-attitudes/media-habits-adults/tuning-into-youtube-uks-media-habits-revealed.
18 'AKBingo!' AKBingo! Season 4. Episode 91. Japan. July 7, 2010. Nippon Television.
19 'AKB48 surpasses Mr. Children as the 2nd bestselling Japanese music act'. March 20, 2019.
20 Oricon News (in Japanese). Oricon. April 11, 2019.
21 KOCCA, 2018.
22 Stimson, Eric (September 20, 2015). 'Idol Fined 650,000 Yen for Dating Contract Violation'. Anime News Network.
23 https://www.youtube.com/watch?v=HF2y45Jl_sI.

References

Achrol, R. and Kotler, P. 1999. Marketing in the network economy. *Journal of Marketing*, 63, pp. 146–163.

Goold, M., Campbell, A. and Alexander, M. 2006. How corporate parents add value to the stand-alone performance of their businesses. *Business Strategy Review*, 5 (4), pp. 33–56.

Kotler, P., Keller, K., Bradly, M., Goodman, M. and Hansen, T. 2009. *Marketing Management*. Pearson Prentice Hall.

McCarthy, E. 1960. *Basic Marketing: A Managerial Approach*. RD Irwin.

Rogers, E. 2003. *Diffusion of Innovations.* Fifth Edition. Simon and Schuster.

Rutkowski, I. 2022. Success and failure rates of new food and non-food products introduced on the market. *Journal of Marketing and Consumer Behaviour in Emerging Markets*, 1 (14), pp. 52–61.

Dal Yong Jin. 2020. Comparative Discourse on J-pop and K-pop: Hybridity in Contemporary Local Music. *Korea Journal*, 60 (1) (spring 2020), pp. 40–70.

9 The Future of Digital Content

9.1 Introduction

In this final chapter we speculate on the trends that may impact the cultural industry in the short to medium term (5–10 years). Anticipating the future is always a challenge, but it remains one of the core roles of the leadership and management of any company. Senior staff are typically charged with creating a vision of the future and how the company will fit into it. Further, they must unite the company behind that vision and ensure that everyone is helping to steer the organisation towards appropriate goals. In order to create such a vision, the senior team first have to develop a view of how the business environment and marketplace is likely to evolve. Thankfully, business academics and practitioners have developed a range of tools and techniques to help them. We will review a selection of them, before applying them to explore how the cultural industries may develop in the next 5–10 years.

9.2 Planning for the future

Looking forward, businesses typically explore a variety of time horizons.

The short term is typically planning for the next year. Planning in this context tends to be driven by the annual budgeting process, whereby estimates are made of the next year's sales and costs. Unless a meaningful change is anticipated in the next 12 months (either within the company or in its environment), budgeting is often driven by relatively broad estimates of whether sales and costs are likely to increase or decline in the next 12 months in relation to current performance. Hence a budget might anticipate that sales might increase by 10% compared to this year (perhaps because of a new product launch), and costs may decrease by 7% (perhaps as a result of incremental improvements in the manufacturing process, or a better deal secured from suppliers), using current performance as the starting point. Typically, each major organisational department, function and project will be expected to project their costs for the next year (which might include hiring new people, investing in new equipment etc.), which are summed to create an overall cost estimate for the entire company. Typically, the sales force, business development or marketing team are then expected to develop a forecast of sales for the coming year, again based on current performance. It is then the role of senior management to reconcile these figures and ensure that revenues are likely to outstrip costs by a sufficient amount to generate the required level of profit.

Of course, if a major change is expected in the forthcoming year, then the basic process of budgeting may not capture the discontinuity, given its reliance on historical

DOI: 10.4324/9781003498599-9

performance as a base point. Perhaps a part of the business is being sold off, so costs and revenues may drop significantly. Perhaps a new office is being opened in a foreign territory, which may dramatically increase costs but also bring in significantly more revenue. Perhaps a new competitor or piece of legislation is anticipated. Using the current performance as a base point is not that helpful in such circumstances, and other tools are called for, drawn from longer-term forecasting techniques.

The leadership team will need to consider longer time horizons, typically the medium to long term, but how this is defined tends to vary according to business sector. In the fast-moving world of technology, the long term can be two to three years in the future. For organisations in the oil and gas industry, typical of capital-intensive industries including pharmaceuticals, the long term may be defined as 30–40 years in the future. Hence the specifics of the time horizon will vary, but in all cases, as the length of time considered extends, uncertainty grows, and forecasts based on current performance become less and less relevant. Hence a variety of approaches have emerged to help the management team peer into the more distant future.

Most organisations develop ever more sophisticated planning systems as they mature. Such systems have annual budgeting at their core, but often look further into the future, developing plans for the subsequent 3, 5 or 10 years. In order to do so, a range of tools are available to the manager, often built into what is called the strategic or corporate planning system. We have discussed some of these already. Environmental scanning using PESTLE, for example (see Chapter 2), can be used to explore potential developments in the political, economic and social environments. Typically, events and trends are identified, supported by an estimate of their likelihood and potential impact. The critical factors that emerge (e.g. the most likely, the most impactful) may then be monitored closely over time and used to develop different scenarios for the future.

Scenarios are essentially forecasts of how various factors may interact to create different environmental conditions in the future. The company may then develop different strategies, appropriate to different scenarios. We may be trying to forecast the development of AI and decide that the speed of evolution of the technology, combined with attitudes to regulation, are the two most critical issues dictating its growth. These can then be used to create different scenarios that require different strategies—e.g. a scenario that suggests rapid technical development combined with limited regulation versus another scenario based on rapid technological development but with extensive regulation from governments and legislators. Each scenario requires a different strategic response from the company. Rather than being precise forecasts of the future, however, scenarios are typically broadly drawn and used to prompt discussion, debate and learning in the planning process.

Whilst scenario planning has grown to be a core element of many strategic planning systems, it has also been subject to criticism. Primarily this is aimed at the managers using the approach, the suggestion being that scenario planning is poor at forecasting highly unlikely events or trends (the black swan criticism—if all you have ever seen is white swans, it's highly unlikely you will forecast the appearance of a black one, though they do exist). Users tend to ground their forecasts in the present, their current understanding of the world, and what seems likely from current market and environmental conditions. Hence, they are less likely to forecast events that seem unusual, or unlikely. We might imagine ourselves as strategic planners in the major record companies in the mid-1980s. Asked to develop some scenarios of the future, it would have been very unlikely that any such planners would have created a scenario in which a tiny piece of computer code (MP3) would emerge to completely change the way in which most popular music was distributed and hence profoundly affect the economics of the industry and their prospects. It would seem too unlikely. Equally the approach is criticised for being too influenced by the users' personal biases (e.g. anchoring bias, confirmation bias) and the danger that scenarios become concrete predictions of the future, limiting flexibility in future decision making and organisational responses to ongoing change.

With these criticisms in mind, other approaches have been suggested designed to encourage the development of more creative and imaginative perspectives of the future. One such approach is ScFi prototyping. This approach, adopted by a variety of technology companies, emerged as a response to criticisms of the scenario planning method. Pioneered by companies like Intel (see Johnson, 2009 for a very good review of the general model), the approach encourages users to think long term, imagining how the business environment might evolve over the next 50 or 100 years. In order to prompt imaginative long-term thinking, planners work with creative individuals (e.g. writers of novels, film makers, playwrights) to create an imagined future, and then work backwards to establish what changes over time might create that imagined future. We might imagine a future in 50 years' time when AI has completely changed the nature of most people's work lives, and 80% of the population does not work. Strategic planners might work with creative individuals (let's say a science fiction author like Liu Cixin) to imagine what that might look like, and what developments need to occur in the preceding 50 years for that end point to be reached. The strategic planners would then work out how their organisation might need to develop to flourish in this future environment. Again, typically the method is not used to try and forecast a specific future which we are certain will occur, but rather to encourage creativity and imagination in the planning process, offering a greater chance of identifying something that might not be anticipated using more conventional planning tools (e.g. scenario planning). For a typical example of such an approach, and an overview of the method more generally, see Roberts and Middleton (2014).

Other functions within the organisation have developed their own methods to anticipate the future. More technical functions (e.g. R&D, engineering) may choose to use technology roadmaps (see Chakraborty et al., 2021), first developed by Motorola and Corning in the USA. This tool is designed to help identify the relationship between current and developing technologies and products over time, focused particularly on identifying technology roadblocks and hurdles that might need to be overcome, and the effects of the complex interaction of technical, economic and social issues. The tool is typically used at the organisational level (what is 'our' technology roadmap?) and at the industry level (how is technology likely to evolve at a more general level through the interaction of different companies, organisations and agencies, that is the stakeholders working in the overall ecosystem?). Some departments will use life cycle or adoption / diffusion models. Other departments might use something like the 'Delphi' method (also known as the expert method) whereby groups of relevant experts work together to establish a consensual view of the future, based on the idea that a prediction from a group of experts is more likely to be accurate than that produced by any one individual. Others may use more numerical approaches like regression analysis.

Combined, these tools and techniques work to create strategic (or corporate) foresight, an organisational capability that allows it to regularly and systematically develop and modify a plausible view of the future and anticipate how the company might best flourish in that environment. 'Strategic foresight is the ability to create and maintain a high-quality, coherent and functional forward view, and to use the insights arising in useful organisational ways' (Slaughter, 1999, p. 287). We can use some of the aforesaid techniques in exploring how digital content in particular might evolve in the short to medium term. But let's start with some history, to understand the drivers and major trends we will be discussing.

9.3 The past and future of digital media

The digitisation of content in its various forms has had a long history. Digitisation in the cultural industries first became evident with the rise of PC-based computing in the late 1970s and early 1980s, following an earlier period when digitisation started to enable the smoother execution of financial transactions, typically between companies. PCs would have a significant effect on work practices within companies, supported by the growth of software tools designed to improve workflows and communication and increase productivity. In some sectors, this change would be hugely significant—e.g. the emergence of MIDI interfaces in the music sector would transform how music was produced, or digital image editing software that would transform how films and television programmes were constructed. Much of this initial transformation was invisible to the general consumer; they consumed the resultant content without any sense of how its production might have changed.

With the rise of digital media formats (e.g. the CD), growth of home PCs and the emergence of the internet, consumers would also start to embrace digitisation personally. The term 'new media' started to be used in discussions around the digitisation of content, describing the conversion of words, images and music into binary code, and its consequently more transportable, manipulable and interconnectable character. Excitement amongst commentators grew, as some discussed the 'democratisation' of media and the revolutionary transformation of the cultural sector, an (overly) optimistic view of a future in which content creation and consumption would be available to all.

In some sectors, at least in terms of pure content creation, it could be argued that a transformation did occur to some extent, as consumers were suddenly able to create content themselves at a level of professionalism that would have previously been impossible. Rather than relying on a record deal to pay for music to be recorded at a high-end international studio, musicians could now call on a range of digital tools to allow them to record and edit their music to a professional standard in their bedrooms or rehearsal rooms. Whilst previously they might have relied on analogue mixing desks (e.g. the Teac M2), which were expensive, complex to use, extremely limited in their functionality and only likely to ever produce a sub-standard quality of recordings, consumers could now use applications like Pro-tools (AVID), Apple Logic Pro or even Apple's GarageBand (which was typically given away with Apple devices), to produce professional-sounding recordings at a fraction of the cost of a professional studio. Inexpensive tools to manipulate digital images and video also emerged, allowing bedroom film makers to edit content on what were essentially home PCs.

With the subsequent growth of VOD sharing platforms like YouTube, and social media applications like TikTok, consumers also had a simple mechanism to allow the distribution of the content they had created (though whether anyone would actually watch or listen to the content was another matter). Part of the reason for the initial excitement around the prospects of digitisation was the way in which new digital platforms promised to be all things to all men (and women). The internet, for example, could be used as a communication method (either one to many or one to one). It could be used as a medium for commercial transactions (e.g. shopping). It was a means of storing and finding information. It was a hugely powerful promotional medium. It was a means to improve workflow and increase productivity in your job. It was a means of providing and experiencing entertainment. It could collect incredibly detailed consumer data. It offered the potential for organisations to establish direct relationships with consumers in a way that was previously impossible. It could do anything that traditional media could, and much more.

Other commentators, particularly academics critical of neo-liberalisation, were more doubtful of new media's ability to democratise content creation and consumption. For them, new media arose at a time when neo-liberalist ideals of free market capitalism and marketisation were in the ascendant. For these commentators, neo-liberalism ensured that all of the inequalities of life that existed before the rise of new media, whether around class, gender, ethnicity or income level, were replicated in the new digital environment. Overly powerful corporations remained dominant, and it was their agenda, rather than consumers', that would dictate the evolution of the new digital economy—indeed it was argued by critics that neoliberal policies would exacerbate inequality and ignore systemic issues like poverty and discrimination.

Some participants in the cultural industries were rather more concerned about the potential of the internet to disrupt existing cultural businesses. As Sparks (2004) notes, the internet was 'always on' and it could encroach on the use of other, traditional media. It eroded the advantages of physical space and control of distribution. It competed with traditional media as a source of advertising opportunities. Others questioned if the internet would add to the overall size of the content market or cannibalise parts of it (e.g. if we sell our films via streaming services, what will happen to the profitable packaged media sector?). Would it add to the opportunities for companies supplying traditional content, or supplant them? Certainly, as early as the late 1980s, some pessimistic commentators were forecasting the death of 'traditional broadcasting' within 20 years, along with the more immediate disappearance of the physical book as a reading medium. Few of these forecasts have come to pass. It appears we regularly tend to overestimate the degree of change possible in the short term, and the speed with which consumption patterns change. As of 2025, traditional broadcasters still have some of the most-viewed television content on their channels and physical books are going through something of a renaissance.

The early history of the internet, at least from a commercial point of view, seemed less than optimistic. Advertising revenues were far slower to develop than forecasts suggested, as advertisers opted to stick to tried and tested advertising platforms like traditional TV and magazines, and the situation was even less promising for content providers. Consumers seemed very unwilling to pay for any form of digital online content, particularly if the content was available easily from other more traditional sources (e.g. newspapers), or if it was available for free through less conventional routes (see Chapter 6 for an overview of the growth of non-commercial piracy in the music sector). Pornography proved to be the saviour of the early internet, the one form of content that consumers seemed willing to pay for. Relatively low barriers to entry also encouraged huge numbers of firms to launch new internet services, backed by overly enthusiastic investors (investment banks, private equity companies, venture capitalists), ensuring low levels of profitability for virtually all companies, given the extreme levels of competition and a cautious consumer. For some content providers, the cost of upgrading to digital infrastructures would nearly bankrupt them. The European cable TV operators faced huge costs in upgrading their networks to enable digital services, in most cases forcing high levels of consolidation and merger between companies as consumer revenues fell far behind rising costs.

The period 2002–2008 proved to be a turning point for the internet. Many of the early entrants to the sector closed down as business plans failed to work out and investment funds were exhausted. Less competition typically meant more profit available to the remaining companies. It was to be a period of consolidation and the emergence of 'business-to-consumer' platforms like Amazon and Ebay, establishing a business model around selling known products (e.g. CDs, books) at a discount price or niche products not typically available in real-world stores. Complementing this was the emerge of what has subsequently become known as Web 2.0, the social web, with the growth of social media networks like Facebook. This would drive the growth of online advertising revenues substantially. Further, the period saw the rollout and beginnings of mass market take-up of the first broadband networks, allowing new services like content streaming, telephony over IP (internet protocol) and new content like the MMOG (massive multiplayer online game—e.g. Warcraft) to emerge. Increasingly the internet was seen not just as a platform for content delivery, but a platform for interaction in all its various forms.

So how has the industry exploited these opportunities, and how is the sector likely to evolve in the short to medium term? Many of the most interesting developments seem to be focused on the dissolution of the traditional barriers between content providers and content consumers.

We have already noted a number of opportunities in the marketing function (see Chapter 8). From being a primarily promotional platform, the internet has emerged as a content distribution and consumption platform. The content being distributed is in turn likely to be increasingly influenced by the vast amount of consumer data being collected by a variety of companies from our interaction with content on digital networks. We noted Netflix's desire to create content that might work better across international territories, driven and guided by the consumer data it has accumulated. Other new forms of content may increasingly focus on the potentially interactive nature of digital platforms, though early attempts to actively involve consumers in deciding elements of the content itself (e.g. the potential ending of a drama series) have been less than successful. But the increasing (if often indirect) involvement of the consumer in influencing what content is created seems assured, at least in the short to medium term. In many ways the marketing techniques developed to promote J- and K-pop are very much in this vein, designed to remove the traditional barriers between the stars (the idols) and their fans and to jointly produce the overall music experience. Hence this may be one of the first areas in which we see efforts to create ever more interactive and accessible content (see the section on AI). The idea of the internet as a platform for coproduction between brands, content providers and consumers is still in its infancy, but we can expect further experiments in the near future.

Where the internet does offer the greatest immediate potential for further marketing innovation is probably in its original role as promotional platform. The consumer data that is collected has uses far beyond the design of content. It potentially allows the development of what has up until recently been the impossible but ultimate dream of marketers, the customisation of advertising for individuals, but on a mass scale. The advertising industry has long been criticised for its inefficiency in reaching target audiences. TV advertising in particular is seen as highly wasteful of advertising budgets. Yes, a television advertisement on a major channel is going to reach a lot of people (typically in the millions), and that reach is going to be extremely expensive, but most of those it reaches are unlikely to be interested in the product or service advertised. A car advertisement may reach five million people, but only a very small proportion of them are currently considering buying a new car. So, whilst television advertising is effective, it's not efficient.

Personalised advertising based on an analysis of consumer characteristics and previous buyer behaviour does offer the prospect of reaching specific target groups much more efficiently and, given the flexibility of digital platforms, promotional messages can be flexed to deliver the right sort of content at the right time in the consumer decision making process (see the AIDA model described in Chapter 8), increasing its effectiveness. Equally, given the flexibility of digital content and networks, the message can be delivered to a variety of devices—the television, the PC, the mobile or a gaming console—based on previous consumer behaviour, with a specific message (and potential incentive) for a specific individual. The promotion might be for a new television series—e.g. 'according to our records you watched three series featuring the Korean actor Lee Byung-hun in the last 18 months. You also like political thrillers. Well, this is a new political thriller series featuring Lee Byung-hun (see a preview by clicking here or read more about the series by clicking here) which can be delivered to your device of choice, and we are discounting the cost if you buy the series now. Just click here.'

With AI driving the process, most of these decisions and interventions can be done with the minimum involvement of (expensive) marketing staff; AI can facilitate the production of millions of customised messages, 365 days a year, 24 hours per day. It can modify or change its approach based on direct, behavioural feedback from the consumer (perhaps they are generally not clicking on an included link or reading a piece of text). Messages can be changed, as can the medium chosen or the specific incentive, far more quickly than any human team could achieve. Indeed, the involvement of AI seems an increasing necessity in such endeavours rather than an option. The sheer volume of consumer data now being generated has created huge challenges of interpretation for human decision makers. There is literally too much of it, flowing into data centres, pooling in what are increasingly called 'data lakes', vast repositories of profoundly detailed records of consumer's digital behaviour and activity. The challenge is to identify patterns and relevant information from such data. Humans are ultimately limited in their ability to do so, we have natural cognitive limits, but AI is built for it—that is, pattern recognition, data categorisation and the extraction of meaningful conclusions. Having mere humans involved is only likely to slow things down, increase costs and lead to errors of judgement—far better to leave it to the AI! But can we say if this is a positive thing for the sector, or a profoundly ominous development?

9.4 AI: the next big thing

When we look at technological developments in the short to medium term, there is little doubt that the next major innovation is artificial intelligence (AI). Although AI has received huge attention in recent years, its core ideas are not new. In fact, the concept has been around for decades. Science fiction has been imagining intelligent machines for well over a century, and the word *robot* first appeared in 1920 in a Czech play titled *Rossumovi Univerzální Robot*. Soon after, in the 1940s, pioneers such as Alan Turing and John von Neumann laid down the theoretical foundations for AI. By the 1950s, computer scientists were creating early applications such as the General Problem Solver (GPS) and 'expert systems', which attempted to enable machines to learn from their experience of performing tasks and improve predictions and performance using collected data.

By the early 1960s, researchers had begun developing programmes that could process language. By 1965, early systems like Shakey and Eliza were already simulating basic conversations with humans. At the same time, expert systems were applied to seemingly simple but instructive tasks such as playing chess and checkers / draughts. These experiments demonstrated that machines could sometimes outperform people in narrow, rule-based domains—an area of research and interest that remains to this day (see Silver et al., 2016).

The 1990s brought a step change. Advances in hardware, data storage and software meant computers were faster and cheaper to use. Moore's Law, which observed that the number of transistors on a chip doubled roughly every year, drove down the cost of processing power. This technological surge renewed both excitement and interest in AI. A key breakthrough came with the development of neural networks, inspired by the structure of the human brain, which allowed computers to 'learn' more flexibly from data.

By the early 2000s, neural networks underpinned new forms of 'machine learning'. Soon *generative applications* appeared, applications that could generate content like images, music and text. These relied on reinforcement learning, where machines learnt complex behaviours—like driving—using relatively small amounts of data. As the supply of data exploded, so did the size and sophistication of training 'sets', allowing much more advanced learning. By the 2010s, executives in many industries identified AI as a potentially hugely disruptive force and in a 2017 Accenture report 85% of senior executives suggested they planned major AI investments within three years.

A decisive moment came in November 2021 with the release of ChatGPT, developed by OpenAI. For the first time, a powerful AI system was placed directly in the hands of the public. By January 2023, it had become the fastest-growing consumer software in history, reaching over 100m users worldwide. By 2025, estimates suggest regular users had risen to 180.5m. This would lead to many new AI applications being launched, including Microsoft Copilot, DeepSeek and Gemini.

To understand why generative AI applications matter for cultural industries, we need to look more closely at how they work. These systems are built on neural networks, which mimic the brain by using artificial 'neurons' (nodes) connected by signalling pathways. Together, nodes process data and solve problems. One of the most influential approaches is the Generative Adversarial Network (GAN). The term generative refers to the ability to create new content—such as text, images, music or video. For example, DALL·E produces images, while natural-language systems like ChatGPT use 'transformers' (the T in ChatGPT) to focus on particular parts of language or images, making their outputs more realistic. GANs are *adversarial*: they pit two AI networks against each other—a generator and a discriminator—so that, through competition, the system produces outputs that appear convincingly lifelike.

So how are these GANS being used in the cultural industries?

Even the most casual review of content on VOD platforms like YouTube reveals that GANS have been rapidly adopted by consumers and content creators. There is a huge wave of AI-generated content on most sites. Whilst this may currently be the province of technically savvy and well-informed 'home producers', the programmes are becoming ever easier to use and are widely available, often for free. Whether it be a song, a video, a set of still images or a piece of text, AI-generated content is appearing everywhere, covering virtually every type of content and genre. Inevitably, some of it is unquestionably awful, but much is presented with a level of professionalism and quality that would have been impossible to achieve by the 'home producer' previously. The boundaries between professional and 'amateur' content creation appears increasingly blurred.

Perhaps inevitably, sometimes this enthusiasm leads the user down darker paths. The growth of 'deepfakes' (a video or image of a person that has been digitally altered so that they look like someone else, often used maliciously or to spread false information), the use of AI to create what has become known as 'revenge porn', and its use to impersonate politicians and spread misinformation are all worrying developments as the boundaries between the real and imagined become less clear.

Companies are turning this to their advantage, however. The digital human and avatar market is already forecast to reach nearly $530bn, far larger than most individual parts of the cultural industries, by 2030.[1] Some stars like American actor Bruce Willis are apparently already licensing their image for use in the creation of avatars (a virtual representation of an individual) for the advertising sector. He 'appears' in a Russian advertisement for MegaFon, a telecoms network, though of course it's not him, but an actor who has had Willis's face digitally transplanted onto his own. Whilst it is debated whether this image appears as the result of a legitimate deal between Willis and the advertising company, Deepcake, or if it was used illegally[2], Willis does appear to be advertising a Russian telecoms network, whether he wants to or not.

But we don't even need to rely on living stars to supply their images as a source for the work of generative AI—we can use dead personalities as well. Why not borrow an image from a previously made film, music video or television programme of an actor who died 20 years ago, but who remains hugely popular? How long might we need to wait to see Marilyn Monroe (who died in 1962 but leaves a legacy of many films and images from which to draw) in an advertisement for perfume, Bruce Lee promoting a new fitness regime or Xie Yuan advertising chess sets? The image rights of deceased personalities are already being traded and the individuals used in advertising—e.g. the British government acquired the rights to use Albert Einstein's image (who died in 1955) in a series of advertisements for energy meters in 2024. What are generally called postmortem (after-death) rights are emerging as an area of particular interest for lawyers in the cultural industries, and with AI's ability to manipulate those images, huge new advertising and content creation opportunities are opening up.

But if we want to see evidence of the use of AI at its most powerful and potentially disruptive today, again we need to look at Japan and South Korea, and its use in the popular music sector. To date, musicians, artists and performers in the music sector have generally been humans, with their huge reserves of innovation and creativity, combined with their built-in limitations, weaknesses and foibles. They get tired, can lack inspiration, deliver poor performances, have arguments with band mates, potentially drink too much or take drugs, behave badly in public, decide not to tour to support a new piece of content, fail to turn up to press events, want to get paid more, get old, lose their looks and charisma etc. Until recently, companies had no option but to work with these difficult, unpredictable but ultimately creative people. But, thanks to AI, this may no longer be the case.

In 2021, Korean idol band Eternity (now renamed Iteoniti) debuted with their new single, 'I'm Real'. The irony was that they weren't; they were an entirely virtual, manufactured band, with 11 digital avatars as members. The band was created by Korean company Pulse9, and the entire process was fan-driven. Initially the company generated 101 faces, dividing them into four categories: cute, sexy, innocent and intelligent. K-pop fans were then asked to vote on their favourites. In-house designers then set to work animating the winning characters according to the preferences of the fans. For live events, videos and online fan meets, the avatar faces can be projected onto anonymous (and hence typically lowly paid) singers, actors and dancers, contracted in by Pulse9.

The avatars are enhanced with the use of relevant 'sources': humans with particularly outstanding skills in specific areas. Do you need your avatar to dance well? Choose the best human dancer you can find as a source and record their movements, which can then be integrated into the performance of the avatar. Do you want them to be great actors, rappers or the best guitarist in the world? Choose the right source, record what you need to, add the appropriate digitally constructed face to the performance and your work is done. Is your new star going to be in an advertisement where they might need to surf on the sea?—not a problem, find the best surfer you can, record their moves and add the capabilities to the avatar's.

Discussing the capabilities of one of the avatars in Eternity, Zae-in, the CEO of Pulse9, Park Ji-eun suggests 'Zae-in has characteristics that most human artists would be hard-stretched to pull off…She can sing very well, rap very well and she can be creative as a (fashion) designer. And she's a natural-born actress.'[3] The idea is simple: with the right source, your avatar can do literally anything, effortlessly.

More significantly, of course, these avatars don't get tired, don't drink or take drugs, don't have romantic partners, don't have a 'bad night' where their performance is poor, are always in tune, are always perfect in their dance moves, don't get old and lose their looks, and don't ask for more pay! They are available to work 24 hours per day, 365 days a year. They can, in theory, speak or sing in any language you want them to, can appear in hundreds of virtual fan 'meet and greets' simultaneously, all over the world, and can perform day after day without complaint. Why on earth would you ever want to work with 'real' artists again?

Digital avatars also have their uses for 'real world' artists. Merely human performers can't compete with digital avatars in terms of the consistency of their performance, their range of abilities and their availability. So why not provide real-world performers with their own digital avatars? Korean girl band Aespa, formed by the increasingly dominant and powerful SM Entertainment, has four real-world singers and dancers, each of whom have their own accompanying avatars who are active in a variety of online and metaverse events, particularly when the human performers are having time off from their commitments. Whilst some fans have complained that the digital avatars aren't active or prominent enough, with some seeing it more as a publicity stunt, this is just the start.

For other bands, their digital avatars are at the heart of new performance opportunities and a resurgence in their careers. *ABBA Voyage* features digital avatars of the Swedish band ABBA, nicknamed 'ABBAtars', depicting the group as they appeared in 1979 and using the original vocals recorded by the group, performed in a dedicated venue in London. None of the aging members of the original band appear, just their avatars, but the concert draws on all of the content created by the original musicians and has proven to be hugely successful. Other aging performers are also exploring the technology as a way of extending their careers. The rock band Kiss, whose members are now in their mid-70s, have decided to end their live touring careers in physical form, but will potentially continue to tour as a set of digital avatars. Combined with developments in postmortem rights management, we may even find bands who disbanded many years ago, or who have lost key members, being reformed; it's probably only a matter of time before a digital version of the Beatles are performing in a venue close to you.

There is no reason, of course, why such avatars might not also appear in other content sectors, particularly film, television and the performing arts. At the time of writing, one of the first entirely virtual actors, Tilly Norwood, a digital avatar, created by AI talent studio Xicoia, a spin-off of AI production studio Particle6, appeared and, according to their creators, was already attracting the attention of major talent agencies and production studios, but was also causing outrage amongst existing, real-world actors.

Equally we may moan the loss of acting talent like James Dean or Laurence Olivier or regret the very premature death of emerging stars like Chadwick Boseman, but perhaps we can find a way of bringing them back through the clever manipulation of postmortem rights. Did you miss experiencing Pavarotti when he performed in La Scala, or Yehudi Menuhin when he performed in London? Perhaps you might get the opportunity to see them in the future. The deals will be hugely complex and difficult to execute (it will be a good time to be a lawyer in the industry), and require the cooperation of a complex range of stakeholders, but this has never stopped the industry from pushing the boundaries of what is possible and acceptable to find new markets and consumers, particularly when the technology is already available to make it happen.

Given this potential, it's likely that we will see significant experimentation around the use of digital avatars by producers in a variety of cultural industry sectors in the next 10 years. But their continued exploitation beyond that will ultimately be driven by the consumer response to them. Will they make it through the 'uncanny valley'? This is a term first coined by Japanese roboticist Mashahiro Mori in the 1970s, who tried to encapsulate his observation that as robots and digital avatars initially become more lifelike, humans are drawn to them and interaction produces positive sensations. However, as they become ever more lifelike, at some point consumers experience a dip in these positive feelings (the valley), and a growing sense of unease, triggering uncomfortable, if rather harder to define, negative emotions. Perhaps there is a warning here to producers not to make their avatars too lifelike.

The implications for real-world performers may be even more stark. We can imagine a generation of content consumers in 20 years who have grown up listening to, watching and interacting with content delivered by digital avatars. The performances are always perfect, singers are on key, instruments are played without the slightest error, dancers always hit their marks. Further, the performers are always available to meet fans in post-event chatrooms and are consistently friendly, enthusiastic and (with the right data and programming) may even know each fan by name. Then our consumer visits a real-world concert, with a very human performer. The performer is late to the stage, they have a slight cold, so their singing is off, they can't quite hit the high notes they did when the music was recorded, the drummer misses numerous beats, the guitarist is slightly out of tune and the dancers seem a little distracted by the explosive on-stage pyrotechnics. At the end of the performance the artist quickly leaves the stage and, without meeting a single fan, disappears to their hotel to nurse their cold. Will that consumer ever go to a live concert featuring a human performer again?

For many current concert goers, the mistakes, the errors, the inconsistencies and the less than perfect reproduction of a recording are the very things that attract them. This is a real performance—it may be full of errors but it's authentic, it's human and, above all, it's unique, never to be repeated in quite the same way again. That is part of the attraction of the concert experience. If you want a perfect reproduction of a musical performance you can stay at home and listen to a recording on your home music system, but if you want to see the artist as they really are, go and see them in concert.

But will this attraction, this authenticity, this acceptance (and indeed love) of imperfection, extend to consumers in the future who have grown up consuming 'perfectly' executed performances from digital avatars? Consumers who have been consuming content from artists and bands that may have been literally designed from scratch for them. No matter how niche your musical tastes, digital avatars can be created to cater for your musical requirements. If there are a sufficiently large number of consumers who want to hear and see Nordic-inspired heavy metal, with emo genre overtones, and lyrics about baking cakes, performed by a band composed of Japanese school girls, we can be assured than someone somewhere will produce it. Rather than searching for just the right human performers with an expensive team of A&R staff, in what will probably be a fruitless effort to find the right candidates, it will be far easier for them to turn to their PCs and design the band from scratch as digital avatars. Our digital consumers of the future will be fed on a diet of perfectly honed performances, from digital avatars designed from the ground up to make them happy. No real-world artist could ever be matched so closely to a consumer's requirements or perform their music quite so perfectly or consistently. At the very least, for these digital natives, their first live experience of real-world performers may be something of a shock. The question of what 'authenticity' looks and feels like in the future is an interesting one, and the degree to which it is valued by consumers, even more so. We continue to discuss this theme in Chapter 10.

Finally, it is worth noting that the next few years will probably be very profitable for lawyers involved in the industry. AI, by its very nature (and the way in which it is trained), draws on existing content from across the internet to generate new content, in a process known as 'scraping'. Often it is difficult to establish what content is being drawn on. But we can almost certainly expect some new AI-generated content in the music sector to sound very like the content it has drawn on in its training. Some will sound so like existing content that it may draw the attention of artists and their lawyers, with accusations of plagiarism and copying. Establishing the veracity of such claims is likely to be a long, complex, expensive and involved process. A great time to be a lawyer, then.

AI won't just affect the content itself; it will dramatically affect how the content is created. AI-enhanced productivity and communication applications are likely to significantly impact things like the animation industry, automating repetitive tasks, improving opportunities for communication and co-creation across long distances and potentially reshaping job roles. Background rendering and aspects of character animation may be handed over to AI tools, creating more opportunities for animators to focus on creative tasks like story development—that, at least, is the optimistic view. The more pessimistic perspective voiced by many in the industry is that AI can radically reshape the production process and cut costs—those costs mainly being in the area of the salaries and fees paid to human animators. Commentators in other sectors—e.g. journalism—see the potential for equally positive and negative outcomes in their sectors.

AI will also be used in managing the internal business operations of companies. AI may assist strategic planners to work through options in release windows, for example. As we noted in Chapter 4, new digital platforms have allowed the evolution of ever more sophisticated release patterns for films and TV content. The challenge is working out the best release pattern to maximise overall revenues and profits for the content. Would it be best if the content had an extended exclusive release window on a specific streaming platform, or if it is sold to a variety of different streaming services for simultaneous release on all of them? Should a film be sold to cinemas, or directly to the streaming platforms? Should the packaged media window still exist? Should it come before or after the streaming window? How will these different strategies affect the valuation of the content in subsequent windows (e.g. traditional broadcasters, pay-TV platforms). How might different strategies affect merchandising sales? These are complex and highly interactive questions requiring the analysis of significant volumes of data. AI is likely to be used extensively to work through these different scenarios and identify the most promising, potentially leading to new and innovative release schedules designed for specific pieces of content.

Inevitably some of the more mundane, routine decision making of leaders may be the first to be automated by AI. Reviewing operational data, actioning routine and well-established decision-making protocols can now be handed over to increasingly 'intelligent' software as an extension of the expert systems companies already utilise. AI will almost certainly take up a central role in developing strategic plans for organisations. Even in the area of human relations, an issue that most leaders may feel will always be the province of human actors, we are already seeing some interesting AI-based developments, which are particularly relevant for organisations in the cultural industries who come in for some criticism in terms of the quality of the human resources function (see Chapter 7).

The oversight and development of more junior management, staff and workers can already be enhanced by AI applications like Amber[4], with the prospect of future applications that can not only collect and analyse real-time, in-depth data about the performance, mood and disposition of a workforce (with data either provided by the staff themselves through surveys, or perhaps more ominously collected from the ongoing interactions of staff with various digital media—e.g. webcam-based eye tracking in virtual meetings) but, crucially, can also take action independently (known as 'agentic' AI). One of the biggest challenges for most leaders has always been identifying and reaching 'the little guy', that individual way down in the organisation who despite their lowly title has a profound impact on the performance of staff around them, and ultimately is a key figure in the distributed creativity of the organisation. The challenge has typically been identifying and developing them, with sufficiently granular attention to make interactions meaningful.

In theory such interactions can now be automated with a previously impossible level of focus on the individual. The importance of a personalised approach in people development, particularly in terms of personalised incentives, has long been evidenced in academic literature (see for example Campbell, 2018), but the difficulty has been putting it into practice, particularly in very large organisations. In theory (a theory which is currently being tested) such new AI-enabled applications might be able to monitor individual levels of productivity, identifying specific learning and development goals and most importantly might offer detailed individual-level feedback and suggestions for improvement. Automated emails might be produced that reach each member of the organisation with a personalised message, based on their specific performance, offering tailored advice and guidance. And such applications can do this 24 hours a day, 365 days a year, to workforces of any size, however geographically diverse.

How will workers respond to such feedback? Will they know it is generated and enacted by AI? How leaders choose to present the involvement of AI in such interactions will be critical. Perhaps the approach of publicly minimising the role of AI in decision making will be natural to many leaders, feeling that staff would prefer such decisions and interactions not to be left in the hands of algorithms. But interestingly there is already some evidence that workers might in some cases actually prefer for such decisions and interactions to be AI- rather than human-driven. Research centred on what is called the 'theory of machine' suggests that workers may feel that the involvement of AI is beneficial (see Logg et al., 2019), as being rational, fair, unbiased, always available and fast. Whatever the decision, to publicly minimise the role of AI in such interactions, or to prominently announce its role, honesty and transparency will be critical.

Of course, such activities (e.g. spotting talent at the bottom of the organisation) already happen to some extent in most organisations—it is the province of middle managers. As we saw in Chapter 2, they have tended to be the interface between the most senior management and those lower down the organisation, bringing that 'personal touch' based on an intimate knowledge of the immediate staff and workers they deal with daily. Perhaps it is this group, then, who have most to fear from the development of AI. As already suggested, since the days of Robert Townsend and his book *Up the Organisation* we have often viewed middle managers rather dimly, as potential obstacles to the free flow of information around organisations, as an unnecessary and highly expensive tier of workers who in the 'flattened' organisations of the future should be the first to get flattened.

Perhaps it is this tier, then, rather than those at the bottom of the organisation who have most to fear from the initial widespread emergence of AI in the business environment. The opportunity for radical organisational re-structuring, hugely significant cost reductions and the fulfilment of the promise of the flat organisation (e.g. the faster movement of information up and down the organisation) are tempting goals for the senior leadership team. Though perhaps such leaders should be cautious, for as well as providing an interface between the top and bottom of the organisation, the middle management tier is typically also the training ground for the senior leaders of the future. Moving through the middle management strata provides a well-structured and established development path for those expected to take the top jobs in a few years' time. Destroying the middle management strata may thus risk not only losing pivotal organisational talent but also the development path and opportunities that such talent relies upon for their career development. This may be equally the case for graduate recruits. Many current graduates bemoan the lack of opportunities to get their first step on the career ladder, with many commentators suggesting that AI is increasingly being used to automate the type of entry-level jobs that graduates might aspire to. Whilst this may save organisations significant costs in the first instance, where will they find the trained middle managers and senior leaders of the future?

Ultimately, the debate around AI within the workplace seems to reduce to one critical issue: will the development of AI lead to people's work lives being enhanced, as optimists suggest, or replaced as others forecast? Certainly, AI has the potential to make people's work lives more productive, easier and potentially more enjoyable. As a creativity-enhancing tool, it has huge potential in the cultural industries. But equally, through automation, and the development of its learning capabilities, it has the potential to replace workers at a variety of levels throughout most organisations, including many in the cultural industries. Perhaps the best career advice at this stage in its development, when so much remains uncertain, is to focus on working out what AI is good and bad at, and to concentrate on developing skills in those areas where AI will perhaps never catch up with the capabilities of the human mind.

9.5 The funding agenda

Another area in which we see the traditional barriers between creators and consumers changing and breaking down is in the area of funding.

We can imagine a future in which consumers have access to everything they need to make professional-quality content. Relatively inexpensive software can be run on home PCs allowing music to be produced, videos created and, thanks to ChatGPT and its peers, novels written. The resultant content can even be distributed to a global audience thanks to the likes of YouTube, Substack and SoundCloud. But something is still missing—that is, funding. This is particularly relevant as the ambitions of our home producers expand, perhaps with the need to secure some additional acting or technical talent, to hire better-quality camera gear, or if the producer wishes to promote their new content with a reasonably sized marketing campaign.

Previously when savings ran out, and no more money could be borrowed from friends, family or the local bank, the artist had no choice but to turn to one of the bigger distribution and funding companies (a Hollywood studio, a major broadcaster, a record label or games publisher) for further funding. The chances of securing such funding were very small, and if it was secured, it usually came with conditions—that is, the funding organisation would exercise its powerful position to influence the production of the content. If the content was to make a return on its investment, it would need to be popular with consumers to some extent, and the funder would potentially direct the producer to make content that was likely to be commercially attractive. Whilst the content might be ultimately created, the ongoing influence of the funder could make the process unpleasant, and the final result would not quite represent the vision the producer or artist originally had. There are many apocryphal stories of record companies interfering in the production of albums they had funded to make them more commercial ('we don't hear a single', 'we need a different producer'), or Hollywood studios insisting on a film's endings being reshot, changing storylines or influencing who was cast in a particular role. This influence might, however, be resisted by the producer, director or artist, who had a specific idea of the content they wanted to create and for some creators the use of such funders was a necessary evil, an unavoidable last resort if other funding sources proved unworkable.

For these maverick creators, new funding opportunities have emerged, however, specifically fan funding. As we have already noted, gaming is one of the top categories of investment on most crowdfunding sites. Equally, musicians like Amanda Palmer and De La Soul have funded the recording of new albums via Kickstarter.

Even well-established creators see the benefits of using fans as funders, rather than large corporations. Spike Lee, a highly regarded and lauded American film maker, raised over $1.25m from over 5000 fans via Kickstarter in 2013 to support the development of a new film project. Why would he need to? He had an excellent history of working with major film companies like Warner Bros., Universal Pictures and 20th

Century Fox, who had previously funded his projects. But the funding, inevitably, came with conditions, which Lee constantly railed against. Working with Hollywood meant making Hollywood films, and if a project did not fit in with this mould, it was unlikely to get their support and hence would not be made. For Lee, fan funding offered the opportunity to work outside the system, to instigate projects that would not normally get funded, and to have a level of creative freedom in the production that would have been impossible if a major corporate funder were involved.

But if we have learnt anything from our previous analysis, it is that we should not overestimate in the short term how disruptive this new funding source might be, and how 'democratic', and available to all, content creation has become as a result of its emergence. $1.25m in 2013 was a lot of money, but it was hardly enough to make a major film. And this was a project proposed by one of the highest-profile film makers in America at the time. If Spike Lee could only raise $1.25m, what were the prospects for a completely unknown film maker working in their bedroom? It's also notable that many crowdfunding initiatives are based on pre-existing franchises that have an existing fan base (particularly in the gaming sector) or are instigated by producers based on brands that have already been built (e.g. De La Soul's previous albums had been promoted by Warner Music Group via Tommy Boy Records). Hence it would appear that fan funding can work, but it really helps if you are an already established artist, with strong consumer appeal or a pre-existing brand that someone else has paid to build. The prospects for our struggling bedroom producer are still less than optimistic.

But in its role as a way to bridge the boundaries between artists and their fans, fan funding does offer some interesting prospects. Certainly, getting fans involved in funding content creation creates a ready-made market for that content, helping to reduce risk. The consumers who have funded it are likely to constitute a significant group of vocal supporters, opinion leaders who might encourage other potential fans to acquire it. Drawing on the adoption / diffusion model mentioned in Chapter 8, they are the innovators and early adopters who will convince the early majority to acquire the content. Consumers may feel closer and more loyal to the artist as they have become, at least superficially, directly involved in supporting their careers. Rather than a pure funding model, then, perhaps the greatest potential for such initiatives is as a marketing tool to build awareness of potential new content, to remind consumers of their favourite games or artists from the past, and to increase consumer loyalty and emotional investment in creators.

Of course, again, there is great potential for misuse of the fan-driven model. We have already seen how involved fans of the K- and J-pop genres are in influencing content creation. They can vote on their favourite band members, who are then preferred in choices around vocal duties on songs or appearances in music videos. They influence what idols look like, how they dress and how they are expected to behave. It might be suggested that their relative closeness to fans is one of the reasons why idols are typically not allowed to publicly date or have romantic relationships. Superfans of idol bands live and breathe their idols, who assume a disproportionately important part in their lives. They might imagine the idols as boyfriends or girlfriends; hence they definitely don't want to see them romantically involved with someone else. But is this too much control, and where does it end?

Perhaps our idols should be allowed to be more human; perhaps the way in which idols are currently developed and controlled by companies like SM will eventually be seen as ethically and morally bankrupt. Perhaps they should be allowed to live their own lives, subject to less of the emotional and physical control that they current endure. But which idol company will be the first to break the mould? Which company will be willing to face the wrath of the superfans, who worship their favourite idols, weave them into their own lives and, significantly, buy more of their content and merchandising and attend more of the meet and greet events than any other fans, by allowing the idol to have a private and personal life not controlled by their company? It will be a brave CEO indeed that proposes this new strategy to their board of directors.

9.6 Challenges for organisations in specific sectors

Hopefully as a result of reading this book so far, you have developed a sense of the diversity of the cultural industries, the wide variety of different organisational structures and operating practices of companies in the sector. It's a far from homogeneous group of organisations. So, whilst there are a number of general trends that are likely to affect the industry as whole in the future, e.g. the impact of AI, individual sectors are likely to respond to these trends in different ways. For some there will be major opportunities, for others, major threats.

9.6.1 Television broadcasting and narrowcasting

In the television sector we have already noted the ongoing challenges for traditional broadcasters. Their decline and eventual disappearance has been forecast for some time now, but they remain, at least to date, remarkably resilient as their channels still host some of the most-viewed programming in most territories. But can this continue indefinitely? Certainly, we are already seeing the troubling movement of younger demographics to new online platforms. Advertising budgets have followed, a significant challenge for commercial channels who rely primarily on advertising for their income. Part of this challenge is that many broadcasters in the past have positioned themselves as 'all things to all men', providing content to all demographics in all genres. This may be part of their reason for existence (e.g. the BBC) and may be a condition of their broadcasting licence. This has also been a key selling point to advertisers, the ability to reach large, diverse audiences simultaneously on a single platform. But these large audiences are increasingly fragmenting into smaller segments across a range of different platforms and types of content.

Broadcasters have a choice, then. They might (and this has certainly been the case in recent history) attempt to re-aggregate these audiences by developing a presence on multiple different platforms. Hence, they may have their own distribution channels (e.g. a digital terrestrial broadcasting service) but also supply their channels to streaming aggregators like Netflix, invest in their own streaming services and catch-up applications and have a significant online presence, particularly on social media platforms. Hence, they will still be able to offer advertisers access to large audiences, even though they are distributed across a range of platforms.

Alternatively, they may decide to focus, becoming niche players in certain forms of distribution or content. Broadcasters typically have developed strong brands around certain of their channels and types of content, and there are numerous examples of this brand equity being used to focus further on specific market targets. The American broadcaster Discovery Communications began its business with a single channel focusing on natural history and documentaries. Subsequently it has drilled down into this genre to launch channels in a wide variety of related sub-genes, covering news, kids, history, education, family, science and health. Discovery complements its television presence with content available via online sources. Hence it is intent on 'owning', or at least dominating in, specific genres and niches, and this is significant, as in most niches in the content business, only the leaders in each segment or niche tend to be profitable (particularly in diverse markets such as Europe and Africa). Being the fourth or fifth company in a small niche tends not to be an economically viable position. Hence broadcasters are faced with an interesting choice. To try and maintain their existing positions, offering a wide range of different content to a large potential audience which is increasingly deserting the platform for other alternatives, or to focus down on specific parts of their business and existing audiences in an attempt to dominate specific niches.

For some broadcasters the challenge is more around remaining large enough to survive independently. In the USA, most major broadcast networks have been integrated into large, multi-business conglomerates like Walt Disney or Paramount Skydance. Hence, they have access to funds and resources which allow them to survive periods when advertising revenue declines and to compete with the likes of Netflix and Amazon for new content. For a stand-alone commercial service like ITV in the UK, this is more of a challenge. It has far lower programming budgets, and when the company has a difficult year in terms of advertising revenue, this has a direct effect on its ability to secure new content and continue to run its business. In such circumstances, it becomes a target for the type of merger or acquisition we discussed in Chapter 5. In the next 10 years, then, we may see a series of acquisitions of these broadcasters by larger conglomerates, particularly those that are cash-rich (e.g. technology companies), looking to diversify their portfolio or those hoping to capitalise on the brand-building potential of the broadcasting platform.

Other broadcasters may choose to focus on content production rather than content distribution. Most major broadcasters typically have their own production operations, and it is these production divisions that appear to have the best prospects for the future. Distribution is becoming increasingly commoditised as a service—there are now so many potential providers. But distributors always need new content, and the ability to consistently create attractive new content remains a hugely valuable capability. Should a large conglomerate express an interest in acquiring a broadcaster like ITV in the UK, it may only ultimately be interested in the production division as a stand-alone operation, rather than the combined content and distribution business.

The ongoing demand for new content should also favour the prospects of independent television production companies, who are now in a better position to retain rights in the programmes they develop, thus building a library of content assets that can significantly increase the value of the company. This is useful as it comes at a time when independent programme producers are increasingly the targets of acquisitions and mergers by major studios and broadcasters. Given our previous assessment of the prospects for most mergers and acquisitions, however, these initiatives will need to be carefully structured and managed if they are to result in increased value and benefit for both companies.

The need to focus may also become apparent amongst the dominant, generalist streaming platforms. Can Amazon or Netflix continue to provide the best content in every imaginable genre as costs rise and specialist providers emerge as competition? Certainly, some providers already appear to be specialising to some degree. Amazon in particular has been making significant investments in the live sports genre, signing deals to broadcast a wide variety of football (soccer) events and leagues, as well as American football, tennis and basketball (with an apparent resulting decline in the amount being spent on new film and television projects). Netflix too appear to have aspirations in the sports sector (offering live boxing and WWE events). Apple TV secured the rights to broadcast F1 races in the USA in 2025. This is an interesting return to the early days of the pay-TV sector, with a focus on securing premium content, not available on any other platforms, particularly in the sports genre (see Chapter 4). We can anticipate the value of sporting rights increasing significantly as competition for them intensifies. Equally we have seen a wide variety of specialist streaming channels launched, focusing on specific genres like film, horror, children, anime, sport and crime etc. We will inevitably see more, and perhaps the development of new, hardware-related streaming platforms (e.g. that provided by LG Channels) that aggregate and distribute such channels, already built into your next television (e.g. Freely on Panasonic televisions).

All sectors in the broadcasting industry are likely to be facing the prospects of increasing costs of operation, particularly in the field of content production. AI, then, is likely to feature prominently as a way to streamline and automate major parts of the production process, though at least at this stage it seems unlikely that the sector will embrace avatars as a source of digital talent to replace ‘real world’ actors to quite the same extent as we may see in the popular music sector. We will almost certainly see it used to automate elements of the production process, perhaps using gaming engines, with potentially significant implications for a workforce that is already suffering from the effects of casualisation.

9.6.2 The music popular sector

In terms of the popular music sector, perhaps the biggest debate is around the continued role and prominence of the three remaining major record companies (Universal, Warner and Sony). Already we see their major roles and functions being divided up amongst a range of new emergent organisations, including artists’ services companies like Kobalt[5] and talent management organisations like SM Entertainment. Certainly, these companies can provide many of the core functions of a major record company, from talent identification and management to marketing and distribution support. Perhaps where they are less prominent is in the area of funding (though talent management companies like SM clearly have aspirations in that area beyond J- and K-pop), which may remain a core function of the larger record companies like Universal. Interestingly this is a position often rejected by the leaders of the major record companies (being reduced to a funding-only business) as they see their overall role in the music sector as more creative, and more focused on nurturing talent. They don’t want to be viewed as banks. Equally, many of the emergent companies tend to focus on specific territories and genres only (though they all have ambitions to be global), so the majors may remain the only ‘one stop shop’ for those artists with genuinely global ambitions in the short term.

Perhaps the major record companies and music publishers’ biggest assets going forward will be their huge libraries of content that still find an audience on distribution platforms. Ownership of master tapes and publishing rights constitutes a significant and valuable set of assets that might be exploited on an ongoing basis. Some of these libraries have been added to through the acquisition of the artists’ share of the rights in their existing music—e.g. Bob Dylan's sale of his music publishing rights to Universal Music Publishing—and may include 'name and likeness' rights offering further exploitation opportunities (e.g. merchandising, experiential events etc.). Sting and Neil Diamond would follow in the sale of shares of the music rights to Universal. Warner Music and Sony Music have been equally quick to acquire major libraries of rights from artists.

It is notable, though, that the major record companies do have competition in this regard. New organisations have emerged like Hipgnosis (now renamed Recognition Music Group) and Primary Wave, who are focused on acquiring music rights and exploiting them in a variety of ways. Hipgnosis acquired 50% of Neil Young's catalogue of music rights, joining artists like Barry Manilow, Blondie, The Pretenders and Shakira. Primary Wave have acquired the rights catalogue of Stevie Nicks (ex. Fleetwood Mac), Disturbed, Burt Bacharach (50%) and Devo. As independent publishers they explore new ways in which such rights might be exploited, as well as utilising traditional monetisation options like merchandising and licensing to film, television and theatre. Companies like Primary Wave also have an artist management division, moving them ever closer to the traditional role of the major record company. The acquisition of libraries of artists' rights is likely to continue to be a major growth opportunity for such companies in the short to medium term.

Prospects in the live music sector appear more mixed. From a consumer perspective, large-scale tours from established artists continue to be popular and generate significant revenues for their many participants (though perhaps not always significant profits). Music festivals continue to proliferate, and large-scale festivals such as Coachella (USA) and Glastonbury (UK) continue to attract customers from all over the world, contributing to the music tourism sector. At the same time niche festivals, whether focused on specific genres of music (e.g. Graspop Metal Meeting in Belgium), activities like snowboarding and skiing (Rise Festival), geographic regions (Lindisfarne Festival in the north of the UK), demographics (e.g. 'family' festivals like Camp Bestival) or even focused on specific companies (SM Town Live in South Korea) continue to add to the total number of festivals consumers can choose from and are helping to drive the quality of consumer experience with greater focus on accommodation, food and drink and the provision of a range of different cultural experiences and VIP services.

Smaller live music venues continue to be under pressure, however, as rents and utilities costs continue to rise, licensing processes involving local government councils become ever more challenging and bureaucratic and audiences appear to be more interested in saving their leisure spending to attend one or two festivals per year, rather than visiting their local music venue every week. We have noted (see Chapter 6) the dangers of this in terms of the development of younger artists who may lose a primary venue to learn their performing craft as a result.

The role of the live tour is also changing for the major record companies and artists. Whilst they still hold their own as a promotional tool, they are also now seen as a major revenue and profit generator, one that the record companies are keen to participate in. As well as more traditional tours, artist-based events like *ABBA Voyage* and *MJ the Musical* have the potential to be significantly more lucrative than musical distribution methods like streaming, Sony Music Group's chief executive Rob Stringer suggesting the opportunity is a potential 'gold mine…that's a revenue stream that is, quite frankly, more lucrative than streaming'.[6] The 360-degree deal in which the record company participates in all of the revenue sources generated by an artist, including live and experiential events, looks set to become the standard model in the industry.

For an organisation like Sony Music, perhaps its future lies with more of a focus on cooperative ventures within the company itself. Given Sony's vast range of businesses, including hardware manufacture, games, television and film, anime etc., the range of potential coproductions with the music division is significant—e.g. Sony's ownership of 50% of the rights to Michael Jackson's music library has subsequently led to a live event (*MJ the Musical*), and will subsequently be leveraged into a feature film biography of the artist.

But again, we need to be critical. Cooperative ventures between content and distribution businesses have proven to be difficult in the past, and balancing the different agendas of different parts of the Sony group will be equally challenging and take a great deal of effort to manage. Establishing the right internal processes, systems and organisational structures to initiate and manage such ventures will take significant time, resources and oversight. Whether such multiplatform ventures are better conducted by large integrated 'super' companies, or alliances of smaller more nimble specialist teams in dedicated organisations, remains to be seen. Of course, for direct competitors to Sony Music like Warner Music, options to develop multimedia cross-platform projects with music at their core are likely to be much more challenging, as they are not part of a larger entertainment conglomerate. Perhaps, then, their future lies in being acquired by one, or trying to become one.

We can be certain of an ever-increasing flow of musical content into distribution channels, from professional and amateur sources. Perhaps the biggest question here is how and by whom the audience's attention is directed. In a hugely crowded and fragmented market, the record company's previous reliance on large-scale promotional campaigns may no longer be sufficient to direct audiences to their new content and, at the very least, these campaigns will need to change in terms of the mediums and techniques used. Certainly there is likely to be a shift in things like promotional music videos, from long-form epics that worked in the era of MTV (Music Television), to short-form videos that can quickly capture the audience's attention on the new MTV, platforms like TikTok, Instagram Reels and YouTube Shorts. The new arbiters of audience attention are more likely to be online influencers that inhabit these platforms, and it will be interesting to see how their relationship with music producers evolves over time.

The other key ingredient in terms of the direction of consumer attention will of course be ever more sophisticated algorithms that can capture data on a consumer's media habits, and recommend new content based on their prior history. Such systems will need to be carefully 'trained' to ensure they balance the consumer's desire to find new content that can be directly linked to content they have previously consumed (i.e. the new recommended content feels somehow familiar), with new content that may be outside their usual listening habits. As with all such deployments, the great benefit is that the algorithms, once calibrated, can operate without human intervention, and given the ability of AI-based systems on neural networks to continue to 'learn', should get better and better at anticipating the consumer's needs and desires.

But perhaps there is a significant danger here, as well. For many in the industry, these AI-based systems will remain 'black boxes', with users having little real understanding of how they work, particularly as self-learning systems get faster and ever more sophisticated and complex. Recommendations are likely to be outputted by the system, and implemented, with little opportunity for those in the business running them to question the way in which the data is being handled (indeed what data is even being used) and how recommendations are constructed. In many ways, the AI system may become the primary point of contact between the corporation and its customer. This is already happening to some extent as AI encroaches on the customer service function in many organisations. The AI systems will collect data, interpret it and potentially handle the direct interactions with the consumer. Yet this is typically the most precious relationship that most companies have, their relationship with the consumer. Are we sure we want to hand it over to a 'black box' we do not fully understand? Yes, it's going to be cheaper and faster than having human beings involved, but will it always result in a better customer experience? We will need to develop the appropriate skills amongst our staff to ask the right questions of these systems, to interrogate their operation, to check their recommendations and to oversee the overall customer experience. But perhaps this will be seen as a major constraint on the operation of AI and hence resisted by many in the industry. Why get subjective, error-prone and cognitively limited humans involved at all? Why go to the trouble of training them? It's an interesting question: do we want our human marketing team or our AI system to be the voice and representative of the consumer in our company?

This is particularly so in the area of ethics. We want AI systems that handle data in an ethical way and make recommendations according to broad ethical and moral standards. AI systems have no inherent ethical or moral standards; they rely entirely on their creators to instil such guidelines and limits on their actions. But will this be a priority for companies? The pain and cost of developing and launching such systems may mean that the initial focus is firmly on ensuring that they make a sufficient commercial impact that they rapidly pay back the investment in their development (hence a focus on raising revenues, increasing profits and cutting costs), rather than necessarily reflecting the ethical and moral standards of the company. Again, do we want to hand over our most precious relationship to a system in which the 'ethical and moral' guidelines were rapidly tacked onto the end of the development process to meet regulatory requirements, without much thought and reflection?

Artists themselves, particularly those with some level of pre-existing popularity, may prove increasingly frustrated with the reported low levels of compensation for their work secured through traditional streaming platforms and opt to pursue direct-to-fan (D2F) opportunities through applications like Bandcamp, Patreon and even Shopify. The question remains whether such an approach can work for emerging artists, without the support of a larger organisation to help build initial awareness and their brand, to the degree to which it allows them to establish successful and long careers. Such an approach may need to be combined with other opportunities emerging from the development of blockchain and NFTs (non-fungible tokens) as additional revenue sources through platforms like Audis, Royal and Opulous. Whilst this all appears to be very optimistic for the artist—that is, the potential availability of multiple different revenue streams that can be stitched together to support a career, particularly when combined with opportunities in the increasingly healthy live music sector—it is worth noting that all of these opportunities require the artist to develop a host of potentially new skills and knowledge. Rather than spending all day writing songs, or perfecting their singing techniques or guitar playing, artists may be reading business textbooks, working through Excel spreadsheets and 'doing deals'. They will increasingly need to develop the business insights and skills that previously could be left to those in the record companies whose sole reason for existence was to do such deals, and who became quite expert in their execution. Artists will increasingly need to be their own business managers and architects of their careers. They will need to navigate an increasingly complex world of opportunities, each of which may be critical to remaining active in the industry. This is a tough, complex and demanding new agenda, and one that many artists may not wish to embrace, preferring to focus on the one thing they love, making music.

9.6.3 Performing arts

Prospects for the performing arts sector remain as challenging as ever in the short to medium term. Over-reliance on government and state funding appears an increasingly risky option. A continuation of the trend for organisations in the sector to refocus on generating their own revenues is likely to become even more prevalent and urgent. Achieving significant profits from ticket sales alone seems unlikely, given the high fixed costs of many such organisations, so the focus may be more on improving the customer experience with enhanced food and drink options, more merchandising, specialist events (the equivalent of the VIP experience in the pop music market) and, away from the venue, the monetisation of digital content. The events themselves will need to exploit all of the capabilities of digital content (including the use of AI, digital avatars and special effects) if performances are to keep pace with developments in other entertainment sectors.

Perhaps the biggest challenge in achieving such change is securing the right business talent, with the right skill set to support such innovative initiatives. In this regard, the sector faces a challenge, in that traditionally it tends to pay far lower wages than other business sectors (and in some cases, as we have noted, relies on volunteers to keep the organisation functioning). If a theatre company wants to secure the best current talent in the field of social media marketing, it's likely to have to 'steal' someone from a major consumer brand. This will be an expensive and risky proposition. As will finding someone expert in digital content exploitation, AI or online community building. The only alternative is to develop those skills within the industry through the provision of better training and development pathways for staff, but this will inevitably take considerable time and resources, time and resources that the sector may not have.

Prospects might be somewhat better for those parts of the performing arts sector that are linked most directly to tourism (e.g. traditional arts, dances and performances linked to a region's cultural heritage), given government interest in growing the tourism business in many regions. Here a critical skill set within the performing arts organisation will be building strong relationships with departments of tourism, local governments and travel businesses, to ensure they are aware of and included in new tourism initiatives. Organisations in the sector will need to develop their open innovation capabilities, becoming part of innovation networks linking organisations from a variety of different sectors and parts of the economy (both public and private).

Any resultant gap in the finances of such organisations will need to be filled with an increasing focus on fundraising, from private (e.g. high-net-worth individuals), state and corporate sources. It is perhaps in this latter, corporate sector that most opportunities may arise, as companies look to associate themselves with 'worthy' organisations in the cultural sector through sponsorship deals and alliances. Again, this points to the need for those in the performing arts sector to develop their skill set in managing innovation networks, focusing on their breadth and diversity. Finding the 'right' partners will be crucial, as whilst corporations may seek worthy and high-profile partners in the cultural sector, not all such corporations will have equally high profiles or reputations. Indeed, the worse the reputation of the business the more likely they are to seek partners who might improve their image.

Again, we are faced with a crucial tension that will need to be managed. If an oil and gas company that has just polluted a major stretch of the ocean, or a clothing company that is rumoured to exploit child labour in Indonesia or bank that is lending money to companies deforesting the Amazon, offers to cover all of your theatre's expenses for the next three years as part of a sponsorship deal in which their name will feature prominently on all of your promotional material, what do you do? Will organisations in the performing arts sector put ethics before continued survival?

Perhaps it will be the audience that decides. This of course highlights the other major ongoing challenge for organisations in the performing arts sector: securing access to and the interest of critical audience segments, particularly younger audiences and those outside major metropolitan areas. The one thing we can be sure of is that the sector can only survive (let alone thrive) if it can continue to secure new consumers for its content. But the sector faces tough competition for consumers from other entertainment sectors (music, film and TV, gaming) and from social media, particularly in younger segments. There are now so many ways in which to consume content, to spend your leisure minute or dollar; why would they choose to use it watching an opera (in a foreign language, which lasts four hours and is a two-hour drive away) or a modern dance performance when they can watch K-pop dancers via YouTube? Radically reshaping the nature of the performance, as is often suggested (e.g. why not have K-pop stars doing classical western opera, why not have a dance performance based on a popular anime series?) is probably not the answer as it risks alienating the current core consumer, and if they desert the sector it really is in trouble.

There is no quick and easy answer here. Organisations in the performing arts sector have been struggling with this dilemma for 40 years and no-one has yet solved the problem. Initiatives to encourage younger audiences to sign up for discounted tickets rarely have a significant, long-term effect. People may sign up for such schemes, but then rarely take advantage of them. Arguably, the problem is not one of price alone. Certainly many performing arts events are expensive (as we saw in Chapter 3) and offering significant discounts on the price of tickets for younger audiences is a good start, but it's hardly enough. Drawing on the AIDA model we discussed in Chapter 8, the problem appears less around decision and action (which is where price reductions tend to have most influence) and more around attention and interest. No matter how cheap the tickets (indeed, they could be free), if younger consumers are not actively aware of and interested in what is happening in the performing arts sector, they will not take up any incentive offer.

Perhaps the focus for most performing arts organisations needs to be more on education and promotion, than price cuts alone. Certainly, many organisations have invested in educational outreach programmes in recent years (again stressing the need for complex and multidimensional innovation networks and the involvement of multiple stakeholders), often linking with local schools and universities to build interest in the sector amongst younger people. Equally promotional budgets have generally increased. These trends are likely to continue, but progress appears slow, and ultimately audiences (and particularly younger audiences) remain elusive. Again, finding the right partners to help the performing arts sector to reach younger audiences, and positively influence their attitudes towards it, is likely to be key.

9.6.4 Electronic gaming

Finally, what can we say about the short- to medium-term future of the games sector? We have noted the way in which developments in AI are likely to have significant effects, from the content production process, through its influence on the development of and use of gaming engines, through the evolution of game modding to games development by amateurs (aided by the popularity of gaming projects in most crowdfunding sites). For the industry, its ability to potentially automate critical elements of the game creation process offers huge potential to restructure the development process and potentially remove cost (for that, read human involvement) from it. AI's deployment in the sector and use throughout the industry is assured; there is little debate there.

Equally we noted that in some territories, technological leapfrogging has led to the mobile device (typically telephone) being the dominant way in which many gamers game, particularly in emerging territories like Africa and parts of Asia. This does lead us to one of the critical questions facing the sector in the next few years, which is subject to widely different views: the future of the console. Perhaps in the same way that commentators forecast the death of traditional broadcasting 20 years ago, some are now proposing a similar fate for the games console.

The markets that are of most interest to the gaming companies, those that are emerging and demonstrate the most significant growth potential, have tended to leapfrog the development of a large installed base of consoles in favour of mobile devices. Consoles have proven too expensive for territories where an average gamer may spend only $5 per year on their gaming habit, particularly when combined with expensive games to run on them. Equally mobile phones have developed to such an extent that they can happily run AAA titles that would previously have only been possible on dedicated consoles or high-end PCs. Such territories may never develop a significant installed base of dedicated games consoles. No matter how advanced and technically leading-edge consoles become, unless their price falls profoundly (and bear in mind most consoles are already sold at a loss), they are unlikely to become a common feature of the gaming infrastructure in such territories. Indeed, the only way in which they might do so is if they are given away by hardware manufacturers, in the same way that set-top boxes were to encourage the take up of pay-TV. Manufacturers would need to be extremely confident that they could recoup such investments through the sales of games for this to be a viable strategy.

For those territories in which consoles are a significant and principal element of the gaming infrastructure, the question is increasingly, what's next? What new technology will be so pivotal, so expensive and so transformative that gamers will continue to be willing to spend significant parts of their salaries on buying the next generation of console hardware? This is particularly so given the increasing power of mobile devices and the move to cloud-based gaming services, that typically require less processing power where the game is being played, and more processing power at the server end of the chain. To consolidate the growth of cloud-based gaming, variants of the console that focus more on mobile gaming, or devices that appear to be small enough to fit onto a USB stick (and hence are just plugged into the back of a television), are likely to emerge in the short term. Further variations of dedicated mobile gaming devices can also be expected. They won't necessarily push the boundaries of processing power, graphics or storage in the same way that previous consoles have, but they will allow increased flexibility in how, when and where games are played.

So, what of the traditional console, the large device that sits next to (or under) the television and announces to the world that 'I am a gamer', drawing on the very latest technologies to explore new dimensions in gaming? Perhaps the most likely potentially transformative applications will be around VR and AR. Whilst early attempts to integrate AR and VR into the gaming experience have met with limited success, developments in hardware and software offer the potential for a more seamless and engaging integration of the technologies, leading to genuinely new gaming experiences. Certainly, a number of hardware developers are investing significant amounts of their R&D budgets in exploring new ways in which such applications might be deployed. Perhaps we will see a renewed focus on the console as the central entertainment device in the home. Already complemented with a range of television, video and music applications, the console as central AR/VR hub might also be utilised in accessing enhanced television, film or music experiences, it may be the central way in which you access the metaverse to meet your new J-pop idol in a chat room, or participate in a new interactive VR-based television show. Again, however, this will involve numerous stakeholders working closely together and hence will take time to emerge. Perhaps it is most likely to emerge from organisations like Sony, who have in-house music, hardware, software, television and gaming divisions who might work together on what might be the most complex, multifaced, innovative (and hence potentially expensive and risky) content ever created. But again, such levels of cooperation and coordination are extraordinarily rare in large firms; it does not just 'happen', it takes time, resources and significant effort, and is more than likely, at least initially, to end in failure or at least some level of disappointment.

A more certain return might be expected from greater levels of investment in what could be called local content—that is, content specifically designed for and drawing on the rich cultural legacies of different territories. Africa is already seeing an explosion in the number of local games developers, and the launch of relatively successful franchises focusing on African history and cultural icons. But a significant challenge is that they are often being funded and supported by non-local publishers, global giants like Microsoft and Sony, and ultimately the flow of revenues tends to favour the publishers, rather than the local developers. Equally such publishers are looking to local content to potentially deliver global hits, content that can transcend local boundaries and work across the globe, and questions are already being asked about the degree to which the very local nature of the content might ultimately limit its global potential. Perhaps local developers will be asked to lessen their focus on the local if they want the support of a global publisher like Tencent or Microsoft, in favour of adopting international cultural symbols and mores that are globally accepted, and at this point the local developer merely becomes part of the global supply chain of development talent that such publishers draw on to develop global content, rather than being core parts of a local set of cultural industries, representing and protecting local cultures. What is clear is that the major global publishers are interested in emerging territories and, at least at the moment, are helping support their development as content suppliers with funding, access to technology and professional support and advice. Whether this route follows the evolution of other global supply chains, driven by large wealthy corporations, claiming to have the interests of emerging territories at heart, whilst at the same time establishing exploitative relationships with them and securing the vast share of resultant profits, or whether a more equitable ecosystem can emerge, is still a subject of some debate.

9.7 Conclusions

As leaders and managers of future cultural industry organisations, part of your role will be to ready your organisations for an evolving and dynamic future. This is hugely challenging, particularly in a commercial environment that appears to represent all of the VUCA qualities (it is characterised by volatility, uncertainty, complexity and ambiguity). But the task remains critical and developing capabilities in corporate and strategic foresight will be a priority for all organisations in the cultural industries. This chapter has outlined a number of tools and techniques used in other business sectors to help us. But it remains an imprecise and evolving art and science.

Perhaps the best advice in this regard is that as future leaders and managers, your job is to at least start a discussion or dialogue in your organisation about what the future might hold, and how your organisation can ready itself. Whilst the output of such a process may ultimately prove to be wrong (a precise forecast of the future is unlikely to be accurate in all aspects), the process of discussion is critical; in this sense, then, planning (the process) is more important than the final plan (the output). Healthy organisations continually discuss and analyse the future; it's something that everyone in the organisation does on a regular basis—everyone is involved. Creating an organisational culture in which this is seen as beneficial and indeed required is a key role for management. Creating the systems and processes (e.g. around planning) that allow everyone to be involved to some extent is the second key objective. When the future is uncertain, having a diversity of views and information is critical.

Hence this chapter does not claim to forecast the future; rather it identifies some key themes and trends as the basis for a discussion. The process of discussion itself is the really useful part, particularly if it allows us to question the status quo, the established view, the consensus upon which all companies are basing their future plans. All of the major record companies in the early 1980s were basing their strategic planning on a singular and shared view of the future in which they remained dominant and nothing really changed. How wrong they were. How valuable it would have been to have one dissenting voice, providing a radically different view of the future, someone asking 'what happens if…?'

This is a discussion which may start in the classroom (if you are currently studying there is a lot of content in this chapter that might prompt debate and, hopefully, disagreement) or in the boardroom of your company, but maximising its value means sharing the discussion with as wide a group as possible. In a university context, for those of you on a specific programme, this may mean sharing the discussion with students from other schools of study. You may be studying on a course hosted by a business school, department of sociology or institute of communications / media studies. But what do students in the school of computing have to say about the future potential of AI (or have they already moved onto the intricacies of quantum computing)? How does the school of design see products and services evolving? What new technologies are the students in the school of electrical engineering working on?

For commercial organisations, the debate about the future needs to be taken up by employees—all employees. For this to happen, employees need to be aware of the issue, appreciate its significance and have the appropriate knowledge and training to make use of the tools discussed in the chapter. They need to be involved in the planning process in some way. The data they generate every day through their involvement with customers, suppliers, funders and creators needs to be collected, analysed and used. Whilst once the sole responsibility of top management, establishing a viable and useful view of the future should now be considered a responsibility of the organisation as a whole—it's everyone's job and everyone's business.

9.8 Activities

- Review how you might be using AI in your daily life. List all of the applications that you might use, from entertainment to communication and productivity services. How might it be affecting what content you are consuming? How is your use of the service regulated by external agencies (if at all)?
- Choose one of the sectors reviewed in the chapter. How might the sector evolve in the longer term? What might television or the popular music sector look like in 20–30 years? What new challenges may emerge for incumbents?
- Develop a set of scenarios around the evolution of AI in the medium term. Identify the critical issues (perhaps through a PESTLE analysis—e.g. technology, social change, legal changes), choose two and develop a 2x2 matrix of four possible scenarios. What are the implications of each scenario for a focal company of your choice?
- Use ScFi prototyping to develop a vision of what online shopping might be like in 50 years' time.

Notes

1 Emergen Research, 2024.
2 https://www.bbc.co.uk/news/technology-63106024.
3 https://edition.cnn.com/style/kpop-virtual-bands-ai-intl-hnk.
4 https://www.infeedo.ai/.
5 https://www.kobaltmusic.com.
6 Interview with Rob Stringer, CEO Sony Music, https://www.youtube.com/watch?v=M7CAXCCWSng.

References

Campbell, J. W. 2018. Efficiency, incentives, and transformational leadership: Understanding collaboration preferences in the public sector. *Public Performance & Management Review*, 41 (2), pp. 277–299.

Chakraborty, S., Nijssen, E. and Valkenburg, R. 2021. A systematic review of industry-level applications of technology road mapping: Evaluation and design propositions for road mapping practitioners. *Technological Forecasting and Social Change*, 179.

Johnson, B. D. 2009. Science Fiction Prototypes Or: How I Learned to Stop Worrying about the Future and Love Science Fiction. Conference: Intelligent Environments 2009: Proceedings of the 5th International Conference on Intelligent Environments: Barcelona, Spain.

Logg, J. M., Minson, J. A. and Moore, D. A. 2019. Algorithm appreciation: People prefer algorithmic to human judgment. *Organizational Behaviour and Human Decision Processes*, 151, pp. 90–103.

Roberts, J. P. and Middleton, A. 2014. Evolving products, from human design to self-organisation via science fiction prototyping. *Technological Forecasting and Social Change*, 84, pp. 15–28.

Silver, D. 2016. Mastering the game of Go with deep neural networks and tree search. *Nature*, 529, pp. 484–489.

Slaughter R. 1999. *Futures for the Third Millennium: Enabling the Forward View*. St Leonards, N.S.W.: Prospect.

Sparks, C. 2004. The impact of the internet on existing media, in Calabrase, A. (ed.). *Towards a Political Economy of Culture: Capitalism and Communication in the Twenty-First Century*. Bloomsbury.

10 Conclusions and Next Steps

10.1 Introduction

In this final chapter we review our findings on the operation of the cultural industries and identify a number of critical trends that may further influence their evolution in the medium term. We discuss issues of a potential resurgence of analogue media, and potential resistance to the further digitisation of the cultural industries. We will explore the implications of globalisation, the ongoing move from distribution- to attention-based economies and the way in which the war for talent may play out.

Further we begin to the explore the implications of everything we have discussed for you, the reader, and your potential career in the industry. We began the book by stressing that its aim was more focused on helping you secure a long-term and rewarding career in the industry as a participant rather than helping you become a better observer and commentator. So, what can we say about the challenges of finding that first job, routes into the industry and the potential for you to start your own business? In doing so we will briefly review academic perspectives on entrepreneurship. Whilst it's a potentially viable route into the industry, it comes with some major challenges and certainly won't suit every reader. Developing a sense of whether it might (or might not) work for you may help focus your career development efforts and, in some cases, rightly, put you off the idea. For those of you who are still keen to 'do it yourself', you will at least have a better idea of the potential downsides of entrepreneurship as a career choice and what would be expected of you if you are to succeed.

10.2 Reflections on our core areas of enquiry

So, having reviewed the structure and operation of several major sectors of the cultural industries, what are our conclusions?

It's clearly a diverse, complex and fascinating sector. It's important, not just for its potential impact on how we live our lives and perceive events around us, but for its sheer economic impact. It generates significant revenues and profits. Governments often see it as a vehicle for economic growth. There are many interesting jobs in the sector, it provides employment and careers—and we will talk about careers in a little more detail in section 10.7. Further, its ongoing growth (with growth rates that often outstrip growth in other business sectors) makes it an interesting place to do business, attracting many investors and entrepreneurs (see Chapters 1 and 2). But we noted that it can also be a dangerous place to do business, prone to rapid and radical change over relatively short time scales. Major businesses can be built quickly, but they can disappear equally fast.

DOI: 10.4324/9781003498599-10

We noted the cultural industries are going through a period of rapid and often radical change at the moment, as a result of the digitisation of content and infrastructures, the growth in competition, the arrival of new forms of distribution and content, the growth in the availability of consumer data and global changes in the ownership of companies (e.g. the trend towards conglomeration). We noted changes in consumer behaviour and hence a requirement for cultural organisations to develop their skills and capabilities in interacting with them. We noted attempts by organisations to break down the traditional barriers between artists and fans, potentially heralding a new era of coproduction between artists, the companies they work for or serve, brands and consumers.

We anticipated that in much of the academic content we would review, the voice of the business sector within the cultural industries would be missing or, at the very least, muted. Equally, based on our initial review of the literature, we felt that the actions and influence of the business community in the sector might be characterised in quite a negative way, as a constraint on creativity, as a group who would always put profit before artistic endeavour, and who ultimately were responsible for a perceived erosion of the quality of content in the sector and a decline in its cultural and artistic variety. This perspective did indeed emerge in much of the literature reviewed in this book. But we also noted that very limited direct primary research had been done on the business community in the industry (other than from the perspective of the creative community) and hence their voice is largely missing from the canon of research. We have only a partial understanding of how the sector operates. Whilst this situation is changing, and academics involved in the study of the sector are increasingly engaging in 'direct talks' with the cultural industry's business community, and publishing their results, this is still an emergent and under-researched area.

We speculated at the start of the book that the cultural industries might be organised and run in a different way to other business sectors. Was this the case? Well, at least in the most industrialised parts of the cultural economy, generally there does not seem to be a great deal of difference. Organisations in the cultural sector share very similar structures (e.g. the bureaucratic hierarchy with specialisation according to role, function and level) and processes (new product development, planning, budgeting etc.) to those organisations in other business sectors. Whilst there may be some differences—e.g. a significant reliance on volunteers in the performing arts sectors (though this is generally the case with most charities), and the presence of specialised functions like A&R or commissioning—this is typical of most business sectors that evolve specialist functions to undertake particular roles. Hence most cultural organisations have broadly similar structures to those in other sectors, seem to follow broadly similar operational practices and share similar forms of organisational behaviour. They face similar challenges in terms of how they might need to evolve and how they are led and managed, and we might argue that those in the industry can learn significant and valuable lessons from how these challenges have been managed in other industries.

Equally, in some areas we noted that other business sectors may be able to learn crucial lessons from the cultural industries. Organisations in the cultural industries have been operating across complex innovation ecosystems for much of their history. In many ways they pioneered the idea of open innovation and finding ways to work with a variety of organisations and individuals outside their own. The continued existence of an independent sector as a source of creativity and new ideas attests to the industry's capacity to deal with the different interests and agendas of a wide variety of stakeholders within and outside their organisations and reach a sufficient consensus for them to work together productively. Cultural organisations have become (relatively) expert in dealing and working with creative talent. These are the very real challenges that many organisations in other sectors are now facing, from technology to consumer goods, particularly as the 'war for talent' intensifies and organisations seek ways to become more innovative, agile and flexible.

Further we speculated that the way in which organisations in the sector operate might be different to other business sectors, particularly the relatively higher levels of organisational conflict we might encounter in their operation. This was based on the idea that there are two very distinct and conflicting agendas at work in the industry, an artistic one and a business one, and that these agendas were ultimately antithetical. Again, our conclusion was that perhaps this element of their operation has been over-emphasised. We noted that conflict appears in the operation of every organisation in every sector, that sometimes it's necessary, and even beneficial. Further we noted that the stark division between business and artistic individuals and their agendas may have been promoted to a level of prominence in research that it perhaps does not merit. In the real world of the cultural industries, the boundaries between the two agendas seems more blurred and permeable, and individuals move between the two worlds to some degree, exhibiting a more artistic or business-related perspective as necessary. Indeed, we noted that in some sectors, like popular music, artists have to become more and more business-like in their outlook as they increasingly take charge of their own careers.

We thought perhaps that the cultural product was radically different to products and services in other business sectors. Again, we found many areas of similarity, from the ways in which products are created (e.g. the new product development process), the kinds of tools and techniques that can be used to analyse them (e.g. product portfolio models) to the ways they are distributed and sold. Even their core characteristics seemed to be a combination of features we regularly see in other types of products and services. We did note relatively high levels of risk associated with their development, however, partly down to the often high costs involved (though, again, we noted other types of product cost far more to create—e.g. a new pharmaceutical) but probably more the result of the difficulties in predicting the consumer's response and hence the content's likely performance. We also noted, however, that significant strides are being made in collecting data on consumers that might be used to make better predictions about how a new piece of content might perform, and that the development of AI is likely to enhance the ability of producers to forecast demand for their new content and plan its release (e.g. windowing).

We did note that marketing, the function that in other business sectors would typically be charged with understand the consumer and forecasting their likely response to new products and services, has been relatively slow to develop to its full scope in the cultural industries; for much of its history it has been focused on promotion and very little else. Organisations often evolved with very limited competition (e.g. the public service broadcasters) and hence didn't really need to develop their range of marketing capabilities. Others were reliant on state support (e.g. in the performing arts sector) and understanding the government's agenda rather than understanding their consumers was critical to generate their funding. Further, many companies did not necessarily have a direct link to the consumer (e.g. the major record companies) and found it difficult to research their behaviour and analyse the results. Finally, there appeared to be a natural reluctance to becoming too market-led amongst some in the industry, particularly those in the creative community who feared the potential impact on content and a lack of artistic variety and opportunity. Again, things seem to be changing, as competition in all sectors has increased, support from state sources has declined and new technologies have emerged that allow the collection and analysis of consumer data in previously unimagined volumes.

Given these numerous similarities, we might well argue that the tools, techniques and perspectives used widely in other business sectors can be applicable and useful to those managing the cultural industries. But they need to be applied carefully, with thought and a clear understanding of their strengths and weaknesses. Having said that, this is typically good advice for users of these tools and techniques in any sector of the economy; established tools of business analysis (e.g. SWOT, PESTLE, value chain analysis) are often used badly, and applied in the wrong way to unsuitable issues and problems. Understanding the origins of such tools, the assumptions they are based on and the specific agenda of those who created them is a key requirement. We have started this process in this book, identifying tools and techniques that might be of use. The reader's work needs to continue, drilling down into these tools and techniques, reading academic and practitioner papers on their practical use and limitations and then practising with them, using them in real-world use cases and assessing for themselves their value. In some cases, they won't be helpful, and new tools will need to be developed to help analyse different business challenges—this is one of the great attractions of having a business career, being part of and contributing to ongoing management innovation.

We can say that it seems challenging to work out what's going to happen next in the industry, given the complex interaction between the social, cultural, technological and political trends and influences to which the industry is subject. But, again, this is probably true of just about every business sector in the VUCA environment. Again, then, we might draw on some of the tools we have identified around corporate and strategic foresight to help us anticipate these future changes.

So, for today's practitioners, some level of knowledge of business practices in other sectors, of the type we have illustrated in this book, can be useful. But, again, their use needs to be carefully managed to ensure they are relevant, useful and doing their job—that is, helping practitioners undertake better analysis and make better business decisions. This is harder than it sounds. It's very tempting to apply the wrong tool to the wrong problem, just because the textbook suggested it, or you were advised to do so by your tutor. Equally, no-one is necessarily interested in the tools themselves; they are interested in their conclusions, their outputs. A useful question to ask oneself having completed a PESTLE analysis, a SWOT, or having examined a value chain, is 'so what?' What are the implications of the conclusions I have drawn from using the tool? The analysis is the start, but the conclusions and implications are the valuable output. To a degree this will only come with practice and experience.

Looking forward, some additional issues stand out as being particularly significant for those of you intent on working in the industry. What tools and techniques will help you deal with these issues and challenges?

10.3 An analogue fightback?

The cultural industries have been surfing a wave of digital transformation for the last 30 years. As we have seen, the wave has had very positive and negative effects. On the one hand it allowed the popular music sector to grow to unprecedented levels of profitability thanks to the launch of the CD, but it also nearly destroyed the traditional industry and dominance of the major record companies thanks to the emergence of digital file distribution. Certainly, it has been the basis for the growth of significant competition in the supply of some cultural content (e.g. television), changing the dynamics of the supply sector, but opening up new options for the consumer.

The consumer, at least to date, has seemingly welcomed all these digital developments. They appreciate the fungible nature of digital content, the huge range of suppliers they can choose from, and ultimately their growing ability to determine exactly what content they consume, how and when. For some consumer constituencies, the growth of digital content creation tools has also allowed them to fulfil artistic and career ambitions as creators.

Will this continue or can we anticipate an analogue backlash? Already on YouTube we can find user videos on how to 'detox from digital', how to rely less on your mobile phone, how to take a break from the constant urge to consume more and more content. In some sectors there has even been a return to favouring analogue rather than digital formats for content.

The return of the analogue vinyl disk to the popular music sector was a surprise to many. Having been the dominant distribution method in the 1960s and 1970s, in the 1980s it was replaced by the digital CD, which offered better sound quality and increased functionality, with vinyl reaching its lowest level of sales in 2006. But for the last 15 years vinyl has been growing in popularity again—in the UK, for example, more than 5.5m vinyl LPs were sold in 2021, according to figures from the BPI.[1] Helped by vinyl releases from major stars like Taylor Swift, with the release of four different vinyl versions of her 10th album *Midnights*, figures from the RIAA[2] show that vinyl LP sales outperformed CDs in the US (for the first time since 1987) in 2022. Just over 41m vinyl records were sold in 2022, totalling $1.2bn of sales. Only 33m CDs were sold, amounting to $483m (ibid).

Why has this happened? Well, many listeners claim analogue vinyl provides a more authentic listening medium than digital—it is claimed to be closer to the sound intended by the original artist when they recorded the content. Conversion to a digital format can lead to problems of compression and limited dynamic range. It can literally change how a song sounds. Better, then, to stick to an analogue format in which every nuance of the original recording can be heard.

For others there is the love of physical items in a digital world. Vinyl disks and the equipment used to play them become furniture, something to be displayed, a way in which one's personality and tastes can be made manifest in the home. For some it's the album artwork, sleeve notes or the physicality of lowering the needle onto the disk. For others it allows them to invest the vast majority of their incomes in high-end audio equipment that brings out the best of the content. The SME Model 60 turntable is currently on sale for £59,000 at UK retailers (and this is far from the most expensive on sale). That's literally just the turntable. Then of course you are going to need the right amplifier, the right speakers and the right cabling. It's very easy to spend over £100,000 on a good system to play your vinyl. The systems also look terribly impressive, particularly compared to your laptop or PC which contains all of your digital music files.

The only problem faced by the vinyl revolution at the moment is that demand is vastly outstripping supply, raising prices. It's a nice problem to have for the industry. According to the head of the Entertainment Retailers Association, then, 'the outlook for vinyl remains extremely positive'.[3]

In other parts of the music sector, digital developments are pushing the boundaries of what an artist is considered to be. At the moment, the emergence of digital avatars is relatively new, and generally of interest and appeal to the consumer. Certainly, in terms of giving a new life to already established but aging artists like ABBA, it's been a popular development. Will it be the same for entirely virtual artists and bands like South Korea's Eternity? These digital idols are certainly attracting a lot of attention, but will consumers build the same types of deep emotional connections they have with 'real world' artists? Perhaps it does not matter. If audience attention begins to diminish in a particular virtual artist or group, the PC can just be turned off, the coding erased.

Whilst we may not need to worry ourselves about their working conditions, or their future career prospects, entirely virtual performers do offer the potential to impact the careers of real-world artists. At the very least they are competition, they contribute to the overwhelming amount of content consumers may choose from, but perhaps more significantly, as we have discussed, they may raise the bar in what is expected from any artist. They sing, dance and can play any instrument perfectly. They can act, be presenters, 'learn' any sport in moments. They are available 356 days a year, 24 hours a day to meet and greet fans (whose first name and listening habits they are likely to know). They don't lose their looks over time, or act inappropriately. More significantly, they don't ask for more pay!

This is a tough agenda for real-world artists to live up to. We might speculate how consumers who have grown up watching digital avatars perform are likely to react when they see their first real-world artist perform. The question we asked ourselves in Chapter 9 is worth repeating here: what is the role of authenticity in this evolving marketplace? Will consumers of the future value the authentic nature (and by that we mean it's typically full of mistakes, errors and unique events) of a performance by a human, or will they see it as slightly less satisfying than what's possible from a digital avatar?

At best we can hope for a mixed marketplace, where digital avatars are available to meet with their fans whenever the fan wants, are able to extend the performing lives of artists who are aging but whom we would miss if they stopped touring and also might extend the activities of musical artists into new spheres (theatre, film, TV and games), but where consumers still value the unique experience of seeing a human perform the content they have created, live, with all of its inconsistencies and imperfections. The role, presence and value of authenticity in the cultural industries will be an interesting trend to track.

Finally, we might want to work out how consumer behaviour is likely to evolve in the future. Forecasters have long predicted a golden age for consumers as a result of digitisation. Rather than relying on large profit-orientated organisations to tell them what content to consume, when and how, consumers can increasingly choose what content they wish to consume, in what form, when and how they wish. Optimistic forecasters predict consumers taking greater charge of their content experiences, wresting control from the big corporations. Well, it's certainly the case that consumers have a much wider range of choices than in previous years. But such choice comes with consequences.

For a start, it's expensive. Yes, you can access 10 or 15 different television streaming services, from broad aggregators like Netflix and Amazon Prime to specialist providers of niche channels like Paramount+ or Discovery, but typically each comes with a subscription fee. Yes, you can sign up to three or four music streaming services, but again expect a monthly fee for each, or having to listen to or watch the advertising that supports the service. You can access electronic games from a wide variety of different games publishers, in just about any genre, but you are probably going to have to buy consoles from all of the major hardware suppliers if you want to play them all. Also, it's likely you will have to sign up to a subscription service if you want to get involved in cloud-based gaming applications. Hence our proactive and 'in control' consumer of the future is going to need deep pockets to make the best of the vast range of content on offer.

Some would argue this expense is not necessary—a lot of content is available on generally free services like YouTube or TikTok. This is true, and that volume of content is growing every day, fuelled by the influx of user-driven content. Equally, it is apparently relatively easy to pirate streaming services and share content for free. The challenge for our consumer, then, is working through all of the content that is available to find that which is actually worth watching. It's a tough and gruelling task, as for every good piece of content found, there are likely to be 100 pieces of potentially terrible content. For every great song you might find on YouTube, you might have to listen to 100 that are genuinely awful. In many ways this search and selection process has in the past been undertaken by the major corporations in the industry. Broadcasters sought the best creatives to make content that they were sure would be of a high quality, and worth watching. They packaged it into convenient channels. They even limited the amount of content that was available (e.g. a limited number of channels), and limiting choice makes choosing easier. They promoted the content they had invested in, making sure the viewer was aware of its presence and where to find it. Equally, A&R executives in the record companies went to the trouble of attending innumerable live performances of new bands and listened to hundreds of 'demo' tapes to find the best new talent. They had to watch and listen to a lot of poor-quality performances, to find the good content. They then produced it, distributed it and promoted it to the audience. As consumers, then, life was pretty simple: you could sit back, let others do the hard work, and wait to be told what to do.

This responsibility is increasingly being handed to the consumer. Yes, lots of videos are available on YouTube, but you will have to sift through them all to find the best or rely entirely on recommendations from friends or the service's algorithms. You are going to have to sort through the 300 channels of television to find a programme that suits your mood. When literally every song is instantly available via a streaming service, which track is the right one? So yes, you can programme your own listening and viewing experience, but it's going to be quite hard work. It takes thought, effort, money and time to find good content—indeed, as some suggest, 'choice is chaos', and working through the chaos of content may not appeal to all viewers and listeners, certainly not all the time. Some will be much happier to let someone else do this arduous work; they don't necessarily want this supreme level of control over every detail of what content they consume. They may be using content to relax at the end of a hard day and don't want to spend two hours searching through a huge list of options and arguing with their family members to find something that suits them all.

Again, we can hope for solutions in either case. Sometimes the consumer may wish to precisely programme their night's listening or viewing. They will want to actively engage in choosing what they consume and as long as they are sufficiently wealthy, patient and determined, they can do so. Other times they may just want to sit back and have the experience programmed for them. This may be an interesting area of growth and development for the future, finding the right 'partners' to help you programme your content consumption, particularly across different forms of content, genres and platforms. At the moment we are typically reliant on the suppliers (and their promotional budgets), their algorithms, critics and internet influencers to guide us, and these tend to work only on specific platforms and often have a very specific agenda (e.g. promoting content they have invested in or have been sponsored to support). In the future we may see the emergence of cross-platform content mediators, drawing on consumer data to programme your entire content experience across multiple platforms and usage situations. This would be a powerful group indeed as they direct consumer attention, in a hugely overcrowded market, to specific pieces of content, irrespective of loyalties to companies, programmes, channels or platforms.

10.4 Globalisation

Developments in most business sectors in the last 30 years have stressed an increasingly global approach to doing business. Global supply chains have emerged, linking companies and countries globally to bring the consumer the right product, typically at the lowest price. Companies have broadened their perspectives, searching out new consumers and markets in international territories. Particularly in western markets, generally considered to be increasingly mature, slow to grow and prone to intense competition (and hence lower profits), companies have sought emerging fast-growth markets overseas to support their increasingly global ambitions and challenging profit targets.

Such trends have also affected the cultural industries. Western companies increasingly look to foreign markets for consumers. Asian companies increasingly seek positions in the western market, often through acquisition and merger with western companies. Certainly, having secured their position in the Asian market, companies behind major J- and particularly K-pop artists are increasingly looking to western markets to provide the next stage in their growth. Companies are in some cases building their entire strategy on creating content that will work for a global market (e.g. Netflix).

As of 2020, it could be argued that things may have begun to change. COVID and subsequent geopolitical events like the war in the Ukraine and that between Israel and Palestine, added to the rise of more popularist and inwardly looking politicians like Donald Trump in the USA, have arguably started to 'put the brakes' on the unrelenting trend towards globalisation. Global supply chains (GSCs), interrupted by COVID, are now being broken up, particularly in response to Trump's wave of tariffs in 2025. As other countries respond with their own tariffs, these GSCs become more complex to manage, and arguably less economically beneficial, hence manufacturers are increasingly investing in building their capabilities in their home territories, minimising their exposure to international tariffs and geopolitical disruption.

It will be interesting to see how this refocus on the 'local', rather than the global, will play out in the cultural industries. Certainly, we have GSCs (e.g. in the area of animation or film production), though they currently seem somewhat less vulnerable to geopolitical changes and the effects of tariffs. Should tariffs begin to be applied by different nations to the service sector (they currently focus almost exclusively on manufacturing rather than services), then these cultural GSCs may come under pressure and need to be restructured.

Political motives may also be behind potential limits on the degree to which companies in the cultural industries can expand their presence globally. The USA already has established limits on the degree to which Chinese companies can supply hardware to telecoms companies in the USA, and companies like TikTok may be forced to sell themselves to an American buyer if they wish to continue to operate there. It is not hard to imagine a situation in which populist politicians make a political issue out of foreign companies buying into the culture-creating industries in their home territories. There is precedent for this—France, for example, has long been careful to limit the amount of American content its television companies can screen in an attempt to protect its own cultural heritage and content-creation industries. Limitations on the degree to which foreign content can be distributed, or on the degree to which foreign companies can invest in domestic parts of the culture industries, have long been a feature of international trade. Will we see these limitations being strengthened in the next 10 years?

The cultural industries have a special place in most economies. They often reflect and represent the very cultural values of their home territories, so if you want to understand the 'American dream', there are numerous American films, books and television programmes that will help explain it (and sell it) to you, from *The Fountainhead* to *Succession* to *It's a Wonderful Life*. Perhaps Donald Trump will not be happy to see Chinese companies owning large parts of Hollywood, potentially influencing the way that America views itself and what it stands for. These views might equally be shared by Xi Jinping in China, Putin in Russia or the leaders of any country. Influence over the culture-creation industry is a powerful position in any country, and the degree to which it should be in the hands of foreign companies will continue to be debated and discussed.

The final question we might ask in this regard is whether there will continue to be a demand for 'global' content. The growth of the popularity of global content has partially been a function of its quality, increased availability (e.g. Koren dramas are now available on many streaming platforms across the world; you can watch AKB48's latest video on YouTube) but also a demand amongst audiences to see life in different cultures, to experience different perspectives on and insights into an increasingly connected globe. How will the turn to the 'local' affect this demand? Will we be willing to embrace a more local focus for our cultural content, content that reflects our history, our values and our population to the exclusion of others? Certainly populist, and particularly right-wing, politicians are encouraging a return to traditional and local beliefs, values and customs; will their presence in positions of power impose ever greater limits on the flow of content internationally? Certainly, in some sectors—e.g. the African electronic gaming market—there is an understandable demand for more content that reflects local conditions, life experiences and stories given the previous dominance of American, European and Asian perspectives and cultural icons. In some cases, this turn to the local then seems very justified, required and perhaps overdue. Again, this is an interesting tension that will play out in the short to medium term.

10.5 From distribution to attention economies: growth and change

Throughout this book we have noted the ongoing decline in the prospects of many previously successful companies in the cultural industries, successful largely because of their previous control of (indeed some would suggest stranglehold on) distribution. Whether they be major broadcasters or major record companies, their previous control of and investment in distribution networks created high barriers to entry for competitors and allowed them to secure a disproportionate share of consumer viewing, listening and ultimately revenues. Distribution was the strategic high ground as there were very limited distribution options; it was hard to secure but, if you did, you could generally rely on accessing large consumer markets. Hence whoever controlled distribution was in a dominant position in the industry.

As we have seen, things have changed. The range of potential distribution routes for a piece of content have exploded in the last 20 years. In theory you can even do it yourself, potentially reaching a global audience via user-based services like YouTube or Soundcloud. It's easier than ever before to get your content distributed. As such the power of those organisations who previously had a stranglehold on it is inevitably diminishing, and many are facing an existential crisis.

The challenge today is not distribution; it is securing the consumer's attention. The growth in distribution routes and growth in the number of providers (including user-generated content) has led to a huge increase in the sheer amount of content consumers can choose from. So yes, you can post your new song or video on YouTube, but along with the millions of other songs and videos available, how does anyone find yours? This is not just a challenge for the user, it's a major challenge for corporations in the industry, some of whom will have invested millions of dollars in the content they are promoting. The challenge is to get the consumer to notice it and consume our content rather than anyone else's.

Promotional campaigns are only likely to get you so far: there are a huge number of corporations promoting their content and it's difficult to be heard amongst all the noise. For some, the answer is getting closer to the consumer, to understand them better and to build a direct and loyal relationship with them. Collecting and analysing consumer data tends to be the starting point for this, particularly as data can now be collected directly from the consumer in a way it could not previously: it is relatively easy to just record their viewing or listening behaviour, how they interact with games or online content etc. Whilst data collection is ever easier, data analysis tends to become more complex and difficult as the sheer amount of data from a diverse range of sources increases. Hence the focus is increasingly on analysing the data, drawing conclusions that are useful and meaningful for business. In the 2010s this led to a global focus on hiring data analysts in all industries, though today the focus is much more on hiring AI experts who can dredge data lakes with appropriate algorithms for usable insights.

Typically, corporations are also focused on building closer relationships with consumers to ensure their attention and loyalty. Online community building has become a core area of focus for many of those in the marketing teams of cultural companies. It is perhaps in this area where we will see further efforts to diminish the traditional barriers between artists and their fans, as both contribute to creating specific ecosystems around content, brands and creators.

Brands (including television programmes, musicians, film franchises and so on) are also likely to work with their distribution partners in the area of recommendation algorithms and placement within the distributor's service. 'Paying for prominence' became part of the music promotion toolkit as radio became more popular in the 1950s. Record promoters working for record companies would do deals with the radio companies to make sure their new content was featured prominently: songs would move into 'heavy rotation' and were constantly played by the radio company. Many such deals bordered on the illegal, particularly those done with individual DJs who did not disclose they were being paid to play (and hence promote) a particular song, and indeed such deals were eventually made illegal (the practice was known as payola in the USA).

In the television sector the practice emerged during the early 1990s in the pay-TV market. As the number of channels grew on services, it was seen to be increasingly important to be the first or most prominent content on the service's EPG (electronic programme guide). Consumers did not want to scroll through page after page of the EPG to find something to watch. When the consumer decided they wanted to watch a film, being the first film channel they saw on the EPG was a powerful position; when they wanted to watch a music video, being the first music channel (typically MTV) was where you wanted to be. Hence deals were executed whereby channel providers might pay for this prominent position. Arguably this prominence has become even more vital as distribution channels have expanded, volumes of content have increased and audience attention has become more distributed, fragmented and valuable. It will certainly be interesting to see if major brands start attempting to influence the operation of recommendation algorithms, ensuring their content always appears on the 'if you liked that programme, you will like this…' screen.

Internet influencers also will play their role in guiding consumer attention, though they walk a delicate path. We may partly listen to their advice because we feel they represent us and our view of the world, they share our values, but also that they are fairly neutral in terms of their recommendations, they are not just advocating a piece of content because they have been paid to do so. Yet sponsorship deals are becoming the most common form of interaction between brands and the influencers they hope will support the promotion of their new product or service. They are often now very clearly being paid to promote a specific item, and their content increasingly appears to take a similar form to traditional television shopping channels. Again, it will be interesting to see how these relationships play out over the next 5–10 years. Will influencers increasingly be seen as merely the mouthpieces of the brands they advocate; will they lose their 'authenticity' and their ability to direct and arbitrate consumer attention as a result? Will we see a splintering of the sector, with some influencers embracing their commercial role as online promoters in return for a fee (they would essentially become shopping channels), whilst others refuse such incentives, offering their unbiased and honest views on what content a consumer should focus their attention on next? The key question for this latter group of course is how they might make a living having rejected the advances of the major brands. Perhaps models like Patreon[4] offer an alternative approach—funding from the fans, rather than the brands.

The move from a distribution- to attention-based economy in the cultural industries has been accompanied by major changes in the structure and operation of those industries: for some firms the value of the distribution infrastructures they built has been vastly diminished and they have had to build new assets and capabilities. In other sectors new competitors have emerged to challenge incumbent (and often previously very profitable) operators. We see some sectors declining significantly and becoming niche propositions (e.g. physical media for the distribution of content?), whilst others grow at remarkable rates (e.g. mobile gaming). Overall, however, the cultural industries appear to be getting larger.

This is obviously good news for those of you hoping to find a job in it. But caution and a critical approach are advisable. Not all sectors of the cultural economy are growing. In some cases, growth in one part of the market (streaming of films) potentially means declines in another (the sale of films on packaged media). Companies in some sectors are likely to continue to expand and grow in the short to medium term; others will decline and potentially disappear. Some sectors are desperately searching for new capabilities and skills (typically in the form of people) to achieve their goals; others are laying off staff and closing their operations. AI will rapidly replace some jobs in the industries, while significantly enhancing others. These are highly relevant issues as you consider your first steps in employment in the industry. Choosing the right sector and company is vital, ensuring you are in one of those sectors that is likely to grow in the short to medium term, rather than decline. So, let's finish with some consideration of your first steps on the employment ladder in the cultural industries—after all, that's probably why you are reading this book: ultimately you want to get a satisfying job and career in the industry.

10.6 How will the war for talent play out?

In most business sectors, recruiters are increasingly engaging in a war with their competitors for the best business talent. Securing the best talent in a particular discipline—e.g. financial management, product design, AI etc.—means that you benefit from it and your competitors do not. We can create a virtuous circle in which we attract the best talent, which makes us the best (e.g. most innovative) company, which helps us attract the best talent, which makes us the most innovative and so on. Certainly this was the model of recruitment that Apple adopted in the 1990s and 2000s, helping its growth to become one of the largest companies in American history. Similar approaches are being adopted by companies like Tesla and NVIDIA. More than ever before, then, it may be the human capital in a company that allows it to develop long-term, sustainable, competitive advantage. Processes, systems, structures, business models and marketing campaigns can all be copied, increasingly easily and quickly. People and their talent can't be copied, though some in the field of AI might suggest this is not very far away.

Talent can be 'stolen', however; indeed, the growth of the executive search industry (focused on the recruitment of senior executives) is testament to this, an entire industry that has grown up on the basis of identifying talent in other businesses and essentially tempting it away to your company. This is the front line of the war for talent, and the continued buoyancy of the executive search sector suggests it will become an even more aggressive and 'hot' war. Even companies like Microsoft are willing to 'steal' talent from their own subsidiaries, evidenced by its attempts to hire Sam Altman from a company it had itself invested in, OpenAI.

The issue becomes even more acute if we look at forecast demographic trends for the next 20 or 30 years, which suggest a decline in the number of young people entering the job market. A battle for the next generation of younger talent is likely to emerge across all business sectors, as even AI systems need someone to ensure they are plugged in and operating!

So, what are the implications for the cultural industries and your career?

10.7 Your business career in the cultural industries

Securing a job in the cultural industries has always been something of a challenge. They are not significant employers in terms of sheer numbers, and many people want to work in the industry, hence jobs, particularly at the entry level, are typically hard to find. Having parents with existing contacts or a role in the sector you are interested in typically helps, as does having parents wealthy enough to support you whilst you do your unpaid intern work in your favourite record company or Hollywood studio. For those of you without access to such assets, expect significant competition for any role you apply to, lots of rejections and a long process. Indeed, many roles won't even be advertised, going to the friends and family of those already in the industry before anyone else has a chance to apply. This may be precisely the situation facing many of you reading this book; it certainly was for the author.

So how might you develop your career in the sector?

The most obvious way in is typically by responding to an advertisement for a job in the sector. But as we have already noted, few of these jobs actually ever get advertised and, when they do, they are hugely oversubscribed in terms of potential candidates. It can be tough to be noticed in the deluge of CVs that are likely to be submitted. This may be even tougher if you have no direct work experience in a relevant sector—e.g. you are applying directly after graduation, having spent the previous three or four years studying, and working in a local coffee bar to help pay for your living expenses. Few candidates will have spent their summers interning in relevant cultural organisations. Company-based placements as part of your programme of study can help hugely in this regard, and this should be factored into your choice of academic programme.

The challenge is always getting the interview, as if you do, obviously, your chances of securing the role are significantly increased, providing the opportunity for you to really display your qualities and to explain how you can contribute to the organisation. If you are not getting interviews, despite numerous applications, experimenting with different approaches to presenting your CV may help. If the typical 'job list'-based structure does not really illustrate your capabilities, try a more skill-based approach outlining what you are good at doing. At the very minimum, do your homework on the target company, demonstrate your knowledge of the organisation and the challenges it faces (typically in the covering letter or personal statement), illustrate how business ideas can help address these challenges and how you can help to implement them.

Very few employees are likely to start their careers in the cultural industries and remain there for their entire careers. Many enter the industry having spent some time developing their skills in another sector. Hence you may begin your career in IT working for a technology company and subsequently move to an organisation in the cultural industries. Certainly, at the moment, the industry is looking for talent to help it navigate the growth and deployment of AI. Little of this talent currently exists within the industry; it will have to be sought in other sectors. Equally many companies in the industry are looking for ways to improve their marketing capabilities and are searching other sectors to supply talent, particularly in the area of customer analytics and social media marketing. Having a successful career in a fast-moving consumer goods company, retailer or a major consumer brand puts you in a great position to make a subsequent move into the cultural industries.

For others (including the author), the route in may be via the types of external advisors that cultural organisations often use—lawyers, accountants and consultants. Typically, when entering any of these professions, which often require specific qualifications or professional exams to be passed first, it's unlikely you will start working directly with clients in the cultural industries. You may start with a more generalist agenda, working for firms in a variety of different sectors on a variety of different projects. Typically, however, in all such service organisations, there are opportunities to specialise in specific types of clients or sectors, and you may choose to focus on the cultural sector. Your career may remain based in a law firm or accountancy firm, serving clients in the cultural sectors, or you may choose to go 'client-side', moving from one of these external service companies to become a full-time employee of one of your clients.

It is worth mentioning here that in terms of career development, not everyone should necessarily aim for the goal of being a great manager or leader. Whilst HR systems often push people into such roles (as a natural reward for their previously outstanding performance), these roles do not suit everyone. They carry significant responsibilities. They require certain skills and knowledge. Assuming that everyone will feel happy in such roles is dangerous, both for the mental health of the individual and for the performance of the company. A more pragmatic approach might be to suggest that many people will be happier as 'followers' rather than leaders and should be allowed to take on and maintain this role. This is an interesting suggestion, as the term follower is often looked down on. You are a follower if you fail to make it, if you are not good enough to be a leader.

Yet if we look at the careers of very successful leaders, they have spent most of their careers following. They learnt from those above them. Even as a CEO, you may have a mentor who advises you, you may receive direction from non-executive directors or have to follow the whims of the financial community. You may follow the guidance of your CFO or head of marketing around issues of strategy. However successful we are, typically we spend much of our careers following to some extent. Yet whilst there is a huge amount of research around leadership, there is far less work done on the idea of followership.

Being a good follower can arguably make as big an impact on the performance of your company as being a great leader. But typically, we don't encourage this perspective, we don't teach this in business school or cover it extensively in textbooks. We seem too obsessed about identifying what makes a great leader and the idea that this is everyone's ultimate goal. But what makes a great follower? One of the first and most influential writers on the subject is Barbara Kellerman, who suggests that great followers have good judgement and a strong work ethic, are competent, honest, courageous and loyal, and are good at managing their own egos. This is a broad and tough agenda, and arguably we need to focus just as much on developing good followers in our organisations as good leaders. Kellerman's book *Followership: How Followers Are Creating Change and Changing Leaders* is a great place for you to start your research if you are interested in this area.

The final route in you might consider is to do it yourself, become an entrepreneur and set up the sort of business you would want to work for. The cultural industries in every region are largely composed of small and medium-sized businesses, set up by entrepreneurs. Why not consider becoming one yourself? Become your own boss! It sounds great, but what are you getting yourself into?

10.8 Entrepreneurship

Entrepreneurship as a field of study is concerned with the examination of how, by whom and with what effects opportunities to create future products and services are discovered, evaluated and exploited. Consequently, the field involves the study of sources of opportunities—the process of discovery, evaluation and exploitation—and the set of individuals who discover, evaluate and exploit them (Shane and Venkataraman, 2000). Academics appear particularly interested in the nature of the entrepreneur, whether they are born or made, their characteristics and behaviour.

Hence academics have spent significant time and resources in studying the personal characteristics of entrepreneurs. Critical characteristics appear to include the need for achievement McClelland (1961); high levels of optimism (Cooper et al., 1988; Hmieleski and Baron, 2009); a propensity for risk-taking (Kirzner, 1977; Brockhaus, 1980); a desire for autonomy and control (Caird, 1991; Cromie, 2000); and a degree of creativity (Whiting, 1988; Ward, 2004). Many of these appear to be admirable and positive qualities, but all of these qualities can have negative connotations—the dangers of over optimism, an over-reliance on 'gut instinct' rather than analysis of data, the illusion of control and a reliance on reasoning by analogy (i.e. in unfamiliar situations, where relevant data is scarce, entrepreneurs will often rely on their past experience as guidelines, even though the past experience is not directly relatable to the new one they face). Combined, we can see why so many new products and services are launched by entrepreneurs, but also why so many of them fail.

Significant attention is often paid by researchers to the early years of the entrepreneur's life, the 'nurture' elements that help develop these qualities in their personalities. Interestingly, these early lives are often characterised by conflicts, losses and difficulties (see for example Yu et al., 2022), which might emerge from the family context (loss of a parent, poverty, illness, the presence of often failed family businesses and bankruptcy etc.) or the challenges of fitting in with 'normal' schooling (e.g. issues associated with autism or dyslexia). These challenges and obstacles in their early lives may motive them to succeed in their later lives.

It is interesting that entrepreneurs share many of these qualities with another group in the population according to researchers like William Baumol (1996): that is convicted, recidivist criminals, particularly in street gangs. Baumol argues that a certain portion of the population in any country has the skills and preferences to become entrepreneurs. The number of people starting productive companies depends a lot on the incentives and context society creates for entrepreneurship. In places where the incentives aren't very good for productive entrepreneurship, or the social and economic context make legitimate routes difficult to pursue, people with the desire and talent to become entrepreneurs often turn to crime as an alternative vehicle for their talent and ambitions.

A second area of research for academics is the entrepreneurial process: how entrepreneurs identify opportunities and create new businesses. The focus here is often on the ability to spot opportunities and the entrepreneurial learning cycle. It is a harsh reality that most new entrepreneurs fail—their first attempts to create businesses don't attract sufficient customers or funders to last more than a few years at best; indeed, many such new ventures may never make it beyond a first draft business plan. Interestingly this failure is generally considered an essential part of the entrepreneurial learning cycle. Whether the failure is due to lack of planning, inappropriate timing, the inability to attract funders or a lack of detailed financial management, what the entrepreneur choses to do when they have failed is critical.

The failure may have huge consequences for the entrepreneur. They may have borrowed money from friends and family. They may have invested their life savings in the venture. The failure may have significant financial implications, but also result in social costs, a breakdown in relationships with those friends and family who supported them, divorces, a decline in social standing and so on. But whilst painful, failure appears to be a central part of creating successful entrepreneurs. They choose to learn from the experience, reflect on it, draw conclusions from it and endeavour not to make the same mistakes again. Indeed, it would appear that the best entrepreneurs make lots of mistakes, but they don't tend to make the same mistakes repeatedly—they specialise in only making 'new' mistakes. This is a valuable principle, applicable to all aspects of working life.

Success is often highly situational, depending on space, time, context and a certain amount of luck. Only a limited amount of this is in the hands of the entrepreneur to control. An idea can genuinely be brought to market 'before its time'—consumers may simply not be ready for it, no matter how good the product or service. Equally everyone may have the same idea at the same time, meaning lots of new entrants to your chosen market, and levels of competition that virtually guarantee no-one will make a profit. It's very easy to fail, no matter how good your idea.

As an entrepreneur, then, get used to failure. But perhaps above all, successful entrepreneurs are resilient: they bounce back from failure and keep trying. Learning in this context requires experience, trying to do it, but also calm reflection and self-analysis, learning from it. When asking the question of oneself, 'do I want to become an entrepreneur?', perhaps the most relevant question you can ask is not 'do I have a good idea?', or 'can I get the funding?', but rather 'do I have the emotional resilience to do this, to fail, potentially multiple times, but keep trying?'

The entrepreneurial process itself tends to revolve around a number of key stages. Firstly, an opportunity needs to be identified. This opportunity may often emerge due to changes in the external environment, new social or cultural trends, new opportunities opened up by changes in laws and regulations, new technologies etc. Hence successful entrepreneurs tend to be very well networked, and they monitor their environment constantly, always on the lookout for an advantageous change.

Once the idea is identified, typically there will need to be some level of verification. Whilst an entrepreneur might have some positive 'gut instinct' around the opportunity, it needs to be established with evidence. Typically, the project will enter a phase of viability and feasibility checking. The potential market will be explored, data will be sought, research will be conducted into the potential consumer response, as it will on the technical viability of the idea, its ability to deliver value to consumers and profits to investors and so on. Often, for very innovative or creative new ideas, ones that may be literally new to the world, such data may simply not exist, forcing the entrepreneur to rely more heavily on their instincts. But remember, many entrepreneurs can tend to be overly optimistic, and in the absence of data or evidence to contradict their views, that optimism may run unchecked. The size of the market may be overestimated, as may the share that the new product and service might secure. The speed of the growth of sales is typically overestimated, and costs incurred and time required to develop the market and the company's position within it are typically underestimated. Is it a wonder, then, that so many new products and services fail?

If a new idea can move through the viability assessment, attention typically moves onto feasibility. Feasibility is typically focused on establishing the precise character of the new organisation that will release the product and service. What will it look like, how will it function? What are its key processes and systems? What talent will need to be secured to run the business? What technology will it utilise? How will it differentiate itself from other potential competitors, how will it position itself in the market? How will it promote itself? Essentially the feasibility stage typically takes the idea and turns it into a business plan that can help the founder raise the required funds to build the company.

In the next phase, initial funds are sought as the entrepreneur talks to friends, family and typically their bank managers to secure the required resources to start the business (often called pre-seed funding). Indeed, much of the life of the entrepreneur is spent fundraising as, even when the company is established, it will almost certainly need further funding to grow and develop. Funding is typically divided up into rounds (typically from pre-seed funding, through a series of stages typically labelled A to D, all the way to IPO—initial public offering). Funds in these later stages may be secured from business incubators, angel investors, venture capital firms or even ultimately the stock market if the company goes through an IPO. Increasingly entrepreneurs may turn to crowdfunding sites to raise the required resources. They may also draw on grants and competitions run by local or central government.

What are such funders and investors looking for? Typically, the focus is on three issues. Firstly, the entrepreneur and their team. Are they credible, well balanced and capable? Do they have relevant previous experience? Indeed, this seems to be the overwhelming focus for the attention of investors: they don't primarily invest in ideas, they invest in individuals. Secondly a strong proposition, a clear identification of an unmet customer need and a method to meet it. In this regard they will be particularly concerned about execution: how the team intend to set up the organisation. It's easy to have a great idea, but much harder to put it into practice. Finally, they expect coherent, robust and well-researched business plans that are viable and feasible.

Equally as an entrepreneur (and probably CEO of your new firm) it's incumbent upon you to find the right funding partners. Not all will be suitable, and just because someone is willing to invest £500,000 in your new business, it does not mean you should let them. Venture capital firms, for example, have a reputation for interfering too aggressively in the firms they have invested in, insisting on having their representatives on the board of the company, directing strategy and pushing it to grow too quickly to the possible detriment of its long-term prospects. It will be important for you to find funders that have a strong history of investing in your type of company, who have good networks of potential suppliers and customers, and who are willing to take a long-term and flexible view of their investment.

Finally, it is worth noting that being an entrepreneur does not limit you to working in small companies and start-ups. Increasingly, large companies—indeed some of the largest in the world—have expressed the desire to become more entrepreneurial in their outlook and working practices. They want workers, managers and leaders who are opportunity-seeking, who like shaking things up, breaking the rules and getting things done. We have noted the earlier criticism of large bureaucracies that they tend to diminish the ambitions of those working for them, and that their sheer size is a constraint on innovation and getting things done. In a VUCA environment, this is a recipe for disaster. Increasingly, then, even major corporations are looking for employees with some entrepreneurial experience (or at least an entrepreneurial perspective) to join and help shake up their businesses. Equally, if you are successful as an entrepreneur, you may find yourself (specifically, your company) acquired by a larger company to secure new assets, capabilities and your culture of entrepreneurialism. Some significant and fast-growing businesses are even structured around combining big-company resources with small-company attitudes and ambitions—e.g. Rocket Internet.

Hence if you plan to become an entrepreneur, particularly in the cultural industries, get ready to fail, a lot. The key requirement does not appear to be the highest IQ or the best qualifications (indeed, many entrepreneurs have virtually no qualifications); you don't need to have attended the best business schools or have done an MBA. You need to be good at three things: spotting viable opportunities, assembling and working with appropriate teams, and dealing with failure. And it's this latter point that tends to differentiate the failed entrepreneurs from the successful ones—that is, their emotional resilience, their ability to bounce back from yet another setback. Without this latter quality, your career as an entrepreneur is likely to be short-lived, unpleasant and ultimately disappointing.

10.9 Conclusions

This all sounds terrible doesn't it! The sector is difficult to get into and tough to work within, salaries often don't match those of other business sectors, and the whole industry is prone to such radical change and disruption that the successful company you finally secured a job with might be out of business by the end of the year. Why would anyone bother?

Well, as the author and many of those he has met in the industry can attest, it's also one of the most exciting and rewarding business sectors in which you might build a career. The products and services it creates affect people at a fundamental level—they can literally change the way someone views the world. The radical change evident in the sector creates as many exciting opportunities as it does threats. It is constantly evolving and throwing new challenges at the people who work within it. If you want a quiet, predictable and ultimately stable career (as many people do, and why not?) then the cultural industries are probably not for you. If you want a challenge, variety and like to learn, then the sector offers unrivalled opportunities.

We hope that this book can help you develop the career you want in the industry. Its insights into the operation and structure of the industry, its key processes and business dynamics, will hopefully mark you out at interview and help you secure that elusive first job. Increasingly, however, this knowledge and insight is likely to become (to use an idea we discussed in Chapter 2) a threshold capability. That is, it will become a minimum requirement for those seeking a business-orientated role in the industry. Luckily, though perhaps somewhat challengingly, business perspectives are constantly evolving. Management innovation is an ongoing process whereby old ideas are discarded and fresh perspectives sought. Like the cultural industries, it is constantly evolving. Remaining at the top of your game from a business perspective means constant change and evolution, a personal development challenge as you too will have to evolve.

To stay in touch with this evolution in the discipline means continuing to learn, reading textbooks, analysing academic papers, reading the business press, being involved in online discussion forums, attending trade conferences and networking widely. It's actually far more fun than it sounds. To make the best use of what you learn, be willing to change your mind and practice, as just because something worked well last week, does not mean it will work next week. An over-reliance on a fixed view of the world and how to do business in it has led many companies in the cultural industries to a dire end (e.g. some of the major record companies). Adopt a stance of self-reflection, regularly review your own practice and perspectives on business and be ready to change and modify your behaviour and views. Be ready to walk away from what has made you successful in the past (a far harder task than it sounds). Feed your knowledge and insight on an ongoing basis: it's your best chance of remaining relevant and valuable. This textbook, then, is hopefully the start, not the end point, of your interaction with business commentary and management innovation.

For some of you, reading this book and working through its references has probably put you off business forever! That's fine—it's an equally valid and useful conclusion for your efforts in reading it. A business career is not for everyone, and finding that out now, at the start of your career, allows you to rethink your priorities and change your career plans before you spend 10 years in a boring office job that you later regret. For those of you still intent on a career leading the cultural industries, good luck, you will need it, but you probably knew that already, that's why you read this book. Luck is where opportunity and preparation meet.

10.10 Activities

- Try and identify the most attractive functions and sectors of the cultural industries for potential employees in the short to medium term. What sectors are growing and changing, what functions are seen as increasingly critical? Where are the talent gaps? How might you fit in?
- Develop an idea for a new product or service in the cultural industries. What is the nature of the opportunity? What unfulfilled consumer or company need does it fulfil? What technology does it utilise? How feasible and viable is the idea? What would be your plan A, but also your plan B (and perhaps even plan C) for when things go wrong?
- Develop a plan for the next set of readings you are going to engage with. What areas discussed in this book excited or interested you? Who are you going to read next to follow up on this interest?
- Apply for a job. If you get it, celebrate and let us know. Well done. We hope we helped. If you get rejected, reflect on the experience: why did you fail and what are you going to differently next time?

Notes

1 https://www.sae.edu/gbr/insights/the-return-of-vinyl-analysing-the-resurgence-of-physical-music-formats/.
2 The Recording Industry Association of America, 2023.
3 https://www.musicweek.com/labels/read/vinyl-destination-can-the-format-s-sales-growth-continue-in-2023/087370.
4 https://www.patreon.com.

References

Baumol, W. J. 1996. Entrepreneurship: Productive, unproductive, and destructive. *Journal of Business Venturing*, 11 (1), pp. 3–22.

Brockhaus, R. H. 1980. Risk taking propensity of entrepreneurs. *Academy of Management Journal*, 23 (3), pp. 509–520.

Caird, S. 1991. Testing enterprising tendency in occupational groups. *British Journal of Management*, 2 (4), pp. 177–186.

Cooper, A. C., Woo, C. Y and Dunkelberg, W. C. 1998. Entrepreneurs' perceived chances for success. *Journal of Business Venturing*, 3 (2), pp. 97–108.

Cromie, S. 2000. Assessing entrepreneurial inclinations: Some approaches and empirical evidence. *European Journal of Work and Organizational Psychology*, 9 (1), pp. 7–30.

Hmieleski, K. M. and Baron, R. A. 2009. Entrepreneurs' optimism and new venture performance: A social cognitive perspective. *Academy of Management Journal*, 52 (3), pp. 473–488.

Kellerman, B. 2008. *Followership: How Followers are Creating Change and Changing Leaders.* Harvard Business School Press.

Kirzner, I. 1977. Entrepreneurial discovery and the competitive market process: An Austrian approach. *The Journal of Economic Literature,* 35.

McClelland, D. C. 1961. *The Achieving Society.* Van Nostrand.

Shane, S. and Venkataraman, S. 2000. The promise of entrepreneurship as a field of research. *The Academy of Management Review*, 25 (1), pp. 217–226.

Ward, T. B. 2004. Cognition, creativity, and entrepreneurship. *Journal of Business Venturing*, 19 (2), pp. 173–188.

Yu, W., Zhu, F., Der Foo, M. and Wiklund, J. 2022. What does not kill you makes you stronger: Entrepreneurs' childhood adversity, resilience, and career success. *Journal of Business Research*, 151, pp. 40–55.

Whiting, B. 1988. Creativity and entrepreneurship: How do they relate? *Journal of Creative Behaviour*, 22 (3), pp. 178–183.

Index

Note: *Italic* page numbers refer to figures.